TRIAL BY FIRE

A Personal Journey of
Consciousness, Power & Freedom

Kaia Anderson

NAMASTE.

PYXIS PRESS

Published by Pyxis Press, 1610 Pace Street, Unit 900-418, Longmont, CO, 80504. pyxispress.com

The intent of the author is only to share her experience and offer information of a general nature. If anyone chooses to use any of the information presented for themselves, the author and the publisher assume no responsibility for their actions.

Cover design: E.L.A. and M. Reynolds
Cover photograph: © Kaia Anderson
Cover portrait of the author, 1976: © Kaia Anderson
Cover portrait of the author, 2014: © Kayla Feldman Photography

Library of Congress Control Number: 2017941086

ISBN: 978-0-9979151-0-5 (trade paperback)

First Edition

Printed in the United States of America

For Mary, who held the lantern,
and my children, who walked with me hand in hand.

Preface

For nearly thirty years, I was terrorized by a madman and sought justice and peace. I'm hopeful it's all behind me.

In all this time, the question invariably posed by reporters and advocates, strangers and friends alike is: How did you cope? Of all the questions, this is the one that burns in their eyes, that reaches out from their hearts with a personal need to know; the one that connects us as human beings trying to make sense of our lives and, at times, to simply endure.

My only true answer is that this is not the question. Had I tried merely to cope, I likely would not have survived. I wouldn't have wanted to.

The question that pulled me inexorably onward in the face of relentless terror, insurmountable obstacles, and unfathomable insanity was: What is the gift in this?

The need to find that answer, that pinpoint of light in the black abyss was my lifeline. Ultimately, it was stronger than fear, anger, or despair. Though perilously fragile at times, my faith that all life experiences are here to teach us, to serve us, kept me going.

From moment to moment, I could not see the path before me. Trapped in a web of violence, ignorance, and cruelty, I could only trust blindly. But with the guidance of my mentor and the burning desire to understand the higher purpose, I worked with my experience and was transformed by it.

This is the story of my journey into the long, dark night and my awakening — a story I offer gladly in the hope that it reaches out to heal hearts and inspire minds.

* * *

"Two roads diverged in a wood, and I –
I took the one less traveled by,
And that has made all the difference."
~ *Robert Frost*

A Note to My Readers

I was born Peggy Anderson. For some years now, I have gone by Kaia, the name I hope you will come to know me by.

To protect their privacy, my children's names are pseudonyms, and the full names of family members and my counselor are not disclosed.

This story is true. All statements asserted as facts are based on careful research for accuracy, and the details of events that follow are corroborated by judicial documents, newspaper articles, and other media coverage listed in the bibliography at the end of this book. Official letters, memos, and emails; copies of evidence; interviews with officials; and my timeline and notes recorded during events, meetings, and telephone conversations were also relied upon to ensure the retelling is true.

I have enlisted minimal literary license with some conversations outside the courtroom in order to convey important information in narrative form. Some court transcripts, official documents, and phone call transcriptions have been shortened, due to space, and some punctuation and small grammar changes have been made in transcripts purely to improve clarity, consistency, and grammatical accuracy; none of these changes alter the content, syntax, or inflections.

Told from a layperson's point of view, this story is not intended to thoroughly describe the law or legal procedures. Nor is it intended to give advice on appropriate safety precautions. And while I mention several types of therapy I worked with, this is not meant as an endorsement or recommendation for others. There are many worthwhile forms of therapy and healing. I continue to explore them myself.

In this story, as in life, I use several names for the divine presence. I do this consciously to open the mind and move beyond the limitations of doctrine. It is not meant to distinguish between believers, to divide or to separate. Quite the opposite. It is to honor the fact that, though belief systems differ, when distilled to their essence, all faces of the Divine — east and west, old and new, masculine and feminine — are one.

PART I

Odyssey

CHAPTER 1

Nightmare

11/11/1997

"Do you believe the work we do here can change this experience for you?" Mary asked me the first day I walked into her counseling room.

My eyes glazed over, I uttered, "Had you asked me that six months ago, or five years ago, or eighteen years ago, my response would have been a resounding 'yes.' But today I have lost all hope of ever changing this experience."

Finally, I'd hit rock bottom.

11/11/1994 – Three years earlier

The phone rang and I reached out to answer the call. "Hello?"

"I just got a phone call from *him*."

Suddenly, the blissfully peaceful day I'd spent with my children spun into a vortex. Terror hit me like a tidal wave. Blood rushed from my head and limbs in a flood. My knees buckled and I sank to the floor. My body shook uncontrollably.

Once again, my life would be completely altered. My family and I were in danger; that was all that mattered. The living nightmare that, like a thread through a tapestry, had been tethered to me for fifteen years had just re-awakened.

There was no question who "he" was.

Bruce's voice shook. "He called himself Frank and asked for you. But it was him."

Overwhelming fear washed through me, commanding control of my senses. Memories I'd long suppressed rushed into the moment, and I struggled to breathe beneath the weight of them. And the all-encompassing question rolled over and over in my mind: *Why is this happening?* I'd begged for an answer so many times before. *Why? Please tell me why!*

The beginning

In 1976, at the age of twenty, I was bursting with the desire to launch my own life. I wanted to move from Missouri, my birthplace, to finish my undergraduate degree somewhere in the Rocky Mountain west; a student of ecology, I longed to live and learn in the majestic landscape I loved most.

Early that summer, Bruce, my high school sweetheart, and I headed west to visit schools. We planned to embark on this new life together.

Odd the moments we remember later in life, the ones that seem so insignificant at the time but, upon reflection, are simply sweet and precious. Stopping for a quick lunch on the road in west Kansas, I pulled out a loaf of bread, opened it, and reached for the peanut butter (we traveled on a budget). In the moments it took me to open the jar and grab a knife, the bread became toast, dry and crusty. Astonished, my brow shot up and I presented the bread to Bruce. Our eyes met and we tumbled into laughter. No doubt about it, we'd left the muggy climate of Missouri behind and entered an exotic, arid land. We were giddy with anticipation.

When at last we approached Boulder, Colorado, both the mileage markers and the mountain tops emerging on the horizon told us we must be close, yet the rolling plains surrendered no hint of the town. On the last rise in the road, a scenic overlook beckoned us. We were on the adventure of our young lives, eager to see it all, and we happily accepted the invitation.

Suddenly, we found ourselves perched high above Boulder Valley, and a breathtaking panorama unfolded. Rugged layers of mountain ranges rolled along the horizon as far as the eye could see. Like great mounds of sleeping giants, all elbows and knees, their jagged peaks poked up at the sky. And tucked neatly into this stunning backdrop was Boulder. The sun was quickly descending, and brilliant rays of light poured between stacks of pink and lavender clouds, spotlighting first one layer of hills, then another, then a lake, then the town. We found ourselves standing on the brink, ready to leap into a future pregnant with promise. I was awestruck. My heart swelled. I felt I'd come home.

Late that summer, we made the move across country and together we rented our first home. Bruce found a good job in his profession, structural design, and I prepared to attend the University of Colorado, CU.

These were the lingering days of the '60s revolution, post-Vietnam, pre-cynicism and greed. It was the era of long skirts and hiking boots, bandannas and headbands. All brothers and sisters, young people were open and free. Liberation was the mantra and the civil rights movement, the "back to nature" movement, and "women's lib" were in full swing. I was swept up in the fearlessness, idealism, and hope that sang on the winds of the time. We were going to change the world, and my first step was my education.

I always loved learning and savored my college years. They were my gift to myself. Working part-time through high school and my first years of college, I saved every penny I earned to pay for tuition, as one could in those days. Before moving to Colorado, I'd attended a community college then Washington University. At both Wash U and CU, the spectacular variety of people and experiences were a balm to my soul, a world apart from my mono-cultural upbringing.

Though I'd chosen my major field of study, my interests ran the gamut from the sciences to art, from dance to philosophy. It was all there for the tasting: music and dance from all parts of the globe; speakers and teachers who inspired bold, new ideas; and an array of new friends to share it all with. The days were filled with excitement, discovery, and the overarching sense that we were bounded only by the breadth of our vision.

When I arrived at CU, I was beginning my junior year, so my environmental biology classes were shared with other students of the same major. A clan of outdoorsy, down-to-earth people, we exuded the camaraderie and playfulness of a pack of pups. As a class we shared field trips, a long excursion through the southwest, and a picnic in the park at the end of term.

Among those I met in the environmental program that year was a rather obscure person named Robert Vinyard. A quiet young man with dark hair and eyes, fair skin that flushed easily, and a thin voice, there was nothing particularly noticeable about him except that he seemed lonely.

I didn't reach out to Bob, but when he approached me for conversation, I listened. I was there for anyone who wanted to talk, and reflecting now on my youth, I realize there were several who sought me out whom I would not have chosen as friends.

Occasionally, Bob talked to me between classes or if we bumped into each other walking home or around town; I walked or biked everywhere.

I don't recall the first time he came to our home. Knowing my habits in those days, I suppose we were talking while walking in the same direction after class. Upon reaching my house, to avoid being rude, I must have invited him in. The details escape me. It was so casual, so insignificant and commonplace, that it doesn't stand out in my memory.

Then one afternoon, while making tea in the kitchen, I saw movement out of the corner of my eye and turned to look out the picture window. It was Bob, striding down the sidewalk, heading toward my front door.

A thick uneasiness filled my stomach. I wasn't sure why. Neighbors and other classmates would occasionally stop by to say hello or invite us to a barbecue or an event on campus. Sometimes to go hiking or just hang out and visit. It was not unusual.

But Bob and I weren't friends, and something about this unexpected appearance at my home felt more than uncomfortable. It felt ominous. It was. Though I had no idea at the time, this one small moment would change the course of my life.

Shoving my discomfort aside, I answered the knock and offered him tea. Our conversation was casual. We likely talked about the classes we shared. We may have discussed our interests and aspirations, topics commonly covered with new acquaintances. What lodged in my memory was my unease, though even that was not so unusual. I'd always been somewhat reserved around people until I got to know them.

I concluded our visit as soon as I felt I politely could and told him I'd see him in class. I didn't invite him back.

But he did come back. Again. And again. Not often, by any means. There were weeks then months between his appearances. So much time between, in fact, that they were always a complete surprise.

I didn't appreciate the visits. Honestly, I dreaded his approach. But at the time, I had no logical explanation for my gut reaction. What's more, I felt guilty for feeling this way. So I did what I was taught to do: I ignored my instincts.

It wouldn't be kind to turn someone away, I coached myself. *Welcoming any visitor, especially one who's just lonely, is the right thing to do.*

I was there for whoever chose to show up on my doorstep, and Bob chose to show up.

Since Bruce worked and I was a student, I did double-duty as the homemaker. A devotee of whole, healthy foods, once my classes were done for the afternoon, I usually headed home to prepare our dinner from scratch, then I'd study while it cooked. Upon his occasional, unannounced afternoon arrivals, I'd invite Bob to join me while I cooked or we'd sit, have tea, and talk. He was intelligent, and I soon learned he was as interested in the mysteries and meaning of life as I was.

I kept a journal of sorts. Actually, it was whatever spare paper I could find in a class notebook whenever inspiration hit me, which I then filled with questions and thoughts about what lay beneath the surface of existence. One night, as memories of the day fell away just before falling asleep, what felt like a profound realization popped into my head and I jotted it down.

The idea stuck with me, and by the next afternoon, the excitement of a breakthrough at hand, I ignored my studies and carried my notes into the living room to follow the thought to fruition.

The universe is a series of patterns, from the smallest atom, electrons circling the nucleus, to the solar system with planets circling the sun. Whole galaxies circle a center.

Of course, this was not a new idea. But at twenty years old, it was new to me, and the question of what unseen forces were at work intrigued me.

Suddenly, a knock at the door. Annoyed, but never to be rude, I pried myself off the couch and answered it.

Bob.

While I put the kettle on, he settled into the couch, and seeing the tablet full of scribbles and sketches I'd abruptly tossed onto the cushion, he picked it up and studied it.

"Wow," he said with genuine curiosity. "What are you working on?"

Brimming with excitement, I shared my idea. With questions unanswered, it became a discussion and I'd found common ground — ground that kept the conversation impersonal, a technique I often used to keep people at arm's length.

One thing I could count on was when Bruce returned home from work, Bob would soon leave. They didn't like each other. Like dogs, it seemed they'd circle one another, growling under their breath. It wasn't that Bruce was jealous. I'd always socialized with both men and women, and from the time Bruce and I first met when I was a freshman and he a senior in high school, we'd been a committed couple. Bruce just didn't like him. I didn't like Bob either but felt it would be unkind to turn him away. Thankfully, his appearances were only occasional. Not too much to tolerate.

To my relief, Bob and I didn't share any classes after that first year, and gradually his visits — a half dozen or so in all — ceased. By late 1977, we saw very little, if any, of him.

During our first years in Boulder, Bruce and I developed a summer ritual. On Friday afternoon, I'd pack up the old Ford Bronco with camping gear and food, and we'd head for the hills, topo maps in hand. Each weekend we took a different route, exploring the history and astonishing beauty of our new homeland. We both loved photography and burned through bins of film capturing our adventures.

Winters, we would cross-country ski, the point of which, I'm convinced, is to place yourself in such mortal peril flying downhill through densely packed trees that the thrill of survival hurls you into a nirvana of nervous laughter. But hot chocolate and chili never tasted so good, and nothing could compare with the silent beauty of the woods in snow as we trekked *uphill*.

In the spring of 1978, I graduated, and Bruce and I rented a new home in town. It was a tiny, lovely, one-bedroom cottage nestled against the foothills, passed down from student to student among friends. The icing on the cake: Rent was extremely cheap.

We didn't realize Bob Vinyard was no longer in our lives. We never considered him a friend and, even now, to speak of our history with him places far too much emphasis on our acquaintance. His absence wasn't noticed. He simply wasn't missed.

Bruce and I had been together eight years when we chose to take our relationship to new depths. He was twenty-six and I, twenty-three. On a balmy, colorful fall day, encircled by family and friends, we gathered in a garden to share our joy as we exchanged our vows.

The sweet taste of our love and hopes for our future together filled our senses and our days — briefly.

When, exactly, the terror began, I can't say. It was such a bizarre experience, we scarcely believed it had happened. I only know it was 1979, soon after we married.

1979

Treating ourselves to a day of leisure, Bruce and I were lounging in the living room, reading, when we heard a knock at the front door.

Delighted to think a friend had dropped by, I hopped up, quickly covered the length of our thimble-sized room, pulled open the door, and through the screen door, saw Vinyard. My heart sank. Then it plummeted.

Something about him was distinctly different, dreadfully wrong. He looked raw, angry, wild-eyed. I didn't recognize the feral person I stood eye-to-eye with. My gut clenched and shivers rolled over my skull.

While I told myself to stay calm and rational, my fingers instinctively gripped the door latch, and in a heartbeat, I realized how thin the screen was that separated us and how tentatively it was secured to a flimsy, wooden door frame.

"Let me in," Vinyard demanded. No greeting, just urgency. "You need to come now and be with me!"

I froze, stunned. There had never been any intimate relationship between us. Not even close.

Utterly perplexed, I stammered, "I don't understand. What are you talking about?"

"Come on, let me in," he insisted as he reached for the handle.

Pulling the latch tighter, my heart in my throat, I tried to appear calm and stalwartly. "You need to leave, Bob," I said, my voice quivering.

At that, he shifted into high gear. Blood surging, a deep red stain poured across his face and neck. His muscles visibly bunched. He was gathering himself, preparing to push his way in.

Vacillating wildly between terror, confusion, and disbelief, I stood there, inanimate, until suddenly Bruce appeared at my side. Together, we slammed the solid door shut, locked it, and pushed hard against it.

The rejection, it seemed, pulled the trigger. Before I could inhale, the screen door screeched and banged as it flew open and slammed the wall. And, like muffled buckshot, an explosion of fists hit the front door so hard that with each blow, I felt the wood bow beneath my palms.

My heart hammered mercilessly against my ribs. Breath came hard and fast. Everything in my being was keenly aware of Vinyard's emotional state and the danger we faced. Digging my bare feet into the carpet, desperately reaching for solid floor, I pushed harder, hoping our weight would hold the lock and keep the door in one piece.

Above the thunderous racket, I heard Vinyard shouting at the top of his lungs. His words didn't register. The overwhelming sensations of fear and shock blocked all else out.

Finally forcing myself to be lucid, I called out, "You're making no sense. Just go away. Leave. Leave now!" He didn't.

Shaking our senses back into play, we found the presence of mind to call the police. Bruce guarded the entry while I rushed to the phone. Then, desperate to stop the invasion, I ran back and yelled through the door, "The police are on their way! They'll be here any minute!"

Gradually the fists and shouts subsided, and our shaking legs giving way, Bruce and I slowly sank to the floor. And huddled against the door, we waited, our eyes darting between the back door and the many large windows we once loved. No longer. For the first time in our lives we realized just how vulnerable we were.

Vinyard left before the officers arrived. A phantom, he vanished the same way he'd appeared — from nowhere it seemed.

We were dazed. What just happened? And why? We had no explanation for the officer who questioned us. The attack defied logic. It was crazy! Our minds raced to put the pieces of the puzzle together while we recalled the events.

He was a gray-haired officer with the confidence of many years on the force. A tall man with a strong and self-assured presence, his face dispassionate, he sat down to record the facts for his report. Then, our story unfolding, his brow furled with insinuation.

"Yeah, I've heard this before," his expression implied.

The conversation that followed is emblazoned in my memory. Quickly, he singled me out.

"What was your relationship with this man?" he asked, looking me over with disdain.

"He was a classmate and casual friend a couple of years ago. We haven't seen him since," I replied.

"Did you have an intimate relationship with him?"

"No, we never had any kind of romantic relationship."

"What did you do to encourage him?"

My gut contracted and a jet of anger gushed up. Quickly, I clamped down on it. "I didn't do anything to encourage him. Bruce and I have been together for a long time, and there was no question that my relationship with Bob was platonic. He knew that, and he never expressed any romantic intentions toward me."

"You're a pretty girl," the officer said.

I'd never considered myself pretty. I was tall, thick-boned and muscular, ash blond and average-looking. The only feature often complimented was my eyes: a pale mix of blues and golds, courtesy of my mother. But my appearance had nothing to do with this. What was he saying?

"Did you ever kiss him? How far did you go with him? Do you think about how you dress? Do you wear lipstick?"

Do you wear lipstick? I was shocked, again. I'd just had the most terrifying experience of my life. We had been violently invaded, and now the person we looked to for help, for protection, accused me. His questions and attitude clearly said more than I played a role in this. This was my fault; I was responsible not the attacker, they declared.

It was a theme that would become all too familiar in the years to come. No matter what I said, the officer's eyes doubted me. And even more disturbing, his conviction cast a shadow of doubt in Bruce — and in me.

Finally, he closed his book and stood to leave. He'd report the incident as "harassment." We were to call if Vinyard ever did this again.

Still stunned, I uttered a small thank you, closed the door, and collapsed into the couch. Then tears and anger both burst in a flood.

I was outraged. I'd heard similar stories of women who had been raped. Now here I was, the victim of an attack, blamed by the police. I was not heard. This officer's internal program was so loud, he couldn't hear me over his own static. I had no doubt that by blaming me instead of the attacker, in his mind he freed himself and all men of responsibility for their actions. The more I thought, the more furious I became.

But my anger also turned inward. What had I done? The tiny seed of self-doubt now planted began germinating in the hidden, fertile earth of my mind. I felt sick. Curling up in bed, I pulled the covers over my head for the night. What a long, dark night it would become.

Months passed. All was calm. In time, we'd nearly forgotten the attack ever happened. It was an aberration; maybe he'd been on drugs, had a "bad trip," we told ourselves. We were certain it would never happen again, and perhaps it hadn't been quite as frightening as we remembered. Or maybe we'd simply overreacted.

1980

The year turned and Vinyard returned. Again. Again. Again. Just when we'd convince ourselves it was over, that now we'd have peace, suddenly he'd appear on our porch. Where did he come from? How long had he been watching?

Startled by the knock, we'd pause and listen. Then, at the sound of his voice penetrating the door, memories of terror sent my pulse surging. Heart racing, my body trembled and I struggled to breathe.

Calling out, he'd beg me to let him in and plead, "Come with me. *Be* with me, please."

Our plan soon became habit. Bruce guarded the door while I rushed to the phone. Then I'd return to his side and shout out a warning, "The police are on their way. Leave us alone. *Never* come here again!"

But instantly, Vinyard's tone would shift, as if a different person stepped into his shoes. Suddenly he was demanding, aggressive. Terrifying.

Each time the police were called. Each time he was issued a warning. They called it harassment. I felt hunted. Stalked.

Then the phone calls began. Long pauses, weeks at least, stretched between Vinyard's appearances, and suddenly we were bombarded with volleys of phone calls — incessant barrages of calls — for hours and days at a time. Over and over and over the phone rang, intruding into our home, forcing him into our life, threatening our sanity.

Afraid that if we unplugged the phone he'd show up at our house, we tolerated the calls. At least they told us he wasn't in the neighborhood (cell phones hadn't yet been invented).

But having seen his reaction when I rejected him, we were torn between trying to reason with him and saying nothing.

At first, we tried reason. We allowed him a moment to speak, but it was always the same: "Bruce, stay out of this. Let me talk to her." Or if I answered: "I need you. Come away with me."

"There was nothing between us," I'd say. "We never had a relationship. You know that."

It didn't matter how firmly or gently I said it. The match struck, his rage ignited, and, the bellowing voice reverberating in my ear, my nerves stood at full alert.

Finally, as firmly as I could muster given the vacuum in my lungs, I'd end the call. "Stop calling. Don't *ever* contact me again."

But as soon as the handset was docked, the phone would ring again, again, again.

All my instincts warned me of danger. There was no rational explanation for the relentless invasions. Something was terribly wrong, and fear was getting an unyielding grip on me.

We always called the police. It was always a different officer, yet the reaction was inevitably the same: skeptical, dismissive, suspicious; insinuating that I was to blame. Even given the history of invasions, they didn't take us seriously and filed no reports on the calls. Before long I felt that, talking to an officer or talking to Vinyard, it hardly mattered. Both were brick walls.

When finally I pleaded with one officer for help, he recommended we ignore the calls and not speak to him. Bruce and I looked at each other, our faces grey. Cutting him off would put us at greater risk. But on the verge of losing our minds, we decided to take that risk.

After that, as soon as we heard his voice (there was no such thing as caller ID), we hung up the phone. He persisted, the clanging bell intruding on the silence, jangling our nerves. Hour upon hour, day after day.

By now we were extremely wary, careful to keep the curtains drawn and doors locked at all times. We surveyed the area before leaving or entering our home. Anticipation and anxiety were our constant companions, and still we had no explanation as to why this was happening.

Then as suddenly as the invasions began, they stopped.

We counted the days that spread into weeks and finally months. Gradually, we put the events behind us, convincing ourselves again that it was an aberration, that it was over. Denial was satiating.

*   *   *

Two years passed in peace. We believed it would last the rest of our lives, and we moved on with ours.

Bruce worked in his profession and to develop mine, in the spring of '83, I enrolled in graduate school at the University of Colorado in Denver. Eager to expand myself in school and build a career, I studied landscape architecture to specialize in environmental planning and restoration.

We worked on projects in teams and the program was intense. Working early morning through many late nights, we saw a lot of each other and little of our homes. Yet in this close-knit studio of students, I was acutely uncomfortable. Something was different.

I was different.

With this feast of new friends laid before me, I didn't partake. When invited to join a group for coffee or dinner, I would decline with some excuse I conjured on the spot then secretly run off to dine alone, eating while walking. Or I'd sink into invisibility on the rare occasion that I sat at a café table. When I did, I'd grab a small table in the corner, my back to the wall, and I'd take a book or newspaper to immerse myself in, clearly signaling I was unavailable. At times, when I felt I really should make an effort, I'd accept an invitation, only to wish I could slink away and disappear.

I had always been introverted and enjoyed time alone. As a child I was painfully shy. Yet in time I'd learned to be at ease with people, and though never a social butterfly, I always had a few close friends and a number of casual ones. But now social settings were deeply disturbing.

When giving a design presentation, I was open and passionate, I allowed myself be seen; it was safe, the subject impersonal. But one-on-one, I was a distinctly different person. It was as though a switch flipped off inside of me and I contracted. Walling myself off, I firmly shut others out and, unknowingly, shut myself in.

If someone looked directly at me, I averted my eyes. The sense that someone was connecting with me was downright terrifying.

I thought I no longer trusted people. The truth, I would later discover, was I no longer trusted myself. Tucked far away in a hidden corner of my mind, that seed planted by the very first responding officer had flourished in my unconscious. I'd assumed some responsibility for what happened, and with no conscious awareness of it, I'd slammed the door on friendships.

Bruce became my only outlet for any kind of intimacy, and we were closer than we'd ever been. But, though only vaguely aware of it at the time, I was deeply lonely and constantly anxious out in the world.

*   *   *

4/2/1983

It was a beautiful April day. The warm rays of the sun pouring through our windows persuaded us to open the front door and welcome the spring breezes into our little cottage. Then as I passed through our tiny living room, I heard the screen door creak and looked up.

Bruce was closer to it than I. Suddenly, a muffled exclamation and the sounds of scuffling and banging shattered the silence.

I was shocked. My heart thundered. No, it couldn't be.

After all this time — more than two years — Vinyard had once again appeared out of nowhere. Creeping silently up the steps and onto the porch, he'd opened the screen door and stepped into our home. With absolutely no warning, he'd crossed the threshold into our private space and into my psyche. I felt deeply, horribly violated.

Bruce had flown to the door to push him out but was not quick enough. The door slammed against Vinyard then banged back open. In a rush of fear and anger, Bruce shoved Vinyard out and over the porch rail. Stunned and horrified, I watched Vinyard scramble to his feet and leap back onto the porch. Lunging, he grabbed Bruce and hauled him down the stairs, and — pulling, shoving, grappling — they were locked in a brawl.

Vinyard was more massive than Bruce (of stocky build, he outweighed my lean husband by at least fifty pounds), and his rage imbued in him a strength that we, gripped by fear, could not match. And we were peaceful people. We had no idea how to defend ourselves.

The sickening image of Vinyard violently attacking Bruce flooding my brain, I tried and failed to develop a plan. First running out the door — to do what? — then turning back, I rushed to the phone and dialed 911. Then, in a vain attempt to stop the fight, I ran out the door and onto the porch and again cried out, "The police are on their way!"

Perched above them, my weight shifting from foot to foot as I searched for a way into the fray, I shouted down at Vinyard to stop. And from that angle, witnessing the savage fury unleashed on Bruce, suddenly the breadth of the stalker's rage and determination hit me like a shot, piercing the haze in my brain.

Until that moment, we'd thought I alone was Vinyard's target. In that instant, I knew. His sight was also aimed directly at Bruce, and he was in mortal danger.

With steely fists, Vinyard pulled Bruce's face in close, and pure vicious hatred shone in this predator's eyes. No one would stop him, those eyes declared; no one would get in his way.

Suddenly, Vinyard slipped on the dirt and gravel that had sprayed across the sidewalk, and Bruce broke free of his grip. Gasping, spent, somehow he found the strength to reach the porch. I grabbed his arm and pulled, and together we stumbled into the house, slammed the door, and locked it.

They must have been in the neighborhood; it seemed less than a minute had passed. When the patrol car rounded the corner, Vinyard tried to flee but was stopped by the officers. One held him in the car while the other approached us for a statement.

Still breathless and shaken, we described the shocking invasion and the stalking history. Now it had escalated to breaking and entering and physical violence. Bruce's clothes were dirty and disheveled. Angry red scratches blossomed on his arms. Stones from the terraces below our porch were strewn down the slope, and the plants lay crushed and broken. They were all physical evidence, proof that our fear of this man was justified. I was horrified it had gone this far.

The officer said he'd take care of it and would be in touch. Together, Bruce and I watched from the dark recesses of our living room as the squad car drove off with Vinyard safely secured in the back seat.

Once out of sight, we breathed a deep sigh of relief. Now we'd be taken seriously, we reasoned. Now this would be stopped.

It didn't stop. For this, Vinyard was given yet another warning. Four months later, he appeared again and was warned again. The police called both episodes harassment. In five years of invasions and terror, there had been no arrests, no jail time, just warnings. That they would do what?

It was then we fully realized the danger we faced. And because there had never been any consequences imposed for his actions, we knew we faced it alone.

I was now uncontrollably hyper-vigilant, always looking over my shoulder, anticipating the next strike.

But again the stalking subsided, and in time, we convinced ourselves it was over. With fierce determination, we picked ourselves up once again and moved on with our lives.

*   *   *

Two more years passed with no sign of Vinyard, and in the summer of 1985, I gave birth to our first child: our beautiful son, Ian. But all too soon our bubble of joy would be punctured.

Bruce had been experiencing muscle weakness and lack of coordination. He was now having problems with his vision. Two months after the birth of our son, he was diagnosed with MS. Multiple sclerosis. We were devastated.

The following spring, I completed my thesis and received my master's degree. The achievement was bittersweet. The life we had dreamed of, worked so long and hard for, would not be as we had imagined. Our future looked fearfully uncertain. I was thirty years old.

CHAPTER 2

Nemesis

"You must do the thing you think you cannot do."
~ Eleanor Roosevelt

I've always been a seeker — of truth, of the meaning of life, of cause and effect. While most kids in my neighborhood were playing foursquare and riding bikes, I could most often be found alone in the woods behind my house, sitting by a trickling stream, contemplating. I was hardly the most popular kid on the block.

I was raised in the Christian church, Lutheran denomination, and always wanting to help people, I volunteered for charitable work. Our church's chosen youth mission was to visit institutionalized mental health patients and offer to escort them to chapel services. How ironic.

Although in my childhood I was a devoted follower of the faith, around the age of eleven, I began seriously questioning. I now affectionately refer to this period as my pre-adolescent existential crisis. I remember a particularly rebellious conversation I had with God in which I declared, "If you really love me, you'll understand my need to question." I still felt guilty, but at least I'd been honest and stated my intent.

By the time I was confirmed in the church, I was ready to search outside its walls for answers. As soon as I could drive, I launched into an exploration of other religious beliefs — at least as far as my imagination, cultivated in a middle-class suburban neighborhood in the Midwest, could take me. I attended services at other denominations of the Christian church.

But my thirst was not quenched, and I had a penchant for historical heretics who, regardless of the sacrifice, searched for truth beyond dogma. By my late teens, I declared myself agnostic. I believed there was purpose beyond the veil of human experience but didn't feel any religious tradition held the answers.

I don't think I've ever lived without a spiritual connection, although throughout all the events of my twenties, I wasn't consciously aware of it; I'd left religion far behind. But I was compelled to follow my inner guidance in my studies and in choosing to have our child. I followed my passions and my principles, and my search for truth and meaning were relentless. Yet over the last decade, each time I'd lift myself up, I was beaten down — hard. And like a wave churned up by stormy seas, I'd rise again, only to be slammed harder into the rocks.

I was angry. I was a good person, and I'd worked hard to build a life of service to the greater good. I trusted that all our life experiences were here to teach us but could make no sense of my own. The abstract mysteries of life always fascinated me: *What is mankind's place in the universe? Why are we here?* Now the question was personal: *Why is this happening to me? What on earth is the gift in all this?* My own life had become the great puzzle.

Starved for an answer, I delved into self-help books and attended lectures and workshops; Boulder was a virtual smorgasbord of spiritual paths. I tried meditation only to find I was what I call a "type A meditator." It seemed impossible to find bliss when my mind kept telling me I wasn't doing it right or trying hard enough. So I listened to tapes of guided imagery. (At least when someone else was talking, my brain shut up.) While the calm, gentle voice painted a scene in my mind and guided my experience, I found I could finally relax and settle into the long-forgotten, comforting sensations of stillness and peace.

I didn't find the answers to my questions, but I was beginning to re-discover my connection to Source. I was reassured there was a benevolent cosmic order, a divine force greater than us, and that there was purpose in all life experiences — purpose that was always for our benefit, never to harm.

I could not fathom the purpose of my own experiences. Though my mind craved understanding, I was forced to rely on faith. My life would be highly challenging; I had no doubt about that now. With roadblocks at every turn, I could not clearly see the life ahead of me. But I no longer felt so alone walking into the fog.

By 1987, two years after the diagnosis, Bruce used a cane to steady himself while walking. The doctors assured us that MS often progressed slowly and that his function might never be severely diminished. We clung to that hope and were assured that with ongoing research there would surely be a cure in the next decade or so.

Taking one day at a time we adjusted, keenly aware we were building our life on shifting sands. But we would make it. We were determined to live a full, happy life together as family. I'm reminded of the sage wisdom: Perhaps the world is round so we may never see too far down the road. Had I known what lay ahead, I don't know that I could have faced it, that I would have had the courage to keep placing one foot in front of the other and continue down this path.

*   *   *

In time, Ian grew to be a bright, active two-year-old, always pushing his limits. Before he could crawl, he rolled across the room to discover what was beyond his reach. As soon as he could walk, he ran. Wide-eyed, mouth gaping open in a great unfettered grin, he'd make a beeline for the next great thing. His enthusiasm could not be contained and he was a handful to keep up with.

I worked at a firm in town, and with little money to spare, we'd stayed in our uniquely affordable, tiny cottage home nestled at the foot of the soaring Flatirons, the solid slabs of rock upended by powerful geologic forces long ago. We often remarked that when the snow was fresh, they looked like giant brownies sprinkled with powdered sugar. Christmas was coming, a cheerful time of anticipation with a toddler in the house.

12/16/1987

It was after midnight on a cold, clear winter night. We were deeply asleep — Bruce and I in our bed, Ian in his crib next to us in the cramped room — when suddenly, leaping out of the silence, the deafening clamor of cannon fire pelting the house pounded us awake.

Instantly, Bruce and I were sitting up, staring at the bedroom window in shock. Disjointed sensations frantically coalescing, the image quickly took shape in our minds.

Vinyard. Outside. Just two feet from the foot of our bed.

Thrashing violently, his feet and fists pummeled the wall and window frame. His words slurred and voice gravelly, he was in a crazed fury, shouting obscenities and threats at the top of his lungs.

"Come out and settle this!" he bellowed. Then, referring to me, he disgorged a spray of revolting sexual slurs and commanded, "Send the bitch out here!"

The ghost of a worn cotton curtain, barely visible in the inky darkness, was all that kept us hidden. Only a thin pane of glass stood between him and us, and with each blow to the wall it trembled. I was terrified he would burst through the glass at any moment.

The phone. How far is the phone? Shadows. Don't cast shadows. Don't make a sound.

Then, as suddenly as it began, the attack stopped. The silence was heavy, dense — electric.

My breath still, I tuned into the void, desperately searching for clues.

Dried leaves crackled quietly under footsteps that turned, paused, turned back, then stopped. He was so close, it seemed I could hear him breathe.

Ian was eerily, profoundly silent. I was torn. Should I pick him up? The truth of it pulled at my heart: If he stayed quiet, maybe Vinyard wouldn't notice him. He was safer away from me.

The decision made, I gathered myself to move to the phone and suddenly, to my horror, discovered that — though my whole body shook uncontrollably — I was completely paralyzed. No matter how hard I tried, I – could – not – move.

With every ounce of willpower commanding my nerves to obey, I gradually regained control of my limbs, and Bruce and I crawled silently off the bed then slid across the floor beneath the windows.

Hands trembling, Bruce dialed 911 and whispered an urgent plea for help. And there, pressed against a small strip of wall between windows, barefoot and in nightclothes, we shivered and waited. Thoroughly absorbed in every sound — leaves rustling, a twig snapping, faint footfalls on the frozen ground — we tracked the predator's movements, guessing wildly at his intentions, his plan.

Finally, silence. Not a trace of sound. Was he gone?

Just as sheer terror began to ebb, an explosion of fists, profanities, and threats erupted. Again and again, long silences broken by violent outbursts crashed over us in waves.

Hours seemed to pass before the police arrived. By then, Vinyard had fled.

Once again, we reported the episode to skeptical officers who had no idea who we were or the history of the attacks. It had been four years since the last invasion.

With little sleep to sustain us, once morning arrived, I quickly prepared to leave for work and take Ian to daycare. Home was no longer a sanctuary and I didn't want to be there. But before stepping foot outside, I peered through the curtains in every direction, scanning for any sign of the stalker. And there, across the street corner, a parked car caught my eye. There he sat. Watching. Waiting.

Through a narrow slit in the curtains, we studied the scene. This time when the officers approached him, like a viper spitting venom, Vinyard slung an angry litany of obscenities at them so loudly, we heard him inside our home a half block away.

The officers inched toward him. While one stood to the side, hands poised over his belt, the other slowly approached Vinyard with one hand up and open, as if coaxing him to calm down. He didn't calm down. Taking a step back then leaning toward them, he grew redder and louder. Profanities poured from his mouth.

The officer approaching him paused. Then, as he slowly stepped forward, I saw his other hand move to his belt. Discretely, he unclipped a pair of handcuffs and eased them into view. Vinyard's head turned toward the cuffs, his body compressed, and he lunged at the officer.

Both officers seized him, and the knot of writhing bodies slowly swam toward the squad car. Then suddenly, the mass stopped and parted. Defiant, Vinyard had spread his arms and legs wide, planted his feet firmly on the asphalt, and was yelling in our direction, "Come on, it's time to go! It's time to go now!"

Finally, with both their bodies pressed against his, the officers held Vinyard face down against the car, cuffed him, and wrestled him into the back seat.

The sight of his violent outburst, even as the police tried to control him, was terrifying. Fueled by his unfathomable rage, he was strong. Our instincts were right. We'd been in serious danger.

Once he was safely locked inside the patrol car, one of the officers approached us for a statement. Then, they were gone.

Collapsing into the couch, we were quiet, thoughtful. He was gone. It was over. We were safe, for now.

Doubt seeped into my gut. I no longer trusted that we'd be protected. But today, we'd seen him arrested and taken away. Today, he had fought with the police; they saw what he was like.

What we didn't know then was that later that day he'd be released on bond. Neither did we know that, at the time, there was no stalking law in Colorado. Surely others had been stalked and there were laws to protect us, we'd thought.

He was charged with trespass and harassment, both third-degree misdemeanors — the least serious of all crimes. A hearing date was set. The bond was conditional: He was to have no contact with us and was not allowed within two blocks of our home.

Our curtains stayed closed at all times. Doors were always locked. The steep, winding path from our door to the car was a danger zone. Anywhere else in our yard or neighborhood without the protection of a car was out of the question. He was out there somewhere, and we were prisoners in our own home.

12/19/1987

When three days had passed, we desperately needed a break from the tension and our four walls, and we gave ourselves a night out. Lingering over our dinner and the welcome breath of freedom, we didn't return until after ten o'clock. Approaching our neighborhood, I slowed the car and we carefully surveyed the area.

Nothing unusual. Nothing out of the ordinary.

Slowly, I pulled into the driveway, parked, and cautiously stepped out. Reaching into the back seat, I quietly released the buckle and gently pulled Ian from his car seat. His head dropped onto my shoulder. Exhausted, he was fast asleep.

While Bruce and I walked up the sidewalk heading toward our door, I scanned the area, and a reflection caught my eye. Pausing to study it, I could just make out the form of a car hidden in the shadows beyond the reach of the streetlight. In an instant I realized that from that position, our front door was easily seen.

Suddenly, the driver's door flew open and a large, dark figure charged out. Gaining ground fast, Vinyard strode directly toward us, yelling, "I don't want to hurt you, but it's time to go!"

By then the house was closer than the car. Leaning hard on his cane, Bruce picked up his pace. Clutching Ian to my chest with one arm, I slipped the other into the crook of Bruce's elbow to steady him and pull him along.

"Just go," Bruce said with conviction.

Quickly, I released his arm and, estimating distance and speed, glanced at the door then Vinyard and flew up the steps.

Hands trembling, I willed the key to find the hole and threw the door open. Bruce was right behind me. Together we stepped up and in, and the door slammed shut just before Vinyard reached us.

We made it. We're safe.

Heart pounding, gasping for air, shaking violently from head to toe, I stood suspended in the pitch black room while the image of the stalker charging and threatening us replayed over and over in my mind. *I don't want to hurt you, but it's time to go.* Everything about his bearing said hurting one or both of us was an option he would readily choose.

He eluded the police. Again, he was gone long before they arrived.

They'd file a report, they said and suggested we contact the district attorney's office to follow up. In all these years, until the arrest a few days earlier, our case had never gone beyond warnings by the police. We were completely ignorant of the criminal justice process and had no idea what the next step was. Now we learned that because Vinyard had finally been charged, the case was in the hands of the district attorney's office, the prosecutor.

The next day, we contacted the deputy DA handling the case and explained the long history of invasions. He assured us that Vinyard's bond would be revoked, an arrest warrant would be issued, and a restraining order would be filed. Finally, we felt the danger to us was taken seriously. A restraining order would protect us. He'd be arrested and jailed.

But in that moment, Vinyard was still out there, somewhere. On pins and needles, we waited and tried to go about our lives.

On December 31, more than a week later, the arrest warrant was issued. To our great relief, Vinyard was soon caught. Then finally, we were handed the information that would shed some light on the violent invasions we had endured for so long. To us it was no less than a revelation, assurance that the attacks would be seen for the terrifying violations they were and no longer be blamed on us.

The DA's office discovered that between 1981 and '83, during our first respite, Vinyard had been admitted to the Aurora Mental Health Center several times. He'd also worked briefly in Alaska and there, was admitted to a psychiatric institute where he was diagnosed, we were told, as schizophrenic and delusional. This disclosure did nothing to calm our fears. But finally, after eight long years, we had some explanation.

The deputy DA continued, "He has fantasized a relationship and is obsessed with you. He requires drug treatment but cannot be required to continue it."

This definitely didn't calm our fears.

We trusted the deputy DA's assurance that his office would prosecute the case and we didn't need to be involved if we didn't want to. We did not want to be subjected to Vinyard in court and were not subpoenaed. We just wanted this all behind us. While we didn't aggressively pursue our defense, we did stay in contact with the DA's office.

Soon Vinyard appeared in court and afterward, the deputy DA called us with the results. As expected, the judge, David Torke, found Vinyard guilty of violating the conditions of bond. But shockingly, the judge then deferred his sentence for twelve months, with the conditions of counseling and "no-contact," the same condition he'd just violated. Now with the sentence deferred, if Vinyard attended counseling, didn't contact us, and committed no other crimes for twelve months, there would be no jail time and the charges would be dropped.

He was to undergo counseling at Aurora Mental Health Center near his home in the Denver area and be supervised by a caseworker in the community corrections department in Boulder. And with that, Vinyard was freed.

We were horrified. How could this be? During this whole episode, we were directly threatened with physical harm, both by actions and words. This predator's rage was aimed at both my husband for being in the way and me for rejecting him. And the attacks had now spanned eight years with no consequences for any of the violations and absolutely no protection for us.

Clearly the judge did not comprehend how terrifying and dangerous this was. But now, there was nothing to do but wait. And hope.

*   *   *

Throughout the years, when episodes of stalking erupted, shattering years-long periods of peace, we debated what else we could do to protect ourselves. If we had to move, we could but not at a moment's notice. And we struggled financially. Our rental was still the cheapest, by far, anywhere in the area, so as long as we stayed in place, we could save for a home of our own — or for a safety net in case Bruce couldn't work. We just needed time to get on our feet and build a stable foundation.

Friends often said they'd get a gun, but I was a staunch believer in non-violence. I would not allow fear to change who I was or what I believed. And even if I turned my back on that, I would never feel safe with a gun in a house with a child. What's more, Bruce was now in no condition to wield a weapon, so it would be up to me. Given my feelings about violence and the disturbing, lingering question of whether I was in some way responsible for Vinyard's obsession, I was sure I would hesitate to pull the trigger, and if I did, the weapon could quickly be turned on any or all of us. A gun was not an option.

Before we married and the stalking began, Bruce and I adopted a dog: a sweet, gentle collie mix. She was so gentle in fact that, to our surprise, she never barked or showed any sign of aggression — not even when Vinyard attacked the house or fought with Bruce. But once Ian was born, and especially when he became mobile, we were grateful that she was so trustworthy. We didn't feel we could trust another, a better guard dog, around a toddler and only hoped ours would protect Ian if he was in danger.

For now, the only other plausible option was to rely on the criminal justice system, created specifically to enforce the law, ensure public safety, and administer justice. The idea that, in a civilized society, we should have to abandon our life and run from a dangerous predator or defend ourselves with a lethal weapon, and in so doing increase the danger to everyone, sickened me. We expected the system to do what it was designed to do and stop this.

*   *   *

More than three months passed. All was quiet. Clinging to hope, we tried to convince ourselves that perhaps this time the no-contact and counseling conditions took hold. Then in April, the peace we enjoyed was fractured. Vinyard, angry and volatile, appeared at our home again and demanded that I go with him. Beyond that, I don't remember the details. I had not yet begun keeping a full record of the invasions. I trusted that all the events from the beginning in 1979 were documented in police reports and that all those reports would be reviewed in court. I was wrong. I only know that on April 23, 1988, Vinyard was again arrested at our home for "harassment."

April rolled into May, and gorgeous spring weather came with it. All Ian wanted was to run outside, dig in the dirt, and explore. And I wanted, more than anything, to throw the door open and watch him play without a care in the world. But the knot in my gut would not unwind. Happiness took a back seat to anxiety. Indoors was safer.

5/2/1988

On a warm, still afternoon, I picked Ian up from daycare after work and headed home. I found no strange cars on the block. I didn't expect to; Vinyard had just been arrested and taken away again.

Bruce was already home, and upon hearing us pull into the gravel driveway, he opened the door and let our dog run out to greet us. Then Bruce closed the screen door and retreated back into the house.

Walking hand in hand down the sidewalk, Ian and I had reached down to play with our pup when suddenly, Vinyard appeared on the sidewalk directly in front of us. Hiding behind a tall, thick shrub next to the walk, the hunter had waited, poised to pounce on his prey.

His intention palpable, he fully blocked my way, and pure terror gripped me. Heart thundering, my body quaked, but my mind was fully engaged: How could I protect my son?

Releasing his tiny hand, I pressed my palm onto Ian's shoulder and gently guided him behind me, trying not to frighten him. He must have sensed danger; my rambunctious, vociferous son followed my unspoken directions without a sound.

My mind raced, calculating. The quickest way to the door was up a winding stone path then up the concrete steps to our porch. How could I get Ian there safely? Could we get there fast enough to lock the door in time? Where was Bruce?

Watching, waiting for an opening, I instinctively stood upright, legs parted slightly for support. Arms dropped at my sides, I twisted my hands behind me to corral my son. The warrior I had not known existed within me emerged. It was instinct; I was the lioness protecting my cub. No matter what happened, I would not allow him to harm my son.

"I see you got a dog," Vinyard snickered.

I got a dog? Had he seen Ian? Up to now, we'd been careful to hide the fact that we had a child. To our knowledge, he didn't know. But now the evidence was right in front of him. Had he not seen him or just chosen not to mention him? Was he afraid of the dog? He reached down to pat her head and she dodged his touch. Then, caught up in the thrill of freedom, she took off, sprinting around the house and deep into the back yard.

"It's time to go," Vinyard said sternly.

How could I stop this without escalating the danger? What could I say?

Desperate to connect with the rational person I'd known years before, I looked into his eyes and deeper. Then forcing air into my lungs, I said, "I'm not going anywhere with you. You need to leave now."

His flesh suddenly deepening to an iron red, he boldly stepped closer and loudly declared, "No, I know you want to come with me, to be with me!"

His rage was building. He was a volcano about to erupt.

Tentatively, I stood my ground. "I've told you many times that we never had a relationship. We don't now. You need to leave. Now."

"How can you say that? That's a lie! You know you wanted me," he shouted.

No matter what I said, he would not hear me. With each rejection, his face pressed closer to mine and his voice grew louder until, the echoes plucking the strings of my nerves, my body visibly shook.

"I know you want me!" he roared in my face.

"I don't want you. I never have. Leave now. Don't *ever* come back here again. Stay away from me!" I said and took a step to the side, plainly signaling I was leaving.

"You fucking *bitch!*" he shrieked as he stepped in and blocked me. A stream of vulgar slurs spewed from his mouth and then, "You're wrong. You do want me. I know you do!"

Time slowed. All the world shrank to the narrow space between us. Though we were nearly the same height, he seemed to grow taller and his angry red face loomed over me, now inches from mine. At any moment, he would either strike or grab me. What followed, I remember as if it were yesterday.

Terrified by the specter of violence and rage, riveted to his crimson face and beady dark eyes, I discovered that, once again, I could not move. I was cemented to the ground where I stood.

Then suddenly, like a tidal wave, my fear washed down through my body and into the earth beneath me. And into the vacuum left in its wake poured a great, vibrating column of energy, so strong, so vivid I could see it in my mind's eye.

In a heartbeat, a profound sense of peace filled me, warmed me, calmed me. I felt immeasurably powerful. Then, filled to overflowing, my heart opened and a conduit of energy reached out directly from my heart to my attacker's. In that instant, we were connected by this inescapable force holding us in stillness. And oddly, the sensation was somehow familiar.

I have no sense of how long it lasted. I only know that while we were linked eye-to-eye and heart-to-heart, calming words came unbidden to my lips and I slowly side-stepped around him so that my son, still behind me, was directly in line with the door.

Gradually, Vinyard's face drew back, his overpowering stance relaxed, and I had my moment. First stepping back then at the last second turning, I grabbed Ian and ran up the steps. Bruce appeared and opened and closed the door behind us. The latch slammed into place. Discretely, we watched as Vinyard turned and scurried down the alley. Then, he was gone.

Bruce hugged Ian and, trying to maintain some sense of normalcy, urged him into the kitchen to get something to drink. Quiet, I sank into the couch and reflected on the moment.

Without a doubt, something mystical had just occurred, something well beyond my comprehension or power.

Perhaps it was divine intervention. Perhaps it was as described in the ancient Chinese practice of Qigong where one draws chi (qi) — the energy field in all things — into the body and directs it out through the chest to meet force not with force, but with control. Or perhaps it was Satori, the Zen concept of the warrior's state of being, when the mind rests in pure awareness, free of thought; the body is active, sensitive, and relaxed; and the emotions are open and free. Perhaps many traditions recognize this miraculous state of being. At the time, I knew of none of them.

However one interprets it, one thing was clear: This was a force much greater than me. The force I felt was divine love and peace pouring into and radiating out from me. Not only were Ian and I protected from serious harm, I was given the gift of certainty that Spirit was alive and *accessible*. And I'd witnessed firsthand that this force was more powerful than the most ferocious rage or the most debilitating fear.

We reported the episode to the police and the DA's office. A full week later, another arrest warrant was issued for failure to comply with the conditions of the deferred sentence, and bond was raised from $1,500 to $2,500. Most bail bonds required only a 15 percent deposit. For a mere $375, this predator could get out of jail again. When he was arrested.

The survival tools we humans carry amaze me. In time of need, they surface: instincts, remnants from our distant, ancestral past. Yet used for long, they come at a steep price.

Above all, we did not want to frighten our son. Swallowing our fear, we carried on as normally as possible. But I felt as if I was severed in two. The face I presented to my child and the world was calm and in control; I attended to work and our home life as if nothing had happened. Yet inside, I was shaken to the core, constantly anxious and on-guard, anticipating the next strike.

For seven months we lived with this threat hanging over us and forced our minds away from it. We were determined not to let fear steal our lives. Then on January 12, 1989, Vinyard was finally found and arrested. The next day, he was released on bond.

A month later, a hearing was held to revoke the deferred sentence. Instead, Judge Torke granted an extension of the already deferred sentence for another six months. The condition: therapy at Bethesda.

We reeled at the news. It was as if a wall of mirrored glass separated us from those who held ultimate power over our lives. We were not seen. We were not heard.

Why couldn't the judge see the truth? Determined to fix Vinyard in lieu of protecting us, he was immersed in an illusion, it seemed.

Trapped in a revolving door, spinning round and round, time and again we were spit out by the system at the exact place we started — terrorized and in danger.

Finally, that spring Bruce and I were able to pave our own way out of the living nightmare. We purchased a home and, on the first of April 1989, moved to Longmont, a small town not far from Boulder. We didn't publish our address or phone number. To take back our lives we, ironically, disappeared.

Shortly after our move, I received a letter forwarded from our previous address. The envelope bore a pre-printed return address from a post office box in Las Vegas, New Mexico, but no name. My name was hand-written. There was no clue who it was from, but fear shot up like a geyser.

Ripping it open, I quickly located the signature — "Love, Bob" — and my hands started shaking so badly, I couldn't read the words. Rushing to the nearest table, I laid down the letter, closed my eyes, and drew long, deep breaths.

It was forwarded. He doesn't know where we live. He can't find us.

Once I'd attained a reasonably calm state, I raced through the letter. He needed me, he said, then apologized for not letting *me* be able to get in touch with *him*. "Please oh please forgive me and come visit me. I'm at the Las Vegas Medical Health Center, Las Vegas, New Mexico (otherwise known as the Looney Bin)."

I leaped to his closing words and a gong of alarm rang through my hollowed chest. "You can save me."

Before we moved, I'd made sure the deputy DA had our contact information. Now I called him to report the letter and was told that two weeks earlier, Vinyard had been arrested in New Mexico for felony car theft and felony receiving and was subsequently admitted to the Las Vegas Medical Center, a psychiatric hospital. "Not to worry," the deputy DA said. "He was found competent to stand trial, and the prosecutor handling the case feels sure he'll be incarcerated there for a long time."

My gut churning, I was simultaneously relieved and infuriated. Stealing a car and receiving stolen property were felonies. For those he'd be locked up a long time. But terrorizing us was a misdemeanor, and in the ten years we had endured this horror, Vinyard had never once served a sentence.

Seething, I breathed deeply and reminded myself that now we were safe; that was all that mattered. In time, I told myself, I'd be able to let it go.

CHAPTER 3

Silence

"There are haunters of the silence, ghosts that hold the heart and brain:
I have sat with them and hearkened; I have talked with them in vain."

~ *Madison Cawein,*
Haunters of the Silence

When it came down to it, it was the view that called us to our new home. Framing an expanse of rolling green, our picture window led the eye and mind to the distant mountain ranges and spectacular sunsets.

Soon our family grew. First, our delightful daughter arrived. The moment she was born, her big, soft, curious eyes melted all our hearts. When Ian, nearly four years old now, first laid eyes on her, his face radiated wonder. Then leaning in to look closely, he said gently, "My beautiful sister, Sophie."

Two years later, our sweet son, Seth, was born. Ian was so excited to play with him that one evening, when I'd laid Seth down in his carrier next to me while I prepared dinner, Ian raced into the kitchen and carefully placed his Legos, one by one, on Seth's belly then eagerly awaited his reaction. I explained that it would be a while before Seth could play with them and, of course, warned him again about the dangers of small objects around infants.

When Seth did become more aware, fascinated by the antics of his brother and sister dancing around him with wild abandon, sharing their favorite books and toys, and inventing games to include him, his smiling eyes crinkled into the most charming crescent moons. Soon he became a remarkably generous child with a strong sense of fairness.

And Sophie, flanked on either side by her brothers, quickly learned to be fierce when needed. A strong-willed girl with a mind of her own, she was both sweet and salty. I appreciated that.

Moving from our tiny cottage, we didn't have much furniture, but the freedom of our sparse, spacious living room was heaven to me. In the center of that room, I would hold my precious children in my arms and rock, gazing out at that long view and breathing peace and serenity deep into my soul. We had taken our life back.

Nothing can give one a new appreciation for life so much as living in fear of losing it. But while our new life together was treasured, the horrors of the past were not easily swept away. Aftershocks from years of terror rolled through me unexpectedly.

For a long time, a knock on the door and I'd hit the floor. All my senses would explode into awareness, and crouched below window level, I'd crawl to the nearest spot I could find that was hidden from all views. It didn't matter if the curtains were closed; there were always gaps one could peer through.

Heart hammering, I'd gasp for breath. Then my rational mind would resurface, and I'd tell myself I was being ridiculous. *It's probably a neighbor or the postman. Just pull yourself together, get up, and answer the door!*

But I rarely did. I was paralyzed. Waiting, listening, I'd track the footsteps as they shuffled across the porch, paused, padded toward the window and back to the door, then stopped. Silent, I'd wait longer. Then louder, persistent knocking, the rising intensity mirrored in my own racing heart.

Finally the footsteps would turn, thump down the stairs, and scrape across the concrete walk. I followed every nuance of sound as a skilled hound tracks the scent of a fox. Listening for the footfalls to diminish — a clear sign the visitor was moving away — I'd then tune into the silence. And still I'd wait until profound silence dissolved into the ambient sounds of nature: birds chirping, leaves rustling. Only then would my heart begin to slow, my breath relax and deepen. And only then would I rise and move ever so slowly and silently to peer through a slit in the curtains, taking care not to cast a shadow. Up and down the street I'd look until, satisfied the intruder was gone, I would sit, calm myself, and gradually let my system recover.

I felt utterly foolish afterward, but there was simply no denying the raw impulses that seized control. And gradually, curtains were seldom left open. Doors always remained locked.

And there were other signs of damage. The slightest, normal threat to the safety or happiness of my children caused a nearly uncontrollable surge of ferocity to rise in me. It was a force to be reckoned with, but I was the one who had to fight it, forcing my rational mind to assume control. These were normal childhood experiences, important for their development and self-esteem, I'd tell myself. But riding bikes and climbing trees sawed at my frayed nerves. And the least bit of bullying and I was over the top; it took every ounce of self-control to keep me from stepping in and roaring over the tiny culprit. I constantly monitored and fought my tendency to overreact and overprotect.

Then there were the nightmares — constant dreams of physically fighting an enemy and dreams of struggling to break through impregnable barriers — over and over and over. I'd wake up more exhausted than when I went to bed. There was no solace in the night.

I'd heard of flashbacks experienced by Vietnam veterans but had never heard of a treatment for it. And I hadn't seen the horrors they had. This wasn't the same, I told myself. The term "post-traumatic stress disorder," or PTSD, did not appear in mainstream consciousness until many years later. To me, it just was what it was. I had to accept that, for now, I was damaged and move on, hoping time, the master healer, would heal even these deep wounds. I focused instead on my family's happiness.

But life would not be as we'd hoped. In time, the course of our lives split in two, simultaneously moving both forward and backward. On the one hand, we delighted in watching our children grow and discovering who they were, each a unique and cherished individual. On the other, Bruce's condition deteriorated rapidly. He could no longer work and succumbed to using a wheelchair. Each day, it seemed, his function was diminished and the disease took its toll on him, and indeed all of us, physically and emotionally.

It was as if an earthquake had crumbled our home, and as I scrambled to pick up the pieces and rebuild, another tremor would hit, dissolving it into rubble. And the tremors kept coming until I finally I accepted that it was impossible to rebuild. The forces of destruction constantly overpowering my ability to create a happy home, all I could do was continually adapt and watch our life disintegrate.

Bruce cared for the children while I worked, and once she retired, his mother moved in with us to help. I had a job in an engineering company and my salary was better than it would be in most firms. For that I was grateful; we desperately needed the income. But I had learned all I could there, my work was no longer fulfilling, I was not living up to my potential, and my future there held no promise of change. Unhappily, I accepted my fate. I was my family's primary support. I would do what I needed to do for them.

But my disappointment at not being free to contribute all I could or follow my passions simmered. In time, my disappointment grew and changed. I felt trapped. I became bitter and apathetic. I thought I'd kept my resentment to myself, but in truth, I let my work slide and my attitude showed. Then in 1992, I was "let go." In all honesty I know that, unconsciously, I pushed my employers to take action. I desperately wanted out but did not have the courage to risk our income and leave on my own.

Once I'd spent sufficient time curled in the fetal position feeling sick and ashamed, I looked at my options. Most jobs in my field were in Denver: more interesting work but less pay and a long commute. I hated the city and the commute would mean at least two more hours away from my family each day. That would not only be emotionally taxing but, given Bruce's condition, unsafe.

Was this my opportunity? Could I make it on my own? Finally, against all odds, I took a giant leap of faith and prayed for a net. I converted a small room into an office, confiscated Bruce's old drafting table and equipment, purchased a computer, and hung out my shingle. Then the tapes started playing in my head.

What the hell do you think you're doing? How will you compete with big, established firms? You've risked everything, your house, your family, and you think you'll succeed?

Then one day, out of nowhere, I got a call from a client I'd worked with briefly before. We still were not listed in the phone book and he'd gotten my number from my previous employers. Because I was on my own, he said, I was now more accessible.

One project led to another, each more engaging and fulfilling than the last. It was like confetti from above telling me I was on the path. Despite the tenacious resistance of my mind, I had followed my heart and it had guided me to exactly where I needed and wanted to be — free to follow the work I was passionate about, free to really make a difference.

But my personal life looked quite different. The tension and discord in our family grew until we were strained to the breaking point. It was not a healthy environment for any of us, but most importantly, it was not good for the children.

Finally, in July of 1994 we went our separate ways. My mother-in-law moved into an apartment she'd wanted in a nearby retirement community. To give the children stability, I stayed in our home with them, and Bruce moved back to Boulder where the services he needed to live independently were readily available to him. Within the month, a more suitable apartment became available, so Bruce moved again and his phone number was automatically published.

Two weeks later, the phone rang. I reached out to answer the call.

11/11/1994

"Hello?"

"I just got a phone call from *him*."

Suddenly, the blissfully peaceful day I'd spent with my children spun into a vortex. Terror hit me like a tidal wave. Blood rushed from my head and limbs in a flood. My knees buckled and I sank to the floor. My body shook uncontrollably. Once again, my life would be completely altered. My family and I were in danger; that was all that mattered.

Bruce's voice shook, "He called himself Frank and asked for you. But it was him."

Overwhelming fear washed through me, commanding control of my senses. Memories I'd long suppressed rushed into the moment, and I struggled to breathe beneath the weight of them. And the all-encompassing question rolled over and over in my mind: *Why is this happening?* I'd begged for an answer so many times before. *Why? Please tell me why!*

11/12/1994

The next day, another call to Bruce. Vinyard's voice.

"Hi, I'm with Allied Siding. I'm conducting a survey on siding." He asked to speak to the lady of the house. Bruce hung up.

Soon after, Bruce called directory assistance to ask that his address and number not be given out. After describing the situation, he was told how to trace a call. Although the caller's location would not be available to us, it would be documented and the police could retrieve the information.

11/16/1994

1:49 PM. Third call to Bruce from Vinyard. He asked for Peggy. Bruce hung up and traced the call: Phillips 66 pay phone, Aurora, a suburb of Denver. Soon we would learn this was just a few blocks from Vinyard's residence.

11/17/1994

7:25 PM. Fourth call to Bruce. Vinyard asked for Peggy. Bruce recognized his voice, hung up, and traced the call: Faith Deliverance, Aurora.

Bruce and I were in constant contact since the first call. We were terrified. Bruce was not physically capable of defending himself. What's more, the prior year, my clients complained that they'd had trouble finding me. We had successfully disappeared. After all this time, we'd felt it was both necessary and safe to list my business number in the Longmont phone book; my livelihood, my income depended on it. Besides, we'd thought, Longmont was long distance to Denver. There was no such thing as people-searching on the worldwide web or an online directory. Our private line remained unpublished.

I didn't have a company name then. My name was my reputation and so, was listed. Now it haunted me. Not only did Vinyard know where Bruce was, he could find me and my children at any time.

I would not let this happen again. Above all, I would not allow anyone to harm my children. This time, I would take charge. From skin to bone, I felt myself shift into the warrior. But mine, I vowed, would be a peaceful battle, pitting sheer determination and wit against all who threatened my family's safety and well-being.

Since the calls were to Bruce in Boulder, it was the Boulder police that would be involved. But I knew that, without knowing the history of stalking, they would not take a few phone calls seriously. I would meet with the police face-to-face, but before I did, I would arm myself with all the information I could gather on the prior invasions.

Over the years, I'd kept scattered notes and scraps of paper with case numbers and contact names. Now I gathered them up, organized them by date, and started a log of events in a spreadsheet format. It was the first time the stalking chronicles would be presented as a whole. In time, this timeline would prove to be an invaluable tool not only to me, but to law enforcement officers, psychiatric experts, and prosecutors.

I then called the county justice center to ask how I would go about reviewing the prior case files. The next day, I planted myself at a desk in the court clerk's office. It was the first time I'd seen any police reports or court documents. I was shocked at how little information the police reports contained. But as I poured through the files, I felt I'd opened a door that had been locked to me before. For the first time, I saw what went on behind the scenes.

Among the pile of papers, I found a series of memos written to the judge by Vinyard's caseworker in community corrections. The first memo, dated May 2, 1988 — the same day Vinyard confronted me and my son — documented the history of Vinyard's mental health diagnosis in Alaska and the Aurora Mental Health therapist's conclusion that he required medication but continued to refuse treatment. Vinyard had hallucinated a relationship with me that never existed, the caseworker wrote, adding, "Mr. Vinyard has broken the no-contact, once again ... suggesting that his control continues to be poor if not deteriorating. ... His lack of control and potentially volatile delusional obsession with the victim elevates the risks in this case."

He recommended that the judge consider competency proceedings, but it was quickly discovered that a competency hearing was not an option during a deferred sentence. Soon, the caseworker wrote another memo to the judge: "The position of Community Corrections regarding this case is that Mr. Vinyard represents a real danger to the victim and her family because he is not able to control his delusional-obsessive thinking without psychotic medication. His refusal to comply with the medication requirement makes him untreatable by the mental health system and Community Corrections."

These memos were the first court-documented confirmation of the danger we knew we'd faced all these years. And there were more.

Memorandum, 1/13/89: "It appears that Mr. Vinyard has continued to refuse mental health treatment since my last memo, and I feel that a more intense supervision strategy through probation would be more appropriate than re-referral to Community Corrections."

Memorandum, 2/17/89, when the judge granted the extension of the already deferred sentence: "Mr. Vinyard has agreed to a 6-month program of therapy at Bethesda."

Memorandum, 6/6/89, two months after we'd moved: "Mr. Vinyard failed to attend more than two sessions and disappeared from supervision in March 1989." The caseworker noted the felony charges in New Mexico and concluded, "We have been attempting to get Mr. Vinyard to comply with treatment recommendations since 2/88, and we do not feel that he will comply no matter what we do. The original case involved harassing a woman in Boulder, and it seems unlikely that he will recidivate (repeat the criminal behavior) in terms of that case. We are closing the case with Community Corrections."

My heart racing, I turned to the next page in the file. The New Mexico case was dismissed. Vinyard had been released.

The following month, he'd failed to appear at a hearing to revoke the deferred sentence in our case. A week after that, an arrest warrant was issued.

Then I saw the final entry. February 28, 1991, nearly three years ago: "Arrest warrant expired … Vinyard not found." The case was closed and archived.

There had been no resolution in our case, no follow-up. Vinyard had disappeared, was never found, and the case was closed. The criminal justice system had simply washed its hands of it. I was horrified.

Now, with Bruce disabled and three vulnerable young children, we were in more danger than ever. In all, we'd had five years of relief from this nightmare. And now it returned with a vengeance.

CHAPTER 4

Convergence

"The spirit that keeps one going when one has no choice must not be mistaken for valor."

~ African Proverb

With the stalking history documented in my timeline, I gathered all my notes and copies and, folder in hand, marched into the Boulder Police Department.

"I'd like to speak with someone in charge."

The receptionist looked at me then my folder and asked what this was about. I repeated my demand and said it was about an ongoing stalking case, and it was urgent.

Did I have an officer's name, she asked? No, I replied.

I would have to wait, she said and directed me to a hard, uncomfortable chair in the empty waiting room.

Quite some time passed, and when I didn't leave, the receptionist finally walked out of view for a minute, returned, and led me to a conference room. Before long a woman walked in, introduced herself as a community police specialist, and asked what she could do for me.

Briefly, I described the situation and, launching into more detail, opened my file and spread my papers across the table. Stunned, she glanced at my timeline and began scanning the police reports. Pleading for help, I stressed that Bruce was disabled and living alone and that I had young children at home.

I left her with copies of my timeline and the county court files spanning the history, 1979 through 1991. She assured me she'd follow up immediately. Someone would be in touch with both Bruce and me. In the meantime, she recommended we both get restraining orders.

Detective Linda Arndt was assigned to the case. From then on, every contact Vinyard made would be reported directly to her. One officer in charge, one point of contact. It was a tremendous relief.

After reading through the file I'd provided, she ordered a computer search of Vinyard's criminal history and called Bruce then me to conduct phone interviews. Finally, when my interview concluded, the detective broke the ensuing silence.

"We need to do something about this before someone is killed," she said gravely.

A wave of relief and gratitude rippled through me. At last, someone in the criminal justice system actually got it and cared. Detective Arndt was our first real ally.

While she followed through with her work, I tackled mine. Soon I discovered that to get restraining orders, we'd have to petition the court and attend a hearing, and Vinyard would have to be notified and allowed to attend and contest it.

We didn't want Vinyard to see Bruce in court. He was paraplegic, obviously unable to physically defend himself. And to file a request, we'd have to disclose the addresses and phone numbers where the stalker was not allowed to contact us. Catch-22. We didn't know if Vinyard had discovered Bruce's address, and it was apparent he didn't know my whereabouts at all. I would do everything in my power to keep it that way. We would face this without restraining orders.

I desperately needed to know all I could about the danger we faced, and Detective Arndt gave me the name of the contact person at the Las Vegas Medical Center in New Mexico. That day, I wrote to her explaining the situation and asking for any information she could provide on Vinyard's mental condition and behavior while he was held there.

Her response was an ironclad "no." I'd run headlong into yet another wall. A patient's records were confidential; she would tell me nothing.

Tapping every resource I could think of, I then called the local safe house to ask what I could do to protect myself and my family: Use good locks, notify neighbors, talk to the police about getting a beeper, and *move*. The word stuck in my craw. I knew that if we could move and disappear again, it was the best way to ensure our safety. But it was so wrong. Mentally ill or not, this perpetrator had violated us, horribly. The consequences of his actions should be his, not ours.

But looking beyond ideology, both from a practical and financial standpoint, moving quickly was not something either Bruce or I could do. I still had a home office, and more upheaval would only increase the impact on the children. There had to be another way.

Bruce lived in a secure building, but it was always possible for someone to get in if they wanted to. I contacted the building manager, who agreed to post a notice to residents reminding them to respect the security function of the building. If I had a photo of the stalker, she would post that too.

Detective Arndt gave me copies of the booking photos from Vinyard's most recent arrest. At my request, she also researched possible vehicles he might be driving. I then asked her for copies of all police reports as the case developed. This time, I was determined to keep my foot in the door, to be involved and informed.

"No problem," she said and followed through. Working hand in glove with the police was an entirely new and empowering experience, one I was immensely grateful for.

Finally, the detective suggested I speak with an advocate at the DA office's victim/witness program. If the program existed before, I had not been aware of it. Its purpose was to inform and support the crime victim throughout the prosecution process. It was a much-needed service.

11/26/1994

9:30 PM. Fifth call to Bruce. Vinyard asked for the lady of the house. Bruce recognized his voice, hung up, and traced the call: Gregories, Denver.

12/15/1994

7:08 PM. Sixth call to Bruce. Vinyard asked for Peggy. Bruce recognized his voice, hung up, and traced the call: Koehnen's Amoco, Aurora.

8:27 PM. Seventh call to Bruce. This time, Bruce let the call go to voice mail and saved the message as evidence. When I heard it, chills raced down my spine.

"Hey!" Vinyard began. Then suddenly his tone shifted to dark, menacing, and slow: "You know who this is."

Then turning on a dime, he demanded, "Where's the bitch? I mean the bitch, the witch bitch. She's a slut. Where's — where'd the slut go?"

He had referred to me in these same vulgar terms and more when I'd refused him before.

From there, the message degenerated:

> Huh. Hey Bruce, whatever your fuckin' name is, if I
> ever see you fuckin' around here, wherever I am — huh,
> oh, oh, okay, I won't show up in Boulder, Colorado,
> but if I ever see you around my neighborhood, your ass
> is shit. I mean butt dry shit. Where's the slut anyway?
> What, she go, go off with another fuckin' [expletives]
> or what? Somebody she really loves? Like I didn't really
> love anybody? Huh? Like I never loved anybody? Do you
> know where I'm comin' from? Huh? Do you know what
> love is about? I doubt it, 'cause if I ever see your fuckin'
> — hey, you don't know what love's about. 'Cause I've
> suffered a lot. Where's the slut? …
> Life's really fair, huh? Really fair. Life ain't fair.

The sinister laugh dripped with disdain.

Bruce traced the call: a pay phone in Aurora.

Inadvertently, the speaker was on when the call came in, and the vulgar threats broadcast loudly into the room. The children were visiting Bruce that weekend. They had been put to bed and fortunately, the younger two were deeply asleep. But alerted by the malevolent voice, nine-year-old Ian, horror-struck, stepped soundlessly into the room. Now he knew about the stalker.

We explained the situation in general terms, making light of it as just an annoyance, nothing to worry about. But fully aware of the contradiction, I asked him what I felt I must. "Don't mention it to your brother and sister, okay? It would only worry them needlessly. They're just too young to understand."

Then blinking back the tears I would not shed, I said, "And don't you worry either. Your dad and I are taking care of it."

It pained me to place this burden on his shoulders, to ask him to keep the secret. For fear distorts secrets, and the longer they are held, the bigger and more frightening they become. And the secret keeper grows bitter carrying the burden alone. I had lived it. I knew the effect well.

So as the days and weeks passed, I kept Ian appropriately informed and brought up the subject casually and lightly whenever the opportunity arose. I was determined not to let fear seize him and I wanted him to know he was not alone. The more it was brought out from under the cloak of secrecy, the more I could relieve his fear.

Ironically, the secret he kept was not the truth. For I too was a secret keeper. I never shared the true horror of the situation with him, and terror held me firmly in its grip.

12/17/1994

9:54 PM. Eighth call to Bruce. Vinyard asked for Peggy. Bruce recognized his voice, hung up, and traced the call: Phillips 66 in Aurora.

With each call, the tension was building.

*   *   *

Concerned for our safety, a dear friend gave me a most generous gift — one I really didn't want. It was a women's self-defense intensive: a weekend-long class in full-force, full-contact fighting against assailants. I understood the need and purpose of the program, but the thought of engaging in physical violence turned my stomach.

I was torn. I would do everything in my power to protect my children, but I still firmly believed that violence was never the answer. And throughout my life I'd lived by my principles, I'd walked the walk. Nothing would sway me from my path, nothing. Yet how could I risk my children's safety?

Reluctantly, I enrolled in the program and struggled with my decision. Then the night before it began, I came down with the flu. With a fever, chills, aches, dizziness, nausea, and a pounding headache, there was no way I could attend. I called the instructor and explained the situation.

"It's a common reaction," she replied.

"You can't be serious!" I exclaimed. "I'm not pretending or imagining this. This is very real."

She encouraged me to come to the class and assured me that, once there, if I wasn't feeling better, I could always leave. In no way convinced these symptoms were the result of my emotional turmoil, I decided to prove to myself that I'd tried my best before quitting. The next night, I pulled on my sweats and dragged myself to the car. Then aching and swaying, I slipped into the back of the room.

The evening began with introductions and a discussion of the evolution of the program. It was designed to be an empowering experience. All the women present were there, I discovered, to overcome their personal demons, whether inner or outer, ghosts of the past or present.

The class began gently. There would be no physical fighting that first night. Suddenly, I realized my flu symptoms were gone — just gone. The power of my emotions to manifest illness truly astounded me.

That night, we did a simple exercise in boundaries. The women stood in two lines facing each other from opposite ends of the room. We were to imagine that the person opposite us was a male stranger. One stranger then walked toward each woman. When the distance between us felt uncomfortable, we were to hold one hand up, palm out, and firmly tell the stranger to stop.

I focused intensely on my stranger and, from the corner of my eye, saw some women stopping their partners when they were half way across the room. Others waited longer. I was unsure of myself and tried to pick up my cue from others. The closer my stranger got, the more confused I became. There had been no threat. It was only a stranger.

Conflicting signals from my head and gut swam frantically in a pool of chaos until suddenly, I mentally disengaged from the exercise. Finally, when the stranger was well within arm's length, I "woke up," raised my hand, and said, "Stop?"

What just happened?

The instructor then emphasized the importance of strong boundaries, but to me it was just words — her conviction, not mine. I would work out what I believed later. In the meantime, I had a lot to process and needed sleep.

The next morning, I hesitantly returned to the class. Now the serious work would begin. We learned basic, effective self-defense maneuvers, and I enjoyed practicing the no-contact strikes with a partner; it was like dancing. Then the assailants, dressed in thick padding, padded helmets, and dark masks with only screened slits for eyes, entered the stage. They were meant to be frightening. They succeeded.

First, we practiced signaling and saying "stop" and "back off" loudly, with conviction. That I could do. But if the assailant didn't stop, we were to defend ourselves physically. I tried but my strikes were weak, uncertain. I was completely torn and the more my classmates encouraged me and cheered me on, the louder my mind declared, *No, I will not do this!*

Finally that afternoon, my mind won the battle. I was attacked and refused to fight. Visibly angered, the attacker shifted into high gear. I didn't budge.

Snarling, he threw me to the ground and himself on top of me. Flat on my back, I stared at his huge head bearing down on me and refused to move. I could barely breathe beneath his weight and felt on the verge of passing out. But I would not surrender my conviction. I would not engage in battle with him. Staring deeply into the dark slit to be sure the person hidden behind the mask saw me, I said, "I won't fight you."

At last, the instructor blew the whistle and ended it. Hissing like a snake, the assailant slowly, reluctantly released me. Leaping to my feet, I thanked the group and announced that I was leaving and would not be back. But before I could walk out, the instructor called a circle (it was an important part of the program to gather in a circle and share our thoughts and feelings during and after class). Knowing I was threatened by a predator in real time, the group encouraged me to finish the class. But I firmly declared that unless something drastic happened to change my mind, I had no intention of returning.

That evening, with the kids at Bruce's for the weekend, I drew a hot bath and soaked for a long time. It wasn't just fatigue or sore muscles. I needed to clear away the violence, wash myself clean. After dressing for the night and wrapping myself in my warm, soft robe, I climbed into bed, tucking my comforter around me and up to my chin. Soon, I drifted off into a light sleep.

Suddenly, shattering the silence, a bell. Instantly I was awake, adrenaline pumping at full throttle. The phone clanged again and as I reached out to answer it, I glanced at the clock: nearly midnight.

My whole body trembled, and catching my breath, I disguised my voice to sound gruff and masculine.

"Yeah," I grunted.

Silence.

I waited. The caller did not hang up and the tension strung between us was palpable. Watching the clock, I waited a full thirty seconds more. Then, sure of the caller's identity, I hung up and traced the call. A recording clicked on: "Trace unsuccessful."

I phoned Bruce. It wasn't him. I had no proof that the caller was Vinyard, but I was sure he had found me. Now he knew where we lived.

The tension that had been building for so long reached its zenith. I was a fiery mass of nerves. Re-dressing in street clothes, I carefully selected layers so I would still be clothed if outer layers were ripped. Then scanning the closet floor, I chose a pair of sturdy shoes with laces and cleated rubber soles. With these, my feet would be protected and I'd have a firm grip on the ground at all times. I meticulously secured them with double knots.

Finally, I studied the layout of the living room, and my gaze locked onto the picture window. Quickly, I rearranged the furniture, placing the couch directly beneath the window. From there, I could see both entrances and would hear the first warning of someone on the porch. Only when all was in order did I recline.

I stood sentry as long as I could. Depleted, the flood of adrenaline eventually waned and I succumbed to exhaustion. Fighting fatigue throughout the night, I wavered between drifting off and waking with a start, heart pounding, nerves on fire, ready to defend.

My classmates greeted me warmly the next morning. I hated being there. We began in a circle. When asked why I changed my mind, I said that, in fact, something drastic did happen and explained. It wasn't coincidence. The timing was perfection. Spirit demanded that I open my mind and engage. And the one thing — the only thing — that would penetrate the wall of my convictions was hanging in the balance: my children's safety.

I completed the class. By the end of the day, the instructor wouldn't call an end to our fights until we'd struck our assailant with such force that, without a helmet, he would have been knocked unconscious three times. I just kept seeing my children's faces and my enemy's. I had no answers, but I let go of my judgments about violence and trusted that I was exactly where I needed to be. For the first time in my life, I accepted not knowing right from wrong.

When it was over I felt different — more grounded, more human than I ever had. I wasn't proud of it. I felt tainted. I had no idea then that I had just turned the first key to unlocking the mystery that had confounded me for so long.

There was a lot to contemplate, a lot to unravel and understand about this experience. In the meantime, I had a new tool in my belt. One I hoped with all my heart I would never have to use.

*   *   *

The next morning, on the off-chance it wasn't Vinyard that called, I contacted the phone company. They placed an emergency update, effective within two hours, to remove my listed business number from directory assistance; I hadn't known that was an option. It would not appear in the new phone book, due out in April. I prayed that, in the interim, Vinyard hadn't found me and wouldn't see the current Longmont phone book.

In the meantime, the results of the computer search for his criminal record had come through. Detective Arndt called me with the shocking results. Vinyard's criminal history spanned more than a decade, 1981 through 1994, the current year. Six aliases and a false birth date were listed, she said. The New Mexico charge was for receiving stolen property. The Colorado criminal history included arrests for flight to avoid prosecution, contempt of court, failure to appear, larceny, DUI, trespassing, harassment, third-degree assault, disorderly conduct, and municipal stalking.

Municipal stalking. Just months before the calls to Bruce began, Vinyard had been arrested for stalking in Aurora, and there was an active arrest warrant for him on another charge there, the detective said. I was so alarmed by the stalking allegation that I didn't ask about the other charge. She'd requested the full police report on the stalking case and, at my request, agreed to give me a copy when she received it.

There had been several arrests during the current year, she said, adding that in each of the last three, records showed the "arrestee was armed with an automatic weapon."

My heart stopped. The words reverberated through me. *Armed with an automatic weapon. Three times in the last few months.* Suddenly, the danger took on a whole new dimension, galvanizing my resolve.

My head was spinning. Obviously, this man was a danger to the community; surely any judge could see that. He was seriously mentally ill with a propensity to violence and no impulse control. He was a serial criminal, had stalked repeatedly, and was armed with an automatic weapon.

How was it possible for someone like this to slip through the cracks of the system all these years? *Had he been convicted of these charges? How could he legally own or keep a gun? Does anyone check his history when he's arrested? Does the court ever look at the whole picture?*

It defied logic. I couldn't fathom it.

Before long, the police report for the stalking allegation came through. The details were hauntingly familiar. The woman claimed that, on several occasions, Vinyard had followed her as she walked home and that a couple of weeks earlier, he had approached her in a store and attempted to remove her infant from the shopping cart, she intervened, and he harassed her. He then appeared at her home and knocked on the door, and when she opened it, he attempted to come into the house, she claimed, adding that she was able to lock the door before he entered and that it seemed Vinyard was then going to come through the door forcibly. Her fiancé intervened and stopped him, she said.

On the date of the police report, the woman said Vinyard again appeared on their porch then made a move to take the infant from her fiancé's arms, and her fiancé shoved him to the ground. Vinyard knew where she lived and she was terrified — afraid for herself and her child — she told the officer and asked repeatedly "if Vinyard was going to be able to bond out and if he did bond out that she would like to be notified as she was afraid he would come directly to her house."

Vinyard, the report continued, was placed in the municipal jail and held on $500 bond. *Five hundred dollars. Unbelievable.*

At the end of the report was a handwritten note: According to the fiancé, Vinyard said "he was going to come back and blow (his) Fucking head OFF."

Clearly, he had the weapon to do it, I thought.

My heart went out to these strangers. I desperately wished I could let them know that Vinyard was safely behind bars, but that was not the case.

Now, once again, I was his target. And my family was in danger.

Detective Arndt presented her findings in an affidavit, and on December 23, an arrest warrant was issued, the initial charges: harassment-stalking and harassment. To my great relief, Colorado now had a stalking law. But shockingly, harassment-stalking was still a misdemeanor, class 1. Harassment was still a class 3 misdemeanor. At the time, theft of property worth more than $400 was a felony in Colorado. It was a dismal reflection of our values and the prevailing ignorance about the danger and emotional violence of the crime of stalking. And, I was told, to be charged with stalking instead of harassment, there had to be a "credible threat."

Bond would be set at his first appearance in court, but the condition of bond was established: no contact with the victims. There it was, the revolving door. But this time, I would not stand back and be run over by the system. Whatever it took, I was determined to stop this.

Christmas came and went. The new year would soon be upon us and Vinyard was still out there, somewhere. On December 30, Detective Arndt phoned the Aurora PD and requested that an officer attempt to arrest Vinyard at his home.

If it was that easy, why wasn't he arrested immediately?

She asked to be notified as soon as he was in custody.

1/2/1995

10 PM. Ninth call to Bruce. "You have a collect call from '___.'"

No name was left in the space provided. There would be a charge of $1.40 to receive the call, the recording said. Bruce hung up and traced the call.

1/5/1995

12:59 PM. Tenth call to Bruce, again collect. This time, when prompted to state his name, Vinyard stammered, "Uuuhh." Bruce recognized his voice and traced the call.

Knowing that all calls from the county jail were collect calls, Detective Arndt contacted the Aurora PD and was told that six days before, on December 31, the Aurora police had arrested Vinyard on the warrant — six days in which we could have had some relief if only she'd been notified.

Detective Arndt called to update me. She'd retrieved the trace records on the two collect calls. Both were from Boulder County Jail, the first on the day of Vinyard's transfer from Aurora.

She'd then called the sergeant at the jail, who confirmed that Vinyard was housed there. "He is not to contact them," she told him sternly, and as the conversation continued, she discovered that on January 3, Vinyard had appeared in court for the arraignment and there, the community corrections caseworker assigned presented a bond recommendation to the judge. Referring to Vinyard's criminal history, including stalking us, he concluded that Vinyard was "an FTA (failure to appear)/danger/

recidivism risk." A substantial cash bond was recommended, with the conditions of further evaluation for bonding purposes and no contact with Bruce or me.

In court, the judge read aloud the no-contact condition. Then he ordered the evaluation and set bond at $5,000.

I was incensed! Once again Vinyard could simply buy his freedom while we were plunged back into this living nightmare. Why did money have any authority here? My whole family was in danger, and we had no protection and no say in this whatsoever. A novice in criminal law, I didn't know the legal purpose of bond, but to me it meant the difference between my family being safe and being thrown to the wolf. Researching it, I later discovered that the two main criteria for bail decisions were flight risk and danger to the community. Time and time again, Vinyard proved to be both. And the caseworker had recognized it and warned the judge.

"The next court date is scheduled for Friday, January 6 — tomorrow," the detective said. Judge Torke was again scheduled to hear the case.

I glanced at the clock: 4:00 PM. Abruptly, I ended the conversation and called D.D. Mallard, the deputy DA now assigned to the case. A kind, intelligent, perceptive woman, D.D. appeared to care deeply about us and this case. I trusted that she would do everything in her power to see that we were protected and justice was served.

She would request an evaluation for competency to stand trial, she said. Vinyard would be held for seventy-two hours for evaluation. If found not competent, he would be committed and treated until competent and then would stand trial. But, she warned, they would not hold him in jail for long before trial on a misdemeanor charge. The maximum was eight weeks.

Why was this a misdemeanor?! It had absolutely no basis in truth. These were extremely serious crimes. As time went on, it was this classification that would prove to be one of the insurmountable obstacles in my fight for justice and peace. Tethered to a wholly inadequate law, our hands were tied at the outset.

Terrified that Vinyard would be released before trial, I desperately wanted the judge to know there were young children involved, but that was a secret I steadfastly guarded from Vinyard. I asked D.D. if I could have a private conversation with the judge before the hearing. That was not allowed, she said. I understood why, but it was infuriating.

Somehow, I had to make myself heard and seized the only option I could think of. I had no idea if it would be read, but that night I wrote a letter to the judge pleading for protection. I asked that he take a few minutes before the hearing to read the letter as well as my timeline and the prior caseworker's report, both attached, documenting Vinyard's mental illness and the danger to us.

"Misdemeanor offense," I wrote, "in no way describes his crimes against us."

Briefly, I described the history of invasions and reminded the judge that six years earlier — after Vinyard had violated all the conditions of his deferred sentence — he, himself, had granted yet another extension and so, placed my family in serious danger. Now the violations were continuing from jail and the danger was escalating, I stressed.

I also reminded him that, in the past, Vinyard had forfeited bond and disappeared, only to commit other crimes in the interim. I begged for the highest bond allowable and, if convicted, the longest sentence.

"He has demonstrated that slaps on the wrist and jail time mean nothing to him. Don't do this again," I implored. "Don't allow his crimes against us to take on a new dimension. Please stop him now. Hear my voice."

Then I took a risk. I wrote that I had small children and asked the judge to keep that information and my address confidential. Finally, printing and signing the letter, I only hoped he would read it.

CHAPTER 5

Quicksand

"There is nothing more frightful than ignorance in action."

~ *Johann Wolfgang Goethe*

The next morning, when the doors of the justice center opened, I walked in to deliver my letter. As I strode past a newsstand, a bold headline caught my eye: *Colorado Daily*, January 6, 1995, "**Judge 'soft' on abusers? Retiring judge is said to be lenient in battering cases.**"

Abruptly I stopped, grabbed a paper, and read on.

The judge, it said, was scheduled to retire that day. Quoted in the article was the executive director of Boulder County Safehouse, saying "of all the judges sitting in Boulder, in our experience, Judge Torke is one of the least knowledgeable about the dynamics of domestic violence. He has most frequently made decisions that place victims in serious danger."

Hands shaking with anticipation, I searched my bag for a pen, circled the quote, tore out the article, and clipped it to the back of my letter. I asked the receptionist to stamp all my copies as proof they were received before the hearing, then I grabbed the one with the article.

"Please see that this is delivered to Judge Torke immediately. It's essential that he read it before a hearing at two o'clock."

I handed her a copy for D.D., as well. The others I would distribute to my police contacts and Bruce, and the last I would keep.

Turning away from the counter, I thought again of the article and gave thanks for this serendipitous gift. Horrendous as this whole experience was, I was reassured that I had not been abandoned. And for the first time, I realized the free press could be an ally in my fight for justice.

Before I left the justice center, there was one more thing I intended to do. Somehow, I'd discovered which caseworker was given the task of evaluating Vinyard, and at that point, I didn't care if the law said I couldn't talk to him.

I walked into the community corrections department and asked to see him. The receptionist asked my name and the purpose of my visit. My mouth clamped shut. I didn't want to be turned away, but not wanting to appear contentious, I finally complied with her request and waited.

Obviously puzzled and more than a little distraught by my unexpected appearance, the caseworker reluctantly invited me into his office, the door appropriately left open. I introduced myself and told him I needed to understand the stalker's state of mind and if it was even possible for treatment to curb the danger to my family. I confided that I had young children at home and asked for his pledge to keep that information confidential. I needed to know as much as possible about the danger we faced, I said.

It was quickly apparent that he was unaware of the magnitude of the stalking beyond the bare bones of the current case file. So I laid out some of the details and described the current escalation.

Quiet, he sat back, paused, and proceeded to tell me that Vinyard's mental health records were confidential. He could tell me nothing, he said and politely moved to usher me out.

It hit me like a shock wave. The injustice was incomprehensible. My family's safety, perhaps our very lives were at stake! But protecting this violent criminal was more important?

For the first time in this whole ordeal, I lost control. The frayed thread that had barely held me together for months finally snapped. Tears erupted, I shot out of my seat, and, unencumbered by thought, I slammed my folders down on his desk. The effect was loud.

Stunned and embarrassed, he glanced in the hall for onlookers, partially closed the door, and walked back to his desk while I paced. Eventually, he asked me to sit.

Look at me! Look – at – me. I am not an anonymous victim. I am a human being. I feel just as you feel. I have children to protect. See me! Hear me!

For a long moment, he stared at me, choosing his words carefully. Finally, he said he had not recommended a competency evaluation; he'd spoken with Vinyard and determined he knew exactly what he was charged with. Vinyard was obsessed with me, he concurred. To divert attention away from Bruce, I asked him to convey to Vinyard that Bruce and I were divorced and no longer in contact and that I had moved out of the area.

Then, in an attempt to clarify the situation, the caseworker explained that the no-contact order was a condition of bond and, since Vinyard was still in jail, his contacts were not violations of the condition.

"Prevention is not part of the law," he said in a tender, condescending tone. "He has to commit a crime."

Shock rippled through me. He had committed crimes against us! Terrible crimes. Regardless of any bond conditions, he had and was continuing to stalk us — from jail!

What were they waiting for, for him to commit something "more" serious? A rape, a murder? My palms shot up to my temples. This was crazy! I couldn't take in any more.

"The truth is, they won't keep him in jail long for a misdemeanor," he added, affirming D.D.'s warning. Then he said, "There's a no-contact condition of bond and will be an evaluation regarding medication."

If I knew how to lose my mind, I swear I would have then and there.

He agreed that the situation was escalating and becoming more dangerous. He suggested I develop a safety plan and seriously consider moving and disappearing again.

Perfect. So this is American justice.

Although the caseworker didn't discuss it with me, I later discovered he'd completed his evaluation report for the judge. In it, he presented a psychological profile of Vinyard based on a standard test — it certainly raised warning flags — and said that the delusion of a relationship with me was "a complete fabrication by Mr. Vinyard."

In conclusion, he wrote:

> I believe the possibilities of dangerousness in this case are medium to high. Case materials indicate that he has never honored the authority of the court regarding the no-contact and treatment conditions. I do not believe that Mr. Vinyard will honor the authority of the court regarding the no-contact condition in this case. I believe any bond conditions should include a medication evaluation as well as supervision by interim treatment.

I called D.D. as soon as I got home. She had read my letter to the judge and felt it and my timeline would be helpful to everyone dealing with the case. The DA's office would offer a plea bargain of no bond and the maximum sentence for all the charges, to be served consecutively. Basically, it was no bargain. If Vinyard turned down the plea offer, he could post bond and be out of jail until the trial date with the bond conditions in effect, she said. She suggested I call the crime victim advocate that afternoon for the results of the hearing.

Nerves bristling, I waited. In no way could I focus on work. I cleaned. I needed to scrub everything clean and put my home and office in order.

That afternoon, I called the advocate. The judge had rescheduled the hearing for the following Tuesday — after he'd retired. The case would be heard by another judge. A breeze of relief rustled through me.

"Bond was raised from $5,000 to $10,000," the advocate added.

No! This is nothing. Nothing. Where there was a flight risk or danger in other criminal cases I'd read about, bond ranged from $100,000 to $250,000 or more.

"The no-contact condition remained," she said.

1/12/1995

11:15 AM. Eleventh call to Bruce, collect. Vinyard identified himself as "Frank." Bruce recognized his voice, hung up, traced the call, and dialed Detective Arndt. The trace and the jail's own phone log both confirmed that a call had been placed to Bruce from Intake Module South.

11:25 AM. Twelfth call to Bruce, collect. Bruce was on the phone with Detective Arndt and the call went to voice mail, where Vinyard's voice identified himself as "Frank." Call trace confirmed by the county jail: Intake Module South.

11:31 AM. Thirteenth call to Bruce, collect, while Bruce was still talking with the detective. A message was recorded: Stammering, Vinyard identified himself as "Ummm, uh." Call trace confirmed by the county jail: Intake Module South.

1:23 PM. Fourteenth call to Bruce, collect. Call trace confirmed by the county jail: Intake Module South. Bruce contacted the jail himself to notify them of the calls.

Vinyard's audacity, tenaciousness, and desperation were building, and our tension rose in tandem. His relentless calls from jail showed complete disregard for the law. Nothing, it seemed, not even steel bars would deter him. Without question, the danger was escalating.

After tracking the calls to the intake module, Detective Arndt called the jail staff to ask again that Vinyard not be allowed to phone Bruce. Then finally, silence. Silence brimming with anxiety, anticipating the next contact.

We'd asked to be notified immediately if Vinyard made bond. But not trusting it, I called often, sometimes daily, to be sure he was still in jail. My whole life, it seemed, revolved around his status. While he was locked up, I tried to focus on work and maintaining a "normal" life. When I imagined his release, full-blown terror gripped me.

Days passed, then weeks. Waiting, praying he would stay behind bars until trial and for a long, long time after.

Our case had never gone to trial before. We'd never been made aware of upcoming hearings nor were we invited to attend. We had no knowledge of criminal proceedings or our role in them as the case progressed. Now the learning curve was steep and fast.

Soon we discovered that once the case was in progress, as the crime victims, our roles were reduced to witnesses for the state, with no more legal status than a piece of evidence. We were not privy to most court proceedings, and until a verdict was rendered, we could only be present during our own testimony, when we were subpoenaed.

We couldn't see in and we weren't seen. And the old adage was confirmed again and again: out of sight, out of mind. We were shut out. We were invisible. We were, it seemed, inconsequential.

D.D. asked me to meet her at her office. There, she related that on January 10, at the hearing postponed until after Judge Torke retired, Vinyard was charged and offered the deal: the maximum sentence for each charge, to be served consecutively. He was overwhelmed, D.D. said, and wouldn't accept two years in jail.

At this point, I'd been dealing with his terrifying invasions for a span of sixteen years. To me, two years of jail was nothing.

Vinyard planned to talk to a public defender and later rejected the offer, D.D. said. Then the other shoe dropped.

As gently as possible, she explained that in trial we could not mention anything about the stalking history prior to the current phone calls and letter at all.

My brain seized, panic coursed through my veins, and I disconnected. I couldn't hear anything she said after that. I watched her mouth
move but could not process the words.

Breathe. This can't be. I must have misunderstood. Relax, focus.

Taking a sip of water, I turned my attention back to her.

Because the prior harassment case was closed, it could not be referred
to in trial at all, D.D. said. Then reading my mind, she added, "And if
you mention anything about it while testifying, the judge will declare a
mistrial."

Catch-22, again. I was stunned. Taken out of context, the recent phone
calls and letter would be nothing. The trial would be nothing more than
smoke and mirrors — an illusion of justice.

This was one long string of violent invasions. We had been horribly
violated all these years and the danger was escalating. But the court
had closed the prior cases without resolution, arbitrarily severed those
offenses from current and possible future violations, and prohibited
mention of them again. The law suppressed the truth. The injustice was
abhorrent. I was steeped in insanity, it seemed.

After giving me a few moments to recover and let this revelation sink
in, D.D. said she'd asked the judge to allow her to call Vinyard up for the
previous outstanding arrest warrant, thus connecting the cases, but it was
quashed. Denied. Locked away. Why?

Pressing on, she said the DA's office had decided that the best option
was to try to avoid a jury trial by offering another plea bargain in the
hope that Vinyard would accept it. It would be a reduction in charges and
so, a reduction in the potential sentence.

My stomach knotted. I couldn't accept it. If we went to trial, there was
still a chance that all the charges would stick and the full sentence would
be served. I would do anything to protect my family from this dangerous
predator for as long as possible.

It was highly unlikely that a jury would find Vinyard guilty on all
counts given the gag order on his previous crimes against us, or that a
judge would impose the maximum sentence, she explained; the most we
could expect was eighteen months. If Vinyard wasn't released on bond
before trial, most if not all of that time would be served by the time we got
through a trial. And if he served the full sentence, he'd be released with no
probation, no supervision at all.

Quicksand. I was hopelessly mired in a pit of inadequate, convoluted laws and judicial decisions, and the harder I struggled, the faster and deeper I sank. I felt sick. We would not be safe for long. And there would be no justice.

Struggling to grasp the twists, turns, and ramifications of all she had revealed to me, I clung to my conviction that this had to go to trial.

"This predator's crimes have to be exposed. The truth has to be told. He has to be stopped!" I declared.

D.D. was deeply sympathetic. But the DA had already decided to make the offer. A criminal case is the state versus the defendant. The DA represents the People of the state. It was the DA's decision and the decision had been made. They believed it would give us the best possible outcome, she said.

I fumed as I left the justice center. The law bent over backwards to accommodate the rights of the criminal at the *expense* of the rights of the crime victim. And we were firmly shut out of the process. Decisions that sealed our fate were made before we were even involved. It was beyond belief. It was so wrong.

For two more months we waited, knowing nothing. Day after day, I worked at letting go of my anger. Borrowing from the Serenity Prayer, the words rolled over and over in my mind: *Please grant me the serenity to accept those things I cannot change.* I needed to care for my children and focus on my business. My work demanded all my mental faculties and my children all the love, support, and security I could give them.

But I was a volcano, my smoldering anger under so much pressure as I shoved it under that at times, when alone, I'd erupt in a fiery rage. I was a jogger then and ran long and hard to vent, burn off pent-up energy, and build my strength. One chilly afternoon, working hard to release my anger, I was lost in the rhythm of my feet pounding the ground when suddenly the path turned, and looking up, I discovered I had no idea where I was; I'd run farther than I ever had before. My aching calves and the stitch in my side begged me to rest, but the arguments chasing around in my head would not be still, and neither would my feet.

Finally, my lungs refused to expand any more. I shuffled to a stop and, collapsing, braced my hands on my knees and gasped for air. Yet still the anger burned in my gut. Then, as I blew out a breath, rage rose up and I rose up with it. Shaking my fist at the sky, I let fly my fury and demanded to know why this was happening.

Once spent, I told myself that far too much of my life energy had been taken against my will by this nightmare. I had to find something positive to focus on. Though merely a crumb tossed my way, the longest time I could possibly hope for now — two years — became my mantra. But I prayed for a miracle.

3/1/1995

It was a weekday when I reached out to answer the call on my business line. I knew it would come eventually. All my senses had been on overdrive for months, ready for the strike at any time.

"You have a collect call from 'Steve Miller.' " The sound of his voice penetrating my home hit me like an electric bolt. Past trauma I'd long suppressed exploded, ravaging my nervous system and seizing control. I could not think, could not move.

Finally, forcing my mind to engage, I hung up and traced the call.

"Trace unsuccessful."

Hands shaking, I dialed the county jail. It was confirmed. A call had just been placed to my phone number from Building A, Special Management. Vinyard was housed in Special Management.

I left messages for Detective Arndt and D.D. Then I had a thought.

I redialed the jail and asked if inmates had access to the Longmont phone book; I knew it wasn't distributed to people in the Denver area, where Vinyard lived. My suspicion was confirmed. How ironic. Incarcerating him for stalking us may have enabled him to find me.

That afternoon, I called my insurance agent to apply for disability insurance, effective immediately. My life insurance was already in order.

3/11/1995

The next week, an envelope arrived in the mail. "Bob Vinyard, Boulder County Jail" boldly occupied the upper left corner. To "Peggy Sue Masters," my address. On the back was an official stamp: "UNCENSORED INMATE MAIL, Boulder County Jail."

It had become his modus operandi. If one channel was blocked, he just slithered through the cracks in the system to find another.

Desperate for any information about his mental state and his plan, I opened the letter. "Happy Valentines Day aka Foolish Love," it began.

Stunned, I leaned back to take in the whole canvas. The letter was deeply disturbing. Chaos enshrined, it was, unmistakably, a portrait of a deranged mind.

Primitive drawings splashed the pages, interrupted by random thoughts scribbled helter-skelter. A big heart pierced by an arrow encircled a stick-figure waving at me, with a comic strip dialogue bubble saying, "Hello, CU later (I hope). Visit me. O.k."

Smaller pierced hearts appeared here and there among the text.

The second page bore a childish mountain landscape, with a smiling sun, three smiling people, and groundhogs, I presumed, the sketch labeled "No Shadow."

Scrawled across both pages were song lyrics:

> "I'm the Burning Bush and she is so cold so goddamn cold. I'm hot for her and she's so cold." … "Go ask Alice. When she is 10 ft. tall When she is 10 ft tall." …

The monikers were all '70s artists: Gracie Slick, Jefferson Airplane, David Crosby, Neil Young, Stephen Stills, Bob Marley, and John "Ono" Lennon — Vinyard had injected John's wife, Yoko Ono, into Lennon's name, as if they were inseparable.

His tangled thoughts rambled on:

> Why didn't u visit or write to me I'm hurt — I've been in here for 7 weeks. … I'm not a cold scientist any longer. The Unconscious mind is Better. "I have a Dream" I need U … Serious is time linear, circular, or spiral? … Stop Making Sense!!

And dark, sinister undertones were beginning to emerge: "For this I can only hope to be rewarded. Its his risk. For I truely do hate the unrewarded. i.e.; I'm only trying to get my way."

Then, "P.S.: John Ono Lennon is God."

Shivers raced over my skin. *It's just a coincidence. He likes Lennon's music; that's not unusual.* But I was hyper-vigilant and couldn't help but make the connection. On December 8, 1980, John Lennon was shot and killed by a psychotic, delusional man obsessed with him.

I called Detective Arndt and soon gave her the letter. But first, I made a copy for myself. No longer would I trust the authorities with evidence. It was our first line of defense; our lives depended on it. From that point forward, I would keep a copy of everything — every piece of evidence, every report, every scrap of paper I had — in my own files. Backup.

With the latest contacts added to the case, the charges were piling up. There were now ten counts, and the DA's office offered Vinyard another deal: one count of extraordinary risk harassment-stalking for the threatening message on Bruce's voice mail and two counts of violation of the court's restraining order. All three charges were misdemeanors with little potential jail time. Vinyard, now represented by a private attorney, agreed to the reduced charges, and a sentencing date was set.

Soon D.D. and I met to discuss the next steps. Because there had been a conviction, the constraints of "witness for the state" were shed, she said. At the sentencing hearing, I would be allowed to make a statement to the judge as the crime victim, not just a witness. And I was not limited to the current violations. In my statement, I could describe any and all past horrors and impacts of Vinyard's predation. After sixteen years, it was only a taste of liberty — my right to be heard — but I'd waited a long time for this, and I savored it.

That afternoon I cleared my desk and, preparing to work on my statement, pulled all my files and stacked them in piles. Overwhelmed by the volume, I decided to start with the current case and work my way back. But when I opened the first thick, overflowing folders, the contents were startling. They were a snapshot of the utter chaos in my life and my struggle to maintain control, to hold it all together.

Torn scraps of paper with case numbers and contacts poured out, along with copies of court memos and reports; hastily scratched notes from conversations with police and the DA's office scribbled beneath, above, and to the side of family to-do lists and my work project notes; lists of questions to ask as I struggled to comprehend legal terms and the bizarre twists and turns of the case; calls to make; and lists and lists of things to do, anything and everything I could think of: "contact victim/witness advocate, burglar alarm, ask for divine intervention, practice self-defense ... " All were thrown haphazardly into my folders and, more often than not, into the wrong folder. And scattered among these were newspaper clippings from other criminal cases, typically with bond amounts and comparative sentences.

Wading through my files, one of these clippings in particular struck me just as it must have the first time I read it. It was a small news brief in the local paper. A man who stole fifteen pigs in Alabama in 1954 had been captured by police. He'd escaped from prison in 1956, after serving two years of his sentence. The sentence was one year in prison for each pig, for a total prison sentence of fifteen years.

Did the world make any sense at all? Had the pendulum just swung way too far the other way?

4/4/1995

When I arrived at the sentencing hearing and faced the courtroom door, the thought of seeing Vinyard made my skin crawl. Quietly, I slipped into the back of the room, as far from his chair as possible. And there in front of me, in a standard-issue inmate jumpsuit, hands cuffed, both ankles cuffed, and a large chain snaked through them all and around his waist, sat Vinyard.

In all these years, I had never attended a criminal hearing before, and the sight of the man chained like a wild animal was at once extremely disturbing and deeply comforting. He was restrained. Shaken as I was, I felt I would at least be safe from physical harm.

It wasn't long before — loudly and entirely out of sync with the hearing — Vinyard, seated at the defense table, asked the judge to uncuff him. My nerves leaped to attention and the judge deferred to the deputies who had accompanied him from jail. They advised against it, explaining that Vinyard was "unpredictable." To my relief, he remained restrained for the duration of the hearing.

D.D. asked that, for our peace and protection, the judge impose the maximum, consecutive sentence for each charge, for a total of four years in jail. The defense attorney countered with mental health treatment as an outpatient. Like a fist to my chest, sheer panic hit me.

Vinyard's brother, who would assume responsibility for him as an outpatient, was consulted. In tears, his brother said he didn't know that he would stay on his medication. *Good,* I thought, *he was honest.* But the point was missed. This was about holding Vinyard accountable for his crimes and protecting us and the community, not just about "fixing" him. I'd seen it so many times before, a judge's decisions based on the grossly simplistic, naive assumption that mental health experts could fix him and the problem would go away. No, not again.

Finally, before the judge passed sentence, I had my chance to be heard. Taking my place at the podium, I drew a deep breath to settle my nerves then looked up at the judge and said, "Your Honor, I would like to make a statement to the court, but first I would like your permission to speak to Mr. Vinyard directly, on the record, in the safety of this courtroom."

The judge's brow shot up. She paused a moment then granted my request. The deputies moved in closer and hovered, hands poised, ready to grab him. A pregnant silence filled the room, and for the first time that day, I looked directly at Vinyard, eye-to-eye. Then I summoned the strongest voice I could muster:

> Mr. Vinyard, I have told you many times to go away and you did not listen. Are you listening now?
>
> I do not want you in my life. I never wanted you in my life, and I will never want you in my life.

A rush of clanging and commotion filled the air as Vinyard leaped to his feet and shouted over me. Indignation gushing up from my gut, to my surprise, it shot out fiercely: "Sit down! You've had your time to speak. This time is mine."

The judge, too, commanded Vinyard to sit and be quiet. Gradually, the room settled and I looked deeply into him, willing whatever part of his mind might remain lucid to hear me.

> It is not because someone else has been between us that I have not wanted you. I never wanted you in my life. We never had a relationship. You have been living an illusion. This is the real me. Listen carefully.
>
> You do not have the right to invade my life. You do not have the right to stalk me. I will not tolerate your invasions. I will do whatever it takes to defend myself. Do you hear me?

As the words were spoken aloud, I realized I was not just addressing him. I was declaring my intention to the universe.

"I am ending this now," I proclaimed, and I meant it. Whatever this was about, whatever contract I may have had when I came into this life, I now intended to break it.

"Don't *ever* try to contact me again. Don't *ever* try to see me again. Do you understand? Leave me alone. Go away."

Taking a slow, deep breath, I drew the echo of my words deep into my soul, solidifying this closure. Then turning my attention back to the judge, I asked for the maximum sentence and explained:

> It is not out of anger or revenge that I ask for this. As you have heard, Bruce and I have been stalked by this man for sixteen years. Nothing has stopped him. ... He has been given every reasonable chance by the justice system and every possible warning, and he's continually ignored them all. ... He has shown that nothing will prevent him from stalking me — not time, not even jail.

Briefly, I summarized the history of deferred sentences with conditions, violation of those conditions without fail, and continued stalking. I quoted his history of institutionalization and the prior evaluations presented to the court. And to demonstrate that the risk and danger were escalating, I summarized his criminal record, noting that in three arrests the previous year, he was armed with an automatic weapon.

With no knowledge of criminal law apart from the crash course I'd had as I floundered through the labyrinth of my case, I relied on common sense. I asked that if he attempted to contact us while in jail or on probation, he be charged again and required to serve the full sentence for that charge. And I asked that he not be released early. I had a decision to make about abandoning my life and disappearing, and I needed to know exactly how long he'd be incarcerated, I said.

In closing, I requested several conditions of probation that I thought would protect my family as much as possible. I asked that he be supervised to the maximum extent possible. Citing his arrest record, I asked that a condition of his freedom be that he turn over all guns and that he be allowed no weapons of any kind. And, in the event that he was arrested on any charge during probation and found to have a weapon, I asked that he be prosecuted to the fullest extent of the law (somehow I'd discovered that in some cases, federal law didn't allow someone under a restraining order to have a firearm or ammunition).

Then, feeling I'd been kept in the dark for so many years, I asked to be kept apprised of the status of his sentence and any changes, and I asked to be notified immediately when he was released.

Though I desperately wanted the judge to know there were small children involved, every fiber of my being told me it was more important to protect this secret. I didn't mention them at all and only hoped this judge had read my letter to the prior judge.

> Your Honor, I fear for my life, for Bruce's, and for those around us. This man is very ill. He is delusional and living in an altered reality. … If he is on the streets, I have no doubt he will try to find me. Sixteen years of this unceasing threat is enough!

Soon, the judge passed sentence. Vinyard had never served the sentences for his previous convictions, she said and proceeded to sentence him to two years in jail, with credit for time served, and four years of probation. The condition: no contact with me or Bruce during the six-year term.

Waves of shock rolled through me. Every nerve in my body tingled, every muscle froze. My stomach plunged. *Two years of protection. Less with credit for time served.*

She ordered a psychiatric evaluation and said that, during probation, Vinyard had to comply with any treatment recommended. If he chose to serve his time at the state mental health institute, he would get jail credit, she said. Intensive supervision during probation was ordered, and he could "possess no weapons."

Concluding the hearing, the judge then sternly warned Vinyard that if he violated probation, he would get the maximum sentence. The plan, it seemed, was to give us some respite during his brief jail sentence and when — not if — he violated probation, to give him more jail time. No one doubted he would violate. The questions in my mind were: When would this ever end? And how?

Two months after the sentence was passed, Dr. David Iverson completed the evaluation the judge had ordered. Though I was unaware of it, it seemed he'd been asked to address the possibility of treatment as an outpatient:

> Clearly, Mr. Vinyard has demonstrated an inability to comply with treatment or court requirements in the past. This makes the decision to recommend in- or outpatient treatment a difficult one. Manic Depression is well treated on either an in- or outpatient basis. Delusional Disorder is very difficult to treat in any setting. It is generally resistant to antipsychotic medication. … I cannot predict within reasonable medical certainty whether Mr. Vinyard would comply, at this time, with outpatient treatment. In general, the best predictor of future behavior is past behavior. Considering the past behavior and future dangerousness, although Mr. Vinyard has never been charged with violence against the two individuals on whom he has been fixated, the possibility of that at some point in the future is not impossible. He has demonstrated a tendency toward violence in the past. … I believe that Mr. Vinyard could pose a physical threat to [them] at some point in the future.

Iverson went on to note that Vinyard intended to continue drinking upon his release and that his level of control was "uncertain, even to himself."

Heeding his warning, the judge upheld her sentence. Whether in jail or the state hospital, Vinyard would serve his time, brief as it was, in a locked facility.

*   *   *

I knew I couldn't relax into this fleeting peace until I had done everything possible to protect my family before Vinyard's release. Researching the possibility of petitioning for involuntary commitment to the state mental health institute, I learned it would be nearly impossible to do; it would be time-consuming, and Vinyard could walk out and stop taking his medications at any time. Apparently, "involuntary" referred only to checking in. Checking out was the patient's choice.

Finally, as horribly unjust as it was, I again had to consider the obvious. The only way we might truly be safe was to move and disappear. We had done it before, though all it took was one small slip to re-open the gates of hell.

Now, disappearing would mean sacrificing my business as well as the home we loved. It meant pulling the whole foundation we had built out from under our children — my work, our home, Bruce's home — at the very time they most needed stability. And even if I was willing to abandon everything I had worked for all these years, the bottom line was I couldn't afford to move. The time and energy consumed by this case had dealt a severe blow to my income, my ability to pursue projects, and my client relations. It was all I could do to try to salvage my reputation and pay the bills.

And in the end, I wasn't sure I could live with myself if I fled again. The injustice I'd seen was abysmal. If this happened to me, surely it happened to others. The abject failures of the laws and judiciary needed to be exposed and corrected. I felt my most basic rights — my rights to life, liberty, and the pursuit of happiness — had been run over and my right to privacy trampled.

I thought, *Every day in schools across the country, children pledge allegiance to the United States, closing with "liberty and justice for all."* When my own children were old enough to learn the reasons for the upheaval of moving and disappearing, what would I be teaching them about our nation? That when threatened, we run and hide? That our own justice system is unjust? Or that we defend our rights against all enemies? That when we see injustice, we work to change it, and in this country we can change it.

The only answer I could live with was the latter. I resolved to stay and defend my life, my freedom, and my rights.

The fact that the judge ordered no contact throughout Vinyard's sentence and intensive supervision during probation did a great deal to calm my fears and allow me to make the decision to stay. The advocate explained that a GPS tracking device would be used. That way, probation officers would know exactly where he was at all times, and he could quickly be captured if he contacted us.

It turned out the law didn't allow electronic monitoring for a misdemeanor. He wasn't tracked. But even mistakenly believing he would be, I vowed to do anything and everything I could to protect my children.

They'd had no time to recover from the divorce when this whole episode began. Just when they most needed the constancy of feeling safe and loved, to be assured that everything would be all right, Vinyard had surfaced and wreaked havoc.

Although Ian now knew a little about the situation, Sophie and Seth were far too young to tell them what was happening, even in the simplest terms; this boogeyman was just too creepy, scary, and dangerous. I was determined to protect them from these horrors and carry on as if all was fine. But in truth, it was like trying to smooth the waves on the surface of the tsunami rising beneath me.

We cannot hide our fear from our children. They sense it in their families and assume it as their own. Signs of my children's fears and anxieties were expressed in ways as different as each of them was unique, but they were, unmistakably, rooted in the terror Bruce and I experienced. Now, with Vinyard in jail, I would turn my full attention back to them and try to soothe and heal these raw wounds.

It broke my heart and stirred my outrage to see how they suffered. When alone, like the pendulum of a clock, I'd swing from overwhelming sorrow to righteous rage. Back and forth, back and forth I'd sway, seeking the stillness of center once again.

CHAPTER 6

Perfect Storm

"There is no greater tyranny than that which is perpetrated under the shield of the law."
~ *Charles de Montesquieu*

Throughout this whole ordeal, I'd had little time to reflect on the purpose of this horror in my life other than to vent my rage and ask why, only to receive no answer.

But there were clues left along the way.

Just when my faith was most fragile, a sign would appear, assuring me I was guided. I devoured those as a starving man would a crumb found in a crack on the floor.

Now, with the immediate threat removed, I again reflected and asked the questions: *What am I to learn? What am I not seeing?* But that was my head talking. In this moment, what I really wanted was calling loudly from my heart. I craved support, comfort, friendship — friends like I'd never known before. It was my heart's desire that was quickly fulfilled.

Within the week, I met two fascinating women at a local Shakespeare festival. I happened to run into one of them again the next weekend. I didn't ask for her friendship, but briefly, I'd shed the armor I'd worn so long and my heart was open; it was one of those rare moments when I was willing to receive. We'd just exchanged greetings when she looked into me and said, "I feel I'm supposed to invite you to our women's group."

Within two weeks of asking, I found myself in the company of soul-friends. These kindred spirits would soon become my center, my home. It was not a religious group. It was a circle of intelligent, compassionate women. Spiritual explorers. We listened and talked and shared the challenges, sorrows, and joys of our lives. And we knew we could always call on each other in time of need, no matter the hour or the circumstance.

Though I shared few details with them, they were well-aware of the stalking and how it had ravaged our lives. Once, during a particularly heartrending conversation, a rather acerbic, outspoken friend said, "We've got a shovel and a truck. Just let us know when and where."

It was a joke, of course, and more. It was a gesture of solidarity come hell or high water. At the time, hell in the form of Vinyard had just surfaced once again.

One evening, the answer-to-my-prayer friends got together to share a guided visualization and potluck. Generally when doing this, once we all reached a meditative state, we began with the imagery presented by whoever volunteered to be our guide then defiantly wandered off into the ether to explore on our own. At the end, our guide would gather us together (I'd done this myself; it was rather like herding cats) and safely return us to the room in present time. Finally, indulging in wine, chocolate, and any less-essential sustenance the participants had brought, we'd share our stories.

On this particular evening, we began at the mouth of a cave and were urged to step inside. My cave glowed brightly. Rustic iron torches lined the walls, illuminating the warm, rich golds and pinks of the stone walls and floor. I felt blissfully safe, there in the womb of the mountain. I was protected, hugged by the solid stone arching gracefully over my head.

We were told to find a stairway and begin stepping down.

The stone steps that appeared to me were hand-chiseled and well-worn in the center. I sensed that, carved by the ancients, these stairs had welcomed the footsteps of many visitors throughout the ages.

Guided by torches along the outer wall, I descended. Further and further down I drifted as the stairs spiraled deep into the belly of the cave. At last, I reached the foundation.

"Look at your feet," our guide prompted.

I looked down: scuffed, laced leather field boots, softened with use to hug every crevice of my feet and ankles while tackling the most rugged terrain.

"Look at your clothes. What are you wearing?"

Slowly, my gaze moved upward: loosely pleated, thick khaki pants; an aged, soft, brown leather belt; a dirty white cotton shirt covered by a well-worn brown leather bomber jacket. On my head, a dusty, brown, hastily creased fedora. Hooked on my belt, a long, coiled leather whip.

I chuckled. *Of course, Indiana Jones.*

"Deep in this cave, a wise one awaits you with a gift," our guide said. "Find this one and accept the gift."

I wanted that gift. I wanted words of wisdom to help me on my path, to help me understand and unlock this vast mystery that had swallowed me whole. This time, I would follow our guide's directions.

Along the walls of the central corridor, arched doorways announced deep, dark tunnels beyond. Ignoring them, I gladly followed the comforting glow of the torches. Corridor after corridor, deeper and deeper into the cave, I wandered, seeking and finding no one.

Please appear. Please.

Finally, the tunnel turned and opened onto a circular room bathed in soft, warm light. There, seated in the center of the space, was an ancient woman, her long gray hair flowing about her shoulders, her layered robes drifting around her like pooling water. Her pale, opaque eyes turned to me. With bated breath, I waited for her to speak. She did not.

The silence that filled the room, its secrets whispered on the echoing walls, was deafening. Did she see me? She was looking right at me. I stared at her more intently, desire pouring from my heart. *Surely you know why I'm here. Please, give me something!*

At last, a soft, gentle, knowing smile graced her lips. She knew a secret but would not share. She was not cruel in her withholding; I sensed she was wise, kind-hearted, and deeply empathetic.

It had taken me a long time to find this woman, and suddenly our guide's voice ringing through the chamber startled me. She was gathering us together, preparing us to return. Quickly, I bowed my head to this strange woman, thanking her — for what, I had no idea — and utterly bewildered, I turned and ran back to the mouth of the cave, sliding to a stop "Indi" style at the entrance.

I hastily checked my gear. Did I have it all? My hat, my whip? *Check.* I patted my clothes. My watch, my compass, my knife? *Check.* Then patting another pocket, I didn't recognize what I felt. I shoved my fist in and pulled it back out.

There, in the palm of my hand, was a small, spiral-bound tablet of paper and a pencil. Stunned, I glanced in the direction of the old woman, nodded, and shoved them back in my pocket. They were a perfect fit.

I had my assignment. It was not a mandate; it was a gift offered, my choice to accept it or not.

I lingered a moment while my mind traced back to the old woman's face, and I studied it more closely. Her expression spoke both of sorrow — a cavernous grief for what I had and, yes, was yet to experience — and her firm resolve not to disclose the meaning I so desperately wanted.

This quest was mine and mine alone her eyes assured me, brimming with the unspoken promise: Seek, and you shall find.

*   *   *

A little over a year after Vinyard was sentenced, our brief interlude of peace was broken. Court proceedings and the uncertainty that always accompanied them once again took center stage.

On May 24, 1996, Vinyard filed a motion for reconsideration of his sentence and attached a letter he'd written to the judge that sentenced him. In it, he claimed he had changed, that he was not violent, and that the sentence was too harsh when compared to other crimes and sentences, which he then described in detail. Apparently he'd used the time to study legal reference books in the jail's library, and it occurred to me that he had all the time in the world to devote to his quest.

The DA's office notified me and, a month later, filed a response asking the judge to deny it. I too had the right to respond and soon submitted a letter to the judge. Once again, I briefly summarized the stalking history and asked the judge to uphold the sentence that now promised us only six more months of peace. In fact, although the judge eventually denied Vinyard's request, our reprieve would last just a few months more.

His release came sooner than expected. I didn't have long to prepare. I felt as if I was preparing for war. But in this war there would be no comrades in arms. There were now allies, a few who cared and helped as they could. But on the front lines, it was a battle I knew I'd continue to fight alone.

On September 9, 1996, seventeen months after the two-year sentence was passed, twenty months from the time he was arrested, Vinyard was released. Now the four-year probation period would begin.

I'd barely had time to breathe. My entire life, it seemed, was devoted to this case, protecting my family, and working to calm the fear that had spread like wildfire, wreaking havoc on my children.

The moment I was notified of his release, I shifted into lockdown.

Now he knew where we lived. He could appear at our home at any time. And so the siege began.

On the day of his release, the phone rang and, heart thundering, I answered. No reply. The silence broadcasting the tension between us lingered until finally the caller hung up. I traced the call.

Over the next two weeks, Bruce and I were both flooded with hang-up calls every day. Most of the calls could not be traced, and with no voice on the other end of the line, we had no proof it was Vinyard. He was playing with us, tormenting us, and both my fear and rage were palpable.

I wanted to take control but could not. Afraid that if I ignored the calls he'd show up at my house, I endured his games, waiting for the chance to catch him. My mind and all my senses fully charged and aware, I was hair-triggered — always working to anticipate his next move, constantly ready for the strike, wherever and whatever it would be.

9/25/1996

10:00 PM. Incoming call. Vinyard's voice. A lightning bolt, it jolted my nervous system. My heart leaped, I gasped for air, my nerves ignited, and I shook uncontrollably.

This wound had not healed. In the brief peaceful interludes of my life, it would recede and eventually rest, lying dormant in my nervous system. But, the mere sound of his voice penetrating my home, my sanctuary, and the wound ripped wide open, fully inflamed.

Pulling deep breaths, I listened carefully for a full twenty seconds to be sure it was him. He posed as a solicitor checking on a lapsed magazine subscription renewal for Maggie Mae Smith. I didn't speak. Was Maggie Mae there, he asked?

Hands trembling, I hung up, traced the call, and dialed 911. The Longmont PD responded. When the unfamiliar officer arrived, I described the call, gave her a condensed history, and handed her a package I had ready and waiting: a copy of the sentence and probation conditions, Vinyard's arrest record, his booking photo, and my timeline.

She took the package and my statement. Then she said if I had a restraining order, she could act immediately. I was confused. I'd just given her a copy of the court's restraining order, the no-contact condition of probation.

Forcing myself to focus on work and my family in the midst of war-fare, I waited. Since the phone seemed his chosen line of attack for now, I gave myself a reprieve. For two days I didn't answer it, hoping he would leave a message. But the only sounds recorded were the clicks of a remote handset contacting its cradle. He'd been trapped by voice mail before. It seemed he was not going to make that mistake again.

9/27/1996

4:00 PM. A ring and I answered the call. Silence. Ten seconds passed before the caller hung up. Trace unsuccessful.

After eighteen days of unrelenting tension, my frustration finally peaked. Casting wildly for sources of help, I alighted on Vinyard's proba-tion officer. Begging for help, I told her about the calls and my report to the police as well as their response.

She was sympathetic and said that Vinyard was required to attend regularly scheduled probation meetings. And, she added, there was a psy-chiatric evaluation done prior to his release: Treatment and counseling were required.

My fury flared. There it was, the old, outworn, broken record.

A full week after identifying Vinyard's voice on the phone, the DA's office brought me in to give an affidavit. Later that day, a detective from the Longmont PD called to say they had gotten the trace information on the same call. It was a pay phone, one block from Vinyard's previous residence in Aurora.

He continued. The department was too busy to issue an arrest warrant for a couple of weeks, and he would not be able to meet with me to start proceedings until the following Tuesday, in a week. I was flabbergasted and tried to explain the urgency, but to no avail.

If I had a civil restraining order, he said, officers were required by law to respond immediately to any contact Vinyard made. Illogically, the court's restraining order did not carry the same weight.

10/2/1996

When I returned to my office after a meeting the next morning, two more hang-up calls had been recorded on my voice mail. Then Vinyard's probation officer called to say that, based on my information, she'd determined that he'd violated the no-contact condition. She'd had an arrest warrant issued; he would be arrested when he arrived at her office for a probation meeting later that afternoon. A rush of relief and gratitude washed through me.

He would be held in the county jail, she assured me, adding that a $10,000 bond was affixed to the warrant. I felt my heart sinking but resolved not to let the low bond extinguish my flickering hope.

Quickly I hung up, called the jail, and asked to be notified as soon as Vinyard was in custody. Hopeful but uncertain he would show up for the meeting, I closed my eyes and asked for help. Then I waited.

7:30 PM. On the first ring, I grabbed the phone. It was the jail attendant calling to confirm they had Vinyard. She didn't sound at all pleased about it and apologized for the delay in calling. He had been difficult, she intimated, but said no more.

10/3/1996

The next morning, I called the crime victim advocate assigned to the case to inform her of the arrest and the results of the trace. She was aware that Vinyard had been arrested and faxed me a brief statement about the arrest and *new* charges.

According to the records, a Boulder police officer, dressed in full uniform, attempted to arrest Vinyard at the probation department. In response, he shouted, "You can't do this!"

When the officer tried to handcuff him, Vinyard raised his balled fists and challenged, "Come on, bring it on."

The officer ordered Vinyard to lower his hands and, grabbing his pepper spray, warned him that if he didn't, he'd be sprayed in the face. Vinyard tried to knock the can away and it burst open. Then while the two wrestled, a picture on the wall broke and glass fell on the floor. The officer said he felt pain as a result either of blows being thrown or hitting a chair as they wrestled. Finally, he subdued Vinyard with pressure to his neck and placed him under arrest.

The new charges were violation of probation and resisting arrest, both misdemeanors, and second-degree assault of a peace officer — a felony, class 4.

Later that day, the advocate called and said there'd been a bond hearing for the new charges and $5,000 was added, raising the total to all of

$15,000 for all the charges pending. Vinyard petitioned for a reduction in bond, she said. Denied. And a felony conviction meant prison, not jail, she exclaimed.

How ironic. Nearly two decades of stalking me were misdemeanors with little jail time. He assaults an officer trying to arrest him for stalking me, and it's a felony. And prison.

For the next two months, Vinyard stayed in jail and my phone number remained blocked. I was keenly aware that he could post bail at any time. Until the court found him guilty, sentence was passed, and he was safely locked away, anxiety droned constantly just beneath the surface.

Finally, in early December, a hearing was held to revoke probation. There were three separate charges of contacting me in violation of probation, including one count of harassment and two counts of violation of restraining order. The defense attorney argued that these should be new charges, requiring that he be proven guilty beyond a reasonable doubt. The judge disagreed and said since there was no civil restraining order, the no-contact order was a condition of probation. Because these were not separate crimes, there would be no new trial and only a "preponderance of (convincing) evidence" was needed, she said.

But she told the defense attorney and the deputy DA to submit briefs to support their opposing positions. She would decide December 16, and if she found him guilty, she would sentence him then.

And so, the process of justice dragged on. I wondered if judges knew that for me, every day without resolution was another day of agony, my family's safety on the line.

12/16/1996

Despite the defense's argument, when the continuance finally arrived, the judge stood by her finding that the three contacts were not separate crimes but were violations of probation. Vinyard was guilty on all counts, she said.

In the hearing twenty months before, when this same judge first passed sentence, she'd said that if Vinyard violated probation, he would get the maximum sentence. It was a warning to him. To me, it was a promise.

Now the judge expressed her concern that jail didn't work as a deterrent and said she didn't trust his ability to comply with the no-contact condition. She was certain he would use up the remaining probation time in stints in jail for continued stalking, she said and sentenced him to a one-year jail term with credit for time served. Then she revoked and re-instated probation for a period of ten years with the original conditions, mental health treatment, and a new condition: monitored sobriety.

My heart plunged. One year. Less with credit for time served. And when he was freed, I would again be condemned to a life of terror. The length of probation was meaningless to me. In the face of all the facts, her rationale completely eluded me. Hope lay in splinters on the floor.

The judge continued. She was open to listening to a convincing mental health evaluation and, if he was improving, reconsidering the sentence.

So after all these years, we were back to square one. Fix him in lieu of protecting us. This was madness! Was this just standard procedure, the pat formula for dealing with such cases with no regard for past failures? Did judges just keep asking for these evaluations hoping they'd eventually get the answer they wanted, that he could be fixed and the problem would go away? What was it Einstein said about insanity, doing the same thing over and over and expecting a different result?

I was livid. Both the excruciating history of stalking and the danger Vinyard posed to us had long been documented in court records. And his propensity to physical violence was becoming more and more apparent; he'd just assaulted and harmed an officer. Why wasn't public safety the first concern?

There was a barrier here I had so long struggled to understand and break through, a field of distortion, it seemed, between what judges saw and the truth of my experience. Vinyard's depraved actions were despicable and absolutely unacceptable under any circumstances, and it was the court's duty to protect us and the community and stop him. But something was clouding their vision.

I wanted to shake the judge. *Look at me! See me! Hear me! Why can't you see the truth?*

I was a caldera. The pressure building, the molten magma of my frustration was churning, boiling, steaming. I felt I would either explode or implode; that fiery energy had to go somewhere. And so my coping mechanism, the pattern I'd established long ago, engaged. I grabbed hold of my fury and shoved it under. And directed inward, my anger became depression, and depression, despondence.

But I could not linger there long. I had to keep fighting to protect my family. Once the shock of the sentence had settled and I'd allowed myself a little time to rest in a cavern of despair, I timidly reached out for an arc of hope and shifted my focus to the only possible promise of some peace.

Ironically, the charge that had the greatest power to protect us, the felony, was not directly related to my case even though the officer was assaulted while arresting Vinyard for stalking me. The cases had to be heard separately; I would not be involved. But a conviction and long sentence for the assault charge was now my only hope. The range of sentence for that crime, I was told, was five to sixteen years in prison.

For four more months I lived in limbo, or more accurately purgatory, waiting for the felony case to be heard. In this, the case that seemed to have absolute power over my family's future safety, I would have no voice at all. Would we finally find solace? Or would we be thrust unceremoniously back into hell? In April, I got my answer.

4/10/1997

The hearing for the felony assault case came to order, a different judge presiding. The deputy DA in that case offered a plea bargain and Vinyard accepted the deal. Just how significant the exchange, recorded in the transcript, would become — not once, but twice — would not be revealed for some time:

> Judge: Are you presently under the influence of any drug, medication, or alcohol, anything that might affect your ability to understand what's happening here?
>
> Vinyard: No, Your Honor.
>
> Judge: Have you had sufficient time to talk with your lawyer about the rights you are giving up and the possible consequences of entering this plea?
>
> Vinyard: Yes, I have.

The judge read Vinyard his rights and reviewed what rights he would be relinquishing if he accepted the plea deal, then continued:

> Judge: ... But all these rights you are forever giving up on these charges. Do you understand that?

> Vinyard: Yes.
>
> Judge: That's what you want to do?
>
> Vinyard: Yes. ...
>
> Judge: You understand that if you were to violate any of the terms and conditions ... then the Court could sentence you on the original charge and you would not have a trial. Do you understand that?
>
> Vinyard: Yeah. Unfortunately, I think this will work out better.
>
> Judge: All right.
>
> Defense: Your Honor, just so the Court is aware, I have gone over and reviewed with Mr. Vinyard this ... agreement and the possible penalties should he be found in violation. And he understands that.

The judge then described the assault charge and asked, "Do you know what you're charged with?"

"Yeah, I know what I'm charged with. Yes," Vinyard replied.

The judge reiterated that the charge was a class 4 felony, and the prosecutor clarified that it was a second-degree assault charge extraordinary risk. It was also a mandatory crime of violence, he said and explained that the minimum sentence was five years in prison and the maximum sixteen.

"All right," said the judge. "Are you aware those are the possible penalties?"

"Yeah, I'm aware because of crime of violence that those would be the possible penalties, yes," Vinyard said.

The judge asked again if, knowing these penalties, he still wanted to plead guilty.

> Vinyard: Well, I'd like to plead to the F-6 but — heat of passion, but —
>
> Prosecution: That's not offered. ... If he wants to do this offer he can do it, but he's not being offered an F-6 at this time.
>
> Vinyard: Well, I still believe that it will work out in my best interests. ...

Again the judge asked if, knowing the possible penalties and the nature of the charges, he still wanted to plead guilty.

"Yeah. I understand the risk and that if I do violate the law, that this is what they will impose. So yes, I do understand," Vinyard said.

The judge then reviewed the second charge, resisting arrest, and the maximum penalty: a year in the county jail and a fine. He asked if Vinyard had any questions and still wanted to enter a plea on that charge.

No, he had no questions, he replied. Yes, he understood, he said. He still wanted to enter the pleas.

> Judge: How do you respond to the first charge I read to you alleging assault in the second degree, guilty or not guilty?
>
> Vinyard: Nolo contendere (no contest).
>
> Judge: Well, you know, I don't know what that means to you, but let me tell you what it means to the Court. It means to me that you're admitting that you're guilty of the crime, and you'll be treated as if you've pled guilty to it. What does it mean to you?
>
> Vinyard: It's like a guilty plea, but you're not really admitting. I'm admitting that I can't prove myself.

The judge read the next charge: resisting arrest.

"Guilty," Vinyard replied.

Interrupting, the prosecution raised the issue of the no-contest plea again. The judge explained that if he entered a no-contest plea, it would have the same consequences as if he was pleading guilty. Vinyard conferred with his attorney.

"I'm taking advantage of the — and I do recognize that in legal aspects that nolo contendere means a guilty plea," he said.

After hearing the details of the arrest and assault, the judge accepted the pleas and said he found there was a factual basis for each charge and that, having observed Vinyard's demeanor, he found that he was not under the influence of any substances and that he understood the nature of the proceedings.

"I further find that his pleas are voluntarily entered, not the result of undue influence or coercion on the part of anyone," the judge said.

The prosecution explained the plea deal in detail and stressed, "The sole conditions on this, other than there be no crimes, is going to be that he have absolutely no contact with these people."

The judge interrupted, asking who we were.

The prosecutor explained briefly then said, "And what we've done with this disposition is place him in serious jeopardy should this continue — his attempt to contact directly or indirectly — of taking him out of the community and placing him in the Department of Corrections (DOC) for as long as we humanly can."

He later added, "And the fact of the matter is we're not messing around with him anymore. If there's any direct or indirect contact, we're going to pick him up and, and I'm not going to be asking to impose a five-year sentence; I'm going to be going to the top of that range. So he's got to be understanding that, that this is as serious as it gets."

Concluding the hearing, the judge warned Vinyard, "Sixteen years is a long time."

"Yeah. Well, I'm sure I won't — I'll be on goody-two-shoes," he replied.

Vinyard signed the agreement, verifying that he understood all the rights he was voluntarily waiving, every one described in detail. And the defense attorney signed, confirming that she had competently represented him, personally explained to him each and every element of the crimes he was pleading guilty to, explained the possible penalties, and personally discussed with him each and every right he would be waiving.

Neither Bruce nor I were consulted before the hearing. When it was over, the advocate called me with the results. By then, contacts from the DA's office had for so long heralded bad news that the brutality of the stalker and the judiciary were inextricably intertwined in my psyche. My physical reaction when called by an advocate or deputy DA, or when walk-ing into the justice center, echoed those I experienced when contacted by Vinyard. My nerves ignited, my heart and breath raced, my body quaked. It was an uncontrollable, visceral response.

Now, with the addition of the assault charge, the predator/judiciary beast morphed into the mythical hydra. Upon cutting off one head — arresting Vinyard for stalking — two had grown in its place. Not only had the hearings, motions, players, and negotiations behind closed doors multiplied, so did the devastation left in the wake of cruel indifference, shattered hopes, and betrayal of justice.

The plea deal offered and accepted was a three-year *deferred* sentence for both counts.

"It was a slam dunk," the advocate said, "a trap."

Horrified, I gasped, and she rushed to explain.

"The DA's office feels sure Vinyard won't comply with the no-contact condition. Then when he violates, the court can sentence him to prison without a trial."

And so, the trap was set. And we were the bait. The tyranny of the judiciary just blew my mind.

"They were concerned that if the case went to trial, there was a chance that a Boulder jury would have just convicted him of resisting arrest and not felony assault," the advocate said. "The stalking was a separate charge and could not be discussed in the felony trial, so the jury would know nothing about it. And if the jury convicted him of resisting arrest, a misdemeanor, it would mean a short jail sentence but not prison."

It was catch-22 all over again. But all I could see was the big picture.

In nearly two decades of stalking, we had been ruthlessly invaded and the danger had continually escalated. Now we were placed directly in harm's way. The DA's office had gambled with our safety, with our very lives, and the judge didn't even know who we were or why we were involved at all.

When I could shake off the shock and take a step back, I understood why the DA's office did it. In the long run, this strategy might give us the best protection the system, as dysfunctional as it was, could give us. But I disagreed with the decision, and worse, we had not even been consulted. We had been stripped of all power and used as pawns. It was an unconscionable, abusive, dangerous move. But there was nothing I could do about it now. It was a done deal.

The deferred sentence would begin when Vinyard was released from the one-year jail term for harassment-stalking and run concurrent with probation in that case. The conditions of the deferred sentence included no contact directly or indirectly with Bruce or me and all other terms and conditions of probation in the stalking case. And according to the agreement, if within three years Vinyard violated any of the conditions or committed new offenses, he'd be convicted of the assault charge and sentenced to prison.

By now, the anticipated date of Vinyard's release was early September, just five months away.

"Call the jail in mid-July to be sure you're on the notification list and to get an update on the release date. And get a restraining order," the advocate said.

And with that, we were left to cope with the consequences of the plea deal on our own.

In the few months remaining, we did everything we could think of to strengthen our defenses. Relenting to the advocate's advice, Bruce and I both petitioned for restraining orders and discovered that, thankfully, the rules had changed: Addresses and phone numbers were no longer required. Bruce had remarried, and he and his wife had moved. Their address and phone number remained unpublished. Now they didn't have to compromise their safety to request protection.

We consulted a private investigator. Hiring a bodyguard was financially out of the question for all of us, but this retired police officer generously helped us develop a safety plan, which we quickly put into place.

I made arrangements for safe places for the children to go in an emergency. In-depth discussions with school principals, teachers, and day care providers followed. And though our youngest children had no idea why, I practiced safety drills with them. I tried to make each drill a game but the kids were confused and resistant. The games were essential to keeping them safe, but fueling their fears was the cost of playing.

Caller ID was now available and I added it to my phone service. Then, discussing my needs with electronics retailers, I found and purchased a recording device that attached to my phone. No longer would I have to wait for a voice mail recording to prove that Vinyard had called. I could now record a call directly onto a tape — hard evidence to give the police.

During the last stalking episode, talking with Vinyard's probation officer had proven invaluable. This time I was determined to meet the new probation officer in advance to be sure he understood the history and the danger my family now faced.

In fact, I found him to be well-informed and sympathetic. He met me at my home and, with my consent, prepared an informational bulletin with Vinyard's booking photo. And going door to door, he distributed it by hand to my neighbors, asking them to be on the lookout for him in the neighborhood while simultaneously calming their fears. Then he offered his availability anytime, day or night, if I needed to contact him. Oddly, during the decades I had endured this nightmare, I rarely cried. But when extended a helping hand beyond what duty required, when offered genuine kindness and understanding, my armor was unexpectedly pierced. Tears long buried welled up and spilled down my cheeks.

Finally, I contacted the Longmont police to notify them of Vinyard's pending release. I asked to discuss the case with a detective. The lack of continuity of officers, prosecutors, and judges all these years had severely hindered justice and impacted our safety. Stalking is, by its very nature, the relentless hunt of a predator. It's the repetitive nature, the whole of the experience, that defines it. Having one police contact in Boulder had been tremendously helpful. I hoped to find a similar point of contact in Longmont and was soon introduced to Detective Sharon Schumann. We met at her office, and while we talked, she did a quick computer search of Vinyard's criminal record. By the time I left, I was assured she took the case quite seriously.

Now, with all our defenses in place, I would try once again to focus on work and easing my children's fears. And, my own fears firing random shots throughout my nervous system, I would wait.

CHAPTER 7

Riptide

"If you are going through hell, keep going."
~ Author unknown

Timeline, personal entry:

I feel like bait. Prey for the predator. We all wait, knowing something will happen. What? His condition has deteriorated. The danger is escalating still.

He has been diagnosed with schizophrenia, delusional disorder, and bipolar disorder, and I believe he is alcoholic. His delusional obsession is untreatable. His level of dangerousness to us was assessed years ago as medium to high. What is it now? Now he has spent time in jail and he assaulted an officer. Now he knows where I live.

Vinyard told [his probation officer] that he might as well give himself up because he could not comply with the conditions of probation. Stalking is called the silent crime that kills. Is this what we're waiting for?

It is absurd this case has come to this. The "justice" system has failed everyone here.

*   *   *

9/8/1997

8:00 PM. Incoming call from the county jail. Vinyard had just been released on probation.

Now the shades would be drawn. I would again sleep fully clothed, in my street clothes and shoes. To keep my family at the ready, for some time now the doors had been double bolted at all times, and the children were never allowed to answer the doors or the phones. Until Vinyard was caught, having friends over and playing outside unsupervised would not be allowed. Once again, while Vinyard was free, we were imprisoned.

But it wasn't just our freedom that was affected. I was in lockdown. I'd felt it so many times before, the sensation, the pattern was familiar. It wasn't a conscious shift, but it was undeniably real. I could almost hear the gate of solid steel slide down over my heart, over any vulnerability. *Sssshhhhh kkknnnngg.* The finality of it echoed in my mind. I was now shut off. The warrior. The sword. Until Vinyard was locked up again, this is all I would be.

Apart from the ever-present love of my children, only two emotions could penetrate my armor. Though I had tried many times to keep them at bay, fear and anger always slipped through. On the one hand, I believed fear kept me sharp; on the other, it interfered with rational thinking and made me more vulnerable, and I condemned it as weakness. And while anger fueled me when needed, it was an ugly place to dwell.

Fear and anger. A toxic combination. I didn't recognize the person I'd become. And I really didn't like her much.

9/9/1997

Bruce's mother, who shared his last name, received eight hang-up phone calls on the first day of Vinyard's freedom and at regular intervals in the days that followed. Terrified, she switched to an unlisted number. Because of my business, changing to an unlisted number was not an option for me. And the stalker already knew my address. If he couldn't reach me by phone, I feared he would take the only other avenue open to him and appear at our home. I needed the line open as much as he did, to catch him before he ever reached my door.

7:52 PM. Incoming call, caller ID: out of area. I answered. No response.

Again, "Hello?"

Silence.

"Hello!"

Pulling the mouthpiece away from my labored breath, I waited, counting fifteen seconds, but the caller did not hang up. My children were nearby when the call came in and now they began talking in the background. Not wanting them to be heard, I quickly hung up and traced the call. Trace unsuccessful.

9/10/1997

6:48 PM. Incoming call. I couldn't reach it in time to answer. Caller ID: out of area. No message left.

9/11 – 9/16/1997

As the week dragged on, the days were becoming a blur, each one punctuated by four to five hang-up calls and two to three calls with dead silence. Most of them displayed "out of area" and most traces were unsuccessful. Although just a forty-minute drive away, at the time, the Denver-metro area was long distance to Longmont, and caller ID and most traces were useless. But one call was from a pay phone in Boulder — closer.

Every call was reported, but with no evidence implicating Vinyard, all I could do was wait.

Finally, a week after his release, the hearing for our permanent restraining order petitions was held. The magistrate had never heard our case before; the hearing was in a different division. Vinyard was notified and appeared in court, but did not contest the orders. I could only guess why he'd come.

It seemed he'd seized the opportunity to be there with me — to stalk me — in court. Irony ran rampant. Though he was ordered by the court to have no contact of any kind with us, getting restraining orders required that he be allowed to attend the hearing. I now understood why the orders were essential, but being forced to stand there before this salivating predator to ask for protection was deeply disturbing and only reinforced his fixation.

With no objection from Vinyard, the magistrate granted Bruce and me each permanent state and national restraining orders against him. From then on, I kept mine with me at all times. Copies were stored in secure locations.

Another week passed and the probation officer called. Vinyard was seen wandering around the justice center and the ramp leading to the employee garage but did not keep his appointment. Wild panic exploded in my chest.

The probation officer had immediately issued a special security alert notice throughout the building that included a photo, a physical description, and a list of Vinyard's crimes. In it, he also advised staff to notify the deputy if Vinyard was seen attempting to enter the building through any entry other than the front door security post. "Justice Center personnel should not attempt to challenge or confront the subject unless properly armed and trained," it warned.

There was some concern that he may have planted a bomb, the officer said. I brushed off that comment and latched onto the imminent threat. This could not happen again. I reminded him of Vinyard's history of fleeing and that in our case, nearly a decade before, he'd disappeared from supervision, an arrest warrant was issued and eventually expired, and the case was closed.

"He has to be caught right away," I exclaimed.

"I'll get an arrest warrant immediately," the officer said.

The next day, the DA's office petitioned for a judgment that Vinyard had violated the deferred sentence conditions, and wrote, "The Defendant has an extensive history of violent behavior, failure to comply, and failure to appear. The Defendant poses an imminent risk to public safety."

The judge agreed and a nationwide arrest warrant was issued. Once again, Vinyard had disappeared.

This time, no one wanted to take the risk of waiting for him to surface or for the Aurora police to find the spare time to make an arrest. A task force was organized to find him.

9/27/1997

Saturday, 8:50 PM. Incoming call: out of area. I grabbed the receiver and, fingers fumbling, switched on the recorder. The squeal of feedback raced through the line.

Heart stampeding, my voice shook. But to my surprise, I found that determination trumped fear. I was on the offensive, working to catch him. I had prepared and waited for this moment, and I planned to get as much information as I could on tape for evidence.

What did he want, I asked? To be with me, he said. "Is my understanding not correct? Did you not paint a picture?"

"No, I never promised you anything," I replied. "Where are you?"

"Uhhh, I just want to trust you first of all. I need to trust you and I don't — I don't appreciate you calling the cops because I'm not that bad of a guy."

Struggling to control panic and my quivering voice, I paused and my breath was audibly ragged.

"I don't really mean you any harm," he said. "I've never hit you or physically assaulted you, and I'm not that bad of a guy, I just — "

"Why are you calling?" I asked again.

"Why?! Because I want to get together with you and, and, and to be together."

"But you know that I've told you many times that I want no contact with you, right?"

"Well you — I, I know how you — but you don't understand how I feel."

Reasoning with a madman is an exercise in futility, and yet I tried. I *needed* to be heard.

Vinyard related stories of meaningless events he believed happened twenty years before. "You once, once on Broadway you got off your bike and you dismounted your bike and you talked to me. ... How can you get off your bike and smile on me and act really super friendly? I mean, if you didn't care you'd just ride your bike on down Broadway without even saying hello, but you took the point and the time to get off your bike and walk with me."

There were two points to these stories, it seemed. One was to validate his delusion that I wanted him; the other, to portray himself as the victim, claiming that I encouraged him. It was infuriating. The more he persisted, the angrier I became.

I wrestled the conversation back to center: "I have done everything in my power to tell you that I do not want contact from you. You have continued to contact me. You have continued to frighten me, harass me, follow me, approach me when you've parked around the corner, beat on my house, called me names that were very vulgar."

"All right, okay, that's all — that's all post, post-marriage. That's all post-marriage. I'm talking about pre-marriage. Before you got married, you were very friendly towards me, very cordial ... "

All I wanted was to scrape this parasite off, but nothing I said slipped through. Circles.

"I'm just — I'm heart — you know how much you mean to me," he said. "You know at one time I was very fond of you and I felt that you were very fond of me."

"I didn't know that you were 'very fond' of me until you started coming around the house and harassing us, and beating on our house in the middle of the night, and frightening us both to death, and walking into my home unannounced, uninvited. I didn't know anything about how you felt, and I never encouraged anything."

But round and round the carousel spun. I felt I would go mad.

"I have — I have done everything in my power to say that I do not want any contact from you. I do not! I do not!" *Stop! Just stop!!*

Still, round and round and round it went. Locked in his selfishness, immersed in delusion, he would not hear me. Pure, unmitigated lunacy was closing in on me from every direction.

Finally, clinging desperately to sanity, I swung the sword of my tongue with all the force of my rage and conviction — at him, at the courts, at the universe: "I do *not* — I will *not* be chased. I will *not* be harassed. I will *not* be violated in any way!!"

"Wwwyyy — would you — www — okay. I want to feel wanted."

That was it in a nutshell. He was utterly, completely narcissistic. My feelings were of absolutely no consequence to him.

"Please deposit fifty cents."

The call disconnected and I dialed the Longmont PD.

Through the bizarre maze of twisted logic, one thing had come to light during the exchange. When I'd asked why he had been violent toward us in the past, Vinyard claimed to have been drunk: something I'd suspected before and was substantiated by the court's condition of monitored sobriety.

Our children had been visiting Bruce and his wife that day. I tried to contact them before they brought the kids home, but they'd already left. Fearing Vinyard might be headed to the area and knowing the police were on their way, I ran outside to wait for them. As soon as the van pulled up, I met them at the street and signaled them to roll down Bruce's passenger window. Glancing into the back, I breathed a sigh of relief; heads flopped to the side, the children were all asleep.

Quietly, I explained the situation and asked them to take the kids back for the night. But Sophie, now eight years old, woke up and, groggy, was confused.

"Why are we going back?" she asked in a voice on the verge of tears.

My own tears rising to meet hers, I brusquely wiped them away.

"Your dad and stepmom have something fun for you to do tomorrow. It just came up," I said as cheerfully as I could.

Unbuckling her seat belt, Sophie crawled over the front seat and into Bruce's lap. Then her small, open hands stretched out the window, imploring me to hold her.

Terrified that Vinyard or the officer would be there any minute, I was torn between clutching her to my chest and rushing them all away. I took a step closer and, with her desperate fingers grabbing my neck, hugged her awkwardly through the window. I looked at Bruce, silently pleading for help.

"We have someplace really special to take you tomorrow," he said as I peered frantically up and down the street. "We'll bring you back right after."

Her stepmother nodded and, reaching across the seat, softly stroked her back. But Sophie would not give in. Tightening her grip on my neck, she cried, "No, I don't want to go. I want to stay with you!"

"Oh, it'll be so fun," I said, squeezing her hard.

I knew what I had to do and it was tearing me apart. My thoughts flashed back to the night the stalker attacked our home, Ian in his crib next to me. Once again, when all I wanted to do was pull my child into my breast, to console her and fold myself over her until all danger had passed, the only way to protect her was to keep her away from me. It was a sickeningly cruel choice.

My chest tight and aching, I pressed my lips to Sophie's forehead then gently but firmly pushed her away and into her father's arms.

Finally, my heart linked to hers by our steadfast gaze, I stepped back, away from my beloved daughter. It would not do to linger. She needed to go.

Bruce pulled Sophie into a hug, but still she resisted. Her glistening eyes now wide with fear, she begged to know I was all right and pleaded with us to let her stay.

"Why are we going?" she demanded and, turning to me, asked, "Are you okay?"

Then struggling to free herself from her father's arms, she declared, "I don't want to leave. Mommy's not okay. I want to stay with her!"

We all did our best to soothe her and allay her fears. But it was no use. She did not believe my invented reason for their return.

Finally, her stepmother gently eased her into her seat and buckled her in.

Bringing my hand to my lips, I blew Sophie and her sleeping brothers a kiss. Then stepping back on the sidewalk, smiling and waving, I felt my heart crumple as I watched them all drive away.

The moment they returned home, Sophie insisted on calling me. Sobbing, she asked again if I was all right. Again, I tried to reassure her. But she sensed danger, and for many months after, she was extremely distraught and clingy.

10:00 PM. An unfamiliar officer responded and took the tape recording. While I was outside seeing him off, Vinyard called again and left a message. The gravelly voice and slurred speech were distinctly different from the earlier call. I'd heard that voice many times before when he'd violently attacked and threatened us — when, as he had just admitted, he'd been drunk.

> Well uh, yeah, thanks for answering the phone. I appreciate talking to you in person. Uuhhh, um, for you and for my own good, I'm leavin'. So you don't have to worry about anything else anymore. And I'm out of the area, and you don't have to worry about me hurtin' you or hurtin' anybody else. I'll be safe and secure. And I was wishing for a happy ending. But I guess not. And, uhh — www, what else is there to say — was — happy ending. But I guess *not*. Uuhhh, mmm.

"End of message."

Now he'd be charged with violating probation and violating the restraining order. But first, he had to be caught.

Both the probation officer and the responding police officer suggested it would be helpful if I could set up a meeting with Vinyard so the police could arrest him. I flushed with fear. If I did as they suggested, I risked revenge, even more danger to my family.

But there was no time to waste. With great trepidation, I resolved to try to arrange a meeting. If he was caught, I told myself, we'd have at least five years of peace while he was in prison. By now, my trust in that promise was shaky at best, but I needed real hope and chose to believe it.

9/28/1997

The next night, at eight o'clock on the dot, the phone rang. As always now, at the sound of the bell, my heart and breath raced. Picking up the receiver, I glanced at the screen: out of area. I pressed "record" and the familiar squeal of feedback penetrated the line.

"Hello." His voice.

My voice thick with anxiety, I uttered, "Yes?"

"Would you want to do that? Why don't you do that because I'm really crazy about you. I am."

"What do you want me to do?"

"I've got a motel room for the night if you want to."

Revulsion twisted my gut, and when I gulped air to force the contents of my stomach back down, my breath trembled loudly. *Get hold of yourself,* I demanded. *You have a job to do. Now think!*

"You got a car. I don't have a car," he said. "It's really hard for me to get up to Longmont. I never been in Longmont. Don't ever really wanna be in — go in Longmont."

"Where are you?"

"I'm on Federal. It's not the best motel, but if you want som'n better, I got money. Do you want me to meet you someplace, halfway in between?" The hunger in his voice made my skin crawl.

My brain, it seemed, was on slow play. A long pause and deep sighs were my only response.

"Do you feel the same way?" he asked.

"I need some time," I replied.

"You need some time?"

"Uh-huh."

"Well, this is encouraging anyway! I'm glad we're at least talking. It's better than calling the cops and all that frustration and everything. I'm glad we're at least talking. That's an improvement."

I needed to put the children to bed so they wouldn't overhear or be heard. Grasping, I said, "Call me in an hour."

"All right, okay, all right. Www — is that gonna be too late for you? Do you have to work tomorrow?"

"It's not going to be too late."

"All right, okay, all right. I'll call you back at nine then. Is that what time it is? It's eight now, eight som'n?"

"Call me at 9:30."

Turning the phone off and on in one swipe, I called the police officer. He was not available, so I left a message. Then I plotted.

Vinyard wanted me to meet him. I had an opening. As repulsive as it was, I knew my best hope was to get into his head, to use everything I knew about how his mind worked, against him. I was reminded of the art of tai chi. When it's used in self-defense, an attacker's energy is collected and deflected back to him; what he gives, he gets back. But in this battle, it was my mind that was pitted against his. My wits were my first line of defense.

The risk to bystanders concerned me deeply. Without a doubt, this could be extremely dangerous. I would find a location away from the public and pressure him to be sober. And I needed to give the officers a day to prepare.

9:30 PM. The phone rang and I switched on the recorder. Again, I wanted as much evidence on tape as I could get and began pumping Vinyard for information. I needed to appear wary anyway. I'd always emphatically refused him before. If I agreed to meet him too easily, I was sure he'd be suspicious. Insane but intelligent — the most dangerous kind of deviant mind. I had to be careful just how I played my hand.

"I need to trust you," I began.

"Yeah, I need to trust you, too."

I asked if he'd been drinking when he'd left the message the night before, and he admitted that he'd "had a few beers." *A violation of the sobriety condition of probation*, I thought.

He'd "technically broken probation," he then confessed, and I realized he was alluding to fleeing supervision. *Good, this shows intent. He understands that he violated.*

"All right, well, so [inaudible], so, I need to trust you that you're not going to turn me in or call the cops 'cause I talked to you," he said.

Even now I found it hard to lie. "You invited me down to your place tonight, right?"

"Right, right."

I had to find some reason for delaying meeting him and said I was concerned he may have been drinking. He claimed he hadn't that day.

"And I just need time to feel comfortable with that," I replied. "Are you planning on being in the area tomorrow?"

"Oh, yeah, yeah. I'm, I'm not goin' anywhere tomorrow."

"Hmm." Struggling to breathe, it was all I could do to steady my voice and think.

"If you don't wanna — if you don't feel comfortable tonight."

"It would help me to have a day to prepare for it, to just prepare myself and feel that I can trust you."

Where to meet was the question. He suggested a mall north of Denver, and an infantry of red flags flew up as I envisioned all the people and chaos in a shopping mall. I suggested a quiet place where we could talk. I needed to draw him closer, away from Denver, but didn't want him anywhere near my home. Boulder was neutral ground between our locations. He had called from there recently. And in his mind, Boulder would probably have some bizarre symbolic lure. It was, after all, the birthplace of his obsession.

"Do you mean like a park-type situation? Do you want to meet at a park?" he asked.

"A park or just an open space where there weren't other people around."

"All right, why don't we meet at Chautauqua then?"

Good, it's at the foot of the mountains, just one block from our previous home in Boulder. After the park closes but before dark.

"Eight o'clock?" he asked.

"No, let's say seven. Seven is better for me. And listen, I need to trust that you will *not* come to my home, you will *not* come to Longmont. You will let me come to you, do you understand?"

"Yes, yes."

"And you also have to promise me that you will not drink or do drugs from here 'til then."

"Yeah, yeah. I'm perfectly, uh — want to be sober [inaudible] drinking and, and I haven't done any drugs since I've been out."

Finally, we were agreed. At seven o'clock the next evening we would meet at the Bluebell Shelter, at the far end near open space. But it wasn't me he would find.

The trap was now set, but it had come at a price. Several rounds of clicks had interrupted the call. I was sure it was the officer trying to reach me and I hoped Vinyard wouldn't notice. I was not that lucky. I quickly discounted them as a problem with the line; I didn't want to draw more attention to them by stopping to answer and was afraid I'd lose the momentum I was building toward the desired outcome — a plan to meet.

But fully aware of the situation and concerned for our safety, the officer rushed to our home. He arrived so quickly that I was still recording the call and, from the lower level, couldn't answer the door. Worried when he got no response, the officer knocked harder and called out, asking if I was all right.

Seth, my youngest, awoke with a start. Terrified and in tears, he ran downstairs to find me while I was on the phone.

"Mom?" he cried, his voice shaking. "Somebody's at the door. You need to get it!"

"Excuse me a minute," I said and shoved the handset into my shoulder.

Seth leaped into my outstretched arm and I pulled him into my lap. His whole body trembled.

Holding him against me with one arm, I lifted the handset to my ear then turned my head and leaned as far away from Seth as I could. But I knew the microphone picked up my son's heart-wrenching sobs.

I had never mentioned the children in court in the hope that Vinyard wouldn't know they existed, at least not more than one. In that instant, I feared he knew. There was simply no way to protect the children from this nightmare when Vinyard was free.

After tucking Seth back into bed, I talked with the officer. Then I called Vinyard's probation officer and Detective Arndt of the Boulder PD to give them the meeting time and place.

It was now in their hands, and I was glad to be rid of it.

9/29/1997

The next day, Detective Arndt gave Bruce an alarm to dispatch, which had been alerted to the situation. The kids would have a long, overnight visit with Bruce and his wife. There was no way Vinyard could find them there, and just in case I was wrong about that, the police would be there in minutes.

"It'll be fun," I insisted.

But by now, the children were extremely insecure. They didn't understand what was happening or why they had to go. In no way did they buy the ruse that it was just for fun, but I had no choice. I had to get them out of the house and into a secure environment.

5:45 PM. The county sheriff had a SWAT team waiting at Chautauqua, and the Longmont police detectives Schumann and Schmad arrived at my home. They had arranged for me to stay in a motel, and Detective Schumann planned to escort me there. Detective Schmad would stay at the house in case something went wrong and Vinyard came to the area. They also had backup waiting in the neighborhood. It was surreal. I'd seen it in films but never imagined anything like this would ever happen to me.

As soon as they arrived, Detective Schmad searched every room — every closet, every nook and cranny of the house — to check for bombs. That's one thing I'd never considered. It just wasn't his MO. But with the probation department and now the police searching for bombs, I was beginning to rethink that.

6:00 PM. Just as I was gathering my things and preparing to leave, the phone rang. I froze and my eyes locked onto Detective Schumann's. She nodded.

I was nowhere near my recorder. I kept it in my office on the lower level, as far away from the children as possible. Racing to catch the call before it went to voice mail, I flew down the stairs and, breathless, picked up the receiver. Vinyard.

He was too scared to go; he just got out of jail, he said.

My heart plummeted. I could not let this happen. Everything was in place. The police wouldn't do this again. He had to be caught that night.

Think. Think fast. I jabbed the record button and, voice trembling, asked how we would ever get together. He suggested giving it a little more time.

"Uh-huh. Well, how would I get ahold of you?" I asked.

"Well, I'm — instead of being my usual lazy self, I'm going to be super busy getting things together and, uh, I will get a phone, and now I feel bad about all those years I was unavailable and didn't have a phone, and that was really unusual, very unusual. And uh, I do want to be more available and be more of a polite gentleman and regular-type guy. And, uh, geez, I just enjoy talking to you, and I think it's amazing that we're talking. I don't know, I just don't feel ready right yet to, uh, to do that even though I'd be the first to, to, you know, love to go to Chautauqua, Bluebell Shelter, and sit down with you and just, just feel great, you know, look into your eyes and, you know, just get a very good feeling. But I, I — just with the cops, I can't take a chance. I'm sorry."

I counted on his obsession to override reason. I'd seen how strong it was all these years. Now I needed it. "Well, if it's too far for you to go to Chautauqua, is there another place I can meet you?"

"Well, yeah, if you really want to come and see me. I mean, uh, I'm staying at a motel that's a lot nicer than the one I was at yesterday."

"Are you still in the same area?"

"No, no. I'm not on the west side. I'm on the east side. I feel more comfortable on this side, on the east side."

"Well — "

"Well, if you want to come down and see me right away, that's — that would be fantastic!" he exclaimed, laughing.

"Well, like I said, I had made arrangements tonight and if — you know, I prepared myself tonight and I wanted to, to do this. I wanted to talk to you."

"Uh-huh, okay. That's great, great."

"Where can I — "

"Well, it's on — you're probably familiar with I-70, right?"

"Right."

"All right, I-70 to Peoria Street."

"Um-hmm."

"Please deposit fifty cents for two more minutes."

"Why don't you just tell me quickly, and — "

"Yeah, yeah. Take, take a right at Peoria Street and it's Traveler's Inn, 104, and, and, you know, I'm really praying to God that I can trust you."

The moment I hung up, I checked the caller ID. It was confirmed: a pay phone in Aurora. Triumphant, I turned to Detective Schumann, but when I saw her face, my own fell.

"It's out of our jurisdiction," she said. "We can't go there."

Nnooo!!

Quickly, she called the Aurora PD, gave them the information, and asked them to pick him up right away. Then she turned to me.

"They said they're too busy to respond quickly. We're going to have to call this off."

I felt something break inside me and before I knew it, my knees buckled and I sank to the floor, arms wrapped around my chest. Nothing existed outside of me. In this small womb that was my world, only the faint beating of my heart could be heard beneath the rushing waters of despair. In that moment, for the first time in all these years, I lost all hope. I was defeated. I was done.

Then somewhere in the distance, I heard the faint beeps of a phone dialing and, as I slowly re-emerged, Detective Schumann's voice asking the county sheriff's team now poised at Chautauqua to go to Aurora and pick him up. In a rush, the officers took the taped conversation, gave me a new tape, and packed up. They'd be in touch, they said, and in a heartbeat they were gone.

Only the quiet, cautious unfolding of hope penetrated the sudden silence.

8:15 PM. The phone rang and I grabbed it.

"They got him," Detective Schumann said, and I burst into laughter and tears.

Finally forcing my brain to engage, I asked if bond had been set. There were two warrants at $5,000 each, for a total bond of $10,000.

"No, it's not enough! He cannot be released on bond," I exclaimed.

"I'll see what I can do," she said. In the meantime, she'd blocked my number at the jail. He couldn't call me.

Within the hour, the probation officer called to say he had a five-day hold on Vinyard and would make a statement to the judge as to why he shouldn't be released. His first appearance was scheduled for October 1, in two days.

I couldn't wait until morning. I drove to Boulder to pick up the kids and bring them home. As soon as I saw them, I swept them all into my arms and held them together in a giggling pile. The little ones had no idea why, but they didn't mind.

For five years at least — maybe, just maybe as many as sixteen — we would live free of this terror, we would have peace.

And again, it struck me. The penalty would not be for stalking me. In the eyes of the law and the eyes of the court, physical assault was a violent, serious crime, punishable by long sentences. But emotional assault — brutal, relentless invasion and terror — and the life-altering wreckage it left behind were not. Justice really was blind.

I soon heard from Detective Arndt and the Longmont officer who first worked the case. They were glad he was caught, they said. Detective Arndt planned to turn her case notes over to the probation officer.

Reflecting on all that had transpired, it occurred to me that, although I was effectively used as bait again when the officers suggested I arrange a meeting, the experience was entirely different than when we were set up by the judiciary. Then we were not consulted, had no say in the decision whatsoever, and were left to handle the fallout from the plea deal on our own. Essentially, we were stripped of our power, placed in danger, and abandoned. This time, the choice was mine and the police had our backs. This time, I was empowered and supported, and that made all the difference.

How would I ever express the gratitude I felt for these officers? I doubted I could. But there was one simple thing I could do, or rather we could do. Ian had been aware of the situation for some time and felt powerless to do anything about it. I wanted to give him some closure. So together, we delivered a note and a cake to the Longmont officers. Then, our arms wrapped around each other, my son and I happily walked out of the building and into our newfound freedom.

And not a single anonymous phone call broke the silence once Vinyard was in jail. Not one.

Now, let the healing begin.

*   *   *

With the nightmare finally behind me, I wanted nothing more than to put as much distance as possible between Vinyard and myself, between the past and the new life awaiting me. Some people get tattoos to mark or initiate change. I chose a new name, a whole new beginning. Since my work relied on my reputation, I didn't change it professionally. It was a name I would go by with family and friends.

Pouring through books, I discovered no names similar to my own that felt right. But having set my intention on finding my name, I began noticing that every night just before drifting into sleep and every morning upon waking, I "heard" the soothing sounds *kI-ah*.

I didn't know Kaia was a name. I wasn't even sure I'd ever heard it before. Digging back into my books, I discovered it had two meanings in two different languages: one was "earth," which related to my career; the other, "season's beginning." Soon it was mine.

*   *   *

During the three weeks Vinyard was free on probation and for many months after, there were signs that my children were suffering severely, and I was riddled with guilt. Should I have run? Could we have disappeared? I knew we were in peril but thought I could protect them. But again, it was made starkly clear that I could not hide my fear from my children.

At the time, Seth was six years old and Sophie, eight. On the cusp of adolescence, Ian was more frightened than he would admit.

One child had chronic stomachaches, a constant sick feeling in the pit of the stomach. One suffered from night terrors every night and feared monsters outside the bedroom window. Schoolwork brought home was laden with pictures of violent, bloody battles with monsters and stories of monsters attacking families. In one story, the only family that survived had fled and found safety.

One child wrote a story of a monstrous spider that wouldn't go away. "A spider lives in my corner and I don't know why. I don't know how to get him out."

Shirts were soaked and lips and fingers raw, all evidence of constant chewing. And fears around sleeping plagued them all.

Night after night, we snuggled together and folded ourselves into the poetry of Margaret Wise Brown and the calm, friendly pictures of Clement Hurd as I quietly read, "Good night stars, Good night air, Good night noises everywhere." Then I'd lead them in a guided visualization, where first we cleared all negativity and allowed it to pass freely from our home, then calling in Spirit, guides, and guardians, we grew a bubble of protection around our home and yard to see us safely through the night.

These sweet, innocent children had no idea why they were so afraid. They only knew what they needed: protection, to feel safe in the world. The torture had to stop.

CHAPTER 8

Crossroads

"When deeds speak, words are nothing."
~ *African Proverb*

I don't know why I thought peace would ensue. It was naked hope, I guess. I needed to believe that after all this, justice would be swift and we'd be safe.

I knew I'd have to be involved in court proceedings at some level, but I didn't see it coming. After all I'd seen, after all I'd been through with the judiciary, I still wasn't prepared for the wild frenzy of legal ping-pong or the quagmire that would soon follow and devour my life.

10/1/1997

Two days after his arrest, Vinyard appeared before the judge. The probation officer presented the new charges, and afterward I was told that bond was raised to $50,000. At last I could be fairly sure he wouldn't be released on bond.

Then later that day, a friend called to congratulate me and tell me she'd heard through the grapevine (a friend who worked at the jail) that Vinyard was "tearing up the jail." I didn't ask for the information, and honestly, it was more than I wanted to know.

"He's kicking and screaming — dangerous," she said.

My breath caught, and my thoughts leaped back to the bond. *Please keep him locked up. Please keep us safe.*

Soon, a form letter landed in my mailbox. By then I'd lost count of the times I'd received the same letter. "The Boulder District Attorney's Office is sorry to learn that you have been the victim of a crime," it began.

James Thurber once described humor as "emotional chaos remembered in tranquility." Until that moment, his words had never meant much to me. But reading the greeting again, I discovered that there comes a time when a situation is so absurd, so preposterous, and when prolonged stress has so exhausted the system that beneath it is revealed, of all things, humor.

I laughed out loud — a rich, genuine, hearty laugh.

You're sorry? Again? Gee, maybe you could — oh, I don't know — do something about it?

True, it was sarcastic humor, but humor nonetheless.

"We have enclosed a brochure explaining your rights as a violent crime victim," the letter read.

At the time, I had no idea of the history behind it, or why the letters only came after the stalking resumed in 1994, or why I hadn't heard about a victim/witness assistance program before then. Soon I learned that a decade before, in response to glaring injustices, the federal government passed the Victims of Crime Act of 1984. The issue gaining traction, the Colorado constitution was amended to include rights afforded to crime victims in 1992. Finally in '94, the state legislature passed Colorado's Victim Rights Act.

I skimmed the brochure again. Emblazoned on the front, in big, bold letters: "**Defendants have the right to remain silent. Victims have the right to be heard**." I snorted.

But in all fairness, the information contained did partially fill the huge gap in communication I'd experienced in the early years of my involvement with the DA's office. It defined the basic legal terms I'd struggled to grasp back then. It provided a list of help resources and described the victim/witness assistance program. It described the safety provisions in court and listed the information a violent crime victim had the right to have: the charges, the police and court case numbers, the judge, the deputy DA and crime victim advocate assigned, and hearing dates.

Scanning the brochure, the first three rights jumped off the page (the emphasis is my own):

- to be treated with *fairness,* respect and dignity and to have a *swift and fair resolution* of your case
- to be *informed of and present for all critical stages* of the criminal justice process
- to be *present and heard in court for any bond reduction, reduction of charges, disposition, sentencing or continuances*

In theory, these were just and good. But in my experience, the judiciary had a long way to go to uphold them.

The advocate assigned to the stalking case soon called to inform me of the new charges. The legalese rolled right over me. All I really wanted to know was the penalties. How long would we be safe?

The deputy DA would discuss that with me, she said. Kathy Delgado had been assigned. Then unprompted, she added, "They think he's scary."

Yeah, he's scary.

The next day, I met Kathy at her office. A tiny, professional woman in a doll-sized suit, she exuded the energy and quick intellect of any three people. With a brief introduction, she launched into the charges.

There were three counts of violation of restraining order and one count of harassment by stalking, she said. The last count was an umbrella over three new harassment charges.

The charges were incomprehensible to me. Evidently, the trauma of recent events had severely affected me. My brain wasn't functioning. In conversation, my words were scrambled and I kept losing my train of thought. Working productively proved impossible, and I wasn't sleeping well at all.

When I slept, I frequently awoke with a start. Heart racing, body tingling, nerves inflamed, I was waiting for the imminent attack, but paralyzed, I was riveted to my bed. Once fully awake, I was afraid of the shock to my system if I tried to move in that state, so I made a practice of lying still and talking myself through it. I assured myself that all was well, took deep breaths, and waited until my heart slowed, my nerves stopped prickling, and my limbs were released before I moved. I just hoped the damage would heal in time.

But while Kathy pushed on, in the jumble of her words, there was one thing I heard loud and clear: Harassment-stalking was no longer a misdemeanor. It was now a felony. Colorado's stalking statute had again been amended earlier that year.

She continued. For a first offense, it was a class 6. But if it was a repeat offense within seven years of the first conviction, it bumped up to a class 5, with a longer presumptive range of sentencing, even if the offender was convicted when it was not a felony. Vinyard would be charged with a class 5 felony, she said.

Struggling to grasp it all, I asked about the penalties. Currently, the presumptive range for a class 5 felony was one to three years, she said. A class 6 was twelve to eighteen months.

My God. How long have I been dealing with this? How many years have I served?

But if a restraining order was in effect at the time, Kathy added, sentences for multiple charges would be consecutive, not concurrent.

Then I heard it — the phrase that, by now, sparked a fiery rage inside me. The prosecution and the defense were discussing a plea bargain. Once again, my family's safety, my freedom from this endless nightmare, justice itself was being negotiated behind closed doors. I would not be involved in the decision; I would only be informed. I was stripped of my voice, stripped of all power.

And it was eating me up that the truth of these horrific crimes had never been spoken aloud in open court. The public needed to hear. Vinyard's crimes had to be exposed, brought out of the shadows and into the light of day. It was wrong and it churned in my gut. But again, I shoved my indignation down, to ruminate on later. Now I needed to focus on what she was saying and think as clearly as possible.

It was true that with only a one- to three-year sentence — which I now knew would likely be one year no matter the circumstances — it didn't make sense to go to trial. Most if not all that time would be devoured by court proceedings. But I was determined that any plea bargain include pleading guilty to the crime of stalking and that it be on record as a repeat offense, an aggravating factor for sentencing. I had learned to look down the road. It was essential that the record be right and clear.

But it was the other case — the felony assault case I'd been counting on all along — that we now turned to. It alone had the power to give us real peace. Vinyard had violated three conditions of the deferred sentence: He had contacted me, fled supervision, and consumed alcohol. We had proof of all three. The deferred sentence would now be revoked.

I chose to trust the promise the deputy DA made in the plea deal. If there was a violation, the minimum sentence would be five years in prison, he'd said. The maximum was sixteen years. I dared not raise my hopes that high — but sixteen years. With that much time, my family's future was wide open. We would be free of this nightmare. We could take back our lives.

10/15/1997

The hearing to revoke the deferred sentence in the felony assault case occurred a week later. This was standard procedure and, I was told, would be straightforward. But I no longer trusted that any court proceeding would be straightforward. I anxiously awaited the news, and when I got it, it hit me like a sledgehammer.

They couldn't — they wouldn't take this seriously. Would they?

Claiming he was unfairly coerced by his attorney to agree to the plea deal, Vinyard wanted to withdraw his guilty pleas.

I was stunned. This treacherous madman was manipulating the system with the deftness of a seasoned criminal attorney.

The hearing was continued with no future hearing date set, the advocate in the assault case said, adding that Vinyard had already gone through several attorneys and said he didn't want a public defender this time. He wanted private counsel.

"Right," I exclaimed sarcastically. A pregnant pause.

"Actually, the court has to provide and pay a modest fee for private counsel."

Terrific. My tax dollars at work.

Again, it was humor that vented my steam. I heard a click and saw it flicker across the screen of my mind's eye: a flashing cellulose strip of black and white images — the *Keystone Kops*. Running around in circles, falling all over each other, prosecutors chased the snickering, conniving criminal in striped prison togs. Vinyard was taking them all for a ride.

But there was nothing funny about it. The film snapped and spun round and round, flapping wildly in the dark.

When the black comedy subsided, I felt adrift in an endless sea of madness. I had to do something or I feared I would go mad myself. I was on the phone, pacing and venting to a friend, when she suggested something I'd never considered.

"Contact the press," she said.

She'd recently read an in-depth article about another case in a small, independent Boulder newspaper. That reporter would be a good first contact, she felt.

My thoughts skipped back to the serendipitous article about the retiring judge, but I was hesitant. I did not want to be in the spotlight and I didn't trust any strangers anymore. I guarded my privacy with my life — literally.

But there was no other way, it seemed. It made sense. And finally, the truth would be told. I hoped.

*   *   *

Upon hearing my brief and likely jumbled history of predation, the reporter for the *Boulder Planet* agreed to meet with me. If nothing else, the length of time I'd been dealing with this harrowing ordeal and the fact that it was tied up in court with no end in sight piqued his interest.

With a down-to-business attitude and sharply discerning demeanor, he struck me as the kind of bulldog reporter that, once he picked up the scent of injustice, you wouldn't want to be caught standing upwind. I was grateful for that.

We met in my home office, and pulling out his tablet and pen, he began. We'd already agreed that I'd use a fictitious name. That eased my mind quite a bit. My youngest children still didn't know about this and my oldest only in the most general terms. I couldn't risk their friends or friends' parents learning about it first. And only a few of my own closest friends knew about it at all; none of my colleagues or clients did. I had been through enough. Notoriety was not something I wanted to deal with. Anyway, my identity wasn't important. It was the story that had to be told.

Pen to paper, he began by asking me to describe the worst of the stalking events. I drew a blank. Grasping, I described the recent phone calls, to which he responded, "Is that all?"

Of course that isn't all, I thought. But I struggled to recall the terrifying invasions of the early years, the ones that lived in my nervous system and re-ignited with every contact Vinyard made and, now, with every contact from the DA's office. When prompted by my timeline, I could recite events, monologues from my head. But he was digging into my emotions — into me — asking what it felt like. That was the heart of the story, he coaxed. I hadn't expected that. I'd thought the story was "out there," not "in here."

Don't ask me to do this. Don't ask me to feel this again. I'd been repeatedly emotionally assaulted and driven to the edge of sanity by the judicial system. Year after year, layer upon layer, I had built this armor just to survive it. Simply shedding it and opening up to a complete stranger and, through him, to the public at large seemed an impossible request. And it occurred to me that there was a fine line between educating the public and voyeurism.

But as he spoke, I understood that I needed to open up. It was the only way others could understand the truth I so desperately wanted told — not just about my case but about the deplorable crime of stalking and the ignorance, dysfunction, and injustice still prevalent in our culture, our laws, and our courts. About the unconscionable acceptance of one person preying upon another.

Taking my cue from my timeline, I searched inside myself for the details he wanted. It was then I first realized I had actually suppressed the vivid details of the earliest invasions. I'd shoved them down so deeply that it seemed I could not access them.

I prodded my own resistance. It was clearly a self-preservation mechanism — a survival tool to prevent me from feeling full-blown terror again, from being re-traumatized and haunted. But I needed to pull those files.

Breathing deeply, I closed my eyes and slowly, gently began navigating the obstacles of my own mind. Sinking deeper and deeper, I touched the resistance, felt it, identified it. It was a deep-seated fear that if I ever fully opened that door, the horror I kept firmly under lock and key would overwhelm and ravage me. I had no idea what it would do to me if I could not control it.

In the end, the "what it feels like" descriptions I gave the reporter merely skimmed the surface. But it was a start. And on October 22, 1997, **"Fear like a shadow,"** the first news article detailing this endless nightmare, was published in the *Boulder Planet*.

"In those times that Robert Vinyard is free, Mary Morgan is a prisoner. … And, as Vinyard awaits another in a long string of court appearances in the Boulder County Jail, Morgan says she feels unprotected by a justice system that has declined over and over again to keep the 42-year-old occasional mental patient away from her."

It was a surprisingly powerful thing to see it in print. A glimpse of the truth — my truth — was finally out.

*   *   *

Soon, a subpoena arrived in the mail. On October 28, I was to appear as a witness at the preliminary hearing for count one: harassment by stalking. There, the judge would decide if there was enough evidence to go to trial. The plea bargain discussed wasn't struck, I guessed — not yet anyway. Maybe, just maybe, he would be convicted and receive more than the minimum sentence. And the sentence would be consecutive, extending his sentence and so, my freedom. *If* the court didn't allow him to withdraw his guilty pleas in the assault case.

No, I told myself, that would not — that could not — happen.

10/28/1997

Although impossible to believe, in eighteen years of enduring this nightmare, I had never been called as a witness in court before and had no idea what to expect. But one thing I knew for sure: I needed my timeline. The history of stalking was so long and complex, I needed to refer to it to be sure of dates and, as I'd just discovered, to prompt my memory of specific events. I only hoped I could tap those memories in the courtroom. It would hardly be the best environment for coaxing me to crack open my armor and negotiate the barriers that protected me from the hellacious memories.

So walking into the unknown, timeline in hand, I entered the justice center on the morning of the hearing and, joined by an advocate, sat down outside the courtroom. Kathy was out of town, and before long her substitute strode down the hall, approached me, introduced himself, and sat down.

"It was decided that you'll be allowed to use your timeline, with one caveat," he said. "The defense attorney and Vinyard had to get copies too."

I hadn't expected that. There were notes about my family in it that I didn't want Vinyard to see. Now, by court order, he was handed the information I'd so long protected. Another weapon in his arsenal.

Ignoring the nausea now squatting in my stomach, I turned my attention back to the prosecutor in the hope of some guidance. Then fumbling through my timeline, he asked, "What exactly did he do that was threatening?"

"I'm not sure I understand what you mean," I exclaimed. "The whole history of stalking is threatening!"

He was insistent. "In the latest contacts, did he ever make a threat?"

I was completely thrown. How could I make it clear? How could anyone not understand that to be targeted and pursued relentlessly against your will, to be hunted, invaded, and constantly held in the cross-hairs of a demented, obsessed predator was threatening? In all these years, I just couldn't understand why judges didn't get it. How could they be so blind? And now the deputy DA, the one I relied on to prosecute this case, didn't grasp it?

But there was no time to discuss it further. He rushed into the courtroom and I was left to grapple with how to explain the obvious. Until I was called to testify, I would not be allowed in the courtroom, and after my testimony, I would not be allowed to remain.

Soon the doors opened and I was called into the theater. My heart in my throat, struggling to breathe, I climbed into the witness box and took the oath to speak the truth. I was glad to do it. That's exactly what I'd wanted to do for an intolerably long time.

In this case, Vinyard was represented by a public defender. "Judge, before we start," he began, "I'm going to ask the court to order the sheriff to uncuff one of Mr. Vinyard's hands to take notes."

My stomach flipped and knotted. My heart drummed my ribs relentlessly, sounding the alarm to flee.

"Sheriffs, how do you feel?" the judge asked. "I know Mr. Vinyard has been somewhat of a problem. Can you — can you cuff him to a chair with the other one? Any objection to that?"

Vinyard was volatile, dangerous. And everyone knew it — even the judge, whom I'd never seen before. But he was uncuffed as the judge suggested. To my relief, armed deputies hovered over him.

My testimony began with direct examination by the deputy DA. The stalking statute included the term "repeated contacts." To demonstrate, he first asked about the general nature of the stalking history, then he continued:

> Prosecution: Between 1977 and now, and in your current frame of mind, how do you feel in having any contact with Mr. Vinyard?
>
> Anderson: Panic.
>
> Defense: Judge, I'm gonna object. I think this is irrelevant. I mean, the cornerstone of this charge is whether or not there's a credible threat. ... [A]t some point, the Court has to hear about a credible threat. And I don't think anything else is relevant until we do.

So that's it. It's the "credible threat" language in the statute that's at issue. Under the law, for his actions to be considered stalking, there had to be a credible threat.

The judge overruled the objection and the prosecution dug deeper into the issue: "In the course of your contacts with Mr. Vinyard, specifically in 1987, were there some events ... which you took to be a threat to yourself?"

I glanced at my timeline. It was the time we awoke to Vinyard beating on the house outside our bedroom window, the night we crawled to the phone. Barefoot, dressed only in nightclothes, we'd been completely vulnerable. And suddenly, it struck me. Was it any wonder that I now slept on the couch, by the window, in my street clothes and shoes when Vinyard was free?

"Yes," I replied and described the attack. Then following his lead, my story unfolded, revealing not only the terrifying invasions but the inherent threat repeated episode after episode, year after year. Gradually, our exchange approached the most recent phone calls (the basis of the current charges) beginning with the call of September 27, 1997:

> Prosecution: What happened during that phone call?
> Anderson: Mr. Vinyard reflected on some things that he imagined having happened between us some twenty years ago —
> Vinyard: I don't want to be part of this hearing now.
> Anderson: He said that —
> Vinyard: You're delusional.
> Judge: Give me a moment. I, I hope and invite you to stay in the courtroom, because that's your right and I want you to be here, Mr. Vinyard. But if you keep interrupting, you'll lose that right, so please —
> Vinyard: It's so one-sided here.
> Judge: Well, you'll have your chance, sir. ...

Eventually, the story of all the recorded calls through Vinyard's arrest unfurled. Then the judge offered cross-examination to the defense.

The defense, too, began with the earliest invasions. I knew it was the defense attorney's job to dismantle the prosecutor's argument and leave doubt as to his client's guilt. I didn't expect outright deception.

Indignation and revulsion rose in my throat. No matter the circumstances, I'd always been true to my integrity. And naive as it may be, I'd
always expected the same of others. But I was about to get my first lesson
in the cunning use of deceit in the pursuit of victory.

At first it was small tactics, like cutting me off to prevent the truth
from being heard:

> Defense: The first incident that you testified to that
> you consider to be threatening was December 16, 1987,
> correct?
> Anderson: It's the first one that I testified to today.
> Defense: Yes.
> Anderson: But that isn't the first one that I —
> Defense: That's my question.
> Anderson: — felt was threatening.

The defense pressing on, his strategy soon became abundantly clear.
His tactic was to limit "credible threat" to the narrowest possible definition: a verbal threat of harm. I found myself locked in a duel. Lunging,
he asked what Vinyard said, whether or not he stated that he would hurt
one of us and if so, how. It was what he did, I parried; his actions were
threatening, not just what he said.

But there was something else in the defense's strategy, something even
more disturbing. Stalking involves repeated invasions. To comprehend
the impact of the crime, the perpetrator's actions must be viewed not as
discrete events, but as a whole; that's the reality for the hunted. The fear
and sense of violation building with each contact, the effect is cumulative.
One incident taken out of context with the others would in no way portray the horror and certainly not the overarching threat.

Yet this is exactly what the defense did. Parceling out each discrete
event, he isolated it from the others and asked what the specific threat was
in each piece. He was dissecting and diminishing my experience, slicing
and dicing it until it was virtually unrecognizable.

He had reached an incident in 1983. I didn't remember the specifics,
and the only information I'd ever found in the court records was that
Vinyard was on our premises, we called the police, and the officer gave
him another warning. But when the defense pressed the issue, I felt myself

simmering, about to boil over. He intentionally distorted the truth, it seemed. It was an ugly thing to witness and I could not let it pass.

> Defense: ... So you can't this morning remember what, if anything, was threatening about that second one in 1983?
>
> Anderson: Right.
>
> Defense: Okay. Go ahead.
>
> Anderson: Other than — because there have been threatening incidences through the continuum of this harassment and stalking —
>
> Defense: Well, I just want to take each one, one by one.
>
> Anderson: I'm sure you do, but I just want to make —
>
> Defense: And I get to ask the questions.
>
> Prosecution: Judge, I object to that. I think she is trying to clear up what [the defense] asked her about that 1983 incident — about why she thought it was threatening — and she's trying to give him an answer to that.
>
> Defense: No, I'm being very specific. I want to know in each incident what was threatening. I know what the prosecution's theory is; I know what law they're going on. I'm not asking about that. I'm asking about each incident.
>
> Judge: Well, let [the defense] conduct his cross-examination and you can straighten everything up if you think it's inappropriate on redirect examination.

Relief rustled through me. The prosecution would question me again. I just hoped he would follow through.

After applying his reduction process to the verbal threat Vinyard made to Bruce the night he attacked our home, the defense then asked about the threat made to me that night:

> Defense: And what did he say he wanted to do with you when you came out?

Anderson: I don't recall what he said.

Defense: Did he — do you recall whether or not he threatened you physically?

Anderson: I think the fact that he was attacking our home, trying to get me out there was, to me, a physical threat. ...

And on and on it went, with Vinyard interrupting my testimony with more bizarre outbursts.

We had come to April 23, 1988:

Defense: Was there anything threatening in that contact?

Anderson: It was either April 23rd or May 2nd. There were two different contacts that I have written here. One of those two was the time that I described earlier where I arrived home and he blocked my entrance when I had my young son with me. ...

Defense: During that contact he never said anything that you interpreted to be threatening, did he?

Anderson: I don't recall him *saying* anything that was threatening. I felt that his physical actions were threatening.

Defense: And what was it about his physical actions that you considered to be threatening?

Anderson: He blocked my way where I wanted to go. As I said "no" to him, to stay away, he came closer and closer into my space. His voice became louder, yelling at me in my face, disagreeing with me, saying no, that I wanted him, etc., etc.

Defense: He never raised his fist, fist as if to strike you, did he?

Anderson: No.

Defense: How close did he come to you?

Anderson: Probably nine inches.

Defense: Never in your relationship has he ever threatened to hurt you physically or emotionally, has he?

By then I'd reached full boil. He hadn't threatened to hurt me emotionally, he *had* hurt me emotionally — severely — for most of my adult life. Why was this discounted, so blatantly disregarded? Why would a punch in the face be harmful and the emotional violation, the taking, the destruction of my life not be?

Eventually, the prosecution questioned me again. It was a relief to respond fully, uncensored. By the time we finished, I was thoroughly exhausted.

At last, there were "no more questions of this witness," and I was asked to step down. I glanced at the clock. I had been on the witness stand, poked and prodded, grilled and turned, examined and re-examined for a full three hours. And this, merely a preliminary hearing.

Rushing out of the justice center, I was swimming in the residue of all that had transpired. I felt sick. Not just exhausted, but distraught, disgusted. Sickened by the games and the perverse use of deception in the name of justice.

And I was sickened by the ignorance and callousness, the casual acceptance of emotional abuse I'd witnessed these many years. It was an insidious undercurrent that seemed to run deep — so deep it was hidden from consciousness. There was something fundamentally wrong with our culture. What was it? Bubbles of meaning were rising just below the surface, but I could not quite pull them up and grasp them.

It was probably best that a good deal of time passed before I saw the transcript of the hearing. As it was, when I read the defense's closing argument, I felt I would spontaneously combust. It belittled the absolute horror I had experienced for so long. It was dismissive. It felt like an outright lie:

> Defense: Judge, it's our position that while there's certainly been violation of restraining order here and harassment of Ms. Anderson and plenty of annoying and alarming contact … what there hasn't been has been a credible threat. It is certainly a huge pain in the neck to her, but it's been pretty clear over the course of their entire relationship, the furthest thing from Mr. Vinyard's mind is to ever harm Ms. Anderson, physically or emotionally, or anyone in her immediate family.

How could the defense attorney live with himself, or did he actually believe what he was saying, I wondered? Whether Vinyard's twisted, psychotic mind intended to harm or not, the harm done to me and my family was reprehensible.

The prosecutor, in closing, reminded the judge that the statute defined a credible threat as "a threat or physical threat or physical action that would cause a reasonable person to be in fear for the person's life, safety, or the safety of his or her immediate family." He argued that, given Vinyard's twenty-year stalking history, his mental illness, his obsession with me, and the physical violence he'd shown at our home, Vinyard's behavior was clearly threatening.

In the end, the judge found probable cause to bind the case over and did so. But during the hearing, an issue had come up. The prosecutor changed the stalking charge from a class 5 to a class 6 felony.

Sitting in the witness box, I desperately wanted to jump in and correct him. It was a class 5, a repeat offense and a longer range of sentencing, dismal as the sentence was. But I could not afford to be thrown by this. Quickly, I reined myself in and made a mental note to discuss it later with Kathy.

As it happens, I didn't have to follow up. The reporter was continuing to follow the case for the *Boulder Planet*. When the hearing concluded, he grilled the prosecutor on that point and on other charges he found that could have been filed. He demanded to know what could be done. No longer was I alone in my fight for justice.

His article appeared in the next issue: "**Woman faces stalker in court**. A Longmont woman who has lived in fear of a stalker obsessed with her for 18 years sat across the courtroom from him Tuesday. ... Now, Vinyard faces 18 months in [jail] on the harassment charge. ... [The prosecutor] said after the hearing that Vinyard was not charged as a repeat stalking offender in the case, giving him a maximum possible sentence of one and a half years. 'We're going to look into the possibility of charging this with a repeat (stalking) offense,' [he] said."

Soon, another letter from the DA's office arrived. It was notification that the arraignment for the same stalking case was scheduled for December 5 — nearly six weeks later. Still the courts moved in glacial time.

I would be allowed to attend the arraignment, where the defendant would enter his plea, it said, but the impact on my work and income had reached critical mass. I could no longer afford to devote my life to these cases. And it occurred to me that, had I not had the flexibility of working independently all these years, I never could have held a job. One may never know the higher purpose of choices of the heart. In this case I did — one purpose, anyway.

I soon met with Kathy and she eased into the subject of a plea agreement again. The agreement could be to simply plead guilty and accept open sentencing like D.D. had first offered, or the charges and sentences could be negotiated, Kathy said.

By now, just hearing the term "plea agreement" sent tremors through me. Closely trailing Vinyard himself and the pathetic stalking law, it had become the third bane of my existence.

If there was no plea deal, she said, the stalking case would likely go to trial in the spring of '98, some six months out. In the meantime, the judge in the felony assault case had still not made a decision as to whether or not he would allow Vinyard to withdraw his guilty pleas.

In both these cases, with all these charges, there still was no resolution. No promise of protection or peace. Nothing.

For so long, I'd fought for our freedom and safety, I'd stood against injustice. But now I sank into silence, reflecting on all I'd been through and all I was yet to face. Stuck in a loop with no end in sight, I felt utterly, utterly powerless.

Numb, I lingered, staring unfocused into the empty space before me. My exhausted mind, shrouded in defeat, registered only static. Then tuning my dial inward, I found nothing. I was empty. Lost. And still I had no answer as to why this was in my life.

Perched on the precipice, about to lose faith, I searched for a clue, some signpost to show me the way, and one thing became abundantly clear: I'd reached a fork in the road. Pushed to the breaking point, I would either lose myself or find myself, but somehow I had to change direction.

When we are truly open and ready to receive, the powers that be respond in an instant. And so it was.

As I pushed my chair back and slowly stood to leave the room, the advocate in the stalking case approached me with an offer. The relatively new victim/witness program included crime victim compensation, a fund financed by fees assessed on each ticket the county issued. There would be no restitution for loss of work caused by the crime or by court proceedings (at this point, the financial impact of both these on me and my family all these years was virtually incalculable). But, she said, it would cover therapy.

"Would you like to see a counselor?"

My knee-jerk reaction was righteous indignation. *So, we can't give you justice, but here's a consolation prize to help you deal with it.*

But like a great gust of wind, the anger blew through me and was gone. I'd lost the will to fight and the timing was uncanny. I desperately needed help — any help that was offered. I asked for a referral and she suggested Mary.

"She can keep up with you," she said.

And so my journey also turned inward. And even if I wanted to, there would be no turning back.

PART II

Nexus

CHAPTER 9

Rabbit Hole

" 'Who are you?' said the Caterpillar.
This was not an encouraging opening for a conversa-
tion. Alice replied, rather shyly, 'I — I hardly know, sir,
just at present — at least I know who I was when I got
up this morning, but I think I must have been changed
several times since then.' "

~ Lewis Carroll,
Alice's Adventures in Wonderland

When I was young, I hadn't yet acquired a taste for the pleasures of reading. But occasionally, I had to amuse myself at our church for hours at a time while my mother attended group meetings. In the basement, there was a small lending library, and I often found myself lingering there. There were two books I checked out and renewed again and again. I didn't just read them; I devoured them. One was the story of St. Francis of Assisi. The other was the life story of Helen Keller.

I'd seen the film *Miracle Worker* when it was first released in 1962. I was six years old and I was riveted. With the help of her devoted teacher and mentor, Helen's triumph over the prison she was born to fascinated me. I imagined what it would feel like to be deaf, dumb, and blind; to live completely in the dark, entirely unaware of the world around you. And I was thrilled when Helen suddenly had a revelation and emerged into waking life. Relentlessly driven by her teacher, at times bordering on cruelty, a miracle had occurred — her epiphany. And in a burst of awareness, the veil that separated her from the true world around her was lifted. The story moved me deeply.

In our children, we often see portents of a child's destiny. Whether we perceive it as a precursor of fate or a reflection of a life path chosen before birth, the truth is the phenomenon occurs. The seed holds the unique plan and potential of the life yet to manifest.

All I knew then was that Helen's story struck a chord deep within me. But now, a reflection of her story had manifested in my own. I found myself utterly in the dark, lost in a struggle I could not comprehend, adrift in the mystery, and suffering. If only I could wake up from this endless living nightmare. I needed illumination. I needed a miracle.

*   *   *

11/11/1997

"Do you believe the work we do here can change this experience for you?" Mary asked me the first day I walked into her counseling room.

My eyes glazed over, I uttered, "Had you asked me that six months ago, or five years ago, or eighteen years ago, my response would have been a resounding 'yes.' But today I have lost all hope of ever changing this experience."

Finally, I'd hit rock bottom.

For some time, sheer will and determination were all that sustained me; I had to protect my children and I had to take a stand against injustice. But at this point, my reserves were depleted. Mentally, emotionally, physically, and spiritually, I was thoroughly exhausted. I was on my knees.

I'd always been introspective, and through journaling, self-help books, seminars, and sharing with kindred spirits, I'd had revelations that fueled my devotion to self-awareness and personal growth. I had also seen other counselors, albeit briefly and with little benefit. But after years of soul searching, I still could not see beyond the veil of this experience. I could not understand the higher purpose of this perpetual nightmare and see what this horror had to teach me. Over and over again I'd asked my closest friends what it was I wasn't seeing, why this was happening to me. They were sympathetic but had no answers.

Now, the only thing I knew was I could not continue being tossed about, ravaged by the storms of fear, hope, anger, and despair anymore. If I was going to survive, I had to find a way to swim deep — fast.

It took a lot of courage for Mary to take me on. I was truly on the edge, and, completely out of my power, I was perilously at risk of further harm and she knew it. She had no doubt that, given a lot of time and hard work, she could help me make sense of the hell I'd been through and become whole. But her first priority was to throw me a lifeline. The problem was, I wouldn't take it.

Struggling desperately against fear, I was rigidly defended. My armor, meticulously applied and nurtured all these years, was thick. Behind it, she saw a tremendous amount of pain. To even begin to relieve it, she focused only on connecting with me. But I resisted. I didn't fully trust anyone, least of all strangers and anyone who claimed to be an authority. And deep down, I was still terrified of connecting with anyone.

As rigid and reactive as I'd become, Mary knew I could bolt at any time. She had to be careful with me; it was clear to her that no one else had been. So taking me under her wing, she hunkered down and, focused and centered, reached out and held a heart connection with me until I was ready to allow it. And it was a long time before I was ready. I was keenly sensitive to the sensation of anyone hooking into me. In fact, I'd refined the skill of scanning for hidden agendas to the level of master. I didn't always know what they wanted, but I sensed their probing and firmly shut them out.

But while I would not connect with her, she anchored me. Even as, like an abused and terrified animal, I balked and pulled in every direction, she tethered me. She was the whisperer I desperately needed. And though I resisted and argued with her, something deep inside me recognized that that calm, that center, that non-judgmental care and compassion was exactly what I needed.

And deeper still, I sensed she didn't carry fear. I was attracted to that. I wanted that. *Okay, Yoda, show me the way. Just don't touch me.*

The unspoken tug of war between us lingered for quite some time. Tentatively, timidly, I'd reach out. Two steps forward, one step back. Again and again. Of course, it didn't help that I was constantly in crisis. The infernal judicial process and my healing process were now moving in tandem — contradictory, to say the least. Just as I'd settle and relax into my work with Mary, another blow would land and my shields would fly up.

But Mary didn't baby me. I doubt I would have stayed if she had. She saw my strength and honored where I was. I wanted answers. And she knew I'd see right through platitudes and wouldn't stick around if she soft-peddled the process; I was more than ready to do the work. So she laid some of the issues, the big pieces of the puzzle, on the table right away and we worked with all of them as I was ready, to the depth I was ready to accept them. I think of it as the "throw it all at the wall and see what sticks" method. And what doesn't stick the first time just might on the second, third, or twentieth toss.

Boundaries, personal power, resistance/surrender, beliefs that don't serve, receiving, integration of shadow — she put it all out there. Some I discounted out of hand and some I found curious, but she challenged me while, at the same time, firmly holding the connection I so fiercely resisted. Looking back, it was an impressive balancing act.

Boundaries. I'd heard the word so many times before and scoffed at it. Why? That one question would involve time and hard work to answer. But I couldn't deny the obvious. While I so fiercely stood by my conviction that it would be wrong for me to have boundaries, I'd constructed the most resolute barrier of all: I had walled myself off behind my shields. No one could get in, and though I still didn't realize it, I — my whole, authentic self — could not get out.

Mary was offering me an alternative: boundaries, not barriers. I hadn't known there was a difference. To me, there were barriers and no barriers. Either-or. Black or white. The concept made sense, but something inside me would not budge.

While my mind resisted and I argued about the value of boundaries, ferreting out the source of my objections, she quietly taught me to feel the difference.

"Where is your awareness now in your body?" she'd ask in the middle of a discussion.

The answer was always the same. My breath was shallow, and as if holding myself up off of icy pavement, my shoulders were raised and tense. I was in my head.

"Relax for a moment and breathe deeply. Let your awareness drop into the center of your body. Now sink down into your first chakra, at the base of your spine. This is your root chakra, your foundation. Relax into it."

Above the base of the neck, where I dwelled, were the fifth, sixth, and seventh chakras: will, self expression; intellect, insight; and wisdom and connection to the Divine, respectively. I was barely in my body, much less on the planet. Below the neck were, in a nutshell: fourth – love, forgiveness;

third – self-esteem, personal power; second – emotion, sensation; and first – connection to the earth, security, and survival.

I didn't want to go there. I knew what would happen; it did every time. When I relaxed and dropped down, tears would well up and my breath would catch as I struggled to control them. I hated feeling so vulnerable, so weak. But Mary just sat quietly, strengthened her connection, and waited until I regained my composure.

"Vulnerability is a strength, not a weakness. It is an aspect of feminine power that has been denigrated and abused for thousands of years."

Another piece of the puzzle I was not at all ready to understand or accept, but it was mind candy and kept me engaged.

A transpersonal therapist, Mary worked with all aspects of the human experience, including those that transcend the physical — in other words, the spiritual. She led me in an exercise. My eyes closed, she began:

> Take deep breaths and relax. Notice the places in your body that are holding tension and breathe into them.
>
> As you continue to breathe, drop your awareness into the center of your body. Now, sink lower, lower. Down into your first chakra.
>
> From there, allow your awareness to reach deep into the ground. Deeper, deeper. Down into the darkness, all the way to the earth's center. You are grounding yourself into the earth. Feel your connection to the earth.
>
> As you breathe in, draw that Earth energy back up into the center of your body. Feel the love that fills you. Rest in this sensation. You are supported.

I'd been working with guided imagery for years, so none of this was unfamiliar. But then she added some pieces I'd never heard before.

"Focus on the center of your body." She placed her hands on her belly, above her naval and over her solar plexus, and she directed me to follow suit. "This is your power center. Sense it. Feel it. You are calling your spirit back, calling your power back."

Following her guidance, my hands on my belly, I felt a warm glow in the core of my body. Intensifying, the glow grew and became the sun in my center, its rays filling my abdomen and chest.

"You are learning to bring your conscious awareness into your body to access your power," Mary said.

After allowing me a few moments to bask in this intense yet profoundly serene sensation, she continued:

> Open your heart.
>
> Now, reach up far above you and out into the space around you. It is filled with light, golden white light. See it. Feel it.
>
> As you breathe in, draw that light into your center. With each breath, you grow fuller and fuller. Feel the love that fills you. Rest in this sensation.
>
> Your energy field extends beyond your skin. At the edge of that space is your boundary. It is not solid, yet it cannot be penetrated. Imagine a grid, a fluid grid of energy and another over it. They move, they flow. They allow in what serves you and keep out what doesn't, according to your own free will. Sense your boundaries holding your space.
>
> As you continue to breathe, drawing in light, allow it to fill and expand your space around you. With each breath, your boundaries grow larger and larger.
>
> Bring your awareness to all your sensations.
>
> This is you in your space. Connected, supported, powerful. Filled with love.

I was so moved, so comforted by the sensations I experienced that tears streamed freely down my cheeks. I had missed this, longed to feel this way and forgotten it was even possible.

The exercise became a practice I would engage in over and over. Her question, "Where is your awareness now?" became, like Pavlov's dog, my cue to relax and drop down into my center, into my emotions. And wait for the tears to clear.

As awe-struck as I was the first time I experienced this exercise, my thoughts refused to settle. While Mary narrated the imagery, my mind was busy sifting through and rejecting some of the concepts.

I still resisted the idea of boundaries. So, she drew some simple illustrations for me and explained:

Without boundaries, we merge with others:

Eventually, this gets uncomfortable and we pull away, erecting walls to protect ourselves:

But eventually, we feel isolated and lonely and go back into merging. This roller coaster of merging and disconnecting never leads to a healthy relationship.

With boundaries, we maintain our autonomy and a heart connection simultaneously. We are connected and we are safe. This is a healthy relationship — one we can sustain, and with both people giving and receiving, one that sustains us:

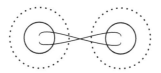

This was a revelation, the first hopeful and intriguing thing I'd heard in a long time. I wanted to learn more and discover the difference for myself. I was hooked.

But other concepts Mary had presented also startled me. When she guided my awareness to my power center, the deep, warm glow in the center of my body felt wonderful: safe, comforting, healing. Still, I recoiled at her description.

"You are calling your power back," she'd said.

Like boundaries, power was a word that made me squirm. Unconsciously, I'd associated the term with power over others and condemned it. The stalker and the courts, it seemed, had all the power, all control over my own fate. I did not want to wield that kind of power; it was immoral. Yet I despised feeling powerless and was, myself, fighting hard to gain control. But control was power over the situation and others. Gridlock.

Most often, instead of answering my questions directly or engaging in the intellectual discussions I relished, Mary turned the wheel and took us down a different course entirely. It inevitably knocked me off balance, as if suddenly I was pushing a rope. It was a conscious move on her part. Firmly and consistently, she was pulling me back from "out there" to within and drawing me out of my head and into my emotions.

"Don't focus on him. Stay in your sphere. Focus on yourself and loving yourself," she'd say.

I'd seen another therapist briefly a few years before. During a form of therapy known as breathwork, a kind of trance work, she had encouraged me to give Vinyard back what was his and take back what was mine. It was necessary to sever the connection between us, she'd said. I was more than willing to take back what was mine. The problem was, I had absolutely no idea what that was.

Now memories of that session stepped forward. Both therapists were guiding me through a separation — something I desperately wanted. But Mary's way seemed to be through the back door. It wasn't necessary for me to understand it all, she said. I just needed to follow her and feel the changes. Comprehension would come if I just allowed myself to feel it.

It was far too right-brained for me. I had always relied on my intellect, my rational mind for navigation. Drifting in unknown waters was not something I was at all comfortable with. My whole quest was to understand, to find enlightenment.

I'd always been a critical thinker and rebellious to boot. So, although I was beginning to accept that Mary had some knowledge I wanted, I wasn't about to follow her instructions blindly. I still didn't trust her or anyone that much. I needed to know.

She gave me more mind candy. "True power is not power over others. That is abuse of power, false power. True power comes from within and is never controlling or abusive." That felt right.

Then she said, "When you are hooked into others and focused on the struggle, you surrender your power to them."

I flashed back to the self-defense intensive when I refused to fight. It didn't work. Disengaging would not protect me or my family. This made no sense.

But it wasn't the struggle itself she was talking about. It was the emotional hook.

"When you get hooked into the stalker's rage and distortions, you surrender your power to him. When you are hooked into the abuses of the courts, you surrender your power to them. The desire to control is founded on fear. When you try to control others or the outcome of situations, you are not centered in yourself and are completely out of your power."

I felt my brain twisting, working to comprehend.

"Whenever you feel hooked 'out there,' turn your focus inward. Focus on yourself. Take care of yourself. Love yourself. Call back your spirit and take back your power."

My head was swimming. It was all a jumble. Some things made perfect sense. Others seemed completely contradictory. I immediately understood that true power comes from within and is never abusive. And I certainly didn't want to surrender my power to either Vinyard or the courts. Although the idea of taking back my power still made me cringe, if there was a way to be appropriately empowered, I wanted to learn it.

I understood that the desire to control was fear-based, but I still felt that in this case it was both justified and necessary.

The focusing on self and loving self parts seemed completely off-subject. They certainly wouldn't have any effect on the outcome of the whole situation, and regardless of her warning, I felt I had to change the outcome. I had to take back control of my own life.

"Control is an illusion. We are never in control," she said. "Surrender is a big piece of this."

I must say, it took a lot of faith for Mary to use the word "surrender" with me. In no way was I ready for that. But she wasn't suggesting I surrender to defeat.

"When you feel you're resisting, surrender. When you feel an emotional hook, surrender it. Surrender your fear. Surrender beliefs that don't serve. Surrender control. They don't serve you or the higher purpose."

At the time I was so strained and exhausted, I could not take in all she was offering. What I could grasp, I grabbed onto like a life preserver. The others I hoped would make sense in time.

I still had no idea what errant beliefs were working against me, and though I tried, under such dire circumstances I could not trust enough to surrender fear or my need to control the outcome.

Finally, after weeks of working with this and feeling utterly incapable of doing it, I threw up my hands and gave it to higher powers. *Please help me understand and surrender. I want to know what's in the way and I want to let it go.* It became my mantra. And without realizing the connection, in asking for help I'd embraced faith once again and, ironically, taken the first step toward surrendering control.

CHAPTER 10

Undertow

"Knowing others is intelligence; knowing yourself is true wisdom."

~ Lao Tzu, Tao Te Ching

Shortly after I began seeing Mary, the advocate referred me to a book, just published, that would finally open a window onto the mind of the delusional stalker. *I Know You Really Love Me: A Psychiatrist's Journal of Erotomania, Stalking, and Obsessive Love* was written by Doreen Orion, MD, a local psychiatrist who had been stalked by one of her patients. To me, her work was more than illuminating. It was a gift of hope.

No longer would judges grope in the dark, not comprehending the true nature of the case. Informed, they could no longer delude themselves, believing that treatment would stop the stalker's behavior. And no longer could judges pretend the danger was not real and escalating.

Orion wrote that in 1987, American psychiatry formally recognized the disorder of erotomania, "the most bizarre disorder of stalkers — the delusional belief that their victims are actually in love with them." In her research, she found "more than twenty mental illnesses in which eroto-manic delusions could manifest, illnesses as disparate as schizophrenia, depression, and manic-depression." This didn't mean erotomanics were not intelligent. "They tended to be older, smarter, and better educated than other mentally ill lawbreakers," she said, adding that this did not bode well for their victims; they "had more resources, intellectual if not financial, to effectively hunt their prey."

In classical cases, the delusion begins with the belief that the person the stalker is obsessed with is the one who started the relationship, she wrote and said that "in their delusional blurring of boundaries, erotomanics often perceive themselves as both pursued and persecuted by their victims." *Yes!* Throughout these many years, I'd been tormented by Vinyard's claims that he was a victim and that I had flirted with him.

It was all a delusion, but I'd seen the effect of his conviction again and again and been astounded by the willingness of police, judges, defense attorneys, even those close to me to believe him and blame me, despite knowing he was mentally ill. The sting of that knife piercing me was felt the first time we called the police in 1979 and had never subsided.

Erotomanics, Orion wrote, are truly narcissistic, believing that only the suffering they have experienced at the hands of their "love objects" counts because "they believe, with all the unshakable conviction of delusional truth, that they are entitled to a relationship at any and all costs to their victims." It was as if she wrote directly from the chronicles of my own case.

She remarked on the seemingly endless capacity erotomanics had for "creative misconception, reinterpreting even the clearest rejections as declarations of love," and said, "While never doubting the love of an object, the erotomanic will rationalize, often quite irrationally, the reason the object does not act on the attraction." It was this misconception of an obstacle to the relationship that had led to attacks on, even murders of the victim's family members, according to Orion. Brutal, violent crimes against stalking victims, their families, and others close to the victims were well-documented in her research. My nerves stood on end. My greatest fear was just corroborated: If family members were perceived as being in the way, they too were in grave peril.

Then, there it was in black and white. Exactly the point I'd tried to make in the preliminary hearing: "All the experts agreed that threats don't count." The credible threat criteria in Colorado's stalking law was completely baseless.

For threat management experts, "the most critical and challenging aspect of their work was distinguishing between those who make a threat and those who pose a threat," she wrote. In her research she'd discovered that, although many stalkers that violently attacked had no history of arrest for a violent offense, a past history of violence was an important factor in predicting the risk of future violence. Other significant indicators of future violence included stalking multiple people and antisocial behavior unrelated to the erotomania. Substance abuse was a double-edged sword, she said, "both increasing the risk of violence and reinforcing the erotomanic delusions themselves." One expert, Dr. J.R. Meloy, also considered the stalker's mobility, the persistence of the obsession, previous reactions to restraining orders, and the nature of the delusion, Orion wrote. A National Institute of Justice report she referenced stated that, while the stalking may temporarily subside, it almost always progressed. And many experts she consulted felt that the longer the stalking continued, the higher the risk of violence.

In nearly two decades, Vinyard had demonstrated every single indicator listed. With all this and the fact that, during several arrests, he'd been found to have an automatic weapon, the danger he posed could not have been more obvious if he wore a flashing neon sign.

Meloy, she said, found that an erotomanic reacts to the shame of being rejected with intense anger, which further fuels the desire to pursue, injure, control, dominate, or in some cases, kill the victim. It seemed an impossible situation. How could one stop a stalker when saying "no" escalated the risk of violence? I'd seen it every time I rejected Vinyard — terrifying red rage and aggression.

Orion also mentioned dramatic events such as intervention by police and the courts that, according to Meloy, increase the risk of violence toward the stalking victim both during and right after. Another reason to, at the very least, hold the stalker for a time when arrested and set a high bond, I felt.

Finally, Orion tackled the issues of incarceration and treatment. Quoting the Department of Justice, she wrote, "It is unlikely that simply punishing the convicted stalker will resolve the problem. ... [Such a] stalker who has been convicted and incarcerated, may be embittered and seek retribution for being kept from the victim, especially if the illness was left untreated during incarceration."

Yet according to Orion, when it came to treatment, psychiatrists generally agreed that delusions were among the most difficult symptoms to treat. None of the articles she'd read mentioned a single case in which a patient with erotomanic delusions had simply stopped.

Her recommendation: mandatory treatment during incarceration and mandatory long-term treatment beyond.

And when it came to sentencing, Orion argued that short jail terms did not deter stalkers and often led to the intolerable situation where perpetrators were imprisoned for far less time than their victims were, emotionally. *Exactly.* Stalking behavior was both chronic and progressive, she noted and concluded that stalking should be charged as a felony, giving stalkers the clear message that their criminal acts would be taken serious-ly. Sentences should be long enough to both deter and punish, she said.

"[P]unishment must be commensurate with the crime," Orion wrote. "Stalking is an act of terrorism against an individual ... and should be treated as such. ... While it is true that one act of terrorism may result in many deaths, the cumulative effects of stalking ravage a far greater num-ber of lives. Stalking has become the most common form of social terror-ism and no less devastating than its political counterpart."

As soon as I dove into her book, I knew Orion would be a tremendous resource in my case, not only by virtue of the printed page but as an expert witness. So, to avoid compromising her objectivity, I could have no personal contact with her. I never crossed that boundary.

*   *   *

Although Vinyard had violated the conditions of probation in the previous stalking case by stalking me again, the latest episode emerged as a whole new case. Then there was the felony assault case. Three cases — all interconnected, all heard separately — were now navigating the courts independently, in tandem. And like boats tied to a dock in stormy seas, the cases bumped and scraped against each other as wave after wave of arguments and motions rocked them all.

Through all these years, different officers, different cases, different pros-ecutors, different judges — even different divisions. This was a nightmare.

Interminably shackled by court proceedings, gagged, and held firmly behind the scenes of the legal theater for so long, my frustration peaked and spilled over. All I wanted to do was barge into the courtroom, tell it straight to the judge, and demand that the maximum sentence he'd promised eight months earlier — eight months in which I'd been to hell and back — be passed and served in full. The assault case was still my only hope of real protection, and I was determined to keep my foot firmly wedged in the door.

So I turned to the only avenue open to me. I planned to write another victim impact statement (a right now afforded by the state's Victim Rights Act) to be presented to the judge in writing and, I hoped, orally in court. But, though Vinyard had violated the condition of the deferred sentence by stalking me, I was not, technically, the victim in the assault case. I had no idea if my statement would be read.

I would write the letter anyway. I needed to believe that I'd have a voice. And frustrated beyond words with the prosecution of the cases, I planned to lead the charge in my own defense.

*   *   *

Before long, I got word that the victim compensation program offered to pay for a women's self-defense intensive.

Biting back my bitter retort, I thought, *Right. We can't offer you justice* or *protection, but we know you're in serious danger, so here's a way to protect yourself.* But the truth was, Vinyard could be released at any time. To protect my family, I had to learn to fight. I soon enrolled.

The class was quite different from the first intensive I'd attended. The woman who developed and taught the program was a local karate instructor. It was not overtly violent and so not as traumatic. That was a tremendous relief.

The first two days we learned and practiced simple moves, refining them and testing their effectiveness on pads and boards. At the end of each day, we'd sit in a circle, feast to refuel, and share. I told my classmates of my reluctance to fight. They didn't push me but did encourage me, as I did them.

With hours on end devoted to practice, my skills improved and my confidence grew, but my heart still wasn't in it. I just did what I had to do. Then before I knew it, the final challenge was upon us. It was graduation day. Attackers would confront us and we'd cheer each other on.

The assailants were select students in the karate dojo, all brown or black belts: well trained, highly skilled, and strong. The attacks came at us from every angle, every position we'd trained for, and with each progressive battle, I felt more and more capable, stronger and stronger. Then came the final assault.

Blindfolded, I was led to the center of the mats and left there alone. Darkness enveloped me. Silence fell over the dojo, and suddenly my nerves ignited. All my senses flared into awareness, past trauma ripped open, and sheer terror gripped me. It was the same sense of anxiety and anticipation I'd lived with for so long. The attack could be anything, come from anywhere, at any time. All I knew was it was coming.

The surface supporting me began to feel slippery as sweat broke out on the soles of my feet. My knees buckled and recovered then bent slightly in readiness to leap. My arms and fingers tingled in anticipation. Blood and adrenaline coursed through my veins in strong, pulsing waves. My muscles twitched in false starts. A cold sweat broke out on my forehead, and the blindfold shifted.

Tuning into the slightest sound, my hearing expanded tenfold, but the roar of my thundering heart and racing breath drowned all else out. Desperate to locate and read the attacker, I focused my intuitive radar and scanned the space around me. Nothing.

Time slowed. Seconds stretched into minutes. The tension peaked, and still I waited. Overloaded, I feared my nervous system would crash at any moment and I wouldn't have the strength to fight. Then finally, it came.

Like the blow of an eagle flying full force at an unsuspecting mouse, it hit me. The attack came from behind and the force of the assailant's body lunging into mine knocked the breath straight out of me. Then before I could even raise my hands, long powerful arms locked around my arms and chest, further constricting my lungs.

Panic swelled. I thrashed, I kicked, I flailed. I had to get air. All my attention went to forcing my lungs open. *Work, damn you, breathe!*

But while I focused on oxygen, the assailant wrestled me to the ground, pinned me, and held me face down with overwhelming strength. My mind raced frantically through the lessons. I wriggled. I struggled. I worked every move, every strategy I could remember. But nothing released me.

All the world shrank to my assailant, me, the floor, and a sinking sense of hopelessness. Defeat.

Suddenly, a voice was bellowing at close range. "Where is your opening? Look for your opening!" the instructor shouted.

My opening. Where is my opening?

Mentally scanning the pressure points in the tangle of bodies and limbs, I found it: one place where the attacker could not bind me, one place where I could move and fight my way out. But now thoroughly spent, somehow I had to find the will and strength to do it.

Mary's coaching surfaced. My "eye" on the opening, I drew a deep breath and my awareness stretched downward. Diving, I plunged into my heart, and there, the fierce love I felt for my children burst into a ball of golden white light. A roaring furnace, it instantly consumed the darkness of despair.

Then diving deeper, I reached out and touched ... rage. Pure, unrestrained, primal rage.

Careening into it, I gathered it, focused it, and pulled it up. It was an unbelievably potent combination. The weakness of my muscles, the limits of my strength were nothing compared to the power I found. In a matter of seconds, I overwhelmed my assailant and, had I not pulled my strikes, would have knocked him out in a heartbeat.

Cheers pealed through the room, and stripping off my blindfold, I stood over my visibly surprised attacker and basked in the sensation of unimaginable power.

That was in me. It's been there all along.

Dumbfounded, I looked to my instructor for some explanation. Beaming with pride, her grin spread from ear to ear. Pulling me into a hearty embrace then holding my shoulders at arm's length, she looked me in the eye and said, "Congratulations. You found your zanshin."

Well, whatever it is, now that I've found it, I will never *lose it again.*

As soon as the class ended and the door opened to release us, the weight of the life I re-entered pressed down on me. In the days that followed, I contemplated my next move. Still stuck in the judicial web that tightened its grip with every move I made, I felt hopelessly trapped and my instructor's words echoed through me: *Where is your opening? Look for your opening.*

Scanning for possibilities, I realized that the only way out of this horrific ordeal was, paradoxically, in. I had tried everything else I could think of over and over to no avail. My only hope for real change was to follow Mary down the rabbit hole. I just had to muster the courage, the will to trust — to trust Source, to trust Mary, to trust myself. To dive deeper and deeper.

*   *   *

Though I still resisted a connection with Mary, when I finally began relaxing into our sessions, I discovered just how much I needed to talk with someone about everything I was going through. In all this time, I really hadn't opened up much, not even with my closest friends. I didn't want to burden them, and I never exposed my vulnerabilities to anyone. My instinct when dealing with emotional turmoil was to crawl into my cave and keep everyone at arm's length. "I'm okay," I'd assure them and try to believe it.

But beneath my relatively calm exterior was so much anger. I barely kept it corked most of the time. Occasionally it would burst through, entirely out of proportion to the situation. Then I'd chastise myself and shove the cork down harder. I didn't want to be an angry person. I had long condemned anger and constantly criticized myself for not overcoming it. But my experience in the dojo changed me. While my mind still struggled to grasp it, somehow I knew that love and anger were not contradictory. Together, they were a powerful force.

In great need of release, I soon used my counseling sessions as platforms for venting. Railing against the stalker, judges, defense attorneys, legislators, even the DA, I spun like a centrifuge, my venomous anger spewing out in all directions. Once uncorked, the vessel seemed bottomless. But each time I'd vent it, my rage would turn back on itself, back on me. I'd condemn myself for being so angry, and as the rage turned inward, it morphed into depression and utter exhaustion. It was a vicious cycle.

The weeks passing, I was truly afraid I would lose myself in the anger, and though she never divulged it to me, Mary was concerned that I was so far out of my power and so much at-risk that if we couldn't get it settled down, we couldn't get to the work. We had to break the cycle.

Each time my anger flared and lashed out, Mary listened and gave me time to release it. Then she reminded me to separate the person and the behavior. "If you judge, judge the behavior, not the person," she'd say. "It's the behavior that is unacceptable, not the person."

I knew what she told me was right. As soon as I made that distinction, I felt the shift. It felt better, more in alignment with truth.

Then Mary asked questions that quietly and consistently redirected my attention away from "them" and back to me. It was a practice in learning to fill my space, hold my boundaries, and pull back my power from all those people and situations I was surrendering it to.

But as soon as my attention turned inward, the critic would grab hold and pull me under again. Intervening, she'd say, "You're terribly hard on yourself," and, "You judge yourself so harshly, you're not allowing yourself to be *human*." That rang a bell.

"Practice being kind to yourself. Be gentle. Work on being open to receiving."

Receiving was something I resolutely resisted. I knew where the resistance came from, or part of where it came from anyway. I grew up believing I was here to serve others and the greater good. It was a belief she challenged.

"Giving to others is a positive thing, but giving without allowing yourself to receive is out of balance. It's not sustainable. If you refuse to nourish yourself, you have nothing left to give."

I understood the logic and actually believed it to be true, just not for me. And I would not let go of that conviction simply because she said it was so. It was too deeply ingrained, tied to my identity and life purpose.

I knew there was more to the resistance. Whenever she pushed me to receive, I felt a firm "no" that didn't explain itself and would not relent. But at the time, I wasn't ready or willing to pursue it further and discover the source of my objection.

"Self-care is an attitude shift," she said.

I didn't budge.

Pushing harder, she warned, "You're giving your energy and power away to your belief systems."

I didn't care. My beliefs, my truth were all that mattered. Truth was far more important than I was.

Little did I know that Mary was, in fact, guiding me directly to it. From the very beginning, her goal was to reveal my own truth to me, truth long hidden from my own field of vision.

Most of the time therapy works from the inside out, but sometimes, I've found, it works best from the outside in. Sometimes I needed to force change to finally embrace it. After weeks of pushing me to take care of myself and to open to receiving with no success, Mary finally proposed a compromise. She suggested I suspend the belief but not let go of it entirely then see how my experience changed.

Closing my eyes, I envisioned the belief that I was to give and not receive as a small, dense ball, and I placed it near the outer limits of my energy field. It was, quite literally, suspended there at a distance from my center. I trusted that it would not drift away, and in my heart, I was finally able to let it go. Temporarily.

My homework then was to practice being kind to myself; big things or small things, it didn't matter. Desperate to break the cycle of anger, depression, and exhaustion, and trusting that I had not abandoned my beliefs, I finally felt free to explore and followed her instructions. In time, I cut back a little on my work, and if I felt like just sitting and staring at the walls for hours or a full day at a time, that's what I did. Often. And the more I took care of myself, the more I settled and was able to focus and discuss the subject of anger and my judgments around it more rationally.

"Our society teaches us that anger is unacceptable, particularly in women. This is an extremely destructive attitude," Mary said. "If you don't allow yourself to feel 'ugly' emotions, you can't release them or use them appropriately. Anger is not inherently negative; it's a tool."

The question was how to use it positively. Anger could be passion. As I had seen for myself, it could be drawn upon to protect my loved ones. It could be a powerful catalyst for change. So how could I channel all the anger I was feeling and use it productively, Mary asked?

I confessed my plan to write another letter to the judge and she encouraged me to follow through. "But it's the prosecutor's job to argue the case. Get out of your head and into your gut," she said.

I half-listened to that advice.

"Your power is in your emotions. Only you know how this has affected you; this is what they're not seeing. Give voice to your emotions. Tell the judge how you feel."

Before long, upon returning home one day from a session with Mary, I found a bag with a note stuck to it hanging on my door knob. It was from a couple of my answer-to-my-prayer friends.

"As soon as we saw this, we knew it was for you," the note read.

I never got gifts for no particular reason! Dropping my things mid-stride, I grabbed the bag with the thrill of a kid on her birthday. Then peeking inside, I was stunned and delighted at the timing and audacity of these wonderful, outrageous messengers.

The book was *Getting in Touch with Your Inner Bitch*, and wrapping myself around it that evening, I found one phrase particularly poignant: "toxic niceness." *Yep. Been there, done that. Not going there again.*

Allowing myself to receive without guilt was beginning to feel good. And the universe was responding.

*   *   *

12/5/1997

In December, the arraignment was held for the new stalking case, in yet another judge's hands. Vinyard pled not guilty, moving the case one step closer to a jury trial.

But both stalking cases now "trailing" the assault case, no decisions would be made in either stalking case until the judge in the assault case made a decision. Still, after months of waiting, there was no word on whether he would allow Vinyard to withdraw his guilty pleas or not.

12/31/1997

On the day of New Year's Eve, the hydra sprouted yet another head. New felony charges were filed against Vinyard. There had been an altercation at the jail. He'd struck and hurt a guard, Kathy said.

Another charge of second-degree assault on a peace officer was added to the list of pending cases. Now there were four.

I dared not hope he'd be convicted of the new charge and that the sentence would be consecutive. I didn't have the stomach to ride that roller coaster any more. But it wasn't long before my stomach lurched again as I plunged down another dip in the track. The potential sentence in the original felony assault case had dropped. Instead of five to sixteen years in prison, the range was now four to twelve. I had no idea why.

Determined to usher in a new beginning, justice, and an era of peace, I symbolically chose to spend the first day of the new year writing my impact statement to the judge in the first assault case: the deferred sentence Vinyard had violated by fleeing, drinking, and contacting me.

Given the convoluted morass of court cases, my first task was to connect the dots and paint the full picture of how the cases were related. Then, armed with the information gathered from Orion's book, I planned to educate the judge and attach key excerpts from the book, my timeline, and the news article that described how it felt to be stalked. Finally, despite Mary's coaching, I wasn't about to relinquish control to the prosecutor. I would do my best to argue my case once again:

> Your Honor, … I am writing to you to ask that you consider my three young children, myself, and my former husband prior to determining an appropriate sentence for

Mr. Vinyard in this case. The charges in the case before you are related to Mr. Vinyard's crimes of stalking me and my former husband ... crimes which have been ongoing and escalating for nineteen years. ... I am not exaggerating when I say I fear for [our] lives ... . And through my research, I have found that this fear is entirely justified. ...

Mr. Vinyard is responsible for his criminal actions against us, and in my opinion, the courts are accountable for past inaction. Allow me demonstrate the impacts on our lives using the case before you as just one example. ... Mr. Vinyard was given a deferred sentence rather than incarceration, thus giving him yet another warning and another chance to stalk me. Given [his] history of consistently ignoring court orders and disappearing from supervision, and the warnings of danger in all of the court-ordered psychiatric evaluations, I believe this inaction recklessly endangered my family. ...

The case before you clearly demonstrates Mr. Vinyard's propensity for violence. [He] physically harmed a police officer highly trained in self defense. My children and I are not so capable of fending off an attack. When Mr. Vinyard is free, we are in danger.

As pen continued to meet paper, word upon word, righteous rage was building inside me. Mary's encouragement to give voice to my emotions and channel my anger in a positive way stirred the embers, and by the time I reached the end, my words charred the page:

In her book, Dr. Orion devotes one chapter, "No Order in the Courts," entirely to the degree court proceedings as they are practiced today escalate the danger in a stalking case and further victimize the victim. Without belaboring my own experience, nor the compelling details of many other similar cases, I will quote this: "Once more, an erotomanic's dastardly deeds went unpunished, a practice that sets up a continually escalating circle resulting in ever more vicious acts, even murder, that finally can no longer go unpunished."

I ask you, your Honor, is this what we are waiting for? What are we waiting for before Mr. Vinyard is forced to take responsibility for his chosen actions? What are we waiting for before my family is protected by a justice system established to do just that for its citizens?

I ask you, what are the messages that have been given to Mr. Vinyard and to me through this calamity of court proceedings since 1979? To me, it seems Mr. Vinyard has been clearly told that his actions are not serious, that he is not responsible for them, that the law cannot control him, and that the harder he works, the more he will get what he seeks: contact with me. ...

And what have I learned and had to somehow explain to my children? That the justice system would sooner put my family at greater and greater risk than incarcerate a criminal — a habitual criminal no less? ...

I am outraged! I am outraged by the many times I was viewed with suspicion by police officers who blamed me for Mr. Vinyard's actions, by the multiple warnings with no incarceration. ... I am outraged by the painfully slow evolution of the stalking law from a misdemeanor equivalent to "spitting on the sidewalk" to a class 6 felony with very brief potential sentences.

I am outraged by the multiple plea bargains, deferred sentences, and minimal sentences given Mr. Vinyard; by "good time" credits granted for simply being in jail; and by the flagrant disregard for how all of this has only encouraged Mr. Vinyard to become more manipulative, devious, and determined in his stalking activities. Words cannot convey how outraged I am by the flagrant disregard the justice system has shown for my family's safety, for our very lives.

Bruce wrote a letter too, concurring with mine. Soon they were in the judge's hands.

CHAPTER 11

Labyrinth

"Under certain circumstances, profanity provides a relief denied even to prayer."

~ *Mark Twain*

As time dragged on, it became abundantly clear that the path to justice was liberally strewn with a tangle of laws, and it seemed Vinyard and his counsel made damned sure we were tripped up and caught on every single one of them. The further we traveled, the more complex and convoluted the journey. Confusion and chaos soon reigned. Truth really was stranger than fiction.

Soon after submitting my statement to the judge in the assault case, I met with Kathy again to discuss the status of all the cases. She had now taken over all four cases for the prosecution.

She was not allowing Vinyard to waive his right to a preliminary hearing on any charges; she wanted it all on record that he was clearly told and understood the decisions. And she was working to ensure there were no mistakes that he could appeal to a higher court where verdicts could be overturned.

She was following up on whether stalking would be charged as a class 5 or class 6 felony. He was convicted of stalking in 1995, she said, not merely harassment.

She wanted the whole picture shown in trial and would submit a motion to allow "prior similar acts," meaning Vinyard's previous stalking, but it would have to be approved by the judge.

A court-appointed private attorney, per his request, was representing Vinyard in the first felony assault case; the public defender was still on all the others. His new attorney was tossing every argument in the book, it seemed, at allowing Vinyard to withdraw his guilty pleas, thus threatening to completely unravel the only case that had any possibility of sending him to prison and giving us peace.

Among other things, she petitioned the court to provide a confidential psychiatric expert, paid for by the state. With the expert being confidential, only the defense would be privy to the findings. The judge denied the request and she petitioned again, insisting she needed an expert to help her decide how to approach the case. While flatly stating the defense was not claiming Vinyard was insane or mentally impaired, she argued that he was entitled to present expert testimony regarding his mental state when he took the plea deal.

It was the best of both worlds — for him. To me, it was pretzel logic and made absolutely no sense.

But still leaning on his mental illness without claiming he was mentally impaired, she argued that Vinyard didn't understand that if he hadn't accepted the deal, the prosecution would have had to prove he *intended* to prevent the officer from arresting him and *intended* to harm him. This, despite the fact that this same judge had read the charges — including the "intent" elements of the crimes — aloud to him in court and asked if he had any questions, to which Vinyard replied, "No," and the fact that he and his attorney had signed the detailed agreement.

While Kathy walked me through the latest twists and turns of all the cases, I was furiously jotting down notes, but struggling to make sense of the whole mess and see a way out of this monumental labyrinth, my brain felt freeze-dried.

Then as we both completed our "to-do" lists, Kathy exclaimed that this was the most complicated, chaotic case she had ever worked on. Exasperated, shaking her head, she confided, "I don't see an end in sight."

The next week, as promised, Kathy prepared her motion to introduce prior similar acts, arguing that they were necessary to prove the charge of stalking itself. Feeling there were too many to list, she asked only to introduce evidence of some stalking events between 1987 and 1996.

The following week, I was again asked to meet Kathy for an update. Ignoring the clatter of my internal alarms, I agreed and, while trying to think positively, braced myself for another round of bad news.

The recent second-degree assault charge for striking and hurting the jail guard was reduced to misdemeanor third-degree assault and obstruction of justice, with a mandatory jail sentence of two years, she said. I was glad I hadn't raised my hopes for that one. A trial in that case was scheduled for April 13.

"But it all goes back to the deferred sentence in the felony second-degree assault," Kathy stressed. "It's imperative that the judge not allow withdrawal of that guilty plea."

There was some discussion about Vinyard going to the state mental health institute, she said, but his attorneys were advising against pleading "not guilty by reason of insanity"; they didn't trust that he'd be released and the DA didn't trust that he'd stay. And given the "not guilty" part of the plea, I knew there'd be no protection for us at all.

Then Kathy said she and Vinyard's attorneys all agreed that the best-case scenario was probably an eight- to ten-year sentence in prison for everything. She had met with them both, it seemed, and the words left unspoken rushed into my head at a dizzying speed: *Plea bargain. They're discussing a plea bargain.*

"You never know what Boulder juries will do," she explained.

I'd heard it so many times before, I began to wonder if Boulderites were from a different planet. Having lived there a long time I knew that in a way they were, but was it really enough to make the DA's office wince and offer a criminal anything time and time again just to avoid a jury trial?

Kathy quickly moved on. A motions hearing was scheduled for February 11 in the new stalking case. She would need me to testify about the prior similar stalking episodes as well as the phone calls charged in the current case. Then she handed me a transcript the defense's own office had made of the taped telephone calls to review.

The defense attorney had already submitted several motions, she said, sighing and shaking her head. He wanted to suppress any statements and physical evidence elicited by officers when Vinyard was arrested. My jaw dropped and she rushed to explain that this was standard practice, to protect the attorney. *Geeezzz. How had the* game *of justice come to this?*

He wanted the prosecution to submit, in writing, all evidence to be presented. It was ridiculous, a delay tactic, Kathy said.

He wanted the trial to be postponed. I had already lost track of the number of times it and all the hearings in all the cases had been continued.

He wanted separate trials for the stalking charges and the restraining order violations. *Of course, slice and dice,* I thought. Kathy assured me she would argue against that.

He alleged that the police and their agents had entrapped Vinyard to commit the offenses. I wasn't sure what was behind the claim, but my mind raced back to the advocate's explanation of the plea deal: It was a trap, she'd said. Then, abruptly turning down another track, I locked onto something else. At the officers' suggestion, I had set up the sting. A distinct uneasiness slid down to my stomach.

He also claimed there were no grounds for the arrest and no authority for Longmont officers to arrest Vinyard outside of Boulder County. That shook me to the core.

And he moved to dismiss the stalking charge, Kathy added, on the grounds that the stalking law was unconstitutional. With that, I felt my head would burst.

*   *   *

I don't know what finally sparked the idea of reaching outside the DA's office for help. Although I knew the prosecutors I'd worked with were dedicated to helping my family, both the DA's and judges' decisions had felt like unscalable obstacles for far too long. And now, working with Mary, I was beginning to feel empowered and was thinking more clearly. I was ready to shed the chains of bondage to the Twentieth Judicial District and felt there had to be another way. So, I walked around the barrier and searched for help outside the county.

As it happens, a friend had worked in the legal field and knew her way around the state legislature, an arena I had no experience with whatsoever. After some networking, she was directed to the Colorado District Attorneys' Council.

With no idea of how to approach the issue, I picked up the phone and, when connected to an associate, blurted out the chaotic story of the cases and stalking history then closed with a treatise on my frustration.

She listened attentively and finally, with an audible sigh, said simply, "They don't prosecute stalking cases in Boulder."

This was a revelation!

She suggested I meet with the executive director and we scheduled a time.

It was truly cathartic to discuss the whole travesty with a highly knowledgeable and experienced attorney outside the walls of the local justice center. He was keenly aware of serious problems with the stalking law and asked that I gather some information on my case for him to review. The next day, it was on his desk. He also planned to contact Kathy. His idea, it seemed, was to use this case as a catalyst for legislative reform.

There was no hope that changing the stalking law would affect my case; it had to be prosecuted under the law in effect when the crimes were committed. But finally, there was movement in a positive direction. If it didn't help me, at least it would help others out there.

I just couldn't consider that I might need a revised law myself in the future. I didn't have the heart to look further down the road than the tower of cases before me. I had to believe that somehow, with all these charges, Vinyard would be stopped then and there.

*   *   *

Within days of meeting with Kathy, I was graced with a subpoena from the defense to appear as a witness in court on February 11. It was the motions hearing for the new stalking case. Like fingernails on a chalkboard, "entrapment" scraped across the edges of my mind.

2/11/1998

Kathy abruptly interrupted my pacing when she threw open the doors and waved me into the courtroom. Quickly scanning the room, I saw the judge, the defense attorney, then Vinyard, thankfully in chains.

Kathy questioned me first and, one by one, led me down the road of the stalking history and current contacts. The defense took a different road and, one by one, asked what the verbal threat of physical harm was in each incident. We had been down that road before, and I was thoroughly annoyed.

He then asked if I'd reviewed the phone call transcription his office had prepared and if I felt it was accurate. I confirmed that I'd reviewed it and, no actually, there were some errors, I replied. He looked puzzled and I explained that the Longmont police had given me copies of the recordings and I'd compared them. Then page after page, I corrected the defense's transcription. Among other things they had completely left out that I'd asked Vinyard why he'd been violent toward us in the past and his response that he'd been drinking. Even after I corrected it, the defense attorney broadly repeated what I said and omitted it. I said it again.

Then the defense took a different tack, his questions probing how much the police were involved in planning the sting and making the arrangements. Not at all, I replied honestly; they suggested it would be helpful if I could set up a meeting, and nothing more was said until I called them with the details.

Finally, I was dismissed and later learned that a number of issues were raised and not resolved, including the credible threat element of the statute. In the end, the motions hearing was continued. In the meantime, the judge did rule on a few things.

The motion to suppress was moot, he ruled; there was no such evidence. The motion for separate trials was denied. The motion alleging entrapment was not relevant. The motion to continue the trial to May was granted.

The judge didn't rule on the defense's motion to dismiss the stalking charge on the grounds that the statute was unconstitutional. And he ordered the prosecution to identify which alleged incidents were credible threats.

Another month of waiting.

3/6/1998

When the continuance finally arrived, the judge launched into a discussion of the defense's argument that the stalking statute was unconstitutional. But now, it was a moot issue. Now, to my horror, it was the prosecution that filed a motion to dismiss count one: felony stalking.

According to Kathy's motion, the judge's comments during the last hearing strongly suggested he did not find that any of Vinyard's telephone calls to me in September of 1997 constituted a credible threat.

To address the judge's order that Kathy identify the contacts that were credible threats, the DA's staff researched the meaning of the term. They consulted with other prosecutors and even listened to tapes of the house and senate judiciary committee hearings. Among the testimony presented in one of the hearings was a compelling description of substantial damage to a man's life, his career, and his family by an erotomanic stalker who had obsessive delusions about him but did not make explicit threats.

He made it clear, Kathy wrote, "that [the stalker's] repeated phone calls and letters had severely impacted his private life and his professional career, and that he believed that those close to him, including his family and co-workers, were at great risk because of the irrational and unpredictable nature of the person's obsession, including the delusion that only those close to him stood between her and the object of her delusional love. But the response from one, and perhaps two, committee member(s) strongly suggested that in the absence of some credible threat beyond that inherent under such circumstances, the stalking statute did not apply and that protection was afforded by the harassment statutes already in existence."

How little they knew.

In my case, Kathy had previously argued that, although there were no explicit threats in Vinyard's phone calls, in the context of his stalking history the calls would cause a reasonable person to fear for her life, safety, or the safety of her family; therefore, his actions did constitute felony stalking. But now, she was forced to concede the point:

> With the utmost appreciation for the very real fear and desperate frustration under which Ms. Anderson has lived for so long, and under which she continues to live as a result of the inability of the system and the unwillingness of the defendant to stop his incessant and unwanted actions, the People have concluded that the court was correct in the attention it gave to the statutory language and the need for the defendant to have made a credible threat for there to be felony stalking. …
>
> There can be no doubt that Ms. Anderson expects and demands that the defendant end his inexcusable and intolerable behavior and leave her alone. This fact is not altered by this motion. It is apparent, however, that the defendant's behavior is not prohibited by the stalking statute, despite the extreme extent to which it has negatively impacted her life.

Instead of forcing prosecution under the current statute, the DA's office would work to change the law, Kathy said. Then she asked the judge to dismiss the felony stalking charge. The charges would now be harassment and violation of restraining order, both misdemeanor offenses.

So the wheels were now in motion, both at the state DA's council and the local DA's office, to change the law. While it was no consolation for the flat-out devastation I felt, it was something. Something that could affect the lives of others unfortunate enough to suffer the same fate as me in the future.

In the meantime, dangling over the edge of a cliff, I clung desperately to the only hope I had left — the felony assault case.

CHAPTER 12

House of Mirrors

"And thus I clothe my naked villany
With odd old ends stol'n out of holy writ,
And seem a saint, when most I play the devil."
~ *William Shakespeare,*
Richard III

3/11/1998

Five agonizing months after the issue was raised, the continued hearing for Vinyard's petition to withdraw his guilty pleas in the felony assault case finally came to order. I was not invited. Kathy met with me afterward and related the events of the day.

When the hearing began, the defense attorney in that case asked if her client could be uncuffed so he could write. The judge allowed it and the deputy interrupted, asking if he could uncuff just one hand. Deja vu.

Kathy had filed an objection, arguing that there was no record of an issue being raised at any of the court hearings about Vinyard's mental health, much less how it impacted his ability to make decisions about the charges. "The People contend the Defendant's reason for his request to withdraw his pleas is because he does not want to face the consequences … and therefore wants to withdraw his pleas and start over. This is not 'fair and just' reason for withdrawal of his pleas," she wrote.

Kathy also wrote, bluntly, "The People are unclear what the Defendant's stated reasons are for the withdrawal of his pleas. The Defendant states that he is mentally ill and was taking lithium at the time of the plea; however, the Defendant is not claiming that his mental illness is a basis for withdrawal of his pleas."

My thoughts exactly.

The defense began by acknowledging that the judge had received some "thick" letters from Bruce and me and asked him to disregard those as well as information about her "client's alleged character or any prior contacts he may have had or ongoing hostilities or whatever with these people." They were irrelevant to the matter at hand, she said and expounded on her argument. She wasn't saying he was so mentally ill that he didn't understand the deal; it was clear he did, she admitted. But, she said, he didn't quite understand and his counsel's advisement didn't help him understand the "intent" element of the crimes he pled guilty to. If he had, Vinyard wouldn't have taken the deal, she proclaimed.

Surprisingly, she then called on Vinyard to testify. He too said the deal was recommended to him without full explanation; he wanted to go to trial.

Since Vinyard had taken the stand, Kathy seized the opportunity and grilled him on exactly what he understood at the deferred sentence hearing about the assault charges, the deal he took, and the rights he relinquished. She asked if he'd had any questions at the time.

He understood them all, he recalled, and no, he hadn't had any questions.

The defense objected to Kathy's detailed questions about what Vinyard understood and said she specifically avoided that line of questioning. If she'd known that's what the prosecution would do, he would have taken the Fifth, she protested.

"The judge blew up," Kathy told me. "He was furious."

The transcript of the hearing plainly showed what she meant. And the transcript of an earlier hearing, when the same defense attorney pushed this judge to appoint a psychiatrist, showed he'd lost his cool before:

> Judge: ... [L]et me tell you something. It occurs to me quite often during these hearings, every time I take a plea I sometimes want to say — I want everybody to have — I want to send him to Switzerland and have him examined by a bearded, old, fabulously well-trained expert to determine if they understand the English language and if they understand the questions I'm asking. I don't get to do that. I have to assume for the most part that the questions I am asking will raise red flags or not. I saw no red flags with Mr. Vinyard.
>
> Defense: Right.
>
> Judge: What I'm saying is, why should I treat this case

different than all the other cases where I'm worried that the person is just not capable of understanding anything? So I just say, "I am sorry, I will take no plea, we are going to trial in every single case because nobody's capable of understanding?" ...

Defense: ... This is a very serious case, Judge. If I am not allowed to withdraw the guilty plea, my client is looking at very serious consequences.

Judge: You're right. He knows it, too. I told him so.

Pushing harder, the attorney said she needed the psychiatrist to help her provide effective counsel. Vinyard had that right under the Sixth Amendment, she declared. The judge's reply echoed my own sentiments:

Judge: I will put down the case law, cite the statute that gives me authority, because I may use it in a lot of other cases. I may, on my own, start appointing psychiatrists to evaluate a lot of people who appear in court. I might even order some lawyers evaluated, but I want to see —

Defense: Judge, this is a case that was —

Judge: — including DAs.

Personally, I would have added judges to the list.

Now, at the plea withdrawal hearing, under pressure from every angle (including Bruce and me via our letters), the judge became livid. Apparently, I wasn't the only one frustrated beyond words:

Judge: ... [Y]ou want me to believe that he didn't understand the specific intent. And yet, if, if he understood the facts, then — I mean, see what this case raises is this whole idea of to what extent does the Court have to not rely on the Defendant's saying, "I understand the nature of the charge," when they're later going to come tell you, "I didn't understand you had to prove culpable mental state. What's that, by the way, Judge?"

What — how far do we have to go? How much do they have to understand? He — he's saying — and if I say — you know, do I have to instruct them on the law of the entire case, the same kind of thing that the jury would understand, and then have — I mean, we're going to have Rule 11's take an hour and a half every single time.

Listen to me. Listen to me. And I understand this, but it just seems to me that if you — you know, you're going to have to say — see, this whole Rule 11 is in a way a sham. And it's a sham because the law seems to say lawyers — the law seems to presume that defense lawyers will not do their jobs and do not do their jobs. Therefore, the judge has to do their jobs. ...

I want to read [the "intent" instruction] because I think it demonstrates what extent am I going to have to rely on or not rely on what the defendants tell me. If they say, "I understand," do I say, "Wait a minute, wait a minute, I need to know your entire educational and psychiatric background. I need to know everything about you to understand whether or not you really understand or not?" ...

You know what I think? ... I think it's more important in this case that he really believed — probably he didn't care about specific intent. He didn't care about whether or not he was pleading guilty to something he did or didn't do. What he thought was, "I'm going to be able to get out of here."

Defense: Well, I would say that my client did think —

Judge: Because if he knew that if he was allowed to get out of here, he's probably going to violate again. That's why I ask him those questions.

Defense: Judge, I agree. And I'll put it on the record, my client thought that it was a pretty good deal and he was willing to go along with it.

Judge: It was an incredible deal. I remember thinking, deferred sentence — the guy who has, you know, all this stuff? I'm sorry to — it's really hard for me to cast from my mind, you know, the whole scenario, the whole circumstances of this case.

Defense: I understand, Judge.

Judge: For example, you know, I want to say maybe it's not relevant, you know. Wait a minute, you know, we live in a society now that's moving towards more of a — some kind of a focus on victims' rights instead of totally on defendants' rights. And I — I'm not sure I agree with that because I think the Constitution wasn't necessarily written for victims. But I'm wrong about that. Now we have constitutional provisions that allow victims to talk and things like that.

You know, how do you explain to a victim — I don't know, if I were a victim in this case, "I don't care about all this. I do not care."

Defense: I understand.

Judge: "Get this man away from me. I don't care whether he has a mental illness. I don't care what his intent was, but he is scaring me to death."

Defense: That may be true.

Judge: "If society can't protect me, then what am I going to do?" So don't give me all this victims' rights junk, it doesn't make any difference.

Defense: Judge, victims say that about every single —

Judge: No, I —

Defense: — little bit of constitutional protections that defendants have. …

I sincerely appreciated the fact that the judge finally understood our frustration with the system and even shared it. But his comments about the rights of crime victims thoroughly shocked me. Now victims are allowed to talk? And, the Constitution wasn't written for victims?

Victims of crime are not a different species! We are among the very "People" the Constitution was written for. What was the purpose of the criminal justice system, after all, if not to protect its' citizens and provide justice for victims of crime?

Whether the judge was referring to the state or federal constitution, I wasn't sure. But the preambles to both were essentially the same. "We, the People, in order to form a more perfect union, establish justice, insure domestic tranquility, and provide for the common defense … do ordain and establish this Constitution," America's founders wrote.

How had our criminal justice system, the light of the free world, strayed so far from its mission? How had it changed from protector to abuser, from defender to oppressor? Like any institution, I supposed, one small step at a time. It was sickening.

The judge made no decision that day — again. Kathy assured me that if he allowed Vinyard to withdraw his pleas, she would appeal. It was purely a legal question, she said.

I was hopelessly stuck in this legal quagmire. I'd risked my life and increased the danger to me and my family by assisting in his arrest; I had done my part. And putting their lives on the line, perhaps even risking careers to do the right thing, the police had done theirs. And now, here at the end zone, again the ball was dropped. It was madness. Incomprehensible insanity.

Finally, after six full months of waiting, one lead weight was lifted. On April 21, 1998, the judge denied Vinyard's motion to withdraw his guilty pleas for felony assault on an officer and misdemeanor resisting arrest. Kathy and I soon met.

The minimum sentence was now four years in prison. She planned to ask for more, she said, but since this was his first felony offense, she would only ask for "a reasonable amount." *What?!*

When Vinyard accepted the plea deal one year earlier, the deputy DA had told him this was as serious as it got. If he contacted us, he would be taken out of the community and placed in the DOC for "as long as we humanly can," he'd said. The maximum had already dropped from sixteen to twelve years. I implored Kathy not to go lower.

She was leaning toward asking for ten years but said she might ask for twelve, assuming he would get eight to ten. I was stunned. How had this been reduced to a heartless game of numbers? This was revocation of the deferred sentence; there would be no jury trial. Why was the DA's office bargaining at all? We weren't haggling over the price of a watch here. The safety of my family and our community was at stake. This was a dangerous predator who needed to be off the streets.

Yet over and over again, the court's lack of consequences only fueled his obsession and reinforced his conviction that what he did was not serious and that he would not be held accountable. It only served to embolden him, to encourage and escalate his relentless predation. Putting it in the context of my own life, it was the worst kind of parenting. It engendered dysfunction. It was archaic and served no one.

I didn't think I could be more disappointed in the criminal justice system. I was wrong. Kathy then informed me that the county jail staff wanted Vinyard out, and she felt obliged to respond to them.

Flaming fury was right on the heels of shock. *Seriously?! It's their job to protect the public!*

He was likely to get a concurrent sentence for the harassment charges; consecutive would have been mandatory only if he'd been convicted of felony stalking, the charge dismissed due to the language of the law, she said. To get him out of jail and into prison sooner, she was considering not pushing for consecutive in a plea deal.

My God! If the jail staff can't handle him, the answer is not to put him back on the streets sooner!

My tongue lashed out: "Only if the prison sentence is a very, very long one. If the jail staff complains, have them talk to me."

I thought of all the years I'd invested in these endless court proceedings, praying for a swift resolution — a right now afforded to me by our state constitution. And now that the jail staff didn't want to deal with him anymore, the DA's office was willing lower its sentencing bid just to speed up the process.

Kathy assured me she wouldn't drop the harassment charges. "He needs to be found guilty for the record."

Harassment. The same misdemeanor crime he'd been charged with since 1987 and received warnings for since 1979.

*   *   *

With each blow the judiciary dealt, I struggled to work with the information Mary was giving me. It was all I had to hang on to.

Breathe, ground, and center. See my boundaries, fill my space with light. Anger; focus and direct it. Call back my power, focus on myself. Surrender — impossible. Be gentle with myself, open to receiving.

None of it came easily, and at times, I was furious that I had yet more demands, more work to do just to function. And when it was too much to deal with, I slid back into old patterns of coping: I shut down and disconnected. "Dissociation" Mary called it and I flashed back to my first self-defense intensive, the boundary exercise. When my rational mind and churning gut were at war, confusion reigned. And when pushed to the critical moment of decision, I'd disengaged.

At this point, I'd honed that escape mechanism to the point that I relied on my note-taking skills to recall events. When overwhelmed, I mentally disconnected.

Dissociating put me at greater risk, Mary warned. "The work we are doing is teaching you to be engaged and fully present, while staying safe."

I knew she was right. If, in that first self-defense class, the danger had been real, dissociating, I would have been at risk of serious harm. Nodding, I turned back down the rabbit hole and kept practicing.

But by now, I was spent — so deeply exhausted that I could hardly complete the most mundane tasks and make it through my days. I wasn't at all sure I could ever recover, no matter the outcome.

Then an old friend called unexpectedly. He was studying hypnotic regression therapy and needed guinea pigs. He offered a session with his instructor. He would observe.

Curious, I asked more about it. In regression, he explained, I'd relive forgotten or repressed experiences which held emotional wounds that had never healed. Unlocking those emotions could shed light on current issues rooted in my past, he said. So the goal would be to take me back to my childhood, pinpoint issues that may be in play in my current situation, and heal them.

I didn't ask Mary's opinion. I told her I was going. I wanted concrete information and whatever healing I could get.

She was concerned. We were just beginning to make progress, and she didn't want anyone messing with me. She insisted on coming along and observing. For that, I was grateful. I was nervous about it; my deep-seated fear of being vulnerable was triggered. But as the method was explained to me, I understood that I would not lose conscious awareness. Ultimately I'd be in control. And my need for answers far outweighed my fear.

Soon we all gathered, and reclining in preparation, I gradually felt myself sinking, my muscles relaxing, my mind surrendering. Gently, I was guided into a trance state. When the practitioner asked if there were any present who were willing to accompany me, I sensed my guides, a large dog, and an archangel surrounding me. I'd never given archangels any thought before. I wasn't even sure I believed they existed. Yet there he was.

I welcomed them all and felt the archangel move to my side. His presence was profoundly comforting. Gradually, I began to trust that I would be guided, protected, and fully supported, whatever may come.

Following the practitioner's guidance, sinking deeper and deeper, I moved further and further back in time. But as random images of my childhood flashed through my mind, none stood out as important.

He asked if I needed to go deeper.

"Yes," I replied.

Following his lead, deeper and deeper I sank until suddenly, an image splashed into every corner my mind, jolting my body.

"Tell us what you see," he said.

I hesitated. I didn't want to believe it, didn't want to see it. But I could not shake the image. I was seized in its grip.

Finally bracing myself, I swallowed my horror and, throat constricted and mouth dry, uttered, "Ropes."

The lens in my mind was focused intensely on a woman's young, feminine hands lashed at the wrists behind her. Tracks of blood, sweat, and dirt traced her desperate struggle against the thick, rough ropes.

"Where are you?"

Something inside me replied, "France," and as the camera in my mind's eye rapidly pulled back, a grisly scene unfolded. A young woman in simple peasant clothing was bound to a wooden stake. Then, through her eyes, I looked to my right. Three other women whom I knew were dear friends were also trussed, prepared for death. *This is a past life.*

Before me, an eager, hungry mob was gathered to witness the spectacle. Eyes ablaze with desire, they shouted, jeered, and waved fists in the air wildly.

Terrified, I scanned the horde of rabid faces. Then abruptly, my gaze stopped and locked on two confused and horrified children — my children — and a third, ethereal figure hovering over them. This boy, I knew, was also my beloved child, one who had died young. He was there to bear witness and comfort his younger siblings and me.

I felt my heart tearing in two. My young children were about to witness my unjust, gruesome death at the hands of my accusers. In a moment, they would be orphaned. Alone in this hideously cruel world.

In the present, profound sorrow flooded me. Tears poured down my face and neck. Choked with overwhelming grief, I couldn't speak. The pain in my heart was unbearable.

How could these people — my people — have been so blinded, so deluded? How could human beings possibly be so cruel? How had mankind come to this? Insufferable grief for my children and all of humanity utterly consumed me.

Sensing the agony that gripped me, the practitioner quickly ushered me back further in time. To change the outcome and heal the experience, he planned to rewrite events from that early childhood forward. But my soul had a will of its own, one I had to honor.

Time rewound then stopped, and I saw myself and other women pushed and shoved by the jostling mob into a church. Earlier that day, the church had been the courtroom. It was the ultimate abuse of power and authority: In the name of God, we condemn you.

Accusations of witchcraft and evil spewed from the mouths of our inquisitors. Demonized, we were not seen for who we were, who they knew us to be. Revered in our village, we were the wise women: intuitives, mystics, counselors, healers — the heart of our community. But the church perceived us as a threat to its authority. To remove that threat, the inquisitors had sparked and fanned unfounded fears, and mass hysteria ignited.

Our frantic protests were lost beneath the cacophony of the mob. The crazed furor of fear, lies, and rage crushed all truth and compassion. We were walled out of the hearts and minds of all who persecuted us. It was madness. Incomprehensible insanity. Cruelty beyond belief.

Again, the practitioner seized the reins and guided me back to my infancy in that life. I tried to follow him, but his scripted words merely drifted by. I saw the story he wove but did not embrace it. My mind was not in charge. The enormous pain in my heart was all that mattered. I was transfixed on the eyes of my children in the moments before my violent death by fire, and there my heart stayed until I was gradually led out of the trance and back to present time.

It soon became clear the experience had not healed. The horror lingered, and immersed in grief and anguish, I barely set foot into the world.

CHAPTER 13

Estuary

"I have lived on the lip
of insanity, wanting to know reasons,
knocking on a door. It opens.
I've been knocking from the inside."

~ *Rumi*

In the days following the regression, the horrors of the past haunted me, mingling insidiously with present day. Lost in the tragedy, I did not sense the separation of time as we know it. The faces of my children — present and past, merging then separating — drifted constantly before my mind's eye. Their suffering tormented me.

The regression had ripped open my emotional floodgates, and an ocean of despair swallowed me whole. All I wanted to do was hollow out a space in time to retreat and grieve, but court was now finally in motion. It would not pause for me.

* * *

Kathy asked me to meet her for an update and discuss the upcoming hearings. After years of experience, I'd become quite adept at the unhealthy art of shoving my emotions under and forcing my mind to engage when needed, but again I found myself struggling to follow the latest twists and turns of all the cases. I felt more disconnected, more detached than ever — as if the cases, the trip wires, the negotiations and ever-changing numbers were all utterly meaningless. The ludicrous mind games bore no resemblance to reality. They were of no importance at all. All that mattered was the weight of this immense sorrow, this agony bearing down on my chest.

As she launched into the litany of cases, her words poured through me and directly onto my paper, not entirely sinking in, until a few things jarred me out of my fog.

Vinyard's attorney in the assault case had finished what the court appointed her to do and the public defender now worked all four cases.

Prior similar acts would be allowed at the harassment trial per Kathy's request. But unless Vinyard took the stand, she couldn't bring up the felony assault conviction or any other criminal history. She couldn't force him to take the stand, and she was sure the defense wouldn't call him.

The stalking charge in that case dismissed, the DA had instead charged Vinyard with three counts of harassment and three counts of violation of restraining order. But it was unlikely he'd be convicted of all six counts, Kathy confessed; we were probably looking at a maximum sentence of eighteen months.

Word upon word, the case and potential sentence were falling like a house of cards. At this point, Vinyard had already been in jail and I'd been trudging through this tar pit for seven months. Even if the judge imposed the maximum for harassment, by the time he was finally sentenced, with credit for time served, there could very well be nothing left.

Then my stomach plunged as the ground collapsed beneath me once again. Kathy and the defense were discussing a plea bargain for both the felony assault and misdemeanor harassment cases but hadn't agreed on the numbers. The defense would probably agree to plead guilty to two of the six harassment and violation of restraining order charges and wanted a total sentence of six years. Kathy was not at all comfortable with six years, especially since a misdemeanor sentence was almost always concurrent if the perpetrator was going to prison for a felony. The defense wouldn't agree to eight years, she said.

The potential sentence had dropped from sixteen to twelve and now maybe eight or even six years, and we hadn't even been to court. I was in a free fall, wondering where and when I would finally hit solid ground.

Kathy moved on to the misdemeanor assault in jail. Vinyard was trying to discredit the jail guards with allegations of police brutality and was sending files on individuals directly to a judge for investigation, she said. His attorney was not privy to those files.

"Vinyard is becoming a jailhouse lawyer and may not listen to his attorney," Kathy speculated.

He'd threatened to file a civil suit for damages against the guard he assaulted unless the officer said the incident was his fault, she confided.

Of course, it's his MO. Blaming his victims.

"I have to talk to the deputies and ask what they want," Kathy said.

But they'd already made their wishes clear: They wanted him out. In a moment of clarity, I asked, "Which case will the credit for time served be applied to?"

She followed my train of thought, "It may be best to apply it to the misdemeanor assault."

She would talk to the probation officer; he was preparing a sentence recommendation. But it was up to the judge to decide, she said.

Finally, our meeting winding to a close, she looked at me apologetically and added, "Vinyard is already preparing appeals. Our office will keep you informed of all appeals."

So no matter the outcome of all of this, the end was nowhere in sight.

The next day, I received two subpoenas to appear in court: one for a hearing in the felony assault case the next week, the other for the harassment trial in three weeks. The pressure reaching full pitch, the new tools I had developed and all the coping mechanisms I'd perfected over the years failed me completely. My anguish evolved into full-blown crisis. I could not think. I could not function. Tormented, I could barely breathe.

Finally, I found the presence of mind to reach out for a lifeline. When she heard of my aftershocks, Mary immediately cleared her schedule. That afternoon, we met.

*   *   *

I wasn't entirely sure why I always found myself propelled to the edge of a cliff before a new path appeared, why I was always knocked to my knees before my trajectory finally changed. But in myth, the phoenix is consumed by flames and reduced to ashes to be reborn. And some say that in its highest form, the phoenix becomes the eagle that sees everything clearly.

Was it because I was working for true transformation, such immense change that I had to be willing and ready to surrender everything — every belief, every ounce of resistance? Perhaps. Perhaps that combined with my willful nature. When challenged, I held onto my convictions with clenched fists. And the harder I was hit, the tighter I squeezed until blood was drawn on my own palms — or wrists — in fierce defiance of the ropes that bound me.

*   *   *

When I took my familiar seat opposite Mary, she took a close look at me and furled her brow. My vacant eyes and pallid complexion revealed how perilously close I was to the edge.

"You look haunted!" she exclaimed. I was.

Pulling her chair in close, she calmly asked what I wanted to do. She trusted my instincts and I trusted hers.

Without hesitation, I said, "I want to go back."

After preparing the space and ourselves, Mary gently guided me into a light trance. My companions in spirit joined me, the archangel so close I felt his warmth fold over me. From there, she let me go. While she carefully monitored my journey, I was free to find my own way.

Instantly, I was back at the scene of my imminent death: hands tied to the stake, my children's terrified faces before me, the fevered mob jostling and shouting for my gruesome execution. Horror gripped me, and there I stood for a long time, searching … searching … searching for the key.

Then finally, gazing into the faces of the delirious mob again, the veil gently lifted and a knowing beyond anything I'd ever experienced dawned. The answer was abundantly clear. Like a warm ray of sun on a cold winter's day, comprehension penetrated me. Down to my bones, it warmed me. Down to the smallest cells of my body, down to my DNA, it changed me.

"Talk to me," Mary said.

"This is an illusion. *All* life is illusion. It is pliable."

It was not just words. Throughout my entire being, I owned this truth. And without question, I knew that I had the power to change the experience.

The fear that had seized me washed down through my body and into the earth below. And into the vacuum left in its wake poured an infinitely powerful column of love and peace.

Then, looking out into the crowd, I opened my heart, channeling that divine grace, and one by one, raised fists were lowered and raised voices receded. Finally they ceased. Silence.

In the eyes of those before me I saw confusion — as if, released from a mass hallucination, my persecutors had suddenly awoken and couldn't remember why they'd been so full of loathing. Blind rage had been transmuted.

All was calm, and as my mind's eye focused on my hands, the knots slipped open and the ropes fell freely from my wrists.

Silently, I stepped forward and the crowd gently parted, opening a path to my children. Scooping them into my arms, I pressed them firmly against my chest and began walking, first through the crowd then over the hills under windy blue skies, to our home.

Once there, I set them down to play and began preparing fresh vegetables for soup, the sustenance of life, while the last vestiges of crimson light poured through our tiny window and the sun quietly slipped below the horizon.

Giving myself time to linger a while in the calm and warmth of our hearth, feeling my love for my children fill me, at last I was ready. Slowly, I walked the path back and re-emerged in present time, at peace.

My eyes slowly opening, I basked in the sensation. I had opened my heart and taken back my power. I had embraced my birthright. This was how it felt.

Though I remembered every detail of that vision, the gnosis I'd experienced in an altered state of consciousness was not easily maintained on the earthly plane. With the passage of time, the sensation faded.

Yet somewhere deep within me, something had shifted. A seed of comprehension, of enlightenment had been planted in my consciousness. And as I continued on the path of self-discovery, unraveling the mysteries of my soul in the months and years that followed, the seed germinated and took root. Upon planting that seed, a quickening had occurred, my awakening had begun. Whatever was yet to come, I would never be quite the same.

The healing had been symbiotic. With the help of my mentor and companions, I had reached from the present across time to heal the past and, in so doing, began healing the present. I felt whole, large, expansive. One living soul spanning the ages.

*   *   *

I don't often remember my dreams, except the recurring nightmares. But I do have a theme dream and it's always good news. It appears in times of great need or major shifts in my life, and it's always a tremendous comfort to me. Cloaked in easily decoded symbols, it confirms that I'm guided, that I'm on the path.

It's a house dream. Most often, although it always looks different, I know it's my house. And clearly my house represents me, my inner realm. In the dream, I always discover parts of my home — myself — that I had forgotten were there. Always, it is a place of unimaginable abundance, even in times of deepest despair.

Once, before I met Mary, when I felt as if my whole world had collapsed, my sleeping mind fell upon that dream. I found myself walking into a thick fog of smoke and stumbled upon my home, burned to ashes, still smoldering. Wandering around the empty lot, dazed and heartsick, I found a small shed hidden behind a thicket of thorny brush choked with weeds. I sensed I had never known it was there. Once white, the tiny shed was scarred by smoke. Creeping up to it, I discovered a small, smudged window. Curious, I rubbed a spot clean then peered inside, and the vision before me stole my breath away.

Brilliant rays of sunlight poured through the glass ceiling, illuminating row upon row of rough-hewn tables filled with vibrant green seedlings. I had a long journey ahead of me, but new life was emerging — a life filled with potential. I awoke deeply comforted, hope renewed.

Now, after healing the regression, I had another dream. The house was mine and yet it was completely different from any I had seen before. In fact, to call it a house at all is a gross understatement. It was extraordinary, huge: a palace. As I entered the central corridor, my eyes wandered up to the dizzying height of the soaring, gilded archways bathed in sunlight.

I was free to explore any room, every corner of this immense place; it was mine, after all. Fascinated, I opened the first beautifully inlaid wood doors I came upon and entered an exquisite study, full of richly polished wooden desks and books stacked from floor to ceiling. All the information contained in those books was there, at my disposal. Every answer I could ever seek, there for me to discover.

Wandering further, I came upon room after room, all stunningly furnished, all beautiful beyond my imagination — although since this was my dream, perhaps not.

Turning the knobs of yet another pair of doors, I was astonished to find myself entering a large amphitheater, copiously adorned with ancient symbols. Gazing over the stage and the crescent of seats engaged with it, I sensed that this was where ancient sacred wisdom dwelled and was disseminated. And it, too, was there for me. All within my grasp. To resurrect, to remember.

Finally, descending into the basement, I began to feel warm droplets of steam condensing on my face and, seeking the source, opened a door onto an enormous pool. I was awestruck, and reflecting on that image in the void between the sleeping and waking worlds, I knew. Beneath the surface, water: the unconscious mind, emotion, hidden wisdom. It was the message of all great teachers throughout the ages: The secret hides within.

*   *   *

Trusting that whatever came up for me was what needed attention, my work with Mary followed my own process. And in time, listening to my gut, connecting with my emotions, and following the threads wherever they would lead became my fascination. It was an adventure of self-discovery like none I'd ever experienced.

Where before, emotional insights were snatched up by my mind and debated, often ending in stalemate, now with a few words of wisdom or questions from Mary, my mind turned in a whole new direction, my emotions leading the way. As she had pushed me to do so many times, I was beginning to shift from my head to my heart.

"The heart is the master; the head is the servant," she'd say, and as insights flowed from one to another, opening doors to new awareness and understanding, I was beginning to accept that my heart held a wisdom my mind could not fathom. But there was one major obstacle to this shift in perception, one deep-seated resistance I had been aware of for many years. And while still battling fiercely with the courts, the agony of it was eating me alive.

It was time to trust Mary more than I had ever trusted anyone. It was time to tell her the truth. For all my blind spots, my internal compass was always strong. If I was not in my truth, if I was not being completely honest, my bearings were off and a persistent hum of disgust droned in the pit of my stomach. And there it had resided for a painfully long time.

All these years, I had been plagued with a secret I kept firmly under lock and key. And throughout endless court proceedings, I'd been sickened by the mask I myself wore: a mask of indifference to Vinyard's fate.

While I fought with all my might for incarceration, I felt dishonest when doing so. I firmly believed that to protect my family and the community, he had to be kept off the streets. Yet knowing he was mentally ill, I questioned whether sending him to prison was the right thing to do. The truth was, when I was not in imminent danger, not steeped in the fear and rage that overwhelmed me when under siege, I felt compassion for him.

Now I dared speak the words to Mary. I flinched as I said it, expecting the same look of shock and dismay I'd experienced before. Roundly condemned whenever I mentioned it, I quickly learned not to discuss it with anyone.

"This man has terrorized you and been a mortal threat to you and your family, and you feel compassion for him?" others had said. And the sympathetic look in their eyes quickly turned to skepticism and judgment. "You brought this on yourself," their glares declared. "This is your fault."

But Mary did not recoil or furl her brow. She didn't jump down my throat or condemn me. Unfazed, she smiled, nodded, and waited for more.

Ever since the stalking began, and particularly after I learned of Vinyard's mental illness, my sense of compassion had tormented me. What I once felt was my greatest gift had somehow become something dark and twisted. The blame and disgust in the eyes of others told me it was so.

Most of all, I dared not show compassion in court. In the context of a case where the predator had distorted the word "love" so grotesquely and blamed me for his obsession, I felt I couldn't risk showing compassion. The court already leaned far in the direction of the perpetrator. I was terrified that if I too revealed compassion for him, I would be seen as culpable, complicit, and my family would be placed in even more danger. So in my fight for protection, I had long condemned the court's sympathy for him. There was some truth to that position, yet it wasn't the whole truth.

I felt torn in two. When I thought of what he'd done to us, I despised him with every fiber of my being. I had no doubt that his predation was reprehensible, absolutely unconscionable regardless of his illness. And yet I felt compassion. The two were irreconcilable, it seemed. So my compassion became my secret and, as secrets do, the secret kept became my shame.

Was it compassion that first invited the darkness in? Was it compassion he'd hooked into and that sustained his connection? If so, was there some truth to his conviction that I encouraged him, that I was to blame? Is this why I reacted so strongly to the first responding officer and insinuations in court that this was my fault? Had their accusations poked at my own raw, painful doubts?

Inevitably, these questions always led to the ultimate torment: Was I responsible for putting my children in danger, for the pain they had suffered? If it was true, it was simply too much to bear. Unable to face it, I'd shoved my doubts down and there, hidden deep in my gut, they loomed larger and larger. And now, while fighting fiercely for imprisonment, guilt's ugly head rose up and swallowed me whole. It was time to dive into the belly of the beast.

"Compassion is humanity's highest expression of divine love, the love we are all called upon to manifest here on Earth," Mary said. "The problem is not that you feel compassion for him. It never was. The problem is that you lack compassion for yourself. It's out of balance."

Those few words held a wealth of knowledge I had so long struggled to comprehend that I could not take in all the ramifications at once. But I latched on to that I desperately needed to hear: I clung to her assurance that compassion was not in any way inappropriate or sick, and the burden of shame I'd carried so long quietly lifted.

"Yes, your heart is always connected to truth. It is the mind, the ego that confuses and distorts the truth."

It was as if Mary's words had cut an old, stubborn knot. And when the thread was finally loosed and began unraveling the tapestry of my life, more and more connections were revealed.

Long ago, soon after the stalking began, I'd shut down and cut myself off from connection with others. At the time, I thought I no longer trusted people, and though I tried to open my heart fully with my closest friends, I knew I was holding back. But now I realized it wasn't others I mistrusted, at least not entirely. Far below my conscious awareness, I feared my own power and mistrusted my own heart. Look what they'd brought into my life, after all.

As one insight led to another, the story woven long ago continued to unfold. Once I'd doubted my heart, my mind quickly seized upon the opportunity. It was my heart, I believed, that betrayed me. It was my own heart I could not trust. From that point forward, I would rely on my mind to solve this mystery and find my way. So all of Mary's work to draw me out of my head and into my emotions, or even to make a heart connection with her, was rejected outright. I had come to Mary for information but was determined to keep my heart firmly locked away. I was shut off from the neck down and refused to reach out for her lifeline.

But now, finally, I understood. My heart had not betrayed me. It was my mind that had. It was my mind that accepted the distortions of others and convinced me to fear my own heart. It was my mind that had imprisoned me.

I had no doubt that what Mary said was true. As these pieces of the puzzle fell into place, the mantle of confusion and heartache I'd carried for so long quietly slipped away, and in its place were clarity and a profound sense of relief and peace. After all this time, my heart was finally emancipated from the bondage of my mind.

As I let this revelation settle into my bones, I gradually felt free to continue our work without holding back. I resolved to trust my heart and was free to follow the threads of emotion to their source and discover the messages, the wisdom hidden there.

Like a flower unfolding within me, each time I relaxed and opened my heart, information long suppressed blossomed. Working with this new-found freedom, I became more and more aware of the subtle shifts in my emotions. And although the guilt did not subside, it did come into sharper focus.

The "what's mine" part of severing the connection haunted me, the question echoing constantly in the back of my mind. Though I still didn't understand what I was responsible for, I knew some of this was mine to own and felt painfully guilty for somehow bringing this into my family's life. And feeling guilty, I still struggled to receive the nurturing and kindness Mary encouraged me to give myself and accept from others. I felt I didn't deserve it. And I still felt guilty for sending Vinyard to prison, as if that was my doing, not his own.

Stepping back and looking at this inner dialog from a distance, I realized I'd always felt responsible for the well-being of others. I carried everything and everyone yet, at the same time, resented all the demands on me. I suppose I was always aware of this fundamental sense of responsibility but accepted it as a tenet of life, not something unique to me and others like me; I'd thought it was true for everyone. Caring for one another, carrying another's burden in times of need was the ideal, utopia. It was what "good" people did.

"You are not responsible for his delusions or his actions," Mary assured me, "and you are not responsible for what happens to him. You are only responsible for yourself."

I'd heard this before. Once, when I briefly saw another counselor, she'd said, "When we carry the burdens of others, we rob them of the opportunity to learn from their own life experiences and the consequences of their own choices. It is not a kindness, but a disservice."

Stunned, I'd fallen silent. This one statement turned my world view on its head. Yet it made perfect sense. I did believe that our souls guide us to experiences to help us grow and evolve and that we had free will to make choices and learn from them. So why had I lacked faith in the integrity and purpose of the experiences of others? Why had I felt the need to protect their feelings, ease their suffering, and carry their burden? And why hadn't this gem of information she'd given me stuck and carried forward into my life?

Then suddenly, it occurred to me that this same scenario had played out again and again in the courtroom. It was the scratched record that looped endlessly. Every time judges withheld the consequences of the stalker's actions from him — incarceration — it was not a kindness, but a disservice. To me and to him. By default, the consequences of his actions were placed firmly on my shoulders, further enmeshing our lives and enforcing the connection I so desperately fought against. And if he was capable of learning, they'd robbed him of the opportunity to learn from his own choices.

The flower of comprehension continuing to unfold, something else then dawned on me. Over and over, I had soundly thrashed judges for focusing entirely on this "poor sick man" with no regard for me. It was a perfect reflection of my own compassion for him and not for myself. My own unconscious convictions were, as in a dream, projected onto the large screen of my experience.

It was right in front of me all along, and yet I had never seen it. The attitudes and perceptions of the judges I'd encountered mirrored my own deep-seated, unconscious belief that he needed compassion, not me, and that I was to ease others' suffering and carry their burdens. *As within, so without. Of course.*

"Yes," Mary said. "You are clinging to beliefs that do not serve. They don't serve you. They don't serve anyone."

So why did I find it so hard to let go of my convictions? Why did I still feel responsible for others, and why did I deny myself the compassion I so freely gave? When she spoke of giving myself compassion, I felt the hook — the same strong emotional reaction I had whenever she told me to stop beating myself up and, instead, be kind to myself. It was a shudder of outright rejection, a resistance I had come to learn was my cue to take a closer look. There was something important here, it hinted. Something buried deep within me was holding me back. Something not yet seen.

As I pondered these questions in the days that followed, the answers didn't come to me. So I pulled out the tools Mary had given me. I'd felt the hook, and instead of lodging it deeper by resisting, I breathed deeply, surrendered the mental gymnastics, and felt myself sinking into the watery depths of my unconscious mind. There, I asked that the reasons be revealed to me. I didn't specify how they would be revealed, only that they would.

CHAPTER 14

Underworld

"Perhaps it is better to wake up after all, even to suffer,
rather than to remain a dupe to illusions all one's life."
~ Kate Chopin,
The Awakening, and Selected Stories

Why did I deny myself compassion? Where was this resistance coming from? I wanted to know, and whatever it was, I wanted to let it go.

I had asked the question, surrendered my mind, and opened myself to the answer, in whatever form it would come. Soon I had a vivid dream.

I was in an odd place, a barren, sterile institution of some sort. When I spoke to those in charge, they could not understand me, nor I them. It was as if our words were scrambled or we spoke different languages. I didn't know why we couldn't communicate. I only knew I could not be heard.

And there was another thing I knew: I had been given the chance to kill Vinyard.

I found myself in a kind of cafeteria line and reached out to pick up a large silver spoon. I then held it out to be filled with poison. Once it was full, I lifted the spoon to my own mouth and began pouring: I was to take half of it. Closing my eyes, I felt the burn spread down the back of my throat. Then suddenly, I realized I didn't have to take it and spat the poison out.

When I turned from the table, a mass of bizarre, scary people spread out before me. All were awaiting their fates at the hands of their victims. Methodically, I walked the aisles between them yet could look at none of them. Though I sensed where Vinyard was, I never saw him.

Finally I reached the end of the aisles, only to find that I had walked full circle and returned to the dispensing table. I'd missed my opportunity. I hadn't done the deed.

Panic setting in, I considered going back but instead lowered the spoon in resignation and uttered, "I couldn't have done it anyway."

Disappointed in myself, defeated, I climbed onto a bus. When the driver closed the door behind me, I found I was not alone. Other victims filled the seats, all ready to be transported.

Once I was seated, the driver took off and turned onto a circular track, but he was going far too fast. Tipping and skidding, the bus was completely out of control and soon plunged into a mud pit, thoroughly stuck. Searching for a way out, I clawed my way to a small window, forced it open, crawled out, and began walking. Then suddenly, I found myself in my home. Yet it wasn't the home I knew.

Brand new rooms awaited me with fresh white walls and ceilings. There was light everywhere. Beautiful, eclectic pieces of furniture adorned the space. They were not mine; they belonged to a friend, one who had given me permission to use them. And I knew it was right to do so.

Reflecting on the meaning of the dream when I awoke, I thought the reason I had to take the poison myself was that I felt responsible for everything and everyone. If I was going to kill another, I too would have to suffer the consequences: I would have to kill myself.

But there was more to it. Much more.

*   *   *

"What do you hate most about him?" Mary asked.

The question took me aback. I didn't want to admit I could hate anyone, but I couldn't deny there were times when I despised this predator more than I thought humanly possible. No sooner had I acknowledged that ugly truth than the answer boiled up and out, with no further thought.

"He's totally narcissistic, completely selfish. He cares nothing for anyone but himself."

"So, if this experience is holding up a mirror for you, what do you see in your reflection?"

That was the question. It was always her question. It was never about others. It was always about me. What was this emotionally charged reaction telling me about myself? What of myself wasn't I seeing?

Our discussion didn't get far that day. I couldn't seem to get beyond the guilt I felt for hating. Sickened by my response, I gazed into the tapestry adorning the wall behind Mary. Remarkably, in color and hue, it was a mirror image of the dark tapestry that had graced my own walls since I was a teenager. They were opposites.

Mary encouraged me to be understanding, to be kind and gentle with myself. Give yourself compassion, she repeated for the umpteenth time. Finally, with the breakthroughs I'd recently had, I was beginning to find that if I imagined stepping outside myself and looked upon me as I would anyone else, or if I imagined what Source would want for me, I could forgive my faults and give myself grace. I softened and I opened.

As the week passed, I didn't consciously seek an answer to the question she'd asked. I just sat with my surprising declaration, let go of self-judgment, and asked that the deeper meaning of my statement be revealed to me. Gazing into the looking glass of my own words, I stared passively at my reflection, and soon a word-play emerged.

Selfish. The mirror image? *Selfless.* Two sides of the same coin. In my mind, one wrong, the other right. The word-play continued. *Self-centered, centered on oneself.* The opposite? *Not centered in self, self-less, without self.* Suddenly, it wasn't so black and white anymore, and the twinge in my gut told me I'd hit on something important.

"That's correct," Mary said at our next session. "If you aren't centered in yourself, you cannot relate to the world in a healthy way. It's my hope that in our work together, you will learn healthy selfishness."

Healthy selfishness? The words were antonyms, incompatible. The whole concept contradicted everything I believed. But it wasn't just me. Our culture and many, if not all, faiths condemned selfishness and revered not only a selfless act, but a selfless life. It was the highest calling.

"And not only that you learn healthy selfishness," she persisted, "but that you learn to do what's best for you first."

My eyebrows reached for my hairline. My eyes rolled involuntarily. I couldn't see myself ever doing that. It would be contrary to all that I stood for, all that I was.

"It's the only way you will also do what is best for everyone else," she said. I was totally confused.

"What do you feel when you hear the word selfish?" Mary asked.

"Disgust. I reject it," I replied.

"That strong, negative reaction is telling you that selfishness is, for you, unintegrated shadow material. It's showing you the selfish side of yourself." I flushed with shame.

"We all — every single one of us — have shadow material that we have repressed," Mary assured me. "From the time we are young children and every day, we assimilate messages from our family, our religion, and our culture of what is acceptable and not, of who we should be and who we should not be. And so, our minds have passed judgment on aspects of ourselves and rejected them. But when we judge, reject, and deny aspects of ourselves, they don't go away."

My mind sprinting, Mary gave me a moment to catch up then continued.

"Shoved down, these rejected aspects of self linger in the unconscious, in shadow. Effectively, we are split in two: the good and the bad, the acceptable and the unacceptable, the lovable and the unlovable. This is duality and it is not the truth. The goal is to become your whole, authentic self. And to do that, you must discover what is hidden in your shadow and integrate it."

The thought of exploring my hidden dark side was beyond uncomfortable. My self-image, my whole identity was threatened. What if I wasn't the good person I thought I was? Had I been living a lie, pretending to be someone I wasn't and hiding the truth of who I really was from everyone, even myself? Some had admired me. Some had loved me. What if they saw only a mask, a persona I'd presented to the world? What if I was completely unworthy?

Sensing my turn down the road of self-loathing, Mary quickly grabbed the wheel.

"The mind — the ego — wants to maintain control and so does not want you to see all that you are. It wants to keep you locked in a self-constructed identity, a self-image that is less than your truth. And holding onto judgments and beliefs that don't serve are some of the mind's tools of control."

A disconcerting mix of concern, guilt, and hope stirring inside me, silence was my only response.

"Our darkness is not the enemy," Mary continued. "It contains great power and wisdom. The question is, will those impulses and aspects of self you've denied and shoved into shadow be used against yourself and others? Or will they be expressed in ways that serve you, others, and society as a whole?"

Scanning, I locked onto anger. Anger wasn't inherently negative; it was a tool, Mary had said. The question was how to use it appropriately, for its highest and best purpose.

"Yes, your judgments around anger shoved it into your shadow. And your beliefs about selfishness do not serve. If you are not centered in yourself, you cannot relate to the world in a healthy way," she repeated. "If you do not live in the world anchored in yourself, you are completely out of your power and unsafe. Your judgment around selfishness is a big part of why you don't nurture yourself and why you felt it wasn't okay for you to have boundaries."

Everything Mary said made sense, yet I still felt the resistance, the shiver of rejection. I could not be selfish. Why? Where was this coming from?

Ever since I'd begun working with Mary, childhood memories had been surfacing, randomly it seemed. But the process of self-discovery and healing is never random. There is purpose in everything that comes up, exactly when it comes up.

Throughout my life, I'd worked to unravel my family dynamic, to understand cause and effect and overcome the challenges of my past. But now, bubbles of memory churned and rose copiously to the surface. It was as if something had punctured the ocean floor and a subterranean airstream raced up from the deep. Oxygen rushing into my lungs, my heart throbbed with expectation, with hope. Suddenly, I saw so many connections more clearly than I ever had.

I was the youngest of four daughters and my family, like many others to varying degrees, was dysfunctional. We were, after all, immersed in a culture that was, in many respects, dysfunctional. I didn't blame my parents. In fact, I believed I chose my family before birth to serve my soul's purpose. But we don't come into this life with a manual on how to cope.

My father was an angry, mean, selfish man. Of course, he was more than that and did have some positive qualities, but those are the attributes that stick in my mind. To my knowledge, he never struck my mother or sisters in anger, other than to grab us kids mid-stride when we ran away from him and spank us with far too much zeal, which itself is no small thing. His method was to degrade, tease, and belittle; and to yell, curse, and throw things for effect.

He was a shotgun, finger perpetually poised on the trigger. The slightest vibration and the explosion unleashed, sending birdshot in every direction. You never knew where it would land or who it would hit, and an array of reactions ricocheted around my family, creating a somewhat different experience for each of us. I can only speak to my own.

Although it was never articulated, the clear message was that we were to walk on eggshells around my father. The whole family's well-being depended on it. Long before I learned to read, I mastered the ability to read my father's emotional state: every nuance of inflection or gesture; every warning of the storm to come, the dam about to burst. My whole focus was on him. Everyone's was. Watching, listening, trying to smooth things over. Working to keep him calm, make him happy. His emotional state was all that mattered, and it was our responsibility to care for his feelings at any cost, including the cost of our own. No boundaries. And the lingering vapors of unfair burdens, sacrifice, and sorrow hung in the air. It was suffocating.

Yet no matter how hard we tried to create peace, the blade of criticism kept cutting, and, the edge honed sharp with shame, the wounds ran deep. The pressure to be perfect, to do everything perfectly was immense. Dodging the pain of shame, I quickly learned to always be generous; to always protect everyone else's feelings without regard for my own; and to be diminished, "less than," both so others would feel good about themselves and to avoid attracting my father's attention and, so, his wrath. Essentially, I learned to be kind, nurturing, and selfless, and to bind my personal power. It was the only way to be accepted. It was the only way to be safe, or so I believed.

Being kind and nurturing came naturally, to a point. But the overwhelming feeling was that this was all so unfair. Yet everyone seemed to accept it without question. Confused, I spent hours upon hours contemplating, trying to make sense of it all. I could not.

Reflecting on this, it occurred to me that we really should listen to children more. Not yet indoctrinated into the mores of society, the things we either blindly accept or sweep under the rug, they embody the truth they came into this world with, and their guidepost is their sensations. It made me sick, the injustice of it. And it made me mad.

We didn't deserve my father's anger. He was cruel to us for no reason. Yet our lives revolved around him. He was the only one who had value. He was the only one whose needs were met. It was wrong, and I desperately wanted to stand up to him.

But sickened by the fighting and wanting peace more than anything for everyone's sake, I avoided rocking the boat, swallowed my anger, rarely confronted my father, and said little. Receding into the background, unseen and unheard, I watched, listened, and felt everything vividly. I took in all that went on and receiving was painful. And when it became more than I could bear, I disconnected. Mentally and emotionally, I disengaged and retreated to my own world.

At the time I believed I was rising above it, taking the higher road. But now, in retrospect, I realized that with no concept of healthy boundaries, dissociation was my only escape. It was instinct, self-preservation.

I'd since learned that dissociation is a common coping mechanism, particularly for children subjected to chronic abuse or a frightening, highly unpredictable home environment. Children are more able to step outside themselves, and the coping tool may continue into adulthood when confronted with trauma. I wanted to know more and asked Mary.

"When confronted with a situation out of the norm that our nervous system perceives as threatening, our system is overloaded and can't process the trauma in the moment. So, our consciousness steps aside and observes — it dissociates — and the body deals with the threat; it's our system's way of protecting us. Then when presented with a similar situation later, our system recognizes the threat and we immediately dissociate again," she said.

It explained so much. As a child I'd dissociated when my father flew into a rage. Then the first time Vinyard confronted us at our home, unable to process what was happening, I just stood there, inanimate, until Bruce took action and I followed suit.

Mary continued. "Stepping aside and observing, our consciousness remembers every detail of the event, but the traumatic memory is repressed and held in our system to process later."

My thoughts leaped back to the first time the reporter asked me to describe the invasions and how it felt to be stalked. I'd struggled to remember the details. Now suddenly I knew why it was so hard to tap those memories. At the time, my memories of those events were locked in my system along with the trauma. It was only by working with Mary that I was finally beginning to fully recall the horrors of the past.

"Exactly," she said. "And if the trauma is not healed, post-traumatic stress develops. To heal, one must access the trauma held in the body and release it."

According to Mary, dissociation was rampant in modern culture. For me, it was the only way I could be in my childhood home and take it. In fact, though entirely unaware of it at the time, I spent most of my youth dissociated to varying degrees; the pain of the world was just too much to bear. But as Mary pointed out, disconnecting from myself and the situation put me at risk of great harm. I hated to think what might have happened if Bruce hadn't been there and taken charge the first time Vinyard invaded us.

In the days that followed, my thoughts kept drifting back to my childhood. I wasn't sure when I began to see my father's flaws as weaknesses, but it was long before I was nine years old, the year he and my mother finally divorced. A child myself, I looked upon him as a younger, hurt child. Though I didn't know why, I knew that despite the fact that he was big, loud, and downright terrifying, he was suffering. And the combination of my general nature, I suppose, the conditioning of my family, and my religious upbringing instilled in me a conviction that stood against the storms. *Turn the other cheek. Be selfless, kind, and compassionate. Forgive him.*

In time, I did forgive my father, or at least honestly tried my best. But I was determined to be nothing like him. I would never be hateful, mean, angry, or selfish like him. I would never make others feel bad about themselves, and I would never, ever wield power and inflict pain. The darker he was, the more determined I was to hold the light. And I was suffering.

Who I had become, how I operated, not only within my family but in the world at large, was all about him and others. And deep within, concealed in the dark recesses of my soul, I was angry that my own needs were dismissed, that my feelings didn't matter; that I was not loved, not even seen. But to feel that was selfish. I would not be selfish. I was better than that. Denying my anger and selfishness, I was determined to rise above them and carry the light. Only the light. And suddenly, I saw it.

The harder I tried to be of the light, the more of myself I'd shoved down in the dark. Swinging the sword of judgment, I had severed my soul and split myself in two.

In that moment, I knew it was the darkness within me — the darkness I'd always felt yet refused to acknowledge — that was the barrier to giving myself compassion. Though I had no idea what it looked like or just how dark it was, I sensed its presence always, and the heavy weight of this formless guilt bearing down on me, I felt I didn't deserve compassion.

The path before me was now abundantly clear. If I was going to heal the duality within me, if I was going to discover my truth and live as my whole, authentic self, I would have to find the courage to walk into the darkest chambers of my soul and look squarely at the faces lurking in shadow — the bizarre, scary faces of my dream, the faces of myself I most didn't want to see.

Was I selfish? I knew I was. I didn't want to always take care of others. I wanted to be nurtured, to be taken care of myself sometimes. I wanted to do things, have things, experience things just for me. And maybe, if I really dug down into the darkness, part of why I chose to be the nurturer, the giver, was because I wanted to stand out and be admired.

And if I mustered the courage to dig deeper still, maybe giving to others was a defensive maneuver to keep all eyes off of me: the real person behind the mask, the person I wanted no one to see. On the other hand, maybe with no boundaries to protect me, it was the only defense I had against emotional abuse.

"That's correct," Mary said. "Being a giver is a form of control, a way to avoid receiving and being vulnerable. And control comes from fear."

It made perfect sense. I didn't want to feel — to receive — what my father gave; it was painful. And if I showed any vulnerability at all, I was immediately pounced upon and attacked. It was the way of bullies. They could smell it, it seemed. Mary concurred and said it was absolute abuse of woman's most basic nature: her vulnerability and receptivity.

Now that I faced it, my selfishness didn't seem so deplorable, and I realized that this perception, this judgment that to be selfish was wrong was so deeply ingrained in me, so hardwired into my identity that I had never before seen it as simply a belief, a choice my mind had made unconsciously long ago. And belief was not always truth. If all our beliefs were true, people wouldn't constantly be warring over them.

No, the face of selfishness in and of itself was not so ugly. In fact, when I took a good, long look at my selfish side, I saw myself as a child, wounded. Of course she wanted attention, to know she was loved and cherished. Of course she wanted to let her light shine brightly into the world, not keep herself small. Of course she wanted to be seen and valued for who she was, not just for what she could do for others. Of course she wanted to be protected, not sacrificed for her father and everyone else.

But from an early age, I had condemned myself for feeling selfish. It was cruel, and all that small child, that selfish side of me wanted was to be seen and heard and folded back into the loving embrace of my soul. In tears, I felt my heart reach out to ease her pain.

"Yes, when we integrate our shadow material, it doesn't look the same," Mary confirmed. "It's not nearly as ugly as we fear it is when we reject it and shove it into the unconscious. Things are distorted and grow larger in secrecy, in the dark."

Until that moment I hadn't known that, all along, Mary had been leading me to my shadow, gently drawing me to those parts of myself I'd disowned: the faces she'd seen clearly from the beginning and reached out to with compassion. She was guiding me to my lost self that, long-buried beneath layers of judgment and errant beliefs, awaited my return.

My mind drifted back to the old woman I'd seen in my vision years before. This quest was mine and mine alone, she'd assured me. *Seek, and you shall find.*

*   *   *

The existence of shadow was a startling revelation. *The secret hides within.* Could the answers I'd been seeking for so long actually be concealed in my own unconscious, here within me?

Once Mary gave me a taste of the shadow, I wanted the whole feast. She referred me to a primer on the subject. Soon I found it, dug in, and, recognizing many effects of unintegrated shadow material, highlighted it profusely. Then, digesting and reflecting on all I was learning, I journaled:

> All life seeks balance, wholeness. An ecosystem destabilized will always evolve toward restoring equilibrium. A body wounded will strive to heal itself. And a soul split in two by judgments of the mind will seek unity, wholeness once again.
>
> Wholeness isn't static; it's dynamic. Without the pulse of contrasts interacting with one another, there would

be no movement, no life. Without darkness, we would not know light. Destruction gives rise to creation. Only together do yin and yang form a whole, each with a bit of the other at its core.

Contrasts — positive and negative, light and dark — are not the same as good and bad; these are distortions born of judgment and fear. And when we perceive the world as black and white, good and bad, duality prevails. Duality: the illusion of separation. The illusion that one is acceptable and one is not, or that one is of Spirit and one is not. This is a fabrication. It is not the truth.

The true nature of contrasts is that each is an essential part of the whole. Without opposing polar forces interacting, bound together by an electromagnetic force, not a single atom or a single molecule would exist. Matter itself would not exist. To believe that one could or should exist without the other is ludicrous. And to believe that we can live in the light and not own our own darkness is a delusion. Yet we try. Every single day we try. So much life energy wasted denying the truth of our existence, the truth of who we are — who we are meant to be.

Every day we judge ourselves, consciously and unconsciously, and cast off those impulses and characteristics, attributes and desires we deem unacceptable. The shadow is our dumping ground where all we do not want to face about ourselves, all we do not want to own, is disposed of. But disowned, these facets of self do not go away. Split off and separated from our conscious awareness, they are banished to the depths of the unconscious.

There is a vast world beneath the ocean floor: fiery, creative forces powerful enough to shift entire continents and create new lands. And when aspects of the self are rejected, repressed, and shoved down into the unconscious, their true nature and wisdom distorted, in darkness and secrecy they operate in our lives in mysterious, powerful, and often destructive ways.

It is our shadow that sabotages us when we most want to succeed. It is shadow that draws to us the thing we most fear or don't want in our lives. When we act outside our integrity, shadow is behind it. When we behave in ways that are cruel then regret it, only to do it again, shadow is working beneath the surface. When we judge, vilify, and demonize people, shadow is showing its face. When, though they appear in different forms, we are repeatedly confronted by the same challenging people and situations, shadow is manifesting in our lives.

Severed from the conscious self and cast out, the shadow self's desire to return — to be seen for what it truly is; to be accepted, loved, and integrated — is immense. And hidden, it quietly reaches out, grasping, creating, drawing us to people and experiences that mirror what begs to be healed within us.

*   *   *

5/6/1998

Now that the judge in the felony assault case had denied the defense's motion to withdraw Vinyard's guilty pleas, the hearing to revoke the deferred sentence finally arrived.

In the hours before the hearing, I gave myself time to prepare. As would become my ritual before going to court, I holed myself up in a solitary space and lit a candle. Calling in Source, my higher self, guides, and guardians, I set up a sacred circle, closed my eyes, and sat in silence.

As Mary had taught me, drawing deep, slow breaths, I dropped my conscious awareness from my head down into the center of my gut then sank into my first chakra. From there, I dropped again. Further and further I descended, grounding myself deep in the center of the earth. Then breathing in, I drew that Earth energy up into my center and consciously opened my heart.

My awareness then reaching up and out, suddenly I was immersed in the most stunning shimmering, golden white light. Inhaling deeply, I drew that light in through my crown and down into my body. With each inhale, light filled me. With each exhale, it pushed further and further out, filling the energy field around me.

I then sensed my boundaries holding my space. Mesmerized, I watched as they danced and glowed. These were not barriers. They were healthy boundaries: fluid; permeable or not, according to my own free will. With each breath they expanded. With each breath, I grew larger.

Thoroughly absorbed in these amazing sensations, I felt energized, peaceful, and whole. Fully connected, I felt safe and powerful.

Then approaching the justice center, old trauma reared its head. My focus became shaky and my heart began to race. A bad case of nerves was quickly setting in. But though I struggled with it, I did remember to breathe, ground, and center from time to time. And occasionally, I remembered to put out a call to Source for help. Like an adolescent going through a growth spurt, I was awkward. It would take time and practice to walk comfortably with one foot in the spirit world and one on the ground under such stressful circumstances. In the years to come, I would have much more practice than I ever imagined. Thankfully, I had no idea of that at the time.

Once again, until the judge made a decision as to guilt or innocence, as a witness for the state, I would not be allowed in the courtroom before or after my testimony. I took the stand and Kathy asked a little about the stalking history. Quickly, she fast-forwarded to the phone calls of September 1997 and played the first of my recordings. Before long, I was dismissed. When it was over, the advocate called me with the results.

The probation officer had testified and said that before Vinyard was released from jail, he'd met with him to review the conditions of his probation. He'd emphasized that he was to have absolutely no contact with Bruce or me, he said.

Vinyard pled the Fifth and chose not to testify. Not taking any chances, the judge reviewed all his rights, asking him if he understood each and every one. Yes, he understood, Vinyard said.

Kathy asked if the judge wanted argument.

"Well, it seems pretty — I guess I want to hear from the defendant. How do I not make a finding that there's a breach of the conditions of the deferred by the telephone call?" the judge asked.

In response, Vinyard's attorney scraped the bottom of the barrel to dredge up a last-ditch defense: The judge could find that Vinyard had not violated the conditions of probation, he suggested, because the order specified my married name, not Anderson. My heart stopped when I heard this. It had, in fact, been an error in the court record. But the judge, I was told, decided that the law protected a person, not a name. Bracing myself, I drew another deep breath.

Previously, the defense had argued that the deferred sentence was a setup to fail. At this hearing, the judge responded. Reading directly from the transcript, he quoted the deputy DA: "What we've done with this disposition is place him in serious jeopardy should this continue — his attempt to contact directly or indirectly — of taking him out of the community and placing him in the Department of Corrections for as long as we humanly can." You were told by the prosecutor that this was a setup, that you will have no contact or you will go to prison, the judge said.

In the end, the judge found that by clear and convincing evidence, Vinyard had violated the terms and conditions of the deferred sentence. It was revoked. Sentencing was set for June 8, in a month, after the harassment trial. Assuming there would be a trial.

Later that day, Kathy called me to discuss the roadblocks ahead of us and her plan to navigate them. She felt the judge would sentence Vinyard to eight years in prison for the assault. It was highly likely, she said again, that he would impose a concurrent jail sentence for the harassment case. And if Vinyard was sentenced to the maximum eighteen months for that, by law the judge could not also impose probation. So, while in prison, Vinyard could buy down his time, "kill his numbers," and eliminate the possibility of parole. With no safety net to track him, he would walk away a free man.

To give us some protection, she felt it was best to plea bargain. Instead of jail time for the harassment charges, she wanted probation, starting when he was released from prison.

"Then the court could impose more jail time when he violates," she said. Not *if* he violates, *when* he violates. Again, no one doubted he would.

She planned to open her bid for probation at ten years — the ten years he'd never served out before — and to give him incentive to agree to the deal, she'd wrap the misdemeanor assault case into her offer. For that, she would offer credit for time served.

In the meantime, I was not giving up on the maximum sentences, served consecutively.

CHAPTER 15

New Moon

"If you don't feel it, you'll never get it."
~ Johann Wolfgang Goethe, Faust

It wasn't long before a plea deal was struck in the three misdemeanor cases. No trial.

The advocate called me with the details. Vinyard would plead guilty to misdemeanor assault, admit to violating the conditions of probation in the 1994 harassment-stalking case, and plead guilty to three counts of violation of restraining order in the current case. The harassment charges in that case would be dropped, she said.

For the misdemeanor assault: credit for time served. For the restraining order violations: probation, the length of which was capped at five years, not ten, and during which the defendant was to have no contact with us. Probation could be consecutive or concurrent with the sentence imposed for the felony assault; that was up to the judge.

The June 8 sentencing hearing would now be for all four cases. And once again, the felony assault was the only case that offered any hope of safety and peace.

The next week, the advocate called again. "The defense attorney thinks Vinyard is likely to file a motion to withdraw his guilty pleas in the assault case again. The judge can hear it if he chooses to. Kathy is concerned."

In fact, Vinyard did file a rather long motion, one he prepared himself. "Defendant, appearing pro se, due to a conflict of interest with the Public Defender's Office, moves this court to vacate ... ." Citing case law, he argued that his attorney provided him ineffective counsel when he took the plea deal. Now it was all her fault. And going "pro se," he planned to defend himself.

The reporter continued to follow the case for the *Boulder Planet* and another local paper, Boulder's *Daily Camera*, soon picked up the story.

6/8/1998

I never heard more about Vinyard's own motion to withdraw his guilty pleas, and though it seemed the day would never come, the sentencing hearing for all the cases was finally upon us, the judge in the felony assault case presiding. Once Vinyard entered his pleas, I was allowed in the courtroom.

The probation officer's nine-page report was presented to the judge. He concluded with his sentencing recommendation:

> Court orders seem to be meaningless to the Defendant and have had no effect in preventing the Defendant from his ongoing campaign of harassment. Though the Defendant has had several treatment episodes with a variety of mental health agencies in the past, it appears that has had little to no success in addressing the Defendant's obsession with women and violent tendencies. Past behavior is often times an accurate indicator of future behaviors. It is this Officer's opinion that when the Defendant is ultimately released from incarceration, he will shortly thereafter resume his campaign of stalking and harassing Ms. Anderson. Ms. Anderson, as well as the public in general, need to be protected from the Defendant for as long as possible.

His recommendation: the maximum prison sentence and the maximum length of probation after.

In the course of the hearing, Kathy called author Orion to the stand to testify as an expert in erotomania, but the defense claimed he was not prepared to cross-examine her. The hearing was continued to July 13.

But before the session concluded, the judge raised questions about Vinyard's diagnosis and treatability — questions asked and answered before. Given the long train of court proceedings over the years with multiple cases, prosecutors, defense attorneys, and judges, I was the only one present who knew the full history intimately. *He had been diagnosed and the delusional obsession does not respond to treatment.* My frustration peaking, it took every ounce of self-control to keep from jumping up and interjecting.

Seated in the audience, I was nowhere near Kathy. Vinyard, on the other hand, seated at the defense table, was passing notes to his attorney.

Then the judge looked directly at me and said he'd read the impact statements Bruce and I had submitted six months before. I sincerely appreciated hearing that; I'd never been sure he would. But when I heard his remarks that followed, I was dumbfounded.

If it was proven that Vinyard was not treatable, he would have no other choice but to sentence him to prison, he said. There it was. After all these years, the either-or again. Fix him instead of protecting us and the public. No accountability, no consequences for his actions. No comprehension that he had committed egregious crimes or that he was extremely dangerous, and as the probation officer had just concluded, we and the public needed protection from this man. There was another answer here: Incarcerate him and provide treatment. It really was that simple.

But when the judge continued, I was utterly astounded. Vinyard's crimes were not as violent as some, he said, adding that if the defendant had hit Bruce or me, the appropriate sentence would be clear.

My blood erupted into full boil. After all this and after reading my statement, he still had no comprehension of the peril we faced or the hell we had endured. I was determined to educate him about violence. And now, with the hearing continued, I would have another chance.

The next day, fear and anger mixed and combusted again. I pounded out a memo to Kathy, listing all my recommendations for the continuance. I'm sure it was a huge annoyance to her. I was not an attorney and didn't know beans about what could or should be done. But I had certainly seen the ball dropped enough over the years to resolve never to let it happen again. Ignoring Mary's coaching, I was desperate to wrestle some control over this whole calamity. My life was at stake. My children's lives were at stake. I could not, would not sit back and trust a system that had so hideously betrayed my trust, a system that had sacrificed us for this predator for nearly two decades.

I was uncomfortably aware that taking charge of my own defense was a mirror image of Vinyard's latest moves. It was as if the attorneys had become intolerable obstacles in the battle raging between us. But I would not let go of the reins. Two steps forward, one step back.

*   *   *

While nothing had changed in the judiciary and I did slip back into old habits from time to time, I sensed that something was different. My work with Mary was beginning to take hold. It didn't happen overnight and despite my regression experience and the revelation of shadow, it was not a Helen Keller-like epiphany where suddenly the true nature of the world was revealed and a life forever changed. It was a process. More, it was my process, apart from the stalking and the judicial process. This one thing was mine and mine alone. No one else could touch it. No one could take it from me. But it was not always consistent, comfortable, or clear.

In the days between our sessions, I worked with all the tools Mary had given me diligently. Still plagued with doubts that it would make any difference, our work was all I had, and I clung to her guidance with all my might.

When I felt resistance, I relaxed and listened closely to what was bubbling up from my unconscious. I wanted that information.

I was aware of my emotional hooks and where I sensed one, I relaxed and worked at surrendering it. When I could surrender and remembered to, I took a moment to feel gratitude for the lessons it had given me, as Mary had encouraged me to do, then I let it go. I saw it as a tightly strung cable that, when unhooked, whizzed back to whatever or whomever it was connected to, outside my field of vision.

Yet surrendering control of the outcome was not something I was willing to do. Fully aware of the fear and emotional hook there, I chose to override them; I could never forgive myself if I didn't do everything in my power to protect my children. It was a conscious choice. I prayed it was the right one.

When fury erupted, as it inevitably did, I could sometimes step back and focus and direct it in a positive way. Then I consciously stopped myself from turning it back on me. And letting go of self-judgment, I suddenly discovered I was much less judgmental of others.

My heart then softening and opening, I gradually allowed myself to receive a little more, and as I did, I found that my intuition was surprisingly strong. It, like compassion, was a gift I'd suppressed and locked away in my shadow long ago. Not everything condemned to shadow is what we commonly think of as negative, I discovered. Light, positive attributes are often imprisoned there as well. It just depends on our own judgments and fears.

Some of the things Mary had thrown at the wall were beginning to stick and sink in. Yet, while recognizing myself that I was making progress, self-doubt rolled through my mind in waves. Was I surrendering or dissociating, trusting or in denial? Was I holding my boundaries? Was my heart open? I was constantly checking in and rarely sure of the answer. My mind was working hard for control, and fear, doubt, and confusion were its tools of choice.

And though I was feeling more empowered, at the same time I felt weak and needy, feelings I strongly criticized. But as I'd start to beat myself up, I'd catch it, soften, and give myself grace. It's okay to be human, I'd coach myself. And as that gesture softened me a little more, allowing me to be vulnerable, tears began flowing freely.

Melancholy rose up from the depths, and pain and a tremendous sense of loss followed in its wake, softening me still further. This was not the depression I'd experienced on the heels of rage. This sadness flowed through me and was released. Yet the depth of my sorrow seemed bottomless. The tears kept coming. At times, it seemed they were all I had left.

I constantly felt drained and slept an inordinate number of hours. I struggled to focus on work. This — feeling all this emotion, being constantly self-aware — was my work, and at the moment it felt much more important than paying the bills. I gave myself time to be fully present with all that was coming up and to listen to the messages hidden in this strange mix of emotions. This, too, was receiving.

It seemed I was holding it all simultaneously, new ways of being and the old. And living two different paradigms at once — one centered in the mind (duality) and one centered in the heart (wholeness) — my system struggled to contain it. Bouts of flu-like symptoms and cold after cold hit me.

"It's a good sign," Mary assured me. "Your nervous system is shifting. This is the way it works. This is what integration looks like."

It wasn't pretty. Though pieces of the puzzle were falling into place, the picture was nowhere near complete. I was a work in progress.

At times it was déjà vu all over again where nothing, it seemed, had changed. I was stuck in the same endless loop.

But ever so subtly, my experience of the nightmare was changing. *I* was changing. It was time to take the next step into the hidden, mysterious realm of the shadow.

*   *   *

"When we repress aspects of ourselves we do not want to see, shoved into the unconscious, this shadow material becomes the dragon in the basement that won't be contained. It squeaks out sideways," Mary said.

It was a light-hearted way of describing something that was anything but. I had seen the dragon "squeak out sideways" myself. Angry with my father and the whole situation in my childhood home, my temper would, on occasion, lash out fiercely toward my sisters, as theirs did toward me. Then, ashamed of myself, I'd force the genie back in the bottle and shove the cork down harder.

Mary continued, "When it is rejected and denied, the shadow is projected out into the world. We all do it all the time. And when the mind is projecting our unintegrated shadow material onto others and our experiences, we can't see them clearly. The image we see is distorted, overlain by our own projections."

I imagined myself in a movie theater, my shadow projecting images of its own making through my mind and onto the screen in front of me. The screen was real, the images merely an optical illusion — an illusion powerful enough to draw me into the story as if, in that moment, what I saw was real.

I then thought of Vinyard's delusions: his conviction that I wanted a relationship with him and his illusions of me. Personally, I never met the woman he was obsessed with. She was a fantasy, a projection of his own making. Was I, too, projecting my shadow?

"We all have positive and negative, masculine and feminine within us," Mary said. "Your father despised and refused to own his positive feminine aspects, and he projected them onto you and the other women in your family. And with no boundaries, you unconsciously carried his projections for him. Then he degraded and belittled you. You took the hits."

In my gut, I felt it was true. I could almost see the tangled web of our family dynamic begin to unravel.

"But your instinct was to resist all the garbage thrown at you — his and everyone else's projections — so you did the only thing you knew how to do. You shut down and closed yourself off from receiving. And later, when you were stalked, your instinct kicked in again and you shut down completely."

Closing my eyes, I tuned into my heart and focused my awareness on the sensation I felt every time Mary encouraged me to open up and allow myself to receive. It was a deep-seated fear that if I opened my heart, everything would come in, including all the pain.

"That's because you had no boundaries, no filter," Mary assured me.

The pieces were falling into place. With no boundaries — no separation between what was rightfully my father's and what was ours — believing we were being kind and trying to keep the peace, we assumed responsibility for and protected his feelings. It was not a kindness, but a disservice. Withholding the real consequences of his actions from him, we'd robbed him of the opportunity to learn from his choices. And carrying his burden ourselves, we suffered — needlessly. It served no one. No one. In fact, it enabled his abuse.

"Your father projected his positive feminine onto all of you, and at the same time, you rejected your father's behavior and chose to be nothing like him. You shoved your own negative masculine aspects into your shadow and, unconsciously, projected them onto your father," Mary said.

He was the angry one; he was the one who was selfish and mean, I'd believed. Mary was right. My mind raced back to the diagrams she'd drawn before, but now more information was revealed:

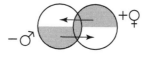

With no boundaries, merged, my whole family functioned as one entity. And — just focusing on my own relationship with my father — with me rejecting my negative masculine and my father rejecting his positive feminine, our shadow projections were reciprocal. We were thoroughly enmeshed.

And when being merged became too uncomfortable, I pushed away and isolated myself:

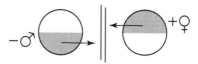

Then suddenly, it dawned on me. Though I eventually liberated myself from my father, I still presented in the world as half the equation, and — life always seeking wholeness, balance — I was a magnet for narcissists. Not always, by any means. But once in a while.

I had long seen the similarities between my father and Vinyard yet had no idea why I was confronted with yet another selfish, volatile, and abusive person: one who believed only his feelings mattered, that I existed only to serve his needs, and that my feelings and desires were of no consequence at all. For so many years, I'd asked why this was in my life. Now finally, after all these years, the missing piece of the puzzle was handed to me.

Condemning my father's behavior, I became everything he was not and nothing that he was. I constructed a self that was, in essence, his opposite. Light to his darkness, I was his counterpart and — half the equation, half the whole — I was locked in duality.

Then when I finally separated myself from my father, it wasn't many years before the stalker appeared. In just about every way imaginable, we were polar opposites.

What does the selfless giver who feels responsible for protecting others' feelings attract? The selfish taker who refuses to take responsibility for himself. The gears meshed perfectly, and I was locked in duality once again. Duality within, duality without.

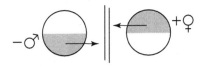

I thought of the needy, self-centered people I'd known before. I was the one they came to for counsel and comfort. It was a repeating pattern in my life and every time, my response was to try all the harder to be a "good" person and to, one way or another, quietly slip away from them.

But, though I was entirely unaware of it, the more I tried to be of the light, the larger my shadow and the brighter my beacon, drawing those I most didn't want in my life directly to me. Those who, unwilling to own their own inner light, wanted mine. Those who reflected my own shadow back to me.

I hadn't known about the existence of shadow, so had not seen it operating beneath the surface nor acknowledged its — my own — power to manifest things in my life. Now and for nearly two decades, what had manifested was a selfish taker in the extreme: a ruthless predator. One who would not be stopped. One who demanded no less than my sacrifice.

"That's correct," Mary said. "He is projecting his light, positive feminine onto you. It's why he wants to merge with you. It's why he chose you to hold onto and do battle with. Your will to hold the light is as strong as his is to have it. Unconsciously, he believes that if he can possess you, he can have his positive feminine and be healed."

Thinking aloud, I uttered the words he'd written long ago: "You can save me."

"Yes, and projecting his light shadow onto you — that part of himself he has rejected — he both loves you and hates you. Unconsciously, he thinks, 'I want you, but I'm going to destroy you.'"

My thoughts drifted back to Orion's book. "What makes erotomanic delusions so tenacious?" she'd asked. "Perhaps it is because erotomanics feel utterly incomplete without their objects. They need to be made whole by some highly esteemed other."

To the erotomanic stalker, the stakes could not be higher; he believes he's dependent on the object of his obsession for life itself, that his very survival depends on it, Orion wrote.

I was to be his savior. And his sacrificial lamb. No, never again. I had no desire to be a martyr, and I would not be sacrificed for anyone.

Vinyard's appearance in my life was showing me aspects of my lost self — anger, power, and selfishness among them — big time. And the larger and more threatening his presence, the more resolutely I'd rejected them until, in my dream, I believed that to finally be rid of those characteristics Vinyard was mirroring, I would have to kill not only him, but myself.

Yet something inside me knew better. I didn't have to take half the poison. I didn't have to eliminate my shadow. I needed to heal it.

But how could I heal my shadow? And how could I sever the connection between Vinyard and me and finally end this living hell? Mary had already shown me the way. I was already doing the work. Wake up! Be self-aware. Bring what is unconscious into consciousness, and embrace all that I am.

Once feared, compassion had been condemned to my shadow. Again, anger, power, and selfishness were banished there as well. Yet all it had taken to begin healing was to recognize the hook when I felt it and, with the help of a skilled guide to hold the light and protect, follow the trail of breadcrumbs into the darkness within. Then, surrendering resistance, judgment, and fear, to open my heart and embrace what was mine.

This was integration, and each time I experienced it, the fog of confusion I'd labored under so long lifted. I felt such relief, clarity, and peace.

"When aspects of ourselves are shoved into shadow and repressed, we are suffering," Mary confirmed, "and when we pull back our projections and integrate shadow material, not only is our suffering relieved, we no longer see the world and others through the mind's distortions. We see things clearly, as they really are."

Pull back my projections, I thought as I closed my eyes and set my intention. Then tuning into the sensation, comprehension dawned:

Pulling back my projections and taking responsibility for what was mine, I was pulling back my power and filling up my space. I physically felt it and I understood.

To know not only why, but how my shadow manifested things in my life — how this experience was drawn to me; how fears, judgments, and beliefs actually shape our reality; and how our projections alter it — was empowering.

Before, unaware that my shadow self existed, much less that it was expressing itself in my life, I felt powerless to change my experience. Now I knew that by integrating those aspects of myself I had condemned to shadow — by drawing them out of the unconscious and into consciousness and love — the choice of how to harness their wisdom, creativity, and power would be mine. My conscious choice how they'd be expressed in the world. My conscious choice what I would manifest, free from the interference of shadow.

A whole new world view had been presented to me. It was the birth of a new paradigm, and the veil lifted, our true nature was revealed. For the first time, I saw just how powerful we are.

I did not have the power to change Vinyard's obsession or his behavior. As Mary had said, "You are not responsible for his delusions or his actions; you are only responsible for yourself." The power to heal the wounds within him was in his hands only.

But beyond a doubt, I had the power to release myself from my connection to him. I had the power to choose not to carry his projections and to pull back my own and, embracing both my light and my darkness, to heal the fissure within me and become whole once again. And when I was whole, the projections of others — be they dark or light, positive or negative — seeking someone to carry them, would not find a home in me.

Within and without, I'd be released from the bonds of duality that had strangled my life and imprisoned me. And boundaries in place, grounded, connected to myself and higher powers, I'd be free to connect with others. Free to open my heart, without fear.

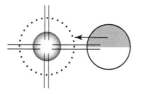

"Take back what is yours and give him back what is his," my first counselor had said. At the time, I had no idea what was mine to own. Now, after all these years, I finally understood.

CHAPTER 16

Full Moon

"Circumstance does not make a man. It reveals him."
~ James Allen

Working with all the tools Mary had given me, with each subtle shift in my consciousness, I was inspired to learn more, grow more, evolve. With every challenge, every clue — inner and outer — I looked inward and asked what it was showing me about myself. This was the quest, and the path led deeper and deeper into the shadowy depths of my unconscious.

What is it that needs to be integrated, I'd ask? *What needs healing? What is mine to own?* And it wasn't long before anger stood front and center, challenging me to deal with it.

Anger. I'd always had a lot of judgment around it, and while fully aware that my anger was justified, I fiercely fought against it. But the enemy never retreated. Repressed, it had only grown larger. Shoved into shadow, locked in the dungeon of my unconscious, it had become the dragon in the basement. It was time to set it free.

Anger was a tool, an aspect of power, Mary had said. My anger, my power — to take responsibility for and to own.

Whatever anger I'd been projecting onto others, it was time to call it back. And whatever anger I was carrying for others, it was time to give it back.

The thought of what the full range of my wrath would look like and do to me given everything I had endured was downright scary. The only way I could even begin to approach it was to ask higher powers for help and trust that help would be given.

In darkness lies illumination, if only we approach it with love, I coached myself. Then, tentatively, I reached out and began.

Please help me. Help me give back the anger that belongs to others, and help me take back the anger that is mine to own and use it for the highest and best purpose.

Day after day, I affirmed my intention and consciously opened my heart, and though I never saw the ugly monster I feared nor understood what anger I'd carried for others, I suddenly found I had more energy than I remembered having in years. And insights, new levels of awareness hit me like bolts of lightning, landing directly in my gut, not my head. I felt them plunge into my lower chakras, particularly my power center.

It was just as Mary had said. Things lurking in my shadow didn't look the same when drawn into consciousness and transmuted by love. Rejected and buried, the shadow's character and dimensions were grossly distorted. But unearthed, its true form was revealed. Integrated, anger was positive, energizing, enlightening — and powerful.

I knew this work wasn't done for me. It wasn't complete. From time to time, my anger still lashed out with a razor's edge. But I marveled at the process and the results. Working with my experiences rather than resisting them, looking into the mirror that each held up for me, and seeking out and healing deeper and deeper wounds, I was becoming integrated and learning to live from my center as my true, authentic self.

It was then I realized that, so much of myself imprisoned in shadow, I had been living an impoverished life. When I opened my mind and expanded my awareness beyond good and bad, beyond black and white, the full range of color — the full richness of my own soul and all of life — was revealed to me.

*   *   *

To my surprise, the saga continued to gain notoriety, and before long, reporters for the ABC news magazine *20/20* contacted the DA's office. They were exploring a piece on stalking and asked permission to bring cameras into the courtroom to film the upcoming sentencing hearing. The DA had no objection. The defense did — twice. I too was consulted and gave my consent.

Word was that Boulder County district judges never allowed cameras to film in their courtrooms. But not taking "no" for an answer, ABC sent an attorney to present its case. In the end, the judge consented on the condition that those witnesses who didn't want to be videotaped would not be. Vinyard chose not to be filmed.

*   *   *

The sentencing hearing drawing nearer, I dedicated myself to writing an addendum to the impact statement I'd submitted to the judge. One morning as I sipped my coffee, bracing myself to hit the keyboard again, I opened the *Daily Camera* and a small article jumped off the page.

"HOLLYWOOD. **Spielberg stalker gets 25 years in prison.** A man convicted of stalking Steven Spielberg was sentenced to 25 years to life in prison Wednesday after the director told the judge he feared for his life. 'If he's out on the street, I will live in fear,' Spielberg said."

According to the article, a few months earlier, the stalker had been convicted of plotting to invade Spielberg's mansion, hold him and his family hostage, and rape the director. Had the stalker actually confronted him, Spielberg said, "I genuinely in my heart of hearts believe that I would have been raped or maimed or killed."

The superior court judge agreed. The stalker was "obsessive and frightening, and I think he does present a danger to society," the judge concluded.

Hot liquid threatening to escape the lip of my cup, I shook off my stupor and quickly righted it. Then slamming my cup on the table, I grabbed the page and ran down to my office. *Thank you. Thank you.*

As I carefully arranged the page on my scanner, the full irony hit me. *He plotted. Had he actually confronted him. Twenty-five years to life.* And in my case, after nearly twenty years of ruthless predation by Vinyard, his consequences and the protection we were now afforded for the "violation of restraining order" charges was probation. The injustice was beyond belief. Renewed outrage added fuel to the fire and soon my addendum was done.

Once I'd recounted the most overt invasions throughout the history of stalking, I tackled the judge's shocking statement that if Vinyard had hit one of us, the appropriate sentence would be clear:

> In terms of physical violence, I firmly believe that the only reason we have not been physically harmed more is because we have always escaped and/or called for protection in time. But I have asked myself how we define violence.
>
> Regardless of the legal definition of violence, I know that we have experienced multiple acts of violence by Mr.

Vinyard. Webster defines violence in several ways, among them: "characterized or caused by harsh, destructive force; marked by intensity of force or effect; exhibiting or caused by intense emotional or mental force; sudden, intense energy."

"Violence," in the true sense of the word, does not dissect us as human beings. It does not merely refer to physical force. If someone has been held hostage at gunpoint and is finally released without a gunshot wound, has she experienced a violent act?

My own experience and all the court-ordered psychiatric evaluations tell me that the defendant is a loaded gun. I have been held hostage by this man nearly half my life. ... Stalking is an extremely violent act on one's emotions and psyche — not at one point in time, but repeatedly. The acts of violence we have endured mentally and emotionally are as extreme, unconscionable, and unjustifiable as any strike. I ask that you very clearly state this to the defendant, in both words and actions.

Searching for a way to get through to the judge, I reflected on all the testimonials I'd written over the years. What more could I possibly say that would open his eyes? What could I say to persuade him to look into his heart? It was my own heart that answered me.

With all the abuses I'd experienced at the hands of Vinyard and the gavel of the court, the thing that tortured me most all these years was seeing my children suffer. In recent months, their anxieties had again manifested in tandem with my own. Their symptoms, both physical and emotional, were heartbreaking.

Now, a cruel dilemma confronted me. Revealing the depth of my love for them and my fear for their safety could redirect Vinyard from me to them. As he had before with Bruce and as was the nature of his delusional obsession, he could perceive them as obstacles, and the risk to them could increase exponentially. But if I didn't expose the truth of their experiences, my only chance for a long period of peace and protection for them might be lost. Vinyard knew of their existence. He'd been handed that information in my timeline.

It was with tremendous regret that, to protect them as best I could, I finally broke my silence:

> In all the information I have previously provided, I have not focused on the impact to my children, not wanting to draw attention to them for obvious reasons. But I am here to tell you the vivid truth of the nightmare we have all endured.
>
> My children have been dealing with this ordeal through most of their childhood — those formative years when they need to feel secure, safe, protected, and cared for by their parents and their community.
>
> My oldest child is thirteen years old. He does not consciously remember the ordeal of being confronted at our home, but I am certain it has deeply affected him subconsciously. Four years ago, he accidentally overheard the unexpected threatening message left by the defendant on his father's telephone. We gently explained the situation as best we could and felt it was best to include him, as appropriate, and keep him informed of the defendant's status. So since he was nine years old, he has had to cope with this horrendous ordeal as an adult would.
>
> I asked him if he would like me to share any of his feelings about his experience. Only now, through counseling, is he able to begin facing his fear and his anger himself. He asked me to tell you, Your Honor, that during the times the defendant has been free and during the harrowing experience of his arrest last fall, he was constantly afraid. He could not concentrate on his schoolwork. He said he was worried for the children's safety, and even more, he was worried about mine.
>
> Repeatedly he asks me, "Why don't they just put him away, Mom? No one should be able to do this to anyone else." My only answer is that I have asked myself the same question many times, that a lot of things need to be changed and with our experience, courage, and strength, we can help change them. I want nothing more than to

be able to tell him he will never have to worry about the defendant again.

I have struggled a great deal to decide what and when to tell my youngest children the truth of the situation. Today they do not know of Mr. Vinyard or of the stalking ordeal. Honestly, it is too horrifying for most adults to cope with, much less young children. I have chosen instead to focus on repairing the damage done with reassurance and understanding, trying myself to be as stable and confident as possible in the face of relentless terror.

We cannot protect them from the fear or the danger. When the defendant is free, I do not let them play outside and friends don't visit them at home because I am never sure it is safe. We practice safety drills with escape routes. When the defendant is free, we are prisoners, ready to defend ourselves at any moment.

During the three weeks the defendant was free on probation last fall, his arrest, and several months following, there were numerous signs that my children were suffering. ...

I described the nightmares, the monsters feared, the stories of families fleeing for safety. The constant chewing on lips and fingers until they were painfully raw. The chronic stomachaches.

I related the story one child wrote about a spider that wouldn't go away, then I attached it to my statement. I disclosed all of their problems sleeping and more.

I shared the fact that, as their symptoms worsened in recent months, teachers began contacting me, concerned for the children's well-being. They told me stories of uncharacteristic classroom behavior and of drifting off into their own private worlds during school. *Dissociation*, I'd thought. *The only way they could escape the pain.*

I felt heartsick as I wrote the words.

There is simply no way that we can protect the children from this ordeal when the defendant is free.

These few examples provide merely small windows into our world because of Mr. Vinyard's escalating campaign of stalking. The ever-present fear has penetrated our lives much more than I can convey. Episodes like this repeat every time the defendant is free.

The last two times Mr. Vinyard was released from jail, he contacted me within three weeks. And each time he is arrested, I spend countless months ... devoting time and energy to court proceedings — time which should have been devoted to my family and career.

We are working hard to heal our family, and I can tell you, it will take a very long time. But it will not be complete as long as we continue to be predated. My children have been robbed of the childhood they should have had, one free of this abominable violation. ...

Determined to present a broader view, to help the judge see the decision before him through our eyes, I then tackled the length of sentencing:

Last fall, in violation of three separate court orders, the defendant contacted me three times shortly after his [most recent] release from jail. He was charged with felony stalking. Due to the interpretation of the credible threat language in Colorado's stalking statute, that was subsequently reduced to three counts of misdemeanor violation of restraining order. For that, the defendant is being sentenced today to five years of probation. ...

His previous probation sentence in the stalking conviction of 1995 was ten years. Of that he spent a total of three weeks on probation before he was finally caught and arrested for violating the conditions of probation. But the ten-year probation period has been dismissed, and now he will serve five years of probation. My feelings about those numbers must be obvious.

I understand that probation provides assurance that he ... will be monitored upon release from prison.

Monitored. Absolutely no consequences for the crimes he committed and absolutely no protection for us during probation, as he has *without exception* violated every court-ordered no-contact condition throughout nearly two decades of stalking.

And in the last year, his level of violence has twice escalated to assaulting peace officers. These are people well trained in self-defense. Imagine my children in hand-to-hand combat. I have seen his rage every time I have told him to leave me alone. I know the danger.

I understand that the potential range of sentence in revocation of the deferred sentence is not five to sixteen years, as was previously stated in the deferred sentence hearing, but is now four to twelve years in the Department of Corrections. In four years, my youngest child will be eleven years old, my oldest seventeen. All still at home, all in adolescence. In twelve years, my youngest will be nineteen, my oldest twenty-five. Perhaps at least my oldest will have escaped any direct threat by the defendant upon his release from prison.

I am well aware, however, that these numbers do not take into consideration the fact that when the defendant serves 30 to 40 percent of his sentence, he will likely be eligible for parole. With a four-year sentence, the defendant could be released in just over one year from the time his sentence will have begun. Exactly when his sentence begins, I'm not sure, but I believe some of the jail time he has served during these court proceedings will be credited to his prison sentence. Even with the maximum twelve-year sentence, it is possible that the defendant could be released in approximately three and a half years.

And each time he is eligible for parole, I will be notified and allowed to testify — more of my life devoted to court proceedings just to ensure we are free from terror. These are the numbers I will have to explain to my children.

Every time Mr. Vinyard acts on his delusion, there are consequences. Up to now, we, the victims, have been forced to bear the burden by default. In and out of courtrooms, with bond releases and disappearances, police warnings, deferred sentences, and revocation of deferred sentences, it wasn't until 1995 that Mr. Vinyard first spent time in jail for his crimes against us. That is a period of fifteen years that we endured the impacts of his actions before he did. ...

One of Webster's definitions of the term "victim" is "sacrifice." Not only has the defendant continually rationalized the sacrifice of me and Bruce to fulfill his delusional desires, but I feel we have been sacrificed to his mental illness by the judicial system. And to what end? What good can possibly come from this? When the defendant is free, we or the next target he chooses for his obsession are imprisoned. Not just me, but my entire family. As I have said before, I fear for our lives, and according to the experts in the field (see victim impact statement, January 1998), this fear is justified.

For comparison, I launched into Steven Spielberg's case. Then I reminded the judge of the deferred sentence hearing, the hearing he presided over himself:

The defendant was clearly told once again that if he attempted any form of contact, he would be placed in prison for as long as possible. According to the transcripts, he was also asked repeatedly if he understood all aspects of the deferred sentence agreement. Without exception, his answer was "yes." The defendant has made his choice. ...

Mr. Vinyard has never taken responsibility for his crimes; he has always blamed me and has continually tied up the court's and my time by filing endless motions and quoting case judgments which he believes will rescue him from accountability. He has negotiated every conviction and then violated every agreement. He has continually proclaimed that his crimes are not serious, and he has never expressed any remorse. In fact, during the first sentencing hearing in your courtroom in June, as I was leaving the courtroom, Deputy DA Kathy Delgado and [the probation officer] both overheard the defendant call out to me, "Next time wear a dress." This is a game to him, with graver and graver consequences.

Not once in all these years has he complied with court-ordered conditions. He has repeatedly made his choice. The consequences are clear. If the sentence is reduced or negotiated, the message given is that his illness renders him unaccountable, allowing him free rein to commit more acts of terror or worse. The long history of this case clearly demonstrates that the lack of consequences has enabled him to delve further and further into his mental illness. It has given him permission and the opportunity to explore the playground of his delusional obsession.

I reminded the judge that Vinyard was not only a danger to us; he'd stalked before. His next target could be anyone, I wrote and stressed, "It has been proven again and again that the sentence withheld from him is the sentence given to us or his next victim."

In closing, I listed all the conditions of probation I could think of to provide us the greatest protection possible. And finally I asked that, before his release from prison, Vinyard be informed, on the record, of any changes to Colorado's stalking statute, including the definition of stalking, conduct that constituted stalking, and the penalties. We were going to change the law, and no way in hell would I be tripped up by "it wasn't explained to me clearly" again.

7/13/1998 - Day of the sentencing hearing

A somber, momentous day, the continued sentencing hearing for all the cases before the court finally arrived. Knowing I would need all the help and support I could get, that morning I visited Mary.

"What would you like to do today?" she asked.

"Guided imagery. I want to see whatever I need to prepare me," I said, surrendering completely to the wisdom of higher powers.

It was always easier to drift into a deep meditative state in Mary's presence. She held the space energetically for me to sink into, and I trusted that she would stand guard.

I began, as always, by walking into a garden. Yet this time, I found myself not in a refined, cultivated garden, but in a dense, wild jungle environment, hot and humid.

Shrouded in a thick, damp fog, I glanced around the clearing and discovered a narrow footpath that reached into a tangle of enormous leaves and vines then quickly disappeared in the tall, crowded growth beyond. Mammoth trunks and canopies towering over my head surrendered only glimpses of the deep indigo night sky above. In every direction, as far as I could see, there was nothing but dense, dark forest.

Mary encouraged me to step onto the path and walk on, noticing the feel of the ground under my feet, the scents in the air, the colors and textures of all the life around me.

"Touch it. Feel it," she urged. "Tell me what you see."

Focusing on my task, I quickly discovered that the ground was so dark and the jungle so dense, it was impossible to get my bearings. Only the moonlight's reflection on dewdrops clinging to leaves and the subtle play of shadows and light guided me. Finally, once my eyes adjusted and I was fully in that place, seeking, Mary let me go. We both trusted the way would be shown to me.

Slowly, I picked my way through the darkness pressing in. My senses heightened, it took all my concentration just to stay on the path. I had begun at the foot of a large hill. Now I gradually climbed, switching back and forth as I inched my way upward.

At one point, when I glanced up to get a sense of where I was headed, a glimmer of amber light in the distance caught my eye. It rose from a small clearing near the top of the hill.

Smoke, I smelled smoke. Then the sound of distant drums, their sober beat pounding a proclamation of undeniable power through the air. I drew closer and, beneath the chorus of drums, heard the low drone of chanting. *People.*

At last, reaching the crest of the hill, I broke through the tangle of forest and crouched at the edge of a clearing bathed in the blinding oranges of arcing flames and sparks that exploded and drifted off wildly into the now black, starry skies.

Tucked in the undergrowth, hidden from view, I watched. *Tribal people.* Garbed in colorful feathers and pale bones, crude spears and loincloths, these people were in a frenzy, chanting, calling, and dancing riotously around a bonfire.

The deafening rhythm of rattles and drums filling the air rose to a crescendo, then suddenly it stopped.

All eyes turned to me. I was expected, it seemed.

Frightened, I called up my courage, walked into the center of the circle, and looked around at the figures surrounding me. Their aged, painted faces were obscured by masks. Their eyes, hidden in the dark recesses, were visible only by the firelight reflected in them. *The tribal council.*

Then beyond the council's circle, a vague, shadowy mass appeared where the forest's darkness met the fire's light. *Other tribal members, the lower rung of the hierarchy,* I thought.

Finally, my gaze landed on the person seated directly in front of me. With the presence of royalty, this rather small man sat on a heavily carved and painted raised dais. *The chief.*

I studied him closely. In his right hand, held firmly upright, was an ornamental feathered spear: his staff. Above his bare feet, a leather strap bearing feathers, rattles, and bones draped his withering calves. Above his elaborate loincloth, his frail, sunken chest was adorned with layers of necklaces so thick and heavy, it seemed they would swallow him whole. His face, too, was painted. He wore no mask.

He was staring me down, but when I looked into his eyes, my own were drawn upward. A gigantic spray of brightly colored feathers adorned his head. From his crown, the gaudy headdress soared to more than twice the height of his torso. Shifting my focus, I took in the whole man. He was, well, ridiculous!

Only the occasional crack of the fire penetrated the heavy silence. They were waiting for me to speak — my last words, as it were, before the chief passed judgment. My fear gone entirely now, I looked them all over again and the words rose up from the depths of my soul. It was my truth through and through.

Facing the chief, I said confidently and authentically, "You have no power over me."

It was an archaic, primitive culture. The chief's presumed authority had no basis in truth.

When I emerged from the jungle and opened my eyes, Mary and I looked at each other and dissolved into a fit of laughter over the heavily symbolic, highly entertaining B-movie imagery presented to me. Spirit, my guides, my higher self — all who conspired to create this vision — had a keen sense of humor, it seemed. And I got the message loud and clear.

It wasn't a lesson learned in my head. It was gnosis: an intuitive knowing, direct divine revelation. A shift in my perception and so, in my entire being.

I owned my true, authentic power. No one could take it from me. No one had power over me.

CHAPTER 17

Eclipse

"The individual has always had to struggle to keep from being overwhelmed by the tribe. If you try it, you will be lonely often, and sometimes frightened. But no price is too high to pay for the privilege of owning yourself."
~ *Friedrich Nietzsche*

7/13/1998 – Sentencing hearing

3:00 PM. When Kathy held the door open and I entered the courtroom, a hush fell over the room, and en masse, the spectators' heads turned toward me. The size of the audience filling row upon row of benches gave me pause. Scanning the sea of strange faces, I seized on the warm smiles of several friends, who had come to support me, and nodded my appreciation.

Stepping into the aisle, a collection of attorneys and uniformed deputies strategically placed around the room came into view. Then continuing up the aisle, my gaze landed on the foot of the bench — the throne — and my eyes were drawn upward. There, in his black, flowing robes, his gavel resting near his hand, sat the judge. And continuing upward, in my mind's eye, a gargantuan headdress of soaring, gaudy feathers, their fine tips bent slightly as they brushed the ceiling. I smiled.

Video cameras poised in the corner, the hearing finally began. Normally, I was told, sentencing hearings lasted about fifteen minutes. This would become a marathon seven-hour event. And though the only felony charge was for assaulting an officer, the entire hearing revolved around Vinyard's stalking.

As the hearing progressed, I noticed copies of Orion's book appearing around the room. It was the bible that everyone carried and referred to. At long last, the stalker's obsession, delusions, and conduct were seen for what they truly were. Ignorance no longer prevailed. *Thank you, Dr. Orion. Thank you from the bottom of my heart.*

Kathy presented a mass of evidence demonstrating the current contacts in violation of the deferred sentence for the felony assault, the long history of stalking me and Bruce in violation of court orders, the long history of refusing treatment, and the long-documented danger. Then she surprised me.

She'd followed up on the stalking and attempted kidnapping charges in Aurora and told the judge that Vinyard was convicted of harassment-stalking and disorderly conduct in that case. According to Kathy, the woman testified that Vinyard followed her, and when she turned around and asked him to leave her alone, he said, "You can run, but you cannot hide, bitch."

Kathy also presented a police report from 1993 (when we had disappeared) from the Town of Fairplay, Colorado. In it were statements from five women who claimed that Vinyard harassed them and wouldn't take "no" for an answer. One woman reported that when she rejected his advances in a restaurant, he grabbed her arm and said, "You lied to me, you [expletive]," and that, as she pulled away and kept walking, he yelled, "You bitch."

Kathy continued, "The officer had an opportunity, Your Honor, to speak with Mr. Vinyard about his behavior at the restaurant, and Mr. Vinyard informed the officer that he wanted to go to — he wanted to go to the Fairplay area with 'victim woman' ... ."

He also followed other women around the town, Kathy said. One was a sixteen-year-old girl.

I'd seen the police report myself. It also included an incident in which an officer said he approached Vinyard for shouting obscenities in a public place — a playground. The officer reported that Vinyard was combative and that when the officer tried to cuff him, Vinyard attacked him. He was booked and processed for harassment, resisting arrest, and second-degree assault on a peace officer. That was familiar.

"I am also trying to contact his mental health caseworker," the officer noted.

Soon, Kathy called a sergeant at the county jail to testify about Vinyard's behavior there. I hadn't heard any specifics about the jail issues before, and as the full story unfolded, I felt my heart racing. By my count, in the ten months since his most recent arrest, there were twelve incidents discussed, including altercations with other inmates and officers; racial slurs, sexual slurs, and obscene language; and on more than one occasion, attempting to make "hooch" in his cell.

When asked, the sergeant said that most of the time he'd been in jail, particularly since his last arrest, Vinyard was housed in either the max module or the disciplinary module, the highest security parts of the jail. Unusual, he added, given that they like to move people out of the higher security areas to less restricted areas of the jail as soon as possible.

Kathy asked if he'd witnessed any of the altercations and, if so, to describe what the defendant was like at the time:

> Sergeant: … I particularly remember observing the one where the officer got involved — to forcibly remove him — and the officer was struck in the mouth. During the course of this incident, in my opinion, he looked like an animal.
>
> Prosecution (Kathy Delgado): Did he appear dangerous?
>
> Sergeant: No doubt in my mind.
>
> Prosecution: As a result of your witnessing these altercations and investigating the evidence, have you determined what it takes for Mr. Vinyard to become angry and aggressive?
>
> Sergeant: No idea.

Three psychiatrists gave expert testimony, including, for the prosecution, Iverson and Orion. When the defense (the same attorney I'd done battle with in earlier hearings) cross-examined Iverson, he began, predictably, by focusing on the physical harm to us, his questions carefully framed to minimize Vinyard's actions:

> Defense: In terms of actual violence — let me rephrase that. In terms of instances where there has been assault, they are relatively few, are there not?
>
> Iverson: Let me refer to Ms. Anderson's timeline.
>
> Defense: Actually, if you would just answer that question. I have more specific questions on that issue.

Iverson: I would say that they are not few and they are significant.

Undeterred, the defense alluded to the physical "altercation" with Bruce on our porch and another incident in the 1980s (I presumed the night Vinyard attacked our home) and continued:

Defense: Okay. And as far as the other instances where there was physical contact, what are those?

Iverson: Physical contact with either [victim] — at the time there is a small collection of —

Defense: I'm sorry. What?

Iverson: Small collection of those. But, as I said, I feel those are significant. There is a history of assault by Mr. Vinyard towards other individuals —

Defense: Right.

Iverson: — and there was —

Defense: We are just talking right now about Ms. Anderson or her husband at that time — actual physical contact with him with those people. I know of those two instances ... . Do you know of anything else?

Iverson: Actual physical contact, I am not aware of.

Defense: Okay and those would have been eleven or twelve years ago?

Soon the defense took a different tack, and I was surprised to discover that I still found his questions shocking:

Defense: In terms of the encounters between Mr. Vinyard and Ms. Anderson over the years, all of those that have been able to be preserved — phone messages or cards or letters — have been sweet and gentle on his part, have they not?

Iverson: Not at all.

Defense: Tell me which ones have not been sweet and gentle.

Iverson: Sir, I believe that any contacts with regards

to Mr. Vinyard towards Ms. Anderson cannot be constituted as sweet and gentle.

Defense: Well, I am not asking you to interpret the
effect on her, but actually what he communicated.

Iverson: I think one has to understand the nature of
contacts — of these kinds of contacts.

Defense: That's fine. But my question to you is, in these
contacts, in terms of words used by Mr. Vinyard, those in
which he has used harsh words have been extremely rare
in the case of contacts with her — nonexistent except for
one, I believe, isn't that true?

Iverson: Again, to answer your question would not
be fair or complete, in my opinion.

I lauded Iverson's integrity, and Orion's words came to mind: "In
letters from someone who is potentially dangerous, you are more likely to
find expressions of shared destiny than of hatred," she wrote.

While on the stand, both Iverson and Orion warned of the danger
to us, and Orion said she believed that if Vinyard couldn't find me, he
would stalk another, just as he had before. Both agreed that, given his
track record, Vinyard's prognosis was very poor and that the only place
he could receive treatment and not pose a serious risk to us was in a
lockdown facility.

The expert for the defense said only that he would need to be someplace with a fair amount of structure and supervision, where his medications and abstention from alcohol could be monitored. There were some
new medications available that might be worth trying to treat the "love
obsessional" delusions, she said, while agreeing with the other experts that
the delusions were harder to treat than his primary diagnoses — diagnoses
which Iverson and the defense's expert disagreed on, technically. But they
did agree on two things: He had a psychotic disorder, manic type, and
erotomanic delusions.

The testimony continuing, it soon became clear that the whole hearing was focused on two issues: Was Vinyard's mental illness treatable,
and what was the risk to us and the community if he was free? The risk.
Not the harm already inflicted, the damage done, but the risk of harm if
he was free.

What if the crime was a murder, I wondered? Would the sentence be based on whether the perpetrator would murder again or the crime already committed? Granted, this sentence would be for assaulting the arresting officer, but the assault stemmed from the stalking; it was just the climax. In my mind, the crimes were completely connected.

While I sincerely appreciated Kathy's efforts to paint the whole picture for the court, all I could think was — after all I'd written in my statements, after all he'd done to me and my family, after all the evidence of his criminal acts, his refusal to comply with treatment, and his flagrant disregard for the law — how could it be that the question of whether or not he was treatable was still the only thing that would dictate his sentence? How could it be that the focus was still on "fixing" him and not on holding him accountable? But the judge's own questions posed to the psychiatrists confirmed that this was, in fact, still the question in play. And Vinyard was not even pleading insanity. He never had.

Soon, Kathy called me to the stand to present my statement. But the "treatability" question now weighing on me, I abandoned my plan and shot from my gut. "Your Honor, I have already submitted two rather lengthy victim impact statements to you directly. And I know that you have read the first … and I sincerely hope that you have read the second … because — "

"I have," the judge interjected.

It appears to have fallen on deaf ears, I thought, and at that point my focus turned to the audience and beyond, to cosmic consciousness, I suppose. *Someone out there, please hear me. Someone wake up and see clearly!*

Exasperated, I shook the foundation beneath the question of whether or not Vinyard was treatable and asked the judge to take a step back and look first at the question of treatment versus incarceration — the same question pondered by judges since the beginning of this whole ordeal. Then I challenged the underlying assumptions.

The first assumption, I asserted, was that it was an either-or scenario. I'd recently learned that a judge couldn't legally mandate treatment and imprisonment simultaneously and said so. But, I said, Vinyard could be offered treatment while he was incarcerated.

The second assumption, I posited, was that if he was mentally ill, he was not accountable for his violent crimes against other people. "And I use the term 'violent' very consciously and very purposefully. ... But I would like to reiterate that because it's hard to convey — and I didn't hear it conveyed today — just how violent these actions are and the impact they have had on our lives."

If a mental illness excused a stalker for his crimes, he'd be given free rein to commit any unthinkable act he chose to fulfill his fantasy with absolutely no consequences, I argued, adding that throughout nearly two decades, the severe lack of consequences had only taught Vinyard how to stalk us better, how to get away with it, and how to spend minimal time in jail.

"He has learned that he is the only one that matters, that everyone will accept that, and others are violated. And to me, in the scenario with no accountability, no one wins. He doesn't win, we don't win, the community doesn't win ... ."

Finally, I pointed out something that occurred to me when I worked to integrate my anger. It was one of the bolts of insight that hit me.

The third assumption, I said, was that Vinyard wanted to be well. "He is mentally ill, why wouldn't he want to be? And we also assume that if he could be healed, we would all be free of the effects of this disorder, and therefore, he should be treated."

Not only did this perception surrender all authority to his illness, I stressed, but it was a projection of our desire for healing onto him, not so unlike his projection of his desire onto me.

"But, as has already been mentioned in the testimony today, consistently and without exception, Mr. Vinyard has demonstrated both by his actions and his statements throughout the history that he does not want treatment, he will not comply. ... [I]n open defiance of court orders and plea bargains he made, after proclaiming he would follow through with treatment — vehemently proclaiming he would follow through with treatment — he never complied."

Then I remembered something Kathy presented earlier in the hearing. I brought it up again.

"I believe Ms. Delgado mentioned a very recent letter that Mr. Vinyard wrote in which he said 'they' wanted him to take psychotropic drugs, and he stated defiantly, 'To hell with them.' For nearly twenty years, the courts have relied on treatment for Mr. Vinyard to make us safe, and every time we have been placed in danger. And the warning of danger has come forward in court-ordered psychiatric evaluations since early on."

I then began reading a combination of my impact statements aloud, but I found myself tongue-tied, struggling to find a way to get through to the judge, to at least open his mind enough to see this from my point of view. Knowing that neither the judge nor the audience would take my word for it that Vinyard's stalking was a violent act against us mentally and emotionally, I again related specific events. Reading aloud stories of the terrifying invasions and relentless intrusions, I occasionally glanced at the faces before me for some sign of comprehension. What I saw was shock and distress. It was reassuring to know that, when viewed from outside the labyrinth of the law, the injustice was glaringly obvious.

And when I reminded the judge that, given the law governing parole and the credit for the ten months already served, even the maximum twelve-year sentence translated into little more than three years of peace where I could be certain my family was safe and we would be free, a ripple of disgust rolled across the audience.

I talked about the impacts to my children at length, though only in general terms. I didn't want to violate their privacy more by having it filmed.

"I have not yet been able to explain to my children," I confessed, "that the court — created to serve justice and protect the People — would sooner put us at greater and greater risk than incarcerate a habitual criminal."

How, I asked, would I explain to them that we were perpetually sacrificed because this man was mentally ill? Seeing them suffer the trauma caused by this man's actions and worrying constantly for their safety when he was free was the hardest thing I had ever faced, I said, my heart aching.

"I am at a loss to alleviate their fears. And my only answer to them … will be the length of sentence you pass today."

In the precious little time I had, I hammered away at every point I'd made in my statements, hitting each hard from every angle.

The question my son asked me, the most simple question:

> Does anyone have the right to do this to someone else? Anyone? To be predatory, invasive, to terrorize them, to stalk them? He doesn't understand it, and quite

honestly, I don't either. He doesn't understand why [this man] is allowed to impact others' lives so violently and so severely. ... Should we, any of us, be sacrificed because of his mental illness? No. This serves no one.

Was the defendant accountable for his actions, I asked?

Yes, I believe he is. I believe he must be. ... If, once again, he is not held accountable, the court will only enable him to further justify committing horrendous crimes against us for his own gratification. ... To me, this is unconscionable and absolutely unjustifiable.

I reminded the judge that every time Vinyard was not held accountable, the sentence withheld from him became ours or someone else's. He alone was responsible for his actions, and he alone was responsible for the consequences, I stressed again.

So I ask you, Your Honor, to direct your attention away from the question of treatment versus imprisonment, the question of how to delicately handle the defendant's illness. It was stated very clearly to the defendant at the first court hearing that if he contacted us again, he would be placed in prison for as long as humanly possible. He stated repeatedly that he understood. He has clearly made his choice, and he can receive treatment in prison if he chooses to. ...

You have the authority to stop him for a period of time, Your Honor. And I ask you to do everything in your power to release us from the burden of his actions.

Stop the dysfunction. Sever the court-enforced enmeshment, I silently urged. *Give him back his power and release us, all of us, from the burden of his illness and his choices.*

Do not pass his sentence onto us again. Do not put our lives at risk again in the hope that he will be cured.

Finally, grant me and my family what is rightfully ours for as long as you possibly can: the maximum time. Grant my children their remaining childhood in a safe environment. Grant all of us our freedom and our own lives. They are our lives, not his for the taking.

And grant the defendant all that is rightfully his: the very real consequences of his criminal actions.

My pleas and arguments exhausted, I drew a deep breath, thanked the judge, and retreated into the audience.

The defense called Vinyard's sister to testify about Vinyard's family history and his mental illness. Then a new argument was introduced.

"I think you told me that there was some issue involving the cost of incarceration?" the defense asked her.

Kathy objected. The judge overruled.

"Okay," Vinyard's sister replied. "This is from the table of Colorado Department of Corrections. It costs the state $30,361 to incarcerate a male for one year, and that was in 1997 — the cost — and the publication was put out in April of '98. So while Robert has certainly done some terrible things, it's my idea that there are more terrible things that have been done and that those spots in jail for an extended period of time do not need to be taken up by someone like Robert, who has a chance of getting better and has not done the worst of crimes."

Before long, Vinyard addressed the court himself. He had prepared a long, meandering statement, and while he read it aloud, his voice occasionally broke. He was now facing prison, and for the first time that I had seen, he was genuinely afraid.

"Your Honor, officer of the court, and ladies and gentleman, I have dreaded this day since I was arrested ... I am scared, worried and embarrassed, ashamed, and understandably, predominantly sad," he began.

In all these years, Vinyard had never apologized to Bruce or me. Now he did, adding that he understood we felt fear. "I can empathize. I have been scared myself. Not as much as you, but I have experienced fear."

"I'm sorry that my indulgence has made me — impacted so many lives. I do not have the right to do that. My, my illusion must die. ... She showed affection for me for only a brief period, just a few months in 1978. In reality, it wasn't all that. We had some great conversations is all."

He admitted that he'd lied to Iverson in 1995. "And even my implying that we had a sexual relationship was wrong. We did not — we did not have a sexual relationship at all. None. ... And then you get reports from Ms. Anderson, 'We were nothing,' which — she is right. But then I have the delusion because I am claiming something that is not real." He would take medication to control it, he said.

But throughout his statement, Vinyard wavered between admitting he had a delusion, committing to treatment for it, and sinking back into it. And as he continued to accept responsibility for his actions, his admissions morphed into rationalizing and minimizing his criminal acts then back again to responsibility and remorse. It seemed clear to me that he'd been coached on what to say and was struggling with it.

"The question is: Why do I bother or continue to harass her?" he asked. "The answer: In the vain hope that we can reconcile. And also, partially, because I am ill. I was in a manic state of my bipolar disorder," he said, adding that his lack of good judgment was compounded by alcohol.

He claimed he wouldn't force himself on me again then wandered back to excusing his actions:

> The point is, I wasn't on my meds. I was ill. The reason I wasn't on my meds, I just couldn't get to them. I was in a situation where I came up to the probation meeting to go with my — to meet my probation officer, and I saw a bunch of cops here at the probation office.
>
> And I felt threatened because that's what happened the last time I come to the probation and that is — that I got arrested, and I felt that they were going to do this again, and that's why I took off and went to Denver. ... And when I was in Denver, I went into manic phase ...
>
> And it wasn't — I was off my meds is the reason, one of the reasons. Not really accepting responsibility would be another major factor.

Soon he returned to the subject of his delusion. "I realize that I do have delusional hopes that some day we will be together, that it will all work out for the best. Because since I have suffered so much and been through great tribulation, I deserve you."

Then he assumed responsibility again. "But now, in order for me to get better, to stop the harassment, I have to admit I have delusions."

He said he would welcome two conditions upon release from prison: court-ordered sobriety and treatment in the form of medications and therapy.

Again, Vinyard expressed regret. Then he addressed the sentence:

> I also feel a prison sentence is justified in the natural progression of this case. ... I ask you, Your Honor, to consider my new commitment to sobriety ... and my willingness to take the medicine and to admit an illness. And, most importantly, a new realistic assessment of my relationship to the victim, Peggy Anderson — we were only friends — shows that I can be rehabilitated.
>
> Your Honor, you have scared the living daylights out of me. I am dead sober and very, very concerned. I am scared to death of twelve years and my family is too.

He asked the judge for compassion for him and his family then resurrected his sister's argument:

> And I think my sister raised this issue: Prison is very expensive. I think the resources of the state of Colorado are better spent on people that do really very criminal — criminal things that are a lot worse than this.
>
> I am not belittling the charge of stalking. But, you know, breaking into your home and stealing items, kidnapping — how terrifying it would be to kidnap a child. So I think there is a lot worse things than stalking to spend our resources on in prison.
>
> But if I do go to prison, I would ask you for the less time as possible.

The idea that his stalking was not threatening and not as serious as some cases was a repeating theme throughout his statement. Pressing the point, he described one case in which the stalker's sentence was home detention, an ankle bracelet, and continued:

So, you know, there is other alternatives to prison in this case. So, Your Honor, whatever you think is appropriate. ... I think I have shown remorse here today. I know I have shown remorse. I felt remorse. Everyone can see that I am very sincere about this.

I feel remorse and the rehabilitation part. I think I am rehabilitated — rehabilitative. I don't have a problem admitting that I have a disease, and taking medicine for it shall not be a problem, especially with the new psychotropic drugs that don't have the bad side effects.

I wasn't so bright. I know that alcohol has been a major factor in the various episodes of harassment ...

In mitigation, you know, alcohol — you can't form a specific intent to intentionally do something when you are drunk.

Anything to avoid responsibility, I thought. *Anything to surrender his power.*

Claiming he'd worked hard to understand his illness and do something about it, Vinyard said he'd read Orion's book. Then he explained in some detail why he felt he didn't fit the profile of an erotomanic stalker.

Finally, to my surprise, Vinyard, himself, addressed the future risk to us. It was not reassuring:

I would like to say there is none. I really would. I would like to hopefully go home tonight and, you know, and let their children do whatever they are going to do and live a normal happy childhood, like the happy childhood I had. I really and sincerely hope that. I don't know if that's possible, but I hope so.

With high regret, I have shown, I think, that it's possible. ... Sincerely, I want to go on with my life and get more — mourn the loss and move on.

Dr. Mullow [sic] says that the number one predictor of violence is mobility. I don't have a car and I haven't had one in some time. ... So I think me not being mobile lessens the threat somewhat.

Again Vinyard expressed remorse and his fear of twelve years in prison. Then, closing, he said, "I only ask that your sentence will tender justice with mercy and grant a short prison sentence. I will not disappoint you."

In his closing statement, the defense attorney claimed he didn't minimize the suffering my family and I had endured "at the hands of Mr. Vinyard." But he disagreed with what we were asking for.

"[W]hat Ms. Anderson ... and I think the prosecution wants — and it's what everyone in the court is entitled to — and that is to live their lives free of intrusion from someone else, or invasion, and to be happy and free to pursue what they want to."

Yes. Life, liberty, and the pursuit of happiness — our fundamental rights.

"But society doesn't have the time or the space to guarantee that for everybody," he claimed. "Everybody that wants a liver transplant doesn't get one. Nobody wants cancer, but people get cancer. ... I'm sure that Ms. Anderson would say, 'Really, Judge, what I would like you to do is put Mr. Vinyard in prison for the rest of his life because I deserve to live my life free from his harassment.' "

It was just a fact that Vinyard's mental illness had fallen on us, he said, adding that the question now was what the court should do about it. "What can society afford to do about it?"

I hoped I would never become so cynical.

Putting Vinyard in prison would be expensive, the defense declared. "Just for example, we don't have the money to spend $30,000 on a man who has not victimized society. This type of conduct doesn't compare to the other types of conduct that the court has seen where people have been actually physically hurt, seriously, and gotten sentenced to the magnitude that they are seeking."

Ignorance does enough harm. Willful ignorance is something else entirely.

With that, it was now in the judge's hands. Several rows behind me, my friends spontaneously clasped hands and sent me strength. In the same moment, I looked down at my own hands resting in my lap, fingers unconsciously interlaced in a mudra of prayer. Then, out of the corner of my eye, I saw movement and turned to see what was happening.

While the judge slowly shuffled his papers, armed deputies standing guard in all four corners of the room moved in unison toward Vinyard, then one quietly reached for the chains, loosely draped behind him. Discretely, the deputy bent down, grabbed them, and pulled them taut.

Judge: The length of this sentencing hearing has exceeded by three times the longest sentencing hearing I have had in the last sixteen years. ... There is no pleasure taken by this Court in arriving on a sentence. There is probably no justice if the Defendant is not held accountable for his conduct.

This case, last year ... was set up. And I have indicated in open Court this plea arrangement with Mr. Vinyard is a setup of Mr. Vinyard. Mr. Vinyard knows it, the District Attorney knows, and the victim knew it. I think she disagreed with it and didn't want it to happen because it was too lenient, but it was, nevertheless — but it was in the best interest of Mr. Vinyard, the victim, and the People, I suppose.

And the Court said — we are all sitting here, as understanding, intelligent human beings — there has not been any accusations that Mr. Vinyard is not a smart person — and the Court said, "You will have no contact — no contact with Ms. Anderson, and if you do, then you will go to prison."

And you said, "No problem. I won't have any contact." Now that's what made so unique this nearly seven-hour hearing, is the circumstance of this case. I have heard persuasive argument from both sides.

It is true that I have never seen a first-time felony conviction sentenced to prison, particularly for injuries to a police officer that were relatively minor. ...

I can't understand this. If we could predict danger to people, my job would be easy. Even the doctors admitted they have nothing — not the foggiest idea whether or not an individual is going to commit a violent act. Neither does this Court. ...

I think there is mental — there is a lot of people in prison who are there partially because of their conduct, but their conduct is partly excused by some mental illness.

I cannot understand Mr. Vinyard's crime in this case. He has continued with this pattern of conduct over the last nineteen years, and it is my responsibility to protect the community and punish the crime. If he can recover from a mental illness, then he should be treated in order to rehabilitate so that he will no longer commit this particular crime.

I happen to accept the testimony in this case on these issues: Mr. Vinyard is not treatable, his conduct proves that he cannot refrain from committing this crime, and nothing he says to me now will convince me otherwise — nothing. Because I remember what he said about the time he entered the plea. I believed him then and I do not believe him now. Definitely, I thought that you were going to abide that time — it was a voluntary plea.

Vinyard: I will just appeal it then, Judge. Go ahead. Damn.

Judge: The diagnosis is — at least that's part of the symptomology, and it is not treatable. So rehabilitation is not likely a result of any sentence to be imposed by this Court. It seems to me — the factors in this case then make the Court's focus on punishment and protection of the victims and the community.

The impact on the victims in this case are severe and long term. I accept the testimony of Dr. Iverson and others with regard to the risk of future danger that this Defendant runs.

I find that he understands the risk he was taking when he rendered the pleas on the subject agreement and he was willing to take that risk, and he still failed to obey the conditions of the deferred sentence. I can only focus on what this Court does know and not continue to focus on the things that the Court does not know about.

What is the appropriate sentence? What do I do so the victims are not frightened? This case has gone on for a very long period of time, and while the actual physical violence toward the victim is not — has not been severe in terms of other cases that have come before the Court, it is clear that this victim — these victims were harmed and remain at risk of harm from him.

Because of that, the Court has the option of probation or prison. I don't have, in this case, other alternatives. I think that in order to protect these victims, the society, and punish the Defendant for his conduct, I am following my promise to him that if you violate, you will go to prison. I am going to do what I said. There is no prejudice in this. I can see no justice in doing otherwise.

I think the length of the sentence has to be taken into consideration the fact that he is not treatable and that society cannot be protected without his being warehoused.

The decision of this Court is twelve years in the Department of Corrections on count one (second-degree felony assault on an officer) ... .

Stunned, I paused to take it all in. My emotions were mixed. On the one hand, I felt victorious when the judge passed the maximum prison sentence, the twelve years Kathy thought we would never get. On the other, given everything I'd seen in the courts, I couldn't trust it. Shock and relief mingled insidiously with the doubt now deeply embedded in my psyche.

Tears washed down my face, and struggling to get my bearings, I slowly stood and found myself pulled into the arms of friends congratulating me on my victory. To privately take in the moment, I closed my eyes. When I opened them, a camera was pressed into my face.

Gradually, the spectators stood and began milling around the courtroom. Then suddenly, the swelling murmur of the crowd was silenced by Vinyard's thin, penetrating voice slicing the air. My nerves stood at full alert and, horror-struck, I turned to look up the aisle.

His face blazing red, blood swelling the veins in his neck, Vinyard was completely unhinged.

Catapulting out of his seat, with three deputies holding him he leaned toward the judge, shouted obscenities at him, and threatened appeal. Quickly, he was dragged out of the courtroom.

Witnessing his violent outburst, I shuddered and past trauma reared its head. My body quaked. My brain seized. The rest of that day was a blank to me.

Several weeks after the hearing, I received another letter from the DA informing me of the disposition in my case. The defendant pled guilty to violation of restraining order, it said, and was sentenced to five years probation *concurrent* with twelve years in prison for the felony assault. It was a bitter pill to swallow.

To my knowledge, ABC's *20/20* did not complete and air the piece. It made no difference to me. From my point of view, it had served its purpose: The maximum prison sentence (the longest period of peace I could have realistically hoped for) had been passed.

The district attorney's office made good on its promise. A threat management unit was formed, and part of its mission was to reform the stalking statute. Kathy invited me to join the subcommittee that would revise the law, and I gladly accepted.

The press spread the news of our plan to amend the statute, citing this case as a testament to the need. We now had the exposure we needed to move ahead and, finally, substantially reform the law.

*   *   *

As fate would have it, the peace we were granted was far less than promised. Thankfully, for the duration of our hiatus, the coming reversal of fortunes was never revealed to me.

CHAPTER 18

Heart of Justice

*"The longest journey a man must take is the eighteen
inches from his head to his heart."*
~ *Author unknown*

Twelve years. While I knew that, in reality, the time granted would
be less, even a decade seemed like a lifetime. Anything could happen.
Yet, with a future of freedom and peace ahead of me, my heart was still
heavy.

In a brilliant closing argument in the 1994 trial for the murder of
Medgar Evers some thirty years before, Assistant District Attorney Bobby
DeLaughter said justice has sometimes been called the soothing balm to
be applied to the wounds inflicted on society and that "where justice is
never fulfilled and that wound can never be cleansed, all it does is just
fester and fester and fester … "

In all this time, with all this work, I still had not found justice. Although the extraordinary sentence was intended to give me and my family
relief and protect us and the community, the perpetrator had not been
brought to trial or sentenced for stalking. Shrouded in whispers, the true
atrocity of his crimes had never been spoken aloud and condemned — not
by the law and not by the courts. And within me and within society, the
gaping wound was still laid wide open. It was time to cleanse and stitch it.

The subcommittee convened to begin work on overhauling Colorado's
stalking statute. Prosecutors, legislative specialists, police, and others like
me whose lives had been shattered by stalking assembled. The prosecution
of many cases had been challenging given the narrow definition of stalking
in the current statute and the minimal penalties. Mine was just the case
that finally made it indisputably clear the law had to change.

How I could still be shocked by anything involving the criminal justice system is beyond me. Yet I was. One of the first comments I heard
after Kathy introduced the group's mission was: "How many prison beds

will it add? We can't make a law that puts more people in prison and adds beds. The legislature won't pass it."

Wow. This was the criteria for writing criminal law? Not justice, not public safety, but to pretend to address a crime without consequences commensurate with the harm inflicted on others and without significant enough penalties to thwart the behavior and keep truly dangerous perpetrators off the streets?

The concern was the cost of enforcing it. What was the cost of not enacting and enforcing the law, I wondered? The cost to me, personally, was crushing, both emotionally and financially. The cost to taxpayers all these years in my cases alone was mind-boggling. Had our civilization really devolved this far?

But it was a numbers game. Before the amended statute moved out of our subcommittee, some magic formulas I didn't understand and didn't want to understand were crunched, and it was determined that the expected increase in the number of prison beds would be minimal. Luckily, we'd passed this appalling test.

As our discussions continued and laws from other states were researched, writing a law that would withstand a constitutional challenge became paramount. During the course of my recent case, the defense had challenged the constitutionality of the law. Unable to imagine that this argument had any substance at all, I'd basically ignored it. But now I discovered that stalking laws were often repealed on the basis that they were unconstitutional, resulting in overturned convictions, prisoners released, and no stalking law on the books at all until another was written and passed in its place. In fact, it had happened in Colorado between my own cases.

The issue, I discovered, was to balance the stalker's right to free speech with the crime victim's right to privacy. *Free speech?* I seriously doubted this was what our forefathers had in mind. Stalking was predatory terrorism, pure and simple. The fact that judges and defense attorneys had, time and time again, turned a blind eye to the emotional violence and devastation it caused still boggled and infuriated me.

In her book Orion discussed the effect on the stalking victim — an effect which, in my experience, neither the legislators nor the courts had even begun to grasp. Two Australian psychiatrists who ran a specialized clinic for stalking victims and stalkers noted the extreme fear produced in most victims by the repeated, intrusive contacts, Orion wrote, adding that "anticipation and not knowing when the stalker might strike next heighten the sense of impending doom and consequent omnipresent anxiety." Three-quarters of the stalking victims treated in this clinic "expressed overwhelming feelings of powerlessness," she said, "and nearly a quarter acknowledged serious suicidal thoughts."

How could a civilized society allow such cruel, inhumane treatment of a human being? What was the purpose of civilization and the establishment of law if not to ensure that no citizen lived in fear of another, thereby protecting and increasing freedom for all? It seemed to me that, even in these United States, the very people we appointed to uphold the rule of law had lost sight of its purpose, the foundation on which it was built.

I kept going back to the fundamentals: my rights to life (the right not to be killed, injured, or abused), liberty, and the pursuit of happiness, free from the interference of others.

In the Declaration of Independence, our founding fathers proclaimed, "We hold these Truths to be self-evident, that all Men ... are endowed by their Creator with certain unalienable Rights, that among these are Life, Liberty, and the Pursuit of Happiness. That to secure these Rights, Governments are instituted among Men ... "

I was no legal scholar, but the meaning of these words seemed perfectly clear to me. Government was created for the purpose of securing these sacred rights.

To me, it seemed these God-given rights our founders recognized were fundamental human rights — rights that our conscience tells us must, above all, be protected. Curious, I delved further into the topic of human rights and discovered that, in the wake of the atrocities of World War II, world leaders gathered to develop a road map to guarantee the rights of every individual everywhere. And on December 10, 1948, the U.N. General Assembly adopted the Universal Declaration of Human Rights.

The preamble to the declaration recognized that the inherent dignity and inalienable rights of all members of the human family were the "foundation of freedom, justice, and peace in the world." It was a beautiful thing to see in print.

"[D]isregard and contempt for human rights have resulted in barbarous acts which have outraged the conscience of mankind," it said and warned that if man was to avoid rebellion against tyranny and oppression, it was essential that human rights be protected by the rule of law.

The general assembly pronounced the Universal Declaration of Human Rights to be a "standard of achievement for all peoples and all nations, to the end that every individual and every organ of society, keeping this Declaration constantly in mind, shall strive … to secure their universal and effective recognition and observance."

This declaration of human rights was not written just for those subjected to the brutality of tyrant dictators or the ravages of war. It was written for all members of the human family, at all times, in all circumstances. *Every organ of society, keeping this Declaration constantly in mind.* With each law that was written and at every moment when applying the law, the justice system had a fundamental responsibility to ensure that these universal human rights were protected and upheld. And being "inalienable," it seemed to me that no other laws created by man could ever undermine or override them.

Riveted, I turned to the rights laid down in the document, and there it was in Article 3: the right to life, liberty, and security of person. Essentially the same rights America's founders spoke of were now universally recognized human rights. Yet it was these very rights that, in my experience, were repeatedly, blatantly ignored by legislators and the judiciary when it came to the crime of stalking.

Then Article 5 leaped off the page. "No one shall be subjected to torture or to cruel, inhuman or degrading treatment … " While all these human rights rang true, it was this that most expressed my own torment. It was inhumane to stand by and allow such torturous, cruel treatment of anyone. Emotional assault was a violation of our human rights, and it was simply unacceptable for the government created to defend these rights to trample them. And so, to the extent we could, we would change the law.

In the end, it was recognition of the cruelty — the emotional impact even in the absence of physical harm or a verbal threat of physical harm — that was the most fundamental, sweeping change in Colorado's new law. For the first time, our state's stalking law defended the heart.

When I read the final declaration of the new statute, I felt a remarkable lightness of being. For so long, I'd wanted the truth to be told, for stalking to be seen for the reprehensible violation that it was. Now, here it was in black and white:

> The general assembly hereby finds and declares that stalking is a serious problem in this state and nation-wide. ... Because stalking involves highly inappropriate intensity, persistence, and possessiveness, it entails great unpredictability and creates great stress and fear for the victim. Stalking involves severe intrusions on the victim's personal privacy and autonomy, with an immediate and long-lasting impact on quality of life, as well as risks to security and safety of the victim and persons close to the victim, even in the absence of express threats of physical harm. ...

Words penned on paper are powerful things; a snapshot of the moment, they become timeless. Words forged into law are enormously powerful. Not only do they establish a code of behavior in a society, they reflect the character and values of that civilization itself. They are a declaration to the gods of who we are today, of how we have evolved.

And that day, in my state, stalking was no longer limited to a threat of physical harm — the emotional and psychological impacts were recognized and the actions that caused them declared criminal. Further, the torture I'd endured was no longer a misdemeanor; it was a felony, a serious crime against a person. That day in my state, stalking, in any form, was no longer acceptable.

The new law severed the crime of stalking from the crime of harassment and expanded the definition of stalking to include not only a credible threat, but specific repeated *actions* "that would cause a reasonable person to suffer serious emotional distress and does cause that person, a member of that person's immediate family, or someone with whom that person has or has had a continuing relationship to suffer serious emotional distress."

A legislative specialist on our subcommittee felt the "reasonable person" clause set an objective standard that would likely survive a constitutional challenge. Whether a reasonable person would suffer serious emotional distress would be up to a jury to decide.

The definition of "credible threat" was expanded to include a threat not directly expressed if the *totality of conduct* would cause a reasonable person such fear. Hopefully, this would also open the door to allowing prior similar acts to be presented in court, even if they were, technically, separate cases. Finally, stalking would be seen for what it was to the victim: one horrendous, cumulative series of violations.

In all these years, the twists and turns of my cases seemed to expose every crack in the system. Now was the time to patch what we could. The revised statute raised the penalties for stalking and cracked down on repeat offenders. The first offense was raised from a class 6 to a class 5 felony, and second or subsequent and aggravated offenses within seven years of the prior offense were raised from class 5 to class 4. But if, at the time of the offense, there was *any* kind of protection order or court order in effect against the perpetrator prohibiting the stalking behavior, the offense was a class 4 felony. And in that case, any sentence imposed for stalking would run consecutively and not concurrently with any sentence imposed for violation of a protection order.

The new law also recognized that stalking was an extraordinary risk crime. As I had seen in the felony assault case, this designation was, appropriately, a sentence enhancer. It was also an acknowledgment of the inherent danger. And because of the danger, the new law also emphasized that it was a peace officer's duty to respond as soon as reasonably possible to a report of stalking.

In May of 1999, the governor of Colorado signed the new statute into law. It was said to be the nation's strongest.

A year later, Kathy would say that the Boulder County judicial district prosecuted ten times more stalking cases than it had in previous years.

CHAPTER 19

Still Waters

"Wherever you go, go with all your heart."

~ Confucius

Now that the sentence was passed and the law reformed, the storm subsided and an eerie silence filled the space left in its wake. The nightmare I thought would never end had ended. The life I thought I may never have again was suddenly mine. The stillness of peace was so unfamiliar that I fidgeted and had no idea what to do with it. And as I looked around me, assessing the storm's destruction, the thought of picking up the pieces of my life again was overwhelming. I couldn't find the will to do it.

I needed time to recover and set aside as much quiet space as I could. But for a long time, the silence was charged, electric — like the air just before a storm. It was coming. I could feel it. At any moment this peace would erupt into chaos and terror. I even feared dreaming of the future as if, somehow, just raising hope would slam the door on it.

While I allowed the feelings to come up and worked to release them, I found no relief. The anxiety was too deeply imprinted, it seemed.

"This is the classic, very real effect of long-term abuse," Mary explained. "Your nervous system is habituated to the other shoe dropping. And the courts are completely unaware of the damage they do."

But one day passed and another dawned. A week passed, a month, then several, and the storm never broke. Moment by moment, day by day, I settled into the silence, praying I could trust it, working to let go of the omnipresent feeling that, surely, a hammer was about to fall.

Ever so gradually, I sank into the still waters, and there I found that all I wanted was to get as far as possible from the courts, the law, and the stalking — anything and everything to do with it all, including my work with Mary. It wasn't that I turned my back on her. I knew my work with her wasn't done, and I continued seeing her for a time. But it also seemed my growth had reached a plateau. Something was holding me back.

Mary understood my need for a break and gave me a long lead while holding the connection she knew I still needed, and my search for healing took me in a whole new direction.

Year upon year, extreme stress had taken its toll. The anxiety and nightmares persisted, and physical pain had increased to the point where it was now crippling. In the aftermath, I was bent over like a crooked tree that had survived against all odds. It was time to undo what damage I could and take care of my body.

*   *   *

"I didn't know you were wearing armor over your heart!" the practitioner exclaimed, grunting with the effort of digging her small fingers of steel into the connective tissue between my sternum and ribs.

Her words rang true. I had worn armor over my heart, and though it was finally shed and replaced with healthy boundaries, the remnants of old patterns, old unconscious beliefs, old wounds and scars still lingered in my body. And until they were released, it could not hold the new, higher vibrations of my expanding consciousness. It was my own body that was holding me back.

Week after week she poked and kneaded, working to pry me open and allow my skeletal frame to relax into its natural alignment. She was a structural integration practitioner. Integration of my soul, integration of my body — it made perfect sense. Restoring my natural state of balance and wholeness required healing and integration of all aspects: spiritual, emotional, mental, and physical. It was deep, cellular work and, as with counseling, I needed help. I needed intervention.

Wincing as she discovered more and more damage and forced me to open up, I leaned on my lessons again and again. *Don't resist the pain, go into it; give thanks for the lessons given and release it; breathe, relax, surrender; open to receiving,* I'd coach myself as she broke through my resistances.

Then, digging in deep, she'd touch something and suddenly I'd burst into tears. It wasn't the pain of her touch, although that was significant. It was the physical release of deep emotional pain: cellular memories. For a while I felt haunted by my own ghosts as, once released from the grave, they floated up into my awareness in a chaotic storm then quietly drifted away.

One afternoon, while she held the pressure and I blew out a deep breath, a small memory long forgotten broke loose and rushed into the moment. Before I met Mary, after Bruce and I separated and the stalking re-ignited, I stumbled upon a psychic while attending a festival with a friend. At the time, plagued with unrelenting terror, I was so distraught that the question burned like a furnace within me: *Why is this in my life?*

Desperate to know, I was on my knees. Yet with a healthy dose of skepticism, I resolved not to tell the psychic anything about myself or pose any questions. But when I pulled back the flap and entered, before I could even sit in the darkened tent, his radiant green eyes seized on mine, and leaning into me with a sense of urgency, he said forcefully, "You must be a stalker!" I froze where I stood.

"Stalk – out – your – wounds," he insisted. "Stalk out your wounds and heal them, and like cutting old growth from a rose, you will create a multitude of blooms in place of the cuts. You will find such happiness and peace."

Every shiver racing over my skin told me this was important. But in the wild frenzy of events that followed, I had completely forgotten his message.

Now suddenly, I remembered. It was what all my work since then had been about. *Stalk out your wounds and heal them. You will find such happiness and peace.* Hope was renewed.

*   *   *

The results of the structural integration were astonishing. I felt I had a whole new body. But it wasn't just the technique itself. It was that I went into it with the clear intention of getting down deep and healing. I was ready and willing to let it all go.

I then turned to homeopathic remedies to restore my system's natural balance and help relieve the effects of trauma. I stretched regularly, and in conjunction with all these, I kept working with all Mary had taught me.

My life force flowing again, more and more information long suppressed was released from the depths of my unconscious. New awareness and insights flowed freely, and every day I felt myself growing larger, fuller, and more vibrant.

Then one morning, as I stretched and breathed into my body's resistance, I unexpectedly touched the deepest wound of all and crumpled onto the floor in tears. "What did you do?" others had asked, inferring it was my fault I was stalked, my fault I was violated.

The wound, laid wide open again, ripped right through my heart. Over and over, of everything I had endured, apart from the pain of seeing my children suffer, this was the most painful wound of all. Just when I most needed comfort, support, and compassion, just when I'd shed my armor and allowed myself to be vulnerable, I was hit with the pain of blame.

Curled up in a ball, I wept. Then finally, my tears ebbing, empty, I listened. And the words that rose up were the most healing I'd ever heard: *All I had learned growing up, all I was groomed to be had put me at risk, not at fault.*

Doing what I thought and was taught was right, I'd unknowingly become a lightning rod. Stretching upward, reaching for the light, the rod does not create the lightning or cause it to strike. The rod merely attracts it more than other objects. Because of my upbringing and the beliefs I'd embraced, I was configured to attract this predator. I was not responsible for his behavior. I was merely more at risk than most of having it land on me.

Relief flooded me and a tremendous weight rose up and out of my body. In every fiber of my being I got it more deeply than I ever had: I was not responsible for his obsession or his behavior; I was only responsible for myself. And I wondered why others were so quick to blame the victim.

Those who bullied and abused blamed their victims. But they were hardly alone. In my experience, victim blaming crossed the full social spectrum: all levels of education; men and women; strangers, friends, even family. Where did this come from? Why were others so cruel as to rush to judgment and blame the victim at the very moment she or he was most vulnerable? Then it hit me.

Vulnerability. Fear.

We want to believe we're in control of what happens to us, that if we're good, moral people, we'll be safe. My situation, like many others', must undermine this belief and trigger a deep-seated fear of being vulnerable and unsafe. It's unthinkable. So, rejected, that fear squats in shadow, waiting to be projected onto the one who reflects the fear. The victim becomes the scapegoat, the one they demand carry the fear that they refuse to own.

Craving a deeper understanding, I journaled:

> Our culture, it seems, has a fascination with "victims."
> We worship, pity, or blame them, all of which are
> projections and none of which empowers them. In fact,
> all these attitudes only cultivate polarized thinking and
> entrench duality — perpetrator/victim duality.
>
> Villain/hero, bad people/good people, perpetrator/
> victim, power-full/power-less; I can see the appeal.
> Preserving the dichotomy, the illusion of absolutes, gives
> shadow projections a home. But entrenched in duality
> we are stagnant, frozen in a state of polarity. There is no
> movement, only the status quo.
>
> Holding on to duality will never engender healing
> and wholeness. In fact, it does egregious harm not only
> to individuals, but to society as a whole. Projecting onto
> the victim or the perpetrator, or both, only perpetuates
> the cycle; it ensures that the struggle and suffering
> continue.

Shadow projections. Of course. For years, I struggled to understand why few in the criminal justice system saw me, the stalker, or the situation clearly. Now I understood. When unconscious, unintegrated shadow material is repressed and projected onto others, reality is distorted. Illusion prevails.

I didn't need to know what each was projecting. I only needed to know that this was the source of my frustration and to consciously choose not to carry the projections of others. While it might not be the whole answer, it was clear to me that the shadow was operating beneath the surface. And not just the shadow of individuals, but of the collective.

It explained so much: the ignorance and callousness, the blind acceptance of emotional abuse I'd seen all these years. There was something fundamentally wrong with our culture. It was the insidious undercurrent that ran so deep it was hidden from conscious awareness. I could feel it but could not quite grasp what it was. Now I knew. It was shadow material, buried in the collective unconscious. And despite all the glaring evidence and all my efforts to bring the cruel reality of emotional violation to light, over and over again truth was obscured by the distorted lens of the shadow.

I journaled more:

> What harm we inflict with our judgments and fears! There is a sickness in our society, a deep, hidden malignancy festering in our collective unconscious. And if we continue refusing to acknowledge and heal it, we will destroy ourselves. We already are.
>
> Judgment is born of fear. It is the mind's primary tool of divisiveness, first within us then between us. Judgment is the sword of separation, and it is brutal. Severing the soul creates duality. And duality — the illusion of separation — gives birth to the shadow. When we judge others, in truth we are judging ourselves, and we are suffering. And every act of judgment only fuels the shadow and increases its power.
>
> The evidence of shadow is all around us. Why have we worked for peace for ages, yet always find it beyond our grasp? Why are our politics more polarized than ever? Why are those who preach the loudest about virtue so often caught in scandal? And why are others so eager to read their stories? Where do the rampant fear, bigotry, and hate; the divisiveness, greed, and extremism we now witness on a daily basis come from? They come from judgment and its creation, the shadow. They come from the shadow's projections.
>
> But as I've experienced myself, when we pull back our projections, surrender judgment and fear, and give ourselves compassion — when we embrace our shadow and restore our soul — compassion for others flows naturally. And taking responsibility for all that is ours, we own our true power and inherently empower others.
>
> In contrast, succumbing to fear and wielding false power, we crush others' power. And denying our own wounds, we blame, project, and inflict them on others, demanding they carry our pain for us.

We inflict pain every day with our projections. We have killed one another to avoid owning what is ours. Taking responsibility for and healing the duality within us is the only way we will end the madness: the prejudice, persecution, and oppression; the political wars and culture wars that constantly tear us apart.

Healing the wounds in our own soul is not only the greatest gift we can give ourselves, it is our fundamental responsibility to one another. For ourselves, our children, and all of humanity, it is imperative that we retrieve our lost selves, become whole once again, and release others from the tyranny of our projections.

The extreme polarity we are witnessing today is a sure sign we're on the brink of change; the tension is always greatest when an era is about to end, a paradigm about to collapse. The turning point is upon us. Which will we choose: love or fear, wholeness or duality, healing or destruction — within and without?

Carl Jung once said, "Enlightenment is not imagining figures of light but making the darkness conscious." If we would just gather the courage to face our own darkness, surrender judgment, open our hearts to compassion, and take back our true power; if we would dedicate ourselves to self-awareness and consciousness, we would free ourselves from the illusion of duality and the suffering it creates and live in alignment with our true, divine nature. If we did just this, it would be revolutionary. One by one, together we would change the world:

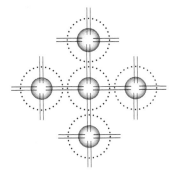

I have no doubt that this is the power of healing the soul. And though this vision of a compassionate and peaceful world may seem forever beyond our reach, I find hope in the words of Arthur Schopenhauer: "All truth passes through three stages. First, it is ridiculed. Second, it is violently opposed. Third, it is accepted as being self-evident."

*   *   *

Progress during this healing time steady and slow, I began to notice that bits of myself long forgotten — aspirations, creativity, inspiration — were re-awakening. A deep sense of fulfillment and gratitude were with me more often. Colors and sounds, the sensual sides of life were once again unfolding before me and in me. It was an unexpected and most welcome experience.

One thing I vowed to do was reconnect to my body and ground myself in the physical world. For so long, I'd been cut off from this vessel I dwelled in, just going through life cramming things into my body to take care of, as if it were a trash can for anxiety and stress. Now, with the structural integration complete, the last thing I wanted to do was imprint my newly cleansed tissues with destructive patterns again. And I hoped to restore a sense of joy of being in my body.

I decided to try a variety of physical activities. I danced again (it had always been a source of joy for me), and I turned to yoga. It had been longer than I cared to admit since I'd worked with it.

I picked up a remarkably beautiful video tape and, stretching, breathing, working my body hard, I was struck by how powerful yet gentle the movements were. Muscles and tendons stretching from one extreme to the other, I felt myself opening and simultaneously felt strong, soft, flexible, and centered. It was virtually the embodiment of all that Mary had taught me.

Finally, I reached the end of the workout. As instructed, I laid on the floor, facing the sky spread-eagle and taking up as much space as I could. Then I was told to let my mind and body relax completely, to just rest in this space, feel it, and be fully aware.

Tuning into the sensations, I felt completely open and vulnerable — and as though I embraced the entire universe. It was ecstasy. This was what

Mary had been telling me. This was the power of being soft, vulnerable, and receptive. This was the feminine aspect of power.

Then suddenly they came, the wellspring of tears. I didn't hold back; I just let them flow. These weren't tears of anguish. They were tears of sorrow, regret, and loss, flowing up and out of me with every breath. And as these were released, gratitude, fulfillment, and joy rose in a swell. Lying quiet and still, I was absorbed in the sensation of this healing balm spreading into every cell of my body.

Then into the long silence, the teacher gently inserted, "Love is what's left when we let go of all we don't need."

Tears now streaming down my face, I experienced this simple truth body and soul. Divine love, self-love, love of life and the world we live in; so much gratitude and so much regret that I'd shut it out for so long washed into and up from my core. My long-held resistances now stretched and released, pure radiance poured into and out of me.

I communed with this luminous sensation for some time, and for the rest of the day, I was more aware of every move I made. Each was a sensual, beautiful act of creation. The day was a walking meditation and more quietly fulfilling than any I could remember. From that moment on, I vowed, I would practice this — receiving this love and being of love in every act.

Healing and releasing the wounds of the past, surrendering and opening to this ever-present gift of love, I was beginning to blossom. And deep within, the delicate seed of new life was forming.

PART III

Alchemy

CHAPTER 20

Elements

*"Hold on to what is good, even if it's a handful of earth.
... Hold on to what you must do, even if it's a long way
from here. Hold on to your life, even if it's easier to let go."*
~ *Pueblo Prayer*

On the morning of 9/11/2001, terrorists struck the twin towers of
the World Trade Center in New York City. America would never be the
same. Suddenly, terrorism — a horror I was all too familiar with — had hit
home, the trauma now embedded in our nation's consciousness.

10/23/2001

When my foot touched the pavement of the parking lot, my heart beat
a tattoo in my chest. As I turned to face the ominous building ahead of me,
its massive rigid form punctured only by shadowy shards of smoked glass,
the facade seemed to drip with symbolism. With each step, my hammering heart pounded steadily toward a crescendo. By the time I reached out
to open the door of the justice center, my limbs were shaking, my muscles
weak. My courage was ebbing.

This is not unusual, I coached myself. *Sometimes it's just best to meet
face-to-face to discuss complex legal issues. This is old trauma resurfacing,
a remnant of the past, that's all.*

Over the last month, my sixth sense had been warning me that something was up around the stalker, around the case, but I got nothing more.
Perhaps it was a gift to help me ease into it, a cushion of time and some
level of acceptance to soften the blow.

My own voice startled me as it broke my introspection and trembled.
I told the receptionist my name and the purpose of my visit, and she led
me to the DA's conference room, where a box of tissues stood prominently
in the center of the table. *I'm sure it's always there,* I told myself, working
to calm my fears.

Settling into a chair facing the door, I closed my eyes, turned within, and walked myself through my exercise. *Breathe. Drop into your center and down. Reach into Earth's center and ground. Breathe and draw that Earth energy up into your center. Open. Reach up and out. Breathe, drawing in light. Sense your space and boundaries. Breathe and fill them with light. Expand.*

I struggled to follow the imagery and, still feeling shaky, silently asked for help. Then I returned to the room and opened my eyes.

Somberly, Kathy and the advocate walked in, nodded, and took their seats. I don't remember how Kathy began. I'm sure she tried to ease into it gently, but I was already in the grips of fear. It was the same sense of anticipation and dread I'd lived with for so long. Watching her lips move, focused only on the words that were coming, I waited for the hammer to fall.

"Vinyard successfully appealed the second-degree felony assault conviction, contending he didn't understand the charges," Kathy said. "The appellate court allowed him to withdraw his guilty pleas and sent the case back to this judicial district — to start over."

The surge of fluid rushing into my head drowned out the words that followed, and seeing my catatonic stare, Kathy paused a moment to allow me to rejoin her before she continued. Rejecting her statement, telling myself there was a silver lining here somewhere, I breathed, focused, and listened as best I could.

It all went back to the "intent" element of the crime, Kathy said. The Colorado Court of Appeals decided that the crime and the consequences of the plea deal offered were not adequately explained to him in light of his mental impairment. "They overturned the conviction," she explained again, making sure I'd heard.

The DA's office petitioned for a rehearing and when that was denied, appealed to the Colorado Supreme Court. But on September 21, she'd received notice that the court refused to review the case.

That was a month ago. Why had I not been informed of any of this?

"The case will probably be heard in this court in the next two to three weeks," she said. "But the officer Vinyard assaulted is no longer here, and it's on the court record that the plea deal was a setup to begin with. That's bad for the case."

With so much against them, she was concerned that the charges would be reduced to third-degree assault, a misdemeanor with up to two years in jail. He'd already been in prison for three. Even if the case went to trial and he was convicted of the lesser charge, his time would already have been served and he'd be released immediately, Kathy said.

Like a bat swung full force at my gut, it hit me. *In two or three weeks he'd be tried and released — immediately.* It was all my mind could grasp.

Old trauma exploded and raced through my body, every nerve fiber crackling in the wake of the surge. All reality shrank to the threat of impending doom. I cracked.

"You can't do this!" I demanded. Kathy tried to explain, but her words were vapor. I had no idea what she said.

"No, you cannot do this to me and my family. We cannot go through this again." It wasn't a plea. It was a statement of fact. I could not survive this again.

Clearly annoyed with me, Kathy said sternly, "You're not hearing what I'm saying." I wasn't. I was shell-shocked.

"It was the appellate court's decision and the state Supreme Court refused to review the case. There's nothing more we can do," she said.

Looking back on it, I'm sure Kathy's snap at me was an outlet for her own frustration. She cared. She cared deeply and felt powerless to do anything about it. Later she would say that breaking this news to me was the hardest thing she'd had to do as a prosecutor.

I felt filleted, exposed. No more armor. Only my speared heart in full view. Tears rained down my cheeks. The air grew still as the faces of my children drifted across my mind. Sobbing, I shook uncontrollably.

Finally, through ragged breath, I uttered the only words I had — "I feel as if you just signed my death warrant" — and collapsed into a pit of despair. Of utter, utter hopelessness.

Kathy had spoken to the judge that sentenced Vinyard and to the attorney general. She said the attorney general was sympathetic toward Vinyard. The district judge, on the other hand, was so furious that he recused himself from ever working another case involving him, Kathy said.

"I'll request a high bond and a new sentencing hearing for your case, but the most we can get for that is probation. You still have the permanent restraining order. We've been able to successfully prosecute stalking cases under the new law, and the statute survived a constitutional challenge. I'll give Vinyard a copy of the restraining order on the record, and I'll read the new stalking law to him, on the record."

She also planned to contact his attorney and his case manager at the prison. "I'll find out as much as I can," she said.

Her assurances seemed so odd, so out of place. They didn't matter. Nothing mattered. The world had just cracked in two.

Suddenly all I wanted was to leave that suffocating room and go home. Quickly, I stood, gathered my things, and was rushing out the door when the advocate approached me. The crime victim compensation program would pay for more counseling and another self-defense intensive if I wanted it, she said. Then she handed me a list of self-defense courses along with a sleek new brochure describing the program, and I wondered: Was the justice system compensating me because I was a crime victim, or was it attempting to compensate for its own failures and abuses? Over and over, the judiciary had not only rubber-stamped abuse, it had participated in it, wielding all the authority of the courts. Not only had it reinforced my role as a victim, it had perpetuated it.

But I was not a victim, and I'd fiercely rejected being called "the victim" in the courtroom, on police reports, in stacks of official documents. The term was thrown around the judiciary so freely, it had long since lost all meaning. *I am a human being. I have a name.*

Somewhere deep inside me, there was still a measure of strength and will. And more than a measure of outrage. No, I would not roll over and accept this. I would fight it with every ounce of strength I had. It was wrong. Just *so* wrong.

Storming out of the justice center, questions and arguments raced around in my skull like a dog hell-bent on his tail:

> *Mental illness is not synonymous with low IQ. Did the court read the transcripts and the full case file? Did it review the psychiatric evaluations or order its own? How did the judges determine he didn't understand the plea deal? He knew exactly what he was doing. Over and over, he'd hidden behind the skirts of his mental illness, strategically positioning himself to strike again.*
>
> *If the assault conviction requires that he intended to harm the officer and the court believes his mental illness renders him incapable of such intent, then he is placed above the law and can never be held accountable. If that's*

the court's conclusion, why can't he be found criminally insane and committed?

We were also victims of the crime. He was finally sent to prison because he violated the conditions of the plea deal by stalking me. Why was I not informed and allowed to testify? Was this a violation of crime victim rights?

It's not fair to move forward with a new hearing without firsthand testimony by me and the officer he assaulted. If the officer is unavailable in the time frame, the hearing should be delayed until he can be found and appear. The probation officer was also a witness and should testify.

I went way out on a limb to testify at the sentencing hearing. I'd emphasized the impact on my children, gambling their safety in the hope of winning the greatest protection I could give them. Each time we take this to court, the stakes are raised and stacked against us. Now he has served time in prison. What will his mental state be when he's released?

As soon as I got home, I headed straight for my keyboard and, mutinous, slammed out a four-page memo to Kathy arguing my points and demanding explanations. The next day, it was in her hands. But in the span of a minute-long phone call, any hope I'd had of changing the outcome was crushed.

"It was a purely legal issue, interpretation of the language of the law. There was no testimony," she said and faxed me a copy of the court's disposition.

Two things were at issue. First, the legal definition of second-degree assault on a peace officer included *intent* to cause bodily injury. Second, the charge of resisting arrest required that he *knowingly* attempted to prevent the officer from arresting him. It was the same "intent" argument Vinyard's attorney had made before the district judge. In the end, that judge rejected it. The appellate court didn't.

"We, therefore, conclude that the trial court was aware of defendant's mental infirmities and should have made inquiries to ensure that the defendant voluntarily and knowingly entered his pleas of guilty," the disposition said.

Collapsing into my chair, I closed my eyes and instinctively breathed, centered, and called on higher powers. In a heartbeat, I realized I had ricocheted right back to my old pattern: fear, anger, control. It had never worked. It would not work now. But there was more to it. The whole time I'd immersed myself in that mindset, it felt "off." It was no longer in alignment with who I was. The coat no longer fit. So what did?

*   *   *

Once I stopped fighting it and faced the inevitable, I accepted that Vinyard would soon be released and we would, once again, live a life of terror under siege until he was caught. Nothing I could do now would change that. But it wasn't my job to change it.

My job was to keep striving for integration, wholeness, and consciousness. To stand in my truth and require that others respond to it. To keep my heart open, be in my power, and trust that universal forces and my own conscious and unconscious interactions with the world around me had brought me to this threshold. And to ask for and surrender to the highest and best purpose of my unfathomable fate.

As I sat in silence, lessons learned long ago in my first self-defense class echoed through my mind: *Open your mind. Engage.* And I realized I was here at this place and this time not only to learn and evolve. My heart linked with Spirit, my feet firmly on the ground, I was to act, consciously, in alignment with all I had learned, with all I had become. *Be the change.*

Recently, I'd come across what I consider a code to live by. I never found the source, but it was presented to me as "Rules of Relationship," meaning relationship with anyone and anything:

> Show up: physically, mentally, emotionally, and spiritually
> Listen: to what has truth and meaning for you
> Tell: your truth, without judgment or blame
> Let go: of the outcome

The more I worked with it, the more I found it spoke to most everything I had learned. And though at first glance it seemed simple, in the most challenging times, it was anything but. If I took no shortcuts, left nothing out, it forced me time and again to be more than I thought I could be. And always, it was "let go of the outcome" that was my biggest sticking point until finally, when I relinquished control, it became my greatest comfort.

*   *   *

Show up, be present. The clock ticking, it was the practical things I turned to first. What did I need to do to prepare for his release?

My children were older; the safety plan would need rethinking. I had to be able to reach them at any time. Cell phones were my first priority.

Then, as vivid memories of life under siege rushed into my gut, it was the doors that captured my attention. Inlaid with windows, the entry doors were not designed for security. Quickly they were replaced, with deadbolts, new locks, and peepholes installed on every one.

The tasks before me were crucial and I undertook them with fierce determination, but to my astonishment, the anger and fear that drove me before were no longer in the forefront. They were there, surely, but this time the work felt positive, empowering. And I knew it was time to empower my children.

My youngest, Seth and Sophie, were now ten and twelve. Ian was sixteen. It was time to explain the situation to them and engage them in their own protection. I'd disclose only what was necessary, not the full horror of Vinyard's predation. And we'd continue seeing Mary. During our brief respite, the children had also worked with her as each of them was ready and willing; there was much healing to be done, much damage to overcome. Now I hoped continued therapy would help stem the tide of destruction I had no doubt was headed our way.

I typed a list of instructions for the kids, including calling 911 and what to say, and posted copies at each door. They had no memory of ever seeing Vinyard, so to help them identify him, I attached his booking photos, buried on the last page so we didn't constantly see his face in our home or our minds.

We reviewed the instructions together. Until he was caught, they were never to be in the house when I wasn't home and were never to answer the door to a stranger.

"Look through the peephole and if you don't recognize the person, man or woman, call me to answer it. Answer the unpublished phone line only, never the listed number; I need to answer the call to record him. Then he will be caught, arrested, and put in prison for a long time."

They were not convinced.

"The stalking law we — all of us — helped change is much stronger than it was," I said. "If he contacts me, he will be stopped. Now it's a felony with a long prison sentence. The law has helped many others in Colorado. Now it will protect us."

By God, I would see to it this promise was fulfilled.

It was actually a relief to talk with the children, to end the secrecy. But as we continued discussing precautions, I quickly realized that I had to tread carefully, balancing informing and empowering them with insisting they let me take charge. I had secured a safe place for them to go. Now we agreed on a code phrase that was their cue to sneak out and go there immediately.

"Don't argue. Just go," I said firmly.

I hoped to instill just enough fear that they would take this seriously but not enough to paralyze them or damage them further. That proved impossible. Sheer terror shone in their eyes, and torn between denial and the need to control the situation, Ian argued with me. A full-fledged teenager, rebellion was well within his repertoire. Challenging me, he insisted on taking the lead.

"I'm not afraid of him. I can keep us safe," he said with conviction.

I wrestled the reins from him. "No, I *know* him. I know how he thinks and how to handle him. I've dealt with this for a long time and we've always been okay, haven't we? Trust me. It will be easier for me to do whatever I need to if I'm not distracted by worrying about what you'll do. I need to trust you to follow directions and not put yourselves in danger."

He relinquished the reins, but his impulses were not so easily dismissed. One day not long after Vinyard's release, I walked in the front door and was confronted by a long sword pointed directly at my chest. Ian had placed it on a cabinet in the entry hall then carefully positioned it so he could grab and plunge it in an instant. There was a long discussion about that, and finally coming to agreement about the danger of wielding weapons without extensive training, it was put away. But before long, at Seth's prodding, we enrolled in ongoing self-defense training.

I was checking off my list of things to do: notify Longmont PD and get a newer photo; talk to neighbors, principals, and school counselors;

check the phone recorder and get blank tapes. What else?

Allies from unexpected places had helped before. I turned to them again. When the last case was drawing to a close, Boulder's *Daily Camera* had followed it closely. The paper continued its coverage throughout our efforts to revise the stalking statute. Columnist Clint Talbott had written several poignant opinion pieces, and when the new statute was signed into law, he summed it up well with the headline, "**And it only took 20 years of stalking**."

Now I reached out and informed him of the turn of events. The stone tossed into the pond, I trusted the ripples to radiate out as they should. I consciously gave it to Spirit then let it go. Four days later, the first in a series of articles that would track this case hit the streets.

The previous year, Bruce had received an odd and ultimately inexplicable collect phone call from an inmate at a different prison facility. In a futile attempt to track the source, I'd spoken to Vinyard's case manager and was told that, due to his violent outbursts, he'd spent much of his time in isolation. Now that information haunted me. I contacted him again but discovered there'd been a fairly rapid turnover. Finally, I tracked down his current case manager and — after explaining who I was, how I was involved, and the current situation — asked for any information about his behavior in prison that would help me prepare for his release. She was hesitant to say anything, but obviously taken aback, she finally confessed she had no idea there was stalking involved.

Of course, he was imprisoned for assaulting an officer. The stalking was merely a sidebar, one no one seemed to notice.

"Well, I can tell you he hasn't improved," she said.

"What exactly hasn't improved?" I asked.

"Stalking." He'd been stalking while in prison.

My breath caught and I gasped, "What's been done about it?"

"It's unlikely that new charges were filed unless CID, the Criminal Investigations Division, was notified. And they probably weren't."

I called a CID investigator and related what I'd learned.

"The local DA at Fremont County would have to decide whether to prosecute," he said. "They don't pursue misdemeanor cases when prisoners are serving long sentences for felony convictions."

But Vinyard's conviction was just overturned. He was about to be released. And stalking was now a felony.

A flurry of emails flew back and forth between the Fremont County DA's office, CID, the crime victim advocate there, the advocate here, Kathy, and me. Soon I knew I was walking a fine line between focusing on protecting us and focusing on Vinyard; my control issues were up again. And when I felt fixation taking hold, I knew I'd crossed the line. It was the proverbial Chinese finger puzzle: The only way out was to stop fighting against it and soften. Consciously, I backed off, breathed, and called on higher powers. *Please help me and give me clarity.*

Surrender. Surrender fear.

Under the circumstances, this was no small task. But with practice, in time I felt it working. I felt myself shifting until I was confident that I was appropriately engaged yet letting go of the outcome and embracing faith. And where before, my interference — my need to control events — was thwarted at every turn, I felt that now, doing the work laid before me and surrendering the outcome, I was working with the fates, not obstructing them. I was allowing the story to unfold as it should. I felt it. I could see it in my mind's eye. It was as if a log jam broke loose and the energy that carried events forward flowed freely, and so did I.

Yet ironically, being fully present, grounded in reality, and surrendering the outcome, for the first time in all these years I accepted the fact that I might not survive this. I contacted an attorney and engaged her services to draft a will, immediately. Time was now terribly short.

The day before the hearing to withdraw the guilty pleas, the Fremont County prosecutor finally returned my call and assured me he would contact the CID investigator to see if they had a stalking case to prosecute.

"But we can't detain him unless and until we have a case," he warned.

11/9/2001

In the blink of an eye, it seemed, the dreaded hearing arrived. The *Daily Camera* heralded the event with the headline, "**Habitual stalker may walk free.**"

Quickly, I read on. "A habitual stalker who made a deal with the Boulder District Attorney's Office in 1998 convinced the Colorado Court of Appeals the agreement was unjust. He may be freed from prison today

— nine years early."

In advance of the hearing, Vinyard had written to the chief judge asking her to hear the case; he didn't want the judge who sentenced him, he'd said. Now he said he didn't want representation from the public defender's office and claimed he'd been represented by about seven different attorneys from that office and gotten "very bad advice." His sense of entitlement was astounding.

The chief judge took the case, denied his request for a private attorney, and appointed a public defender. Vinyard's guilty pleas were vacated and the judge set a conference in two months to sort out all the cases. A trial was scheduled in March — four months out.

I had no delusions that this would ever go to trial. In fact, I was beginning to wonder if the DA's office had forgotten what a trial looked like. But, four months out. Would Fremont County have a case by then? And would Vinyard stay behind bars until then?

Finally, the hearing drawing to a close, the judge addressed that very question and set bond at $50,000. At that, Vinyard bolted out of his seat, cursed at her, and was hauled out of the courtroom.

*   *   *

Soon, Talbott wrote another blistering column for the *Daily Camera*:

> **A danger, not an idiot** … Robert Vinyard is a dangerous, incorrigible stalker who should be locked up. Vinyard wants freedom and might even win it. That's our judiciary at work. The victim lived in abject terror. Judges sent Vinyard to treatment, but he refused to go. Courts ordered him to stay away from the victim, but he harassed her anyway. … Vinyard had zero respect for authority, boundaries or, most importantly, the victim. …
>
> The appeals court said Vinyard may not have understood the crime he pleaded guilty to. He is insane, but he's not an idiot. Vinyard's criminal file includes legal motions, written in his own hand, arguing arcane legal points.
>
> Vinyard's five-page criminal history includes three arrests for second-degree assault. He recites the elements

of second-degree assault like a lawyer. His claim of legal
ignorance, like much of his behavior, is manipulative,
delusional and downright scary. ...

Like nothing I'd ever encountered, Talbott's words were a comforting
palliative. Finally, someone saw the truth and said it like it was. Finally,
what I'd seen and experienced were validated.

*   *   *

The days rushing by, my mind was working all the angles. I needed
to know if I was still a target and called the maintenance supervisor, who
handled the phones at the jail, to see if my published number was blocked.
It had been blocked since 1996, he said, and I asked him to unblock it
immediately. Done.

Vinyard would not be notified, so if there were no calls, it would be
inconclusive. If the calls resumed, I could block my number again at any
time, and I'd know I was still his target.

But unknown to me, while I was strengthening our defenses, Vinyard, too, was working hard behind the scenes. He filed a motion he'd
prepared himself asking the judge to lower the bond from $50,000 to
$10,000. As grounds, he claimed his crimes were not as serious as some
with lower bonds and that the allegation he was stalking DOC personnel
was false or they would have charged him by now. Then he enlightened
the court: His mother had died and he had inherited, so he'd be able to
meet a $10,000 bond of his own accord without placing a burden on his
family.

And, though I was unaware of it, he'd pushed for a bond before. While
the DA's petitions were pending in the state's appeals court and Supreme
Court, the defense had asked for an appeal bond. The district judge denied
it and, eventually, so did the state Supreme Court. But clearly, Vinyard
wanted out, badly. And soon.

1/7/2002

The motions hearing for the re-trial came in January. I anxiously
awaited the news.

To my surprise, Kathy filed a motion asking the court to allow her to
add an additional charge of second-degree assault on a peace officer while

in custody. She was shrewd. The new charge was similar to the original, but the intent standard didn't apply. The additional charge was warranted, she said, because "he was lawfully in custody when he applied physical force."

The latest in Vinyard's long string of public defenders asked the judge to consider the statute of limitations of the crime — three years unless the court considered the case a pending prosecution — and the possibility of double jeopardy in filing the new charge.

And so, the pieces now placed on the board, the game of justice commenced. But while anarchy continued to rule the court, something had changed. The winds of chaos ripping around me, I found myself standing in the eye of the storm. No longer a tattered flag of flimsy cloth to be whipped about by every crosswind, I was less triggered by the events around me. I felt separate. Boundaries in place and heart open, connected to Source and surrendering the outcome, I was fully present and felt safe.

The feeling would come and go, but I had touched something, experienced something profoundly different. Clutching the sensation to my chest, I told myself to remember. It was my touchstone that, in time of need, would lead the way home. I journaled:

> I see that I have changed. Although I have my moments when fear takes hold, I feel that is an old program that no longer serves me.
>
> The warrior emerges but feels entirely different. Before, I was closed and armored. Now I remain open and connected, with healthy boundaries.
>
> *This* is integration and the clarity and power it holds.

2/12/2002

I wasn't subpoenaed to testify at the preliminary hearing. Itching to do something while waiting, I emailed the Fremont County DA again to ask the status of the stalking case there. His reply soon dinged my inbox.

He'd talked with the investigator, who told him they lacked sufficient evidence to proceed with a new criminal case. "I wish you well in the upcoming trial. He needs to return to prison where he can't stalk you." And with that, another door slammed shut.

I flushed with the shock of it and the tingling sensation slid down to my fingertips. Then filling my lungs, I closed my eyes and listened.

Let it go. Just let it go and move on.

The pressure of the hearing now amped up, I paced while awaiting the results. But when some of the details were related to me, I burst into laughter. *How bizarre*, I thought. Either I was losing it or getting healthier. Maybe both.

Thankfully, the arresting officer, now working in another state, agreed to testify. On October 2, 1996, he'd struggled with Vinyard while attempting to arrest him at the probation office, the officer said, adding that Vinyard struck him four to five times on the head and refused to comply with verbal commands when told he was under arrest.

Responding to Kathy's additional charge, yet another new defense attorney argued that the officer had failed to place Vinyard in handcuffs and, therefore, did not have control of him. Then she offered the court clarity. Vinyard couldn't be guilty of assault on a police officer, she said, because a person must be in custody before assaulting the officer to be legally charged with assault. Assault on an officer before being in custody should be considered resisting arrest, she concluded.

The judge interjected, "Why is it a worse crime to punch a police officer after you're in custody than before you're in custody?"

I laughed. My thoughts exactly.

Case law stated, the defense replied, that such a crime was worse because once a suspect was arrested, the officer would have let his guard down, so he'd be less alert and less able to respond quickly to an attack. My lack of reaction to this statement concerned me. Was I too becoming desensitized to the idiocy of our laws?

Arrestees also have a moment of reflection after being arrested to make a conscious decision to lash out at an officer, the defense said.

Kathy shot back: Case law and the circumstances surrounding the incident proved that Vinyard "knew exactly that he was under arrest." He consciously made a decision to struggle with the officer, she declared.

The judge decided to review the case law and said she would rule on the new charge in the next few days. I had not allowed myself hope that the additional charge would stick. Now I had little hope that the original assault charge would either. And I wasn't sure it really mattered.

Somewhere, I had lost the thread that connected the assault conviction to my current plight. And rather than hold onto the hope of a favorable outcome, I seemed to grab onto the lighter notes of the hearing to buoy me — Vinyard's motion to reduce his bond, for instance.

In response to the motion, the judge pointed out his unstable behavior patterns, including an outburst the last time he appeared in her courtroom. Then before she could give her ruling, Vinyard interrupted her loudly.

"See?" she said and denied the motion.

*   *   *

While the case was, once again, slogging through court, I had several interesting, congruent experiences.

Soon after my initial meeting with Kathy, I took the advocate up on the offer of another self-defense intensive and this time, something clicked into place. I felt no resistance, no hesitation. I couldn't quite grasp what had changed; the answer was teasing at the edge of my consciousness. Then before long, I had an unexpected encounter.

I was resting on a bench downtown when an acquaintance, whom I hadn't seen in some time, approached me and sat down at the other end. I'd always avoided this man whenever possible. This time I stayed in my seat.

We exchanged polite greetings, but it soon became clear he was still on a mission to, as he'd said before, "save me from going to hell."

"I'm worried about you. Do you go to church?" he began.

Surprising myself, instead of excusing myself and walking away, as I would have in the past, I turned to face him and said, "I don't want to have this conversation. I'm not here to debate religion." Then I sat back and relaxed.

He did not let it go. Leaning in closer, insistent, he demanded to know what I believed. But I was no longer a projection screen for others.

Genuinely calmly, I looked him in the eye and, holding my boundaries, said, "I do not force my beliefs on you. Do not force yours on me. It's inappropriate. It's your choice to simply accept me or not."

He pushed harder. Four times I repeated it, "It's your choice to accept me or not."

His anger building, he would not relent, and with each verbal shove he inched closer, way beyond my comfort zone.

Finally, without thought, I raised my hand, palm out, and said firmly, "Back off."

To my astonishment, I wasn't angry or lashing out at him. What I felt was a deep, abiding compassion for myself, and I knew the encounter was a gift to challenge me and witness my growth in action.

"I feel attacked, invaded, and disrespected," I said. "That is unacceptable. I will not allow it."

The words spilling out, I realized I'd finally given myself and him a great gift — the gift of my truth. It was, of course, his choice what to do with it; I let go of the outcome. My heart swelled with gratitude. For Spirit, for Mary, and for him.

Feeling ready to move on, I stood, wished him well, and turned to walk away.

Then he grabbed my arm, and my nervous system kicked in.

Instantly, my body was prepared. I didn't have to work to engage my brain or limbs, and no effort was needed to keep from overreacting and attacking. It was all there, working in harmony. I was not hair-triggered; I was simply in a state of readiness, that's all. I could trust my instincts to respond appropriately. Surrendering all interference from my mind, I had freed the wisdom of my body.

The fog of confusion I'd always experienced around such challenging people lifted, replaced by remarkable clarity. No longer did I question whether to protect his feelings or myself. I simply loved myself too much to allow anyone to harm me, invade me, or demand of me what I did not want to give.

I turned to face him and silently held my ground. Our eyes locked and for several tense moments, my gaze held his. Then slowly, he softened and released his grip. And without further incident, I turned and walked away. To my astonishment, during the whole encounter I'd remained open, soft, and vulnerable. And felt immensely powerful.

Then it dawned on me. *Self-defense.* How had the meaning eluded me for so long? *Self-defense.* At the heart of it was — not fear, not hate or anger. At the heart of it was love. Love of self. This was the piece I'd been missing.

Denying myself love and compassion, I could not see beyond the violence and ugliness of it all. I could not accept it. But now, having opened my heart to receiving, having let go of beliefs that didn't serve, having explored and become more my authentic self, I loved myself and knew I not only deserved unconditional love, it was my birthright. And without hesitation, my body had responded.

There was no question of the appropriateness of defending. There was no question of the inappropriateness of self-sacrifice for anything less than worthy. The choice wasn't between violence or non-violence, either-or, black or white. Love embraces all, and firmly centered in love's radiance, all was within the realm of choice.

Over the next several months, these same lessons were hammered home. In business, I had several unusual confrontations with demanding, manipulative clients who wanted to use my reputation but not my advice. And each time, with a clarity and ease that surprised me, I stayed centered, held my boundaries, spoke my truth, and stayed in my power — even if it meant losing the job. No fear. As it happens, not a single project walked out my door.

I also had several personal encounters with manipulative people: less than ethical contractors, insurance reps, and salesmen, to name a few. Each time my response was, effectively, "No, this is what I want, deserve, and will and will not accept." It was not emotionally charged. I was merely stating my truth.

What a transformation of my life! The perpetual loneliness I'd felt for so long was gone, and even in the most challenging situations, I felt comfortable, connected, and safe. Each time, I was fully aware that it was my own experience that was important, not how the other person reacted — and not the outcome. That would take care of itself. Without exception, it did.

Soon my inner work also manifested in my dreams. House dreams. Night after night, I dreamed that people I did not want to see or talk to kept knocking on my doors. Sometimes they'd sneak around outside the house and peer into windows, trying to see me and get me to answer. My heart stampeding, I'd hone in on their location, creep silently away from them, and hide, crouching behind anything I could find. Then suddenly, I'd find myself outside my home, confronting the intruders and telling them firmly to leave.

The story was simple. It was the emotional shift that was profound. I was practicing — practicing what it felt like to shift out of fear and into my power. To shift out of contraction and into expansion. To shift my focus from others to myself and, solidly centered in myself and my truth, to act.

In the half-wakened state, I'd feel the changes ripple through my body, realigning my nervous system, altering me down to the cellular level. My body was virtually being reconfigured to hold my newfound power and freedom.

Yet in the face of all this progress, as Vinyard's imminent release drew nearer, I found it harder and harder to stay centered. All, it seemed, was flipped upside down. To handle all the energy surging through me, I needed a lot of rest, but the nights were restless, sleep best snatched in the light of day.

In sleep I found some measure of peace. When I awoke, life was a nightmare. Each time I opened my eyes, a lump of dread filled my gut as it dawned on me that I faced another day.

Finally, the continued hearing just around the corner, the storm of emotions brewing inside me broke. I was fed up with rising, only to be slammed into the rocks. Swept up by the wave — fear, anger, rage, depression, exhaustion — my deepest fear became fear itself. With a flick of the finger, it inevitably triggered the ripple effect of emotional collapse.

To top it all off, I was disgusted with myself. How, after all this work, could I still succumb to this? My expectations had been so high. Too high. Transformation moves in small steps, often retracing the path just walked. The shifts were not — had never been — accomplished in one great leap.

My work with Mary was intense now. She was the rock I stood on.

"Let yourself be human," she reminded me. "Give yourself grace. Don't fight your emotions, feel them. Your feelings are your truth. They don't discriminate between good and bad; that's your mind interfering. You cannot hold the light and fear the darkness. When you block negative, ugly feelings you shut all feelings down. Set aside time for yourself to feel and just *be*."

Consciously intervening and breaking the cycle of self-deprecation, I felt myself soften. And centering and surrendering to the truth of my feelings without judgment, they rolled through me faster, the crashing waves easier to ride out. Finally the crippling despair broke, but in the aftermath I didn't care about living.

*   *   *

4/12/2002

There was no trial. A plea bargain was struck, and in mid-April, Vinyard appeared in court and pled guilty to a lesser charge: one count of attempt to commit criminal assault, a felony, class 5. The original charges were dismissed and all other open cases were closed.

Repeatedly, the judge asked Vinyard if he understood what he was pleading to.

"I'm pleading guilty to attempting to assault a police officer," he replied. "I understand the charges."

He said he was taking lithium to control bipolar disorder, and the judge said she was convinced he was thinking clearly. Then, surrounded by deputies, Vinyard received his sentence. He had now served nearly five years in prison and jail before that. The judge credited him for the time served and sentenced him to two years mandatory parole. And, she warned, if he violated the conditions of his parole — including staying away from us — he could be imprisoned for two years.

I ignored the lame threat. No longer would I be chained to his sentence for assaulting an officer, or "attempting" to assault. I would rely on the new stalking law to address his behavior directly.

Parole, I was told, would be transferred to Denver. His parole officer would decide the conditions of parole.

The next day, the news hit the papers. "Vinyard seemed to be in a light-hearted mood," the *Daily Camera* reported, "joking that the only clothes he had available included an orange jumpsuit with 'DOC' on it. While he told a reporter that he was an alleged stalker — 'Put that in the paper,' he said — police say he stalked the same woman for two decades. His parole terms include staying away from six people."

The six were me, Bruce, his wife, and the children, who remained unnamed.

Six days later, Vinyard was released on parole. I wasn't notified.

CHAPTER 21

Mercury Rising

"The door is round and open
Don't go back to sleep!"

~ *Rumi*

4/30/2002

Nearly three weeks had passed since Vinyard was sentenced to parole. Nerves stacked like a heap of kindling, I'd been perched on the edge of my seat waiting to be notified of his release. We were as ready as we'd ever be. I just wanted to get this over with. What was taking so long?

Finally, I contacted the DOC's victim services unit and learned he'd been released nearly two weeks earlier. Fury and fear gushing up from my gut, it was with great effort that I remained lucid enough to ask for his parole officer's contact information.

Contacting a new police, probation, or parole officer was always awkward. How would I stuff this whole decades-long nightmare into a nutshell and introduce myself? But soon after launching into my loosely rehearsed prologue, the parole officer interrupted and said no explanation was necessary. He knew the case well; Kathy had spoken with him for over an hour.

To my great relief, he explained that it was his job to deal specifically with sex offenders, stalkers, seriously mentally ill perpetrators, and high-profile cases. He assured me he knew exactly what Vinyard was about and said he'd pushed for him to be classified as a sex offender. And, he said, he'd told Vinyard that he would not tolerate his attitude or his antics, that he was a stalker and if he made one mistake, he was in prison.

"I'm keeping him on a very short leash," the parole officer said.

He gave me Vinyard's DOC ID number for quick reference and told me that, since he was convicted of a felony offense, the global tracking ankle bracelet the judge had ordered seven years before — ordered but could not impose for a misdemeanor — was now required for the first four months of intensive supervision. But he planned to recommend global tracking throughout parole. He would know where Vinyard was at all times, he assured me.

Parole was now scheduled to end June 2, 2003, in a little over a year. Then Vinyard would be discharged. Still it amazed me how, with the wave of a wand, the duration of sentences shrank.

The officer reviewed the conditions of parole. Vinyard had to stay at least two miles from our homes; avoid alcohol, drugs, and liquor stores; attend weekly meetings; stay away from weapons; not drive; get a job; stay on his meds; and not associate with anyone with a criminal record.

"He will have psychological and psycho-sexual evaluations too," the officer said. "The results may indicate more conditions including those typical of a sex offender, like not being allowed to go to parks, be near children, or view pornography."

By the time our conversation ended, I was more reassured than I ever expected to be.

"Call me for any reason," the officer said. "And if you can't reach me immediately, talk to my supervisor; she knows the case well too." Then he paused a moment and added, "I can't even imagine what this whole ordeal has been like for you, but I sincerely sympathize and will do everything in my power to protect you and your family while the state is supervising."

Choking on the tears that suddenly erupted, I clumsily thanked him, hung up the phone, and wept. I had not been abandoned. Someone who really understood. Someone I could lean on, even just a little. It was so rare and precious. Or was it?

Had I always insisted on being independent, going it alone? Mary had long said the goal was not independence, but healthy interdependence. Fearing connection, convinced it led only to pain, had I never allowed myself to be vulnerable? Resisting receiving, had I never fully opened the door to anyone to lean on or ask for help until I was in crisis? I wasn't sure.

But there was one thing I was sure of: I wanted to live differently, to be my authentic self. And the truth was, I was vulnerable. I needed help. And when I finally softened and opened the door, the parole officer, for one, had stepped through it, rising to meet the need.

I supposed it was a gift to him too. By giving him the opportunity, he could do what he did well; he could follow his own calling. I remembered

Mary's counsel. Long ago, she'd said it was her hope that I would learn not only healthy selfishness, but to be in my truth and do what was best for me first. It was the only way I would also do what was best for others. Finally, I was beginning to understand what she'd meant.

The next day, I enrolled in the DOC's victim notification program. I hadn't known I needed to; I'd thought that, naturally, I'd be on the list. A full month later, a letter confirmed I was enrolled. That was not reassuring. The letter explained that I would be notified of Vinyard's transfer to a minimum security or community corrections program; parole applications, parole decisions, and parole revocation hearings; and escape from custody, discharge, or death. In a flash of dark humor I thought, *The latter would be nice.*

Day after day, I tried to go about my life, always sensing the unyielding threat that — like a panther poised at the tip of a branch over my head — loomed over me. I could almost feel the puffs of hot, rank breath drifting down on me.

Riding the waves of anxiety, fear, and rage that would not subside, I tried not to obsess over the situation. My work was overflowing. Deadlines were pressing down. But when it came to my emotions, resistance was futile; self-awareness was now a way of life. Depressed again, angry, feeling overburdened and overwhelmed, I felt myself disconnecting, seeking refuge in dissociation.

Show up, be present.

I reached out to Mary and together we set an intention: I am not willing to entertain anything that is not in my highest and best interest. Stating it out loud over and over to myself, my guides, and my guardians, it became my mantra — a potent one at that. The nightmarish thoughts invading both my dreams and waking hours waned, and I listened to the whispers of wisdom heard only in silence. Then taking it a step further, knowing I was diligently doing my work of evolving, I asked that my lessons come in kinder and gentler ways, and a strong sense of peace and safety poured into me. And in asking this, I shifted, softened, and was kinder and gentler to myself.

7/1/2002

On the first of July, victim notification informed me that, two weeks earlier, Vinyard had been arrested for a parole violation. *Kinda late to tell me, isn't it? Immediately would have been good.*

In all, he'd been free a total of two months.

The psycho-sexual evaluation had been completed and more parole conditions, including psychiatric treatment, were added. "He refused," the parole officer said. "He denies he has a problem and uses the excuse that stalking was not why he was convicted." The officer saw right through it and felt he should go back to prison.

A couple of weeks later, I received a letter from victim notification informing me that Vinyard would have a hearing before the parole board within the next thirty days to decide if he would be continued on parole. A month after that, I was notified that the hearing was delayed due to Vinyard's request for private counsel.

Oh my God, here we go again.

I am not willing to entertain anything that is not in my highest and best interest. Breathe, surrender, let it go, move on. Focus on yourself, call back your power, fill up your space, sense your boundaries. Stay connected.

8/23/2002

Parole was revoked. As soon as the hearing concluded, the parole officer's assistant called me directly to give me the news.

Vinyard was temporarily moved to the Denver Reception and Diagnostic Center, but even a small breathing space was just not to be.

9/13/2002

Mail was an open channel and it wasn't long before a letter arrived, addressed to P.J.A. Enterprises. Panic coursed through me. My last drop of hope that he had moved on evaporated. Now there was no doubt he was still obsessed with me. All too soon he'd be released and I was still his target.

Quickly scanning, my eyes caught on several phrases that pulsed on the page. While all the letters he'd sent me were deeply disturbing, this revealed a new, darker twist. It was sexually explicit and promised another sexually graphic letter he had written but not yet sent. My stomach heaved and I panted, turned the letter over, and walked away.

Once I'd talked myself down and felt sufficiently detached, I reviewed it again for any clues I might find about his plans. It was not his plans I found, but an even more ominous depth of determination:

> I'm not scared anymore. All warriors must overcome
> fear. A warrior must act as if it is the last battle on earth.
> I'm not in control of what will happen. The mood of a
> warrior is to be in and out of control.

A local officer responded, took the letter, left me a copy, and said he would forward it and his report to the DA's office. I left messages for the parole officer and Detective Schumann. I needed continuity in the police department, but she was now working another beat. Kathy had been promoted to judge in another district.

Finally I contacted the crime victim advocate and asked her advice on how to proceed. She said she would pass the information on to Tim Johnson, deputy district attorney and resident domestic violence expert. She would get back to me, she said.

The next day, the parole officer returned my call and asked me to fax him a copy of Vinyard's letter. In the meantime, the responding Longmont officer was investigating the letter and the mail process at the prison facility. Panic rose in a flutter. I told them both firmly that if he was attempting to contact me, this was continued stalking and he should be held accountable.

"Please make sure that any mail he sends me is not blocked by prison officials," I said. I wanted him caught before he ever reached the exit door.

Nearly a month passed and I felt I would jump out of my skin. Finally I got word that when a perpetrator was already incarcerated, a new case had to be tried within ninety days of filing the charges; the DA's office was preparing its case. The Longmont officer was investigating the mail system to prove the letter was from Vinyard, the advocate said. *It had the Denver Reception and Diagnostic Center's official stamp on it, with Vinyard's name in his own hand!* Tim, the deputy DA, was researching whether or not he could charge more than violation of restraining order; the sentence for that was just eighteen months. *Hell yes! Stalking was a class 4 felony with enhanced sentencing due to extraordinary risk of harm.* I asked to meet with Tim. More than one letter would help, the advocate added and said she would contact the parole officer to be sure Vinyard's mail wasn't blocked. *I did that a month ago!*

Obviously, I needed to pull myself together. I was scattered like birdshot again, my life force and all my power flying out in all directions. *Focus within and call back your power. See your boundaries. Fill up your space.*

"And open your heart to receiving love," Mary added. "Love is the only truth, all else is distortion."

"But they're not doing it right!"

"Your head is your biggest hook," Mary said bluntly. I knew it was true. I always wanted to get into my head, root out the source of the problem, and fix it. It was a huge part of my identity. To change my approach to life felt like I was abandoning my God-given talent.

But she wasn't suggesting I abandon it, only that I put it in its place.

"The heart is the master, the head the servant," she reminded me. "Relax and get in touch with your gut. Your feelings are your truth. Surrender to your truth. Trust it."

Trust. I flashed back to my revelation years ago. Until I trusted myself, I would not trust others. But how could I trust them? Long after this whole nightmare began more than twenty years ago, when the case finally crossed the threshold of the courts, we sat back and let the DA's office handle it. We trusted them. To trust them now flew in the face of all my experience, all I'd learned since I'd stepped up and taken … control.

As soon as the thought was completed, I realized that what we did in the past and what I was asked to do now were completely different, and I'd been confusing the two. In the past, steeped in fear, we surrendered our power to the prosecutors. Then having "learned my lesson," it was fear that drove me to grasp for control. But control was an illusion. The idea that to trust meant relinquishing my power was a belief that did not serve, and the perception that I was powerless was an illusion.

My job was to be in my truth and in my authentic power, and the only way to do that was to surrender my fear and open my heart. Only by receiving the love that was always there for me would truth be revealed.

Truth doesn't come from fear. It never comes from fear. Love is the only truth. All else is distortion.

Trust your heart. Surrender control. Each time I felt myself steeped in fear and flailing, I forced my focus back to center. The harder I was pushed by external circumstances, the more fiercely I worked to turn inward, allow my feelings to flow, and receive the wisdom found only in love.

In time, I trusted more and more — not the prosecutors, I wasn't ready for that. But I knew that, ultimately, they weren't in control any more than I or anyone was. To the best of my ability, I trusted higher powers and my inner guidance.

There were now eight months of parole left — eight months that Vinyard would spend behind the bars of a prison. The parole officer contacted the prison investigator and requested that all mail from Vinyard to me be pulled and turned over to him or the DA's office. He was giving me relief. The DA would have the evidence, but the letters would never reach me. No one was sure if, in the interim, any mail had been stopped.

I told the advocate of the plan and asked to be notified right away if the DA's office received more letters. And I asked again to meet with Tim before the letter was charged. I'd seen things drag on in the courts far longer than eight months. The clock was ticking, but I seemed to be the only one concerned.

News of Vinyard's arrest and the letter he'd sent me from his holding cell hit the local papers and spread to *USA Today*. Soon, the meeting I'd asked for was arranged.

11/7/2002

Preparing to meet with Tim, I studied the new statute again as well as the range of penalties. I couldn't help myself. I didn't want the salient points overlooked, and I'd never met the man. Trusting him was simply not in my vocabulary. Instead, I practiced my "breathing, grounding, centering, and filling my space" exercise and by the time I arrived, I felt fully connected and open to receiving help.

It was quickly apparent that Tim was highly intelligent, kind, passionate about his work as a prosecutor, and familiar with the history of my cases as well as the relevant law. Before long, he brought up the need to wait for another contact, a comment the advocate had made and I'd brushed off.

"To prove stalking, we need more than one contact," Tim said. "He was convicted and served his sentence for the 1998 contacts. He cannot be tried for the same crime twice; that's double jeopardy and it's unconstitutional."

I was floored. In all my preparation, this one critical point had never crossed my mind. I just couldn't believe that the decades-long history was not a factor in charging this as stalking. But stalking constituted and the law required more than one contact. And although the sentence for the '98 contacts was merely probation, the charges were prosecuted. Catch-22 — or was it catch-103?

"Theoretically, some charges dropped in 1995 could still be charged," Tim added. "In the new law, there's a seven-year statute of limitations for stalking. But the 1995 statute was later declared unconstitutional, so those can't be prosecuted. And if the new letter was charged now as a violation of restraining order, the maximum sentence would be eighteen months and it couldn't be used to prove stalking later. That, too, would be double jeopardy."

Why had I expected anything different? It was the same pretzel logic, the same chaos made manifest I experienced every time I stepped foot into the alternate universe of the criminal justice system. And, hand in glove, Vinyard's obsession, intellect, and insanity fit perfectly into it.

But there was no way around it. Once again, we were starting from scratch. We had to wait for another contact. Three would be best to ensure that a stalking charge stuck, Tim said.

Numb, I sat for a moment, staring at my hands on the table and trying to swallow the bitter fruit, forcing it down past the leaded lump in my gullet. Then feeling the need to somehow convey the magnitude to him, I inquired, "May I ask how old you are?"

"I'm thirty-two," he replied.

Quickly calculating, I said, "I've been dealing with this since you were eight years old."

Lowering his gaze in humility, Tim studied his own hands and said, "I realized that when I was reviewing the files."

Lumbering out of the justice center, examining the floor, I was deep in contemplation. The stalker's patterns of behavior would not change. And though the stalking law was better, the fundamental dysfunction of the criminal justice system would not change. The system was broken. In my opinion, somewhere along the way it had lost not only its mission and conscience, it had lost its soul. The only thing that could change this experience was me, bringing to the situation all I had learned and all I had become.

When I glanced up from the floor to get my bearings, the door seemed a mile away, and I realized that ever since I'd arrived, my heart was racing, my breath was shallow, my body felt shaky and weak. Now my knees were buckling. I knew what this was.

Whether it was an invasion from the stalker or contact with the police or DA's office — or even just a message from anyone involved — my reaction was always the same. With the pull of any one of those triggers, the bullet released rocketed down the same entrenched neural pathways. Hardwired by decades of recurring trauma, they were embedded in my psyche. And once that bullet unleashed, all hell broke loose. The chain reaction — fear, rage, anxiety, exhaustion, depression, despair, hopelessness — was set on its inevitable course.

My rational mind could not alter it. My new neural net could not override it. It was not a reflection of who I'd become. This was old damage, wounds that had never healed. And until they did, I had no idea how I would handle what I now faced.

4/4/2003

Five months later, I received a letter from the DOC reiterating that the stalker's release date was June 2 — in two months — and may move forward at a rate no greater than ten days per month. In as few as six weeks, he could be out.

4/15/2003

Another week passed and Tim unexpectedly called me. He'd received a letter from Vinyard, now at Centennial prison, thanking both of us for not prosecuting the letter he'd sent me from his holding cell and asking Tim not to extend his incarceration.

The letter was vintage Vinyard, swinging from the adept use of legal references to the far side of lunacy — his extended, hand-written signature, for instance: "AKA Pepe Le Peuh' mi amore Peggy Puissant; THE GRATEFUL DEAD SIDE OF DEAD. Bob Marley is kingbird. Bob Marley Legend Da Best. '3 Little Sparrows' hopeful. Bob will respond to signals from 'Centennial'."

Pepé Le Pew, the *Looney Tunes* cartoon character. A deluded skunk who relentlessly pursues a cat while she frantically tries to flee from him, Pepé was, essentially, an erotomanic stalker. And not at all funny.

That, Tim felt, was disturbing enough. But the reason he called me was the post-script:

> P.S. I'm scared to death of the restraining order and legal complications. However I need to communicate w/ Peggy. May I write to her. Just one time is all I need to convince her. Please mention to her this letter and see if I may have one chance to convince her.

The request for Tim to convey a message to me was "attempted contact through a third party," a violation of the restraining order. It was also a violation of the new stalking law. As soon as there was another contact, Tim planned to file a stalking charge. "It's a class 4 felony that carries up to sixteen years in prison," he said.

Two down, one to go — before his release, I prayed.

6/2/2003

Apparently, the answer to my prayer was "no." On June 2, 2003, Vinyard was released from prison. I notified the Longmont PD.

The shades were drawn. All doors would be double-bolted at all times. Fortunately, we had not abandoned the habit of keeping the doors locked since the last siege.

That day, as I would every day Vinyard was free, I dressed carefully, choosing clothes that allowed me to move freely and fight. Then, wanting nothing more than to take charge and act, I contained myself and waited.

6/4/2003

12:35 PM. Incoming call from a pay phone. At the sound of the bell, old wounds already inflamed ruptured, and, terror and anxiety unleashed, fury rushed to the front lines.

Now under fire from outside and in, the damage entrenched long ago ricocheted me right back to old reactions: My shields flew up and I clamped down. Before long, the incoming assaults would threaten to dismantle not only all the work I had done, but my sanity.

The number was logged on caller ID, and soon a blinking light signaled that I had a message. Someone had started to speak then coughed and hung up.

I called the phone company. They could only identify the general area: Capitol Hill, Denver. I left a message with the Longmont PD and notified Tim. I had no proof it was Vinyard, but I knew.

6/7/2003

Saturday, 5:53 PM. Incoming call from a cell phone, number logged on caller ID. My daughter, now fourteen years old, accidentally answered it.

When Vinyard went to prison five years before, our use of the two phone lines changed. The unpublished line was for faxes, the listed number for business on weekdays and personal use after hours. It was the only line with caller ID and answering it had become a habit for all of us, especially on weekends.

As soon as I heard the phone ring, I rushed into the room and watched in horror as Sophie's face blanched and screwed into a frown. The receiver was pressed to her ear.

The man claimed to be a Regional Transportation District (RTD) bus driver calling to tell us that someone had left a bag and to pick it up at the Boulder bus station's lost and found. Sophie knew as well as I did that none of us had ridden a bus or lost a bag. Suspicious, she asked whose name was in it. The caller spoke with someone else then said something to the effect that he didn't know and we should just pick it up. She turned off the phone and, her voice quivering, related the story to me.

I grabbed the receiver and hit "redial." The voice was not Vinyard's. I asked the man his name and if he was an RTD employee. Complying, he gave his name, said he was on his way back to Denver, and no, he confessed, he was not an employee.

I demanded to know what had happened when he called. He was reluctant to say anything, but I had his number, literally, and he knew it.

"An RTD employee asked me to call to report the bag," he said.

"Are you sure the person was an employee?"

"No," he replied. "It was kinda weird because he didn't say whose name was in it."

I explained my suspicion that this could have been a stalker and asked him to describe the person who gave him the information.

"I'm sorry," he squeaked. "It was a man, about five-foot-eight, chunky, with glasses."

"Was he balding, with dark hair?"

"Yes."

"You are a witness. I'm calling the police. They'll probably contact you." I distinctly heard a low moan as I dropped the handset into its cradle.

Vinyard was trying to lure me to the bus station. He could still be there.

I called 911. An officer would call me back.

By the time I finally spoke with an officer, forty minutes had passed. It was my own fault. In my rush to call the police, my shaking hands had bumped and muted the ringer. I hadn't heard the return calls.

In the meantime, waiting for an officer to call, I paced while I fumed. *He didn't even have the guts to call me directly. Slinking around in shadows, he tried to lure me blindly into his lair.* I was livid.

Finally, I called the police again and reached Officer Rachael Sloan. She arrived quickly. I asked if the police could go to the bus station and explained the urgency. She was not familiar with the case and was obviously assessing my nutcase probability quotient. I shoved my carefully prepared "for just this purpose" files at her.

From our living room, she placed some calls to check into the case then called the Boulder PD. They had no cars available. She then ran a criminal history of the caller. He was a parolee.

When she reached him, he was a profusely apologetic parolee who was ready to talk. He was in the bus station when "this guy paid him five bucks to make the call," he said.

The officer told him she'd be in touch. Then handing me her card and the new case number, she closed her book and headed for the door.

Overwrought, I blurted out the first impulse that shot straight up from the torrent raging inside me. It was impetuous, it was dangerous, and she strongly advised against it. I closed the door behind her.

Officer Sloan had warned me. She had done her duty. Now I would do mine.

I was scheduled to take the kids to their father's for a visit and we were now late. He was in Boulder. The bus station was in Boulder. As calmly as possible, I told the kids not to worry about the call; the police were on it and we would be safe. I asked them to get ready and withdrew to my room to get ready myself.

Throwing on my old jeans, steel-toed field boots, and a denim shirt over my T-shirt, I checked that I could move freely and that my shoes were secure. Screwing my hair up into a knot, I covered it with a cap, then I donned my sunglasses. Peering at my reflection in the mirror, I nodded. My best friend wouldn't recognize me at a distance. A little closer and one might guess I was a woman.

Stuffing my messenger bag with binoculars, my folders, and other essentials, at last I was ready. The stalker had just traumatized my daughter. He would never do that again. I intended to see that he was arrested and locked up that night.

We piled into the car and I did my best to appear unfazed on the drive to Boulder. Hugging them all, I said my goodbyes quickly and drove straight to the bus station. By now, several hours had passed but there was still a chance. On the one hand, it felt good to have an outlet for my pent up anger and anxiety; I told myself I was directing them into something positive and acting. On the other, my gut was sounding the alarm. This did not feel good. I ignored my gut.

The bus station sprawled over a full block and I cruised the perimeter, eyes peeled for the predator and the best view of the waiting area. The wall was all glass. Parking across the street, I pulled out my binoculars and studied every chair, every corner, every inch of floor space for a long while. No sign of him. I drove around the area. Nothing. Back to the bus station, eyes on the waiting area. No Vinyard. Finally, I walked in.

Quickly, I searched the platform and interior, then I approached the counter staff. They hadn't seen him. He had already left.

The next day I learned that an hour earlier, the Boulder police had also taken photos to the bus station and asked if anyone had seen Vinyard. No one recognized the face, and there was no lost and found.

6/8/2003

Sunday, 9:51 PM. Incoming call from a pay phone.

One of the kids forgot the new rules again and grabbed the phone. A male voice asked for Peggy Anderson. When asked who was calling, he replied, "A friend." I flew down the stairs, picked up the receiver, and pressed record. Feedback squealed through the line.

"Hello?" Silence. "Hello?" I hung up.

9:53 PM. Incoming call, same pay phone.

In a moment of indecision, my finger hovered over the record button. Then choosing not to risk getting feedback again, I grabbed a pen and paper and, pulling a deep breath, picked up the phone. The voice was Vinyard's.

"Who's calling?" I asked.

"You know who this is." I didn't speak.

He "really" wanted to talk with me, he said. "I'm really stressed. I really need to be with you."

"Where are you?"

"Denver."

"Where in Denver?"

Stammering, he asked if I would call the police. He couldn't trust me, he said. Then he asked why I didn't press charges for the letter he'd sent and declared that I must have wanted to be with him. Disgusted, I jabbed the "off" button.

10:09 PM. Incoming call, same pay phone. We now had plenty of evidence for a stalking charge, so I took the risk and pressed record but refused to engage with him.

> ... Would you please talk to me? Please. I'm — I've been in love with you for a long, long time. And, uh, that's all I can say. I've been in love with you for a long, long time and I need to talk to you. I mean this is — you're the only woman I've ever loved in my whole life, and I know we didn't have sex, but we could have, I mean it just didn't work out. And if you want me to leave, I'll just leave, all right? I don't want for you to press charges. I don't want my family to go through what they've been through. I don't want to be in the papers again. And I'm leaving it up to you, if you want me to go, I'll go. And I will just leave like the last time. I'll just leave with a broken heart, all right? But if that's what you want.

I'd seen it so many times before, the turn on a dime from pleading juvenile to raging tyrant:

Can't you say something? Say something, ya know. What are you tryin' to get this on some voice recording so you can take it all into a court presentation, so you can win your case? You know, I been givin' and *givin'* and *givin'* and I don't get *nothing* from you! Why don't I get something from you? Can't I receive something, hear your voice or anything? Oh man, you're just recording this aren't you?

Never mind, ya know, if you want me gone, it's better for everybody that I'm gone, an' I'll be the sad one, you stay here and be happy, all right?

Short of breath, my voice quaking, I wrapped up the recording — "This is 10:09, Sunday, June 8, I think. I'll double check that date" — and called Officer Sloan.

She traced the number to a pay phone in Denver and called the Denver police, but they refused to respond until an arrest warrant was issued.

"There's a permanent restraining order," she reprimanded, and they agreed to check the phone booth. By then, he was gone.

10:59 PM. Incoming call logged on caller ID. Officer Sloan was at my home when the call came in. I didn't answer it. She traced the number to Broadway Motel in Denver, took the evidence, and left.

11:49 PM. Incoming call from another pay phone. Staring at the phone, I tapped my foot and waited. Finally the light blinked. I had a message.

Like thunder in the distance warning of the coming storm, the gravelly voice and slurred speech rumbled through the air. I was sure he was drunk.

Uh, yes I was — I was wantin' to know if you would give me a chance and not report this to the police, and give me a chance to turn my life around, get something accomplished in Denver — like the summertime. ... And, I'll see ya in the fall maybe at — see you in the fall in, uh — maybe, uh — see you in the fall in the solstice on, uh — or what is it, the vernal equinox? On September 21 at the Bluebird Shelter. And I'll be there and you can see what I look like. And, uh, you're partly responsible for this too 'cause, uh, 'cause you flirted with me and made me interested in you. And don't say you didn't 'cause you know you did, so you are partly responsible for how I feel.

And I'm gonna get off for a while, and, um, whatever you want to do. If you want to send a bunch of cops to the Bluebird Shelter like you did last time, you can do that, it's up to you. Or if you want to come alone — if you want to come there with somebody to kill me, go ahead, 'cause I'm gonna be there. I'm gonna be there on, uh, on the day — the evening, be evening. And, uh, hopefully you give me a break and you're not reportin' this to the police, and, uh, 'cause I'm not gonna call you anymore. You're not gonna see nothin' from me. Not gonna hide-'n-go-seek an' run up there in Boulder 'n play hide-'n-go-seek an' play some kinda outside game ...

I was stunned. He just admitted he'd tried to lure me to Boulder. I had no idea what the Bluebird Shelter was. Racking my brain, my best guess was a homeless shelter. I called Officer Sloan.

This had to stop now. The cross-jurisdictional barrier was ludicrous. It was time to set up a sting. It had worked before. It seemed the only way now. But I might have to agree to meet him in another jurisdiction. Then it hit me. The "Bluebird" shelter he'd mentioned was the Bluebell Shelter, Chautauqua, where the last sting was planned six years before.

Tim agreed it was a good idea, but said we needed to wait for the felony warrant; the Denver police wouldn't arrest him without it. The misdemeanor warrant done, he was working on the felony. The full case had to be documented for that.

Following up, the Longmont police contacted the bus station caller to identify Vinyard in a photo lineup, and during the interview, the caller inadvertently dropped a small bombshell. When Vinyard approached his unwitting pawn in the bus station, he'd just disembarked from the Longmont bus. My heart stopped. He'd been to my home.

That was it. We had to make a change. The children were never to be in the house when I wasn't home and were to stay away from the house as much as possible. It wouldn't be easy. This was their summer break.

CHAPTER 22

Flashpoint

"What lies behind us and what lies before us are tiny matters compared to what lies within us."
~ *Ralph Waldo Emerson*

"I really can't take this much longer," I said, squirming in Mary's chair, desperate to crawl out of my skin.

She knew it wouldn't serve to raise false hopes and asked how I would cope if he wasn't caught for several weeks or more.

Nnooo! I wouldn't accept it. Grasping the power of symbols I declared to her and the universe, "Summer solstice is mine."

6/10/2003

It was a Tuesday, just two days after the onslaught of phone calls. Wound up like a jack-in-the-box, I'd been ready to spring into fight mode at any moment for days on end. Constantly on guard, I was hyper-vigilant, jumping at the slightest movement or sound.

I'd been trying to work but had developed a whopping tension head-ache. Finally relenting, I washed down some pain reliever and headed upstairs to rest.

Just as I reached the main floor, Seth, now twelve, unlocked the front door and walked in with a friend. Caught in my puzzled glare, my son explained that they were just stopping by for a bite to eat before they went to their self-defense class. It would only be a few minutes, he said.

My eyes pinched tight against the blinding pain, I muttered, "Okay, I'm really not feeling well and I'm going upstairs to lie down."

I closed the door most of the way, pulled the curtains, and slithered gently onto the bed then pressed my forearm over my eyes to block out the last remaining whispers of light.

Our doorbell was quiet. I didn't hear it. Suddenly, Seth burst into the room, his flushed face an alarming blotchy red in the glare of the light pouring in through the door. Out of breath and shaking, he gasped, "I think the stalker's here. He gave you a present."

Leaping off the bed in a full sprint, I hurtled down the staircase while my mind raced around his words — *a present* — and latched onto something planted there long ago. *A bomb.*

Rushing into the living room, scanning for the intruder, I felt my son's friend shove something hard into my hand. I glanced down at the CDs and the boy, his expression a mix of pride and confusion. I ignored the distraction, tossed them aside, and looked around for the stalker. The front door was closed.

"He just left," the boy said.

"Stay back," I commanded, my arm stretched out in warning as I bolted to the door to confront Vinyard.

But as soon as I touched the handle, I stopped. My first priority was the boys' safety. I didn't open it. Instead, I peered through the peephole but the view was distorted. All I could make out was a man in a red cap rushing around the front of a compact white sedan parked on the street. Quickly, he slid into the driver's seat and took off.

Throwing the door open, I rushed onto the porch and searched for a bomb. It didn't take long to see there was nothing unusual or out of place. Confused, I ran into the street, but he sped off. I couldn't make out the license plate.

Shaking violently, struggling to get air, I was a jumble of nerves and disjointed thoughts. Flipping the deadbolt behind me, I flopped into a chair to collect myself.

"He gave you these," my son's friend said and handed me the music CDs I'd tossed aside.

Then I saw the note: "Thanx for letting me out, Schools out." The writing I recognized.

Unaware of our peculiar house rules, the boy had answered the door. Horrified, my son peered around the corner and found himself staring at the stalker, in the flesh, standing in the open doorway.

Vinyard had asked if Peggy was available. The boy knew me as Kaia and thought that was strange, but he knew I'd gone by Peggy before.

"She's upstairs, but she's busy," he replied.

"Take these," Vinyard said, and as my son rushed up the stairs to get me, he shoved the CDs at the boy, turned, and left.

I called the police. Then I feared he might return. I had to get the boys safely out of the house. But I had to stay and wait for the police, and if the stalker came back, I needed to be there to detain him. I was deeply shaken and could not think clearly.

Vinyard had not seen my son; he wouldn't be recognized. But I needed to disguise his friend. Trying not to alarm him, I asked the boy to change into one of my son's shirts and wear a cap. He happily obliged. I then walked into their route to be sure the stalker wasn't there and sent them out to walk to safety.

Within minutes, I realized what a dreadful idea that was. Vinyard was out there, in a car, driving in the neighborhood. And in the mad rush, we'd forgotten my son's cell phone.

Officer Sloan rushed over. Throwing the door open with keys in hand, I exclaimed that I had to go and find the boys. No, I didn't have time to talk to her; I had to find them right away, I said and left with her in tow.

Calling and searching to no avail, I finally stopped at a friend's house nearby. As soon as I stepped out of the car, her door opened and she crossed the road.

"They're fine," she said. "They're here."

I'd never heard more beautiful words in all my life.

Later that day, the felony warrant was issued. Bond was set at $20,000. I felt sick.

6/12/2003

Headline, *Longmont Times-Call*: "**Convicted stalker is sought by authorities.**"

Damn, I thought as I read around Vinyard's mug shot staring menacingly out from the article. I was sure if he saw this, he would lay low for a while, dragging this nightmare out longer. The next day, the Boulder paper ran the same information in its police blotter. *Damn*.

I could not control the situation and protect those around me. Every time one of our defenses was out of place, even for a moment, this predator slipped right through the crack.

The tension in our home was now so thick and toxic that, as soon as they walked into the house, the children were hit with bouts of nausea and vomiting, nervous ticks, headaches, and fatigue. I watched their suffering in horror. It would end now. Until Vinyard was caught, they would stay at separate safe havens — separate to lessen the burden on our generous hosts. I felt awful about it. I had no idea how long this might go on.

They didn't want to go. Just when we needed each other most, we were torn apart. Once again, the only way to protect them was to send them away from me. It was heart-wrenching.

I promised we would talk and visit often. I kept that promise, and each time we talked, their worries about my safety filled the hollow space between us. I worried more than I can say about the effect all this was having on them. Holding myself together during our visits, as soon as we said our good-byes, I'd break down and cry. At times, arms clutching my chest, I'd find myself rocking and moaning until, throat raw and eyes swollen shut, there were simply no more tears to shed.

I couldn't even think about what we faced when all this was over. *One step at a time*, I told myself. *One step at a time.*

*   *   *

Soon I discovered that, with the children out of the house and knowing they were safely out of harm's way, an enormous burden was lifted. No longer was I frantically tracking their every move, terror tugging at me from all directions. Now it was just him and me, and this time, I would do it differently.

No longer would I fight for control over all the external factors that would always be out of my control. This time I would turn my attention inward, on myself, trusting that if I held my boundaries and remained grounded, connected, and open, all action radiating from that center would serve the higher purpose.

Immediately it was apparent that the first thing I needed to do was take care of myself, and not just physically. Physically, mentally, emotionally, and spiritually, my well-being was paramount. The next invasion could be anything, come from anywhere, at any time. To sustain a state of readiness, being consciously aware of how I was feeling and what I needed at all times was crucial. And my first need was staring right at me.

For the first time in decades of stalking, I told my clients that I had a family emergency and needed to take time off work until it was resolved. Since I worked alone with no one to cover for me, this was no small request; I worked in teams on public projects and delays were unacceptable. But graciously and without question, every one of them gave me my space. Now I was free to focus on one thing and one thing only: catching the stalker. As soon as possible.

Pacing, taking stock of the situation and searching for options, I quickly realized I was again focusing on the stalker and flinging myself at the bars of my imposed prison. *My prison.* That was a matter of perception.

Consciously shifting my focus from "out there" to within, my perspective changed and suddenly, the view looked completely different. I was relieved of the burdens of work and worrying about my children's safety, so the time and space were mine — mine to focus entirely on the task at hand and caring for myself, mine to connect and commune with Spirit. My prison could also be my sanctuary, and I chose to see it as such.

If I held my arms out in a broad arc in front of me, this shift was the difference between holding my hands palm out and holding them palm in. And small as this gesture may seem, it was in fact the paradigm shift — a new way of being in the world, even when under attack.

Care for yourself. What do you need?

Staying healthy and strong was essential. I needed to replenish my depleted reserves but had no appetite and soon realized I'd hardly eaten anything for days. I consciously reminded myself to eat and keep up my energy, but I also needed to strike a balance. I was a powder keg of nervous tension and needed to defuse it. I worked my self-defense moves rigorously and felt more fit than I'd been in a decade, but the stress was still overwhelming.

Struggling to cope, I turned to the homeopathic remedies I'd relied on before and added to my stockpile. The essences and remedies helped a great deal, but the nights were taking their toll. Insomnia hit and night after night, I watched the dark hours tick away while my mind raced around in circles. Finally, as the hands of the clock approached four in the morning, I'd drift into sleep, only to wake with a start in a full-blown panic attack.

With so little sleep, I felt rational thought beginning to slip, and I caught myself staring at walls in a daze with no idea how much time had passed. I couldn't risk sleeping too deeply but couldn't be ready without enough rest. Finally relenting, I turned to a mild sleep aid for help. The question was, when was it safe to sleep?

While caring for myself physically was challenging, it didn't come close to the work of caring for myself mentally and emotionally. Though I wanted nothing more than to charge in and get the stalker, all I could do was wait. And in waiting, there was silence. And in silence, there was a battle raging inside me.

Wave after wave crashed through me, and when I felt myself resisting — clamping down on the inescapable terror, rage, and despair — I'd catch myself. If avoiding the pain, I resisted feeling emotions, I could not release them. If I was armored and shut them down, I could not open and pull in my power. Mary had said it so many times, "Your emotions are your truth. Trust them. Accept them all without judgment. Open your heart and let your feelings flow."

Day after day the battle raged on, and finally it occurred to me that, apart from the stress swamping me, this was the ultimate clash between my ego, clinging to fear, and my soul showing me another way, the fight so fierce it felt like the last stand: the battle to the death between distortion and truth, between fear and love.

Now, in my darkest hour, what was required of me was faith. Faith beyond anything I could imagine. Faith that no matter how horrific the situation was, all was as it should be. *The universe works perfectly. My soul is guiding me. Trust it. Surrender.*

This didn't mean surrender to the will of others or sit back and accept everything that happened. I was to act, and I asked for and envisioned what I wanted: my family living in freedom and peace with all this behind us. But I also needed to let go of attachment to the outcome. Asking over and over for the highest and best outcome for all, I had to embrace faith — blind faith — and surrender to the higher purpose and the wisdom of Source.

I could not see the whole picture. I was not in control. I could not know what the outcome would be, and I was not deluded. Embracing faith didn't mean this would end the way I wanted it to. My children could be harmed more than they had already been. I could die. But even if I died, my soul would not be damaged. My soul would have evolved. Death of a life was nothing compared to that gained.

Trust that whatever happens serves a higher purpose, one I may never know. Have faith that I am guided and that all I need will come to me if I just open myself to receiving. And have faith that within me is more than enough if I allow myself — all of who I am — to emerge. It is encoded within me, the answers accessible. Listen. Listen to it all.

Finally, in perfect trust, I strengthened my connection to Earth's center and Source, breathed deeply and dove. The force of the emotions released was alarming. I felt I would be swallowed whole. But deeper and deeper I dove until, simultaneously, I rose higher and higher.

I was holding it all, and a sort of dynamic equilibrium emerged where all my emotions — fear, anger, sorrow, courage; and love for the Creator, myself, family, friends, and all of life — flowed. And I realized that, by releasing judgment, for the first time in all these years I was engaged in the full breadth of the experience. My heart open, accepting it all — the darkness and the light — I was fully present and connected. And every waking moment became a walking communion with cosmic consciousness.

*   *   *

Police cars patrolled the neighborhood frequently; Tim had requested an extra watch on our home. And throughout the region, law enforcement was searching for Vinyard. I hoped it wouldn't be long now.

Greg Malsam, an officer in Longmont PD's domestic violence unit, had taken charge of the case. Since my case never involved an intimate relationship, it wasn't domestic violence. But because stalking cases often did, officers and prosecutors with expertise in domestic violence had the most experience and training in the crime of stalking. I was deeply grateful for his help.

Before long, working as a team as the case progressed, Greg and I were on a first-name basis, though out of respect, he called me "Ma'am" in equal measure. We had met briefly before when we both worked on the subcommittee to change the law. I had no idea then how vital that work would be to me now, just a few years later; Vinyard was supposed to be in prison for twelve years, not three.

I wasn't aware of all the work going on behind the scenes. It was extensive. Greg was making contacts, gathering information, tracing the phone calls, coordinating with police in other jurisdictions, following up on leads, making arrangements to have an alarm system installed in our home, and preparing reports and getting them to Tim.

He also contacted Vinyard's former parole officer, who gladly shared all his information and said he was aware that Vinyard had called me from some motels on South Broadway. He'd kept close tabs on him while he was out on parole and knew where his haunts were, he said. Then he volunteered to make flyers and distribute them to businesses in the area. Greg gladly accepted his offer.

Soon the parole officer's own investigative report was faxed to Greg. "Mr. Vinyard portrays himself as a victim, with everyone out to 'get him,' yet takes no responsibility for his actions over the past twenty-plus years," he wrote. "He shows little if any victim empathy. He is a severe public safety threat, especially to women. ... Contrary to Mr. Vinyard's objections and opinions, he does display the traits and behavioral characteristics of a sex offender."

By now we had more than enough evidence to prove stalking and I resolved not to answer any more calls. If he left a message, great. More evidence.

Holding my boundaries and filling my space, I consciously gave the stalker back all that was his. Whatever he did, whatever he projected would reflect right back to him, including his own power — power he had long surrendered to me.

"You can save me," he'd written.

No, only you are responsible for yourself and your choices. Only you can save yourself.

6/14/2003

7:22 PM, Saturday. Incoming call from a pay phone, logged on caller ID: Colorado Springs area, south of Denver. No message.

6/15/2003

12:28 PM, Sunday. Incoming call from a pay phone, Denver area. No message.

8:59 PM. Incoming call from a pay phone, Denver area. Message left and recorded.

Two weeks had now passed since Vinyard's release. A friend who worked in the mental health field said that by now, the medication would be wearing off and he'd be losing control. It seemed to hold true. With the passage of time, his messages grew more bizarre and unpredictable, and the confidence he projected even more disturbing.

Uh, yeah! Yeah, I know ya got caller ID, so, uh, why don't you just give me a buzz here? I'll be here for a little while. And uh, uh, the reason I'm callin' you is I'd like to see you again, and if not, then I'm gonna be goin' in here pretty soon. But I would like to see you and uh, if you want to, give me a call. I'll be here for a while.

9:28 PM. Incoming call from a pay phone, Denver area. Message left and recorded:

Yeah, I have to keep moving, you make me nervous — you 'n the cops. Why didn't ya — in the paper — why didn't you report that I came to your door? Yeah, all right, John, John makes me, all right. He might be a li'l bit better 'cause he makes me. But sometimes I — sometimes I feel like I just can't get outta Denver sometimes.

See, uh, went to the zoo today. And, uh, had a good time. It was all right, wasn't too bad. I've already — I've already seen the elephants. Uh, yeah, so I'm pretty much the same. I haven't committed to one or the other. Um, actually, I prefer this way better. Um. And, uh, I really want to see you. And, uh, I — and I would like for you to come to Denver for a change 'cause I'm always — I'm tired of goin' to your place all the time, ya know. If you want a friend, I'll be here, I'll be that friend here. I'm so sick and tired of always goin' to your place. If you want a friend, I'll be here in Denver. And, uh, yuh, you have the number, caller ID. And give me a call, and we'll talk. In the dark. Don't you like the dark?

He'd seen the paper. He was on the move. *Damn.*

But he just admitted he'd come to my home. That would be helpful, when he was caught. In the meantime, not knowing when or how this would finally end, his closing remark reverberated through me.

6/16/2003

10:50 AM. Incoming call from a pay phone. No message.

The calls were relentless. With "crazy" bombarding me constantly, I felt I would go mad myself. And I was furious. Once again, Vinyard was dictating the narrative, calling all the shots. I hated that I couldn't unplug the phone; we needed the evidence, and if he couldn't access me one way, he'd just choose another — like coming to my home.

Every day was devoted to collecting and recording the evidence both on tape and in my timeline, staying in contact with the police and Tim, and exchanging recorded tapes for new ones. I also needed to listen to the messages, and tracking him, scanning for hints of his next move, I strategized constantly. Alone and on guard every minute of every day, I was completely boxed in. Home was no longer a sanctuary. It felt like a prison again.

6:14 PM. Incoming call from a pay phone. No message.

Pacing like a caged lion, I could not stay in the house any longer. I desperately needed a break.

"The calls are still coming, but I'm leaving," I told Greg. "I'm going to a friend's house to visit for a while."

Knowing I'd been wrestling with sleep, he replied lightheartedly, "Good, but you might want to avoid coffee."

It was a great relief to have one point of contact at the Longmont PD again, especially one as dedicated, experienced, and good-humored as Greg.

*   *   *

If Mary was the rock I stood on now, my friends were my sustenance. Fully aware of the situation and concerned, they'd been reaching out to me, asking how I was and offering support.

For as long as I could remember, whenever I'd been in crisis before, I'd isolated myself. I told myself it was to protect others, and there was some truth to that; when Vinyard was free, I would not risk anyone else becoming a target. But unconsciously, I also did it to protect myself. Rigidly defended against the onslaught of emotional assaults and having no concept of healthy boundaries, I did the only thing I knew how to do: I shut down, refused to receive, and built a wall around myself. In time, I'd become a master mason. Isolated, lonely, I disconnected from everyone and suffered alone. And isolated, I was in even more danger.

This time, I vowed to do it differently. No shutting myself off and going it alone. No going off to my cave and licking my wounds out of view. And no protecting others from the experience. I trusted that all involved, at whatever level, were in this for their own higher purposes. Mary had assured me of that.

I would be cautious, of course. I'd perfected the art of being sure I wasn't followed and never had friends over when Vinyard was free. But I could stay connected. *I am vulnerable. I need care and compassion. This is my truth.* I reached out and clasped their outstretched hands.

*　*　*

Heeding Greg's advice, I chose herbal tea, and my friend listened patiently while I ranted and raved, paced and sat, leaped up and paced some more, then exploded, punching and kicking the air. Finally, the edge wearing off, I shared some of the more ludicrous details of the ongoing saga and together we laughed — we actually laughed. What a welcome release.

When I returned home feeling clearer, exhausted, and ready to sleep, I first followed through with my work. Picking up the phone and scrolling through the call list, I accessed my messages, the recorder on. It was a mistake. It would be hours before I could unwind enough to sleep.

8:07 PM. Incoming call from a pay phone. No message.

9:03 PM. Incoming call, logged on caller ID. Message left:

> Uh, yes, this is Bob. Uh, yeah, uh, let's finish this. Uh, uh, I spent a lot of time and effort, and, uh, you know, I wanna finish. Why not? I got some'n to share with you, you seemed interested at one time. And you can give me a call at, uh, [number provided], and uh, I'll be here for a short while, and I'm hoping that you feel the same way and want to finish.

9:15 PM. Incoming call from the same pay phone. Message left. After some legwork, Greg later traced the number to a Hooter's restaurant in Denver.

> Hey, you're probly wonderin' why I'm callin' you. Uh. You know, I been here twice as long as you have. I'm

Colorado native, twice as — born here, born and raised in Colorado. Twenty years longer than you ever been here. Now you get your ass here! You understand me?! *Here!*

Day after day culminating in stalemate, I found that a pattern had formed. Upon waking each morning, I felt fully charged and ready to get this done. But unable to do anything to stop it, by mid-day, hope turned to anger. As the day pressed on, anger gave way to depression, and the dominoes continued to fall until hopelessness and despair washed all color from the sunset and the day ended in blackness. It was a reflection of the stalker's pattern, the calls always peaking at night. I had to break the cycle. I had to retrieve my power and stop reacting to his behavior.

Finally, the walls closing in, I resolved not to contract within them. When darkness descended, I marched out the door, locked it behind me, and walked back and forth to the ends of the block. Patrolling the area, I owned my space.

Pacing a path from my door to the sidewalk, I occasionally stopped at the edge of the walk and, arms crossed, stood guard over my domain. Then across the street, just out of reach of the streetlight, I confiscated a small mound of grass. Perched there, I could see my yard clearly and worked my self-defense moves hard until, muscles burning and out of breath, I was soaked with sweat. It quickly became my evening ritual.

6/18/2003

Two days passed without contact. The police hadn't found him. He could be anywhere, across the country or around the block.

It was intolerable. No way could I live like this with no end in sight. He had to be stopped now. I felt strong and powerful, and I told Greg it was time to set up a sting.

He agreed and said if it was in another jurisdiction, he'd have to confer with the local authorities and would need more time to prepare. He suggested someplace like the Denny's restaurant in Longmont.

All my alarms went off. Vinyard was dangerous and I'd trapped him before. He'd be suspicious and could be armed. I didn't want bystanders caught in the crossfire. There had to be someplace safer in town. Where? And when would he make contact again? And how?

6/19/2003

2:03 PM. Incoming call, no information on caller ID. Voice mail message left:

> Hey, yeah, look at the lotto numbers for Wednesday, June 18th: 2-24. Yeah, I kinda like John making me do this, get up and around. That's exciting. Don't you like the horse that come in second? Colorado native, Pat Day. Huh, well, yeah. Give me some credit 'cause I been working hard. Call me back.

7:02 PM. Incoming call from a pay phone. Heart hammering, I picked up the receiver and pressed record.

" — uh, come to my motel."

I was struggling to breathe and didn't want him to know how shaken I was. I'd keep my reply short.

Lobbing the conversation back, my voice trembled, "Where are you staying?" Then closing my eyes, I began inhaling and exhaling deeply, and my awareness dropped down.

" — meet me someplace. What?" he asked.

"Well, I don't know — I don't know where you're staying. I have plans tonight." The oxygen was working. I was regaining my composure.

"You have plans?"

"Yeah, I do and um — "

"All right, okay, all right. Wow, this is pretty much surprising to even talk to you!"

"Well, you know you left me a lot of messages, and it seems like you were assuming that I'm by the phone all the time, and actually, I travel a lot. I'm not around here a lot."

"Uh, yeah. Right, right, all right, all right. Understandable. Yeah. Uh-huh. So, so what is your business?"

"Um, I don't — I don't really feel like talking to you over the phone about it."

"Oh, all right, all right. You don't feel comfortable over the phone?"

"No, no."

"Uh-huh."

"And I'm really about to take off right now, so — "

"Ah, well don't, don't — hey wait a minute, this has been a lot of trouble for me, I don't wanna just say hello-goodbye type situation. Aahh, why don't you change plans for me?"

I laughed. "I've got other plans." I felt the shift. I was in my power and the conversation turned.

"Come on, I've done a lot — "

"Look, look, look, look, look — " He was talking over me and my voice grew stronger. "Are you gonna just talk and — so that you just want to talk to my voice messaging system again, or do you want to listen for a minute?"

"Yeah, sure, I'll listen."

"Okay, I've got other plans right now. I'm going to be leaving town and let's see, what's today, Thursday? I'm going to be leaving town Saturday evening and I've got a lot going on until then. So, you left me messages saying that you wanted to meet with me. Let me check my day timer and see."

"Wwwe — I can — I can be up in Longmont tonight if you want."

My gut clenched and I sighed loudly. "Actually no, I've got other plans tonight. So — "

"You got what — all right, all right."

"And listen, listen — "

"I seen you. I seen you were driving the Suzuki. I know you got your plans and your Suzuki, but — so you're in control, ya know, so."

"My Suzuki."

"If I could just see you one time to convince you that, you know, I'm for real and I really, really, really, really want you real bad. Badly."

"All right, listen to me. My Suzuki is one of my vehicles, and it's my older one and I don't drive it that much. So, it's here a lot when I'm not here. But don't think about coming to my house because I have a really good burglar alarm system. So — "

"No, no, I don't really want to come to your house. I rather you meet, meet away somewhere."

"All right, um — " My mind was a blank. I hadn't come up with an alternative since I'd talked with Greg.

"When are you going to be to in Denver anytime?" he asked.

"I don't like to go to Denver, so listen. Tomorrow night, I have a meeting and then I have a class, but actually, like tomorrow night about this time, seven o'clock, if you want to meet with me, um, let's see. There is a — oh, let me think." *Why can't I think?!*

"Wwwe, it's gonna be really hard to trust you."

"Oh, listen, you know, it's up to you. You want to meet with me — "

"Yeah, yeah, but I mean, you gotta look at my position."

"No. You know what, if you want to meet with me, you're just gonna have to trust me. Look, I've worked with the police, I've worked with the law, I've worked with the justice system, and none of it's worked for either of us, right? It's been bad news for both of us. I don't want to deal with them anymore. So, you're either going to have to believe me or not. If you want to see me, I guess you're going to have to trust me 'cause I don't know what else to do. So if you want to meet with me, tomorrow night I am available at about seven o'clock. Um, I could meet you — there's a — let's see — are you going by bus or by car or what?"

"I, I — you, you know, you seen me come up in my car, you seen me do — I — "

"So, you got a car."

"Didn't you see me the other day when I brought you the presents?"

"Ah, I — no, I didn't. But anyway — "

"Uh, no, I got a car." He sounded suspicious.

"All right."

"Did you get my presents?"

"Uh, yeah I did."

"Did you — did you like 'em?"

"I — I'm really not sure why you gave them to me, but we can talk about this tomorrow night. I've got to get going. So tomorrow night, seven o'clock, there is a Denny's — do you know where Twin Peaks Mall is since you've been to Longmont?"

"No, no. Let me — let me tell you some'n. The crow showed me a way. The crow says a good place to meet you is at McDonald's on north Main."

"North Main of what?"

"North Main is McDonald's, there's two McDonald's."

Kids! Not where there are kids.

"In Longmont?" I asked.

"Yeah."

"Why, why do you — "

"That's where the crow told me — "

"Where the *crow?*"

"Oh, you don't understand."

"No, I don't understand."

He laughed. "You never read any Carlos Castanada?"

"Ah, no I didn't, but listen — "

"All right, all right — "

"Look, I've got to go. So you either listen or you don't. If you want to meet with me, you meet me at the Denny's restaurant which is in the parking lot of the Twin Peaks Mall. You can find it; you seem to know your way around Longmont. And I will be there at about seven o'clock. Is there some way that I can reach you if, um, I am running late?"

"Uh-huh, uh. All right, all right, um. Uh man, it's really hard to trust, trust you."

"Well — "

"I mean, I gotta — I gotta a place I can stay in now, and I got a home phone and everything like that, but I don't wanta give that away right now."

"All right, but — "

"I'll just leave it up to you. You're goin' to be at the Denny's on Twin Peaks Mall," he said.

" ... Okay, seven o'clock tomorrow night, and if I'm running late, I guess I don't have a way to get ahold of you, so just wait for me."

"Uh-huh, all right, all right. I'm *used* to waitin'."

"So, what kind of car are you driving? I think I'll take my Suzuki."

"Uhh, uh, it's up to you. Um, what other vehicles you got?"

"Look I've got to get going."

"Hey, hey, hey, ya know, I'm taking a big chance here, ya know?"

"Yeah, I guess you are and I guess you're just going to have to take that chance."

"No, now, you really wanna see me or are you just — "

"Yes, I really want to see you," I said.

"All right, okay, okay, I'll be at the Denny's at seven o'clock tomorrow, and I'll wait for you."

"All right, bye."

*   *   *

I made arrangements to pick up the kids in the morning. We would spend the day together in a nearby town before I met the law enforcement team in the afternoon to prepare. They didn't feel a stand-in would work; it would be best if the stalker saw me go into the restaurant so he didn't bolt before they could stop him. We would go over the plan ahead of time, and they'd fit me with safety gear.

In the meantime, dusk descending, I felt I wanted something, a talisman of sorts, to carry with me — something to connect me to Spirit and my loved ones, something to give me courage. Riffling through my jewelry, all the old necklaces of wooden beads and colored string my children had made for me over the years surfaced, along with hot tears that now soaked my cheeks. These treasures were the hallmarks of innocence, never to be tainted with something so ugly. Coarsely brushing my tears with the back of one hand, I plunged the other back into the drawer and focused, but nothing I found felt quite right. Maybe it would come to me later. Or maybe it didn't matter at all.

I then sent an email to friends asking for affirmative prayers and intentions and was preparing a quiet space to take it all in and just "be" when there was a knock at my door. Concern lining her face, my friend said she wanted to give me something to carry with me tomorrow, and she pressed something into my palm. Slowly, I unfolded my fingers and my mouth dropped open. I hadn't mentioned a talisman to anyone. I hadn't even asked the cosmos. I'd simply desired it.

I now had no doubt. I was being watched over, and this time my good friend was the messenger. She related the story.

Her grandfather was a soldier who served during World War II. In the spring of 1945, the Third Reich was falling; the war would soon end. The front line advancing then retreating, suddenly, her grandfather found himself separated from his unit. Alone, he was trapped behind enemy lines.

His best hope of survival was to shed his uniform and, somehow, find his way home to his family, some two hundred miles away. It was an extremely dangerous proposition: German soldiers penetrated every path and road. Terrified, he knocked on the doors of several homes but was turned away. Then he approached a farm house.

A young woman appeared and, with great risk to herself, gave him sanctuary in her barn overnight. The next morning, she offered him civilian clothes and a bicycle: probably her husband's, he thought. Had her husband been killed? Or was he too lost in a perilous distant land, just trying to get home?

Finally this courageous, compassionate woman, whose name he never knew, handed him a locket to ensure his safe journey home.

The photos it once contained were long gone, but the locket had since been passed down through my friend's family, always reaching the one in need in times of great personal challenge. Infused with the timeless story of the call to courage in the face of fear, with compassion and comfort for the one alone and suffering, and with the bonds of love that led the way home, it had now come to my hands.

My eyes brimming with tears, I nodded and hugged her. The gratitude I felt for her and all those souls it had touched before me stifled all words. Stroking it gently, I tucked it securely into my pocket where I vowed it would stay until I, too, was safely home.

That night, I pictured all those who would happen to be in tomorrow's scene and set my intention. *Let no innocents be harmed,* I prayed.

CHAPTER 23

Chrysalis

"To me every hour of the light and dark is a miracle ...
What stranger miracles are there?"
~ *Walt Whitman, Miracles*

As it did for me the morning of the sting operation, there must come a time in all our lives when time stands still and rushes by all at once, a moment so full it can't be contained. When every hue of the grasses, trees, and sky are so vivid, you wonder how it could be that you didn't see their full expression every day. When the life force all around you vibrates and glows before your eyes, yet it must have done that all along. And you feel so small yet so profoundly a part of the vastness, the greatness of it all. How indescribably rich and precious it all is. How truly magical.

*   *   *

6/20/2003
All the little stories and laughter didn't mask the grave concern underlying the conversation my children and I shared that morning. None of us wanted it to. Best to accept and honor the fact that this was a solemn, formidable day and that every moment we shared had the potential to become a treasured memory.

We all fell silent as I drove the kids to their dad's, where together they would wait to hear it was over and that all was well. Pensive and yet on fire, I felt a palpable mix of gaping sorrow and the fullness of love, hope, and oddly, free will. And I realized there is a subtle yet profound difference between being forced into the arena and choosing to enter it, between being dragged and walking freely to one's destiny. The essence of this distinction is, paradoxically, surrender — surrendering to the power of love unmatched by the fear that rushes in to fill the space left in love's absence. It was this choice, it was the presence of love that made all the difference.

2:30 PM. Just as we approached their father's street, my cell phone rang and all eyes leapt to it. It was Greg. Vinyard had been arrested.

Abruptly, my nervous system shifted from high gear to a dead stop. Shocked, I couldn't move or speak. Time slowed. The distinct sensation of fluid draining down through my body and out my limbs overwhelmed me, and I realized I'd been pumping adrenaline for three weeks straight. Now as it poured out, draining my life force with it, I was completely depleted.

He'd been arrested in Denver around midnight the night before, Greg said. Completing the paperwork needed if Vinyard was taken into custody, Tim had just searched the computer system and discovered the arrest. He called the Denver County Jail and it was confirmed: Vinyard was being processed. Tim immediately called Greg.

I shook my senses back, and the urgency of taking the next step — getting a high bond — hit me. Greg said he would write a new warrant for the most recent calls and ask the judge for a high bond to ensure that Vinyard wouldn't be released overnight. He'd do his best to have it signed that day, he assured me.

As soon as I got home, I called the Denver County Jail to be sure Vinyard was in custody and that I would be notified of any release or transfer. That evening, Greg called again and apologized for the delay.

He'd completed the warrant with a $100,000 bond, and at 5:30 PM, the judge that sentenced Vinyard to prison signed it. But because he'd recused himself from any further cases involving Vinyard, he followed up and discovered the warrant was null and void. He called Greg and suggested he contact the chief judge, who was still at the justice center. Greg rushed back, found her, she signed it, and within minutes he faxed the warrant to the jail. The chance of the stalker being released on bond was finally, relatively slim.

6/21/2003

Rising early the next morning, I rummaged through my closet and pulled out the most feminine, soft, flowing clothes I could find. Consciously, deliberately, I adorned my ears, neck, and hands with the most iridescent pieces of jewelry I owned. Pulling a brush through my hair, I let it fall freely around my shoulders. Day and night for three weeks solid, I had dressed for combat: rugged layered clothing, shoes tightly laced and double-knotted, hair tied back, and all jewelry that could be torn off removed. I studied my reflection and a smile crossed my lips. I looked like a woman again.

Alone, I walked into my garden and felt the cool, moist grass cushion and caress my bare feet. I covered the table with a cloth and, in the center, placed a small vase of flowers fresh from my garden. After lighting a candle, I reached into my pocket and gently placed the locket on my small altar. Then breathing deeply, I closed my eyes and drank in the scents and sounds of life awakening in the breaking dawn.

It was summer solstice, when the dark night surrenders to the longest light of day. And just as I'd declared in my session with Mary weeks before, this day was mine, living free and in peace.

My awareness reaching deep into the ground then out to the infinite field, I was overcome with gratitude. I was alive. No innocents had been harmed; they had never even been in harm's way. It was more than I'd asked for. It was a miracle.

I reached out to all the spirit workers — ethereal and earthly, past and present, known and unknown — who had supported and protected us. The gratitude I felt filled me to overflowing. *Thank you. Thank you all.*

I pictured my children and my love for them grew warm in my chest. With each breath, it filled me more, and expanding far beyond the limits of flesh and bone, I linked with overwhelming love radiating from Source. My heart, fully open, soared.

Basking in this magnificent beauty, tears welled up and spilled down my cheeks. *This — this amazing love — is the truth of our existence, here for us always just beyond the veil of ugliness and heartache we've created in our world. It is so beautiful. How have we drifted so far? Why do we choose to live as we do when such a treasure awaits us at every moment?*

I lingered in the timeless communion then snuffed the candle and gathered my things. I'd been invited to join some friends for brunch, and I packed a basket of food.

As hugs and greetings were shared all around, I found I was subdued. Oddly, I had no desire to tell my tale or join in the conversation. It was more than enough to be among these wonderful people and watch. It was as though I was snapping photographs in my mind, recording the memories as they occurred, fully aware of how precious they were and would become.

I didn't stay long, and as I drove home, like a fog rising from a deep pool at dawn, sadness engulfed me.

I wouldn't resist it. Softening, I surrendered, and as the days passed, the droplets of sorrow coalesced into a flood of grief. Sinking deeper and deeper in the bottomless pool, I grieved. For all my family had suffered. For the immense chasm of loss.

*   *   *

Studying police reports and following the papers, I pieced together the details of the arrest. Vinyard had called me twice from Longmont — my heart skipped a beat — and four times from phone booths along Broadway in Denver, among others. The police had received a tip that he was staying at a hotel on South Broadway. I didn't know if it was the parole officer's flyer that led to the capture, but from the depths of my soul, I thanked him all the same.

The hotel was in Englewood, a suburb of Denver. According to the arrest report, the Denver police had watched his room for about five hours and had just called the Englewood police to meet them there, when Vinyard drove into the lot and walked into his room. The officers reviewed his criminal history and found multiple arrests for resisting arrest, obstructing police, assaulting police, and other assaults. The report also noted that the Denver police believed Vinyard had obtained a gun since his release. My blood turned to ice.

Six officers were on the scene. With a liberal dose of obscenities, Vinyard reportedly refused to come out and, his anger building, yelled at the officers through the window then broke the glass with his hand. The scene echoed in my memory: *Only a thin pane of glass stood between him and us, and with each blow to the wall, it trembled. I was terrified he would burst through the glass at any moment.*

When finally coaxed out, the police reported, he came straight toward the officer in charge with clenched fists and refused to comply with the order to get on the ground. A brawl erupted and it took three officers with batons deployed to restrain and secure him. And somehow, my children and I were supposed to defend ourselves.

Charges were pending in Englewood for resisting arrest, Tim said. Later, he told me that when Vinyard was transferred to the county jail, he came completely unglued, tore off all his clothes, and attacked a guard.

"There may be new charges for that," Tim speculated. "The other guards on the scene had to forcibly restrain him."

In the meantime, my phone had been blocked again and his mail would be screened at the jail.

The press was buzzing. Journalists at the *Daily Camera* contacted me with questions and, with my permission, published my birth name, Peggy Anderson. I'd given them permission to publish it before, when the new statute became law four years earlier. Though I'd still been concerned about the notoriety of the case and didn't want clients constantly associating me with it, I'd refused to hide any longer. Instead, I had begun using my new name — Kaia — professionally, and gradually it had taken hold. By now, few of my clients realized that Kaia Anderson was Peggy Anderson, the woman stalked by a madman for decades. For me, it was a welcome degree of anonymity and separation. Two identities, two separate lives.

So by now, I had no reservations about the papers continuing to use my birth name. What I didn't know was that once that Pandora's box was opened, it couldn't be closed again. The news went out on the AP wire and I was deluged by journalists. Tim was contacted by *NBC News*, *48 Hours*, *20/20*, *60 Minutes*, *John Walsh TV*, and local news channels. They wanted cameras in the courtroom and interviews with us both.

Tim wasn't concerned about the cameras, but this was not the time for interviews. We needed a fair trial in Boulder County and too much publicity might force a change of venue. We were not about to provide ammunition for an appeal on the basis of an unfair trial. Finally, I unplugged the phone.

Within the week, bond was raised to $150,000. Vinyard, of course, complained it was too high.

"It sure is, and that's where it's staying," the interim judge said. "You pose a significant risk to this person."

The preliminary hearing was set for the next month. Determined to focus on my family and work and not get caught up in all the eddies and backwaters of the judicial process, I told Tim I saw no reason to testify. There was more than enough hard evidence to prove probable cause, and the Longmont police could identify Vinyard in court as well as describe the emotional impact on me. With "serious emotional distress" now being the key element of the stalking charge, each time Greg responded to a new contact, not only had he verified my claim of a contact and gathered the evidence, he'd also asked what effect the contact had on me and my children, emotionally. It was all in the police reports.

Tim wasn't sure if he'd need me to testify or not. But, he said, since Vinyard refused to disclose the status of his inheritance, the court hadn't appointed a public defender and he was currently without lawyer. If he was not represented at the preliminary hearing, Vinyard would have the right to cross-examine me directly.

"I need to know how you'd feel about that," Tim said.

"Oh my God! Can this really get any more horrendous? Can't the court demand disclosure or just assign a public defender?"

I was completely depleted and my brain felt like a bowl of raw eggs that a heavy hand had taken a whisk to, savoring the omelet about to be fried. When my children complained independently that they too could not focus, their words were scrambled, and they lost their train of thought mid-sentence, dipping into the vast well of my experience, I told them these were common PTSD symptoms that would pass in a month or so. It was true. What I didn't say and only worried about were the countless symptoms that could very well surface later.

Then the first letter arrived. Once again, Vinyard had slithered through the cracks in the system.

7/15/2003

My daughter reached the mail before I did and, a puzzled expression crossing her face, handed me a thick envelope then studied my reaction.

There was no jail stamp, but who else would use the weird, invented name "PJA Associates, Personal Consultants"?

I tried to maintain my composure, but my hands shook uncontrollably, and worry creasing her brow, Sophie stared at them wide-eyed.

"It's all right," I said and quickly retreated to my room, closed the door, and worked to slow my heart and breath.

Before I called the police, I needed to be sure it was from him. Carefully slicing open the envelope, I skimmed the first paragraph. It was definitely from Vinyard. But there was no jail stamp. Was he out?

I was scheduled to leave for a meeting, but terrified of leaving Sophie home alone, I called the jail and was assured that Vinyard was still in custody. Still, I bugged out of the meeting.

Greg arrived quickly. It was an eight-page handwritten letter begging me not to prosecute. Clearly, Vinyard understood the new law and the potential penalties. Then rambling on, dipping deep into the inkwell of his psychosis, he added a new twist and blamed his actions on a cult and orders of the crow.

In closing, he wrote, "You will keep this private." It sounded like a threat and landed the charge of tampering with a witness.

When Vinyard was arrested and safely placed in custody a few weeks before, we began to relax. We were assured that his mail was screened and our phone number was blocked, and I felt we could finally focus on recovering and healing. Then the letter came. I was still so thoroughly exhausted that when Greg asked me how the letter affected me, staring at the walls, all I felt was numb.

It wasn't until the next day that a black despair descended. I didn't have it in me to hope anymore.

New charges were filed for the letter and another $100,000 bond was added. But it didn't stop the invasions, and now there were three separate new cases: one for contacts before the arrest, one for contacts after, and one for tampering with a witness. More heads on the hydra.

Tim kept me abreast of the ever-shifting charges and potential penalties. I listened and took notes but didn't have the heart to believe any of it. I just wouldn't subject myself to that kind of devastation again. Living in the moment and trying to recover was quite enough to deal with.

Two counts of stalking, each carrying a maximum sentence of sixteen years in prison, plus seven counts of violating a restraining order, each punishable by up to eighteen months in the county jail, was the soup de jour according to the papers.

The preliminary hearing was postponed, replaced by a discussion about the defendant's competency to stand trial. Vinyard decided he didn't want to play and refused to come to court. The judge ordered a competency evaluation, and the preliminary hearing for all the cases was moved to September 4. It would, of course, be delayed again. Then I got the form letter: The DA's office "is sorry to hear that you have been the victim of a crime." I was too raw to laugh.

Eventually the results came back and, as always, Vinyard was found competent to stand trial. *Insane, not an idiot.*

Via a spate of emails, Tim and I discussed the possible charges, pleas, and outcomes, including the dreaded insanity plea, ad nauseum. Twisting my mind around it, all I could grasp was there were no clear answers. Once again, it was all melding into one big, amorphous mass of uncertainty.

The attorney who'd fiercely defended Vinyard in the assault case was now working this one. Tim said she planned to challenge the constitutionality of the stalking statute — again. I swore it would be a miracle if I wasn't declared insane myself when and if this ever ended.

I was climbing a trail of switchbacks to the top of a "fourteener," the nebulous peak hidden somewhere up there in the fog. The fact that I'd seen this all many times before didn't make it any easier. But the uncertainty and delays were new to my children. Anxiety was palpable, tempers were short, endless bickering broke out in our home. We desperately needed closure.

Then the phone rang.

11/21/2003

Friday, 7:35 PM. I was on a ladder painting a wall when a call came in on the unpublished line, usually reserved for faxes. I asked Seth, standing next to me, to answer it.

Suddenly, his eyes glazed over and all color drained from his face. Shoving the receiver away from his ear like a hot potato, he handed it to me. As it moved through the space between us, I heard a recorded voice say it was a collect call and there'd be a charge of $1.80. Hands shaking, I slammed the "off" button. Neither of us heard the name of the caller.

My head pounding with the force of the fury that erupted, I called the maintenance supervisor at the jail to ask if the call had been logged and if that number was blocked, but his office was closed until Monday. I left terse messages for him, Greg, and Tim.

When the tumultuous day began to settle, a small voice arose from a quiet corner of my mind: *How did he get that number?* Worse, that line had no caller ID and no voice mail, and I couldn't attach a recorder.

The next morning, the *Daily Camera* announced, "**Accused stalker enters innocent plea.**" I spent the day nursing a headache and nausea. I couldn't think clearly; my brain was misfiring again.

First thing Monday, I was on the phone with the jail's maintenance supervisor. The call came from "the back" where Vinyard was housed, and according to the log, fourteen calls had been placed to that number in the last month. If I accepted a call, he explained, the conversation would be recorded at the jail. More evidence. It was a plan.

"The back," Greg said was "disciplinary," where Vinyard had been held the whole time he'd been incarcerated.

11/30/2003

Sunday, 2:40 PM. Collect call from the county jail on my unpublished phone line.

This time I was fully aware it was a combination of PTSD and my barely controlled outrage that caused my voice to quake. Panic hit, my heart pounded wildly against my ribs, my lungs compressed, and I was spitting fire.

"Uh, yes. Hello," Vinyard said.

"*How* did you get this number?!"

"Uh, someone gave it to me."

"*Really.*"

"Yeah."

"*Nobody* knows this number. How did you get this number?!"

"Uh, somebody gave it to me."

"Nobody gave it to you."

"Yes, they did."

"*How* did you get this number?!"

"I wanted to call you."

"*How* did you get this number?!"

"I wanted to call you. I need to talk to you. Please talk to me."

"Tell me how you got this number!"

"Somebody gave it to me."

"Who?"

"An inmate here."

"Right. This number is unpublished. No inmate can know this number."

"I wanted to talk to you."

"How did you get the number?!"

"Somebody gave it to me. What I wanted to say is that I have a make-up gift that I got for you and I was hopin' that you would just please get it and not report it to the police, please."

"A make-up gift."

"It's a make-up gift to, to, to express how I feel."

Knowing the call was being recorded, I was determined to expose him.

"And how is that?!" I asked.

"I'm sorry and I feel bad, really bad about what happened between us. Really bad."

"Then why are you calling me now?!"

"Because I wanted to say before — not to surprise you by giving you the gift in the mail because you seem to be — I've gotten the message that you don't want me mailing letters to you."

"And that's the *only* message you've gotten?!"

"Yeah, yeah, I haven't, have, have — as far as I know, no one — I haven't gotten any more complaints against me except the letter that I, in uh — in uh Ju, July."

"And so you think that it's okay to call me?! That it's okay to contact me in any way?!"

"I need to make up with you 'n, ya know, I know you got the restraining order, and I know I didn't do a good job when I went to the hearing last time in September 16, 1997, when you had the permanent restraining order in front of [the magistrate]. And there were so many people there, I couldn't really express myself. Ya know, I had stage fright. I'm not — I don't do well in front of the public. There was a lot of people there. I didn't get a chance to express myself. It wasn't — what I wanted is, if there's any way possible, if I could have another chance to express myself to other people as well as just you, privately, that — of how I feel about you — why, why I think we should be together."

"Don't call this number again!"

"All right, all right, all right, don't let's. Ya know, I don't want to argue any more — that you don't feel — I'm just, ya know, you're the only one that's ever — that I've really felt close to in my entire life. I'm just bein' honest. And I, I got you a gift to express myself to music and I, I wanted to let you know that I have that coming your way."

"What does that mean, you have that coming my way?"

"I got a gift sent to you and I hope you don't, you know, report that to police and it's held against me. And anyway, expressing feelings. There shouldn't be a law against expressing feelings."

"Really! I've expressed my feelings that I never want any contact from you again for twenty-five years. That doesn't mean anything, huh?!"

"People, people make up. I mean, ya know, it doesn't have to be this way. We can make up as friends. I don't care how we make up. I don't care if we make up one way or the other. I mean — "

"Apparently, you don't care anything about my feelings whatsoever! I never, ever want any contact with you *ever* again!! I haven't for twenty-five years! We never had a relationship! Stop!! I've done everything I know within the law to make you stop!"

"Ah, I. Ya know. I, I disagree with that. I disagree with what you said. Ya know, um, there were certain things that you did twenty-some years ago to make me feel that you did want a, a relationship, ya know. Uh, you know, time I did come over to your house that you acted very — "

I slammed the phone down and called the jail then Greg.

When the call came in, I'd closed the door, but the kids were all in the next room and they overheard me shouting. I think anyone on any floor of the house would have heard me shouting. I explained what was happening but was in no shape to calm their nerves.

The rage writhing inside me oozed from every pore, and waiting for the police to arrive, I found myself scrubbing the bathroom.

"Why are you cleaning?" Seth asked, his face creased with concern.

"Sometimes when you feel violated, it just feels good to clean," I replied, digging the brush into porcelain, desperately trying to scrub every trace of him out of our home.

Greg picked up the recording at the jail, and as soon as he'd verified the recording was audible, he had that phone number blocked too.

The nightmares returned and the next morning, a headache and nausea surfaced again from the rank debris. I was completely depleted. I tried to work but finally gave up and put myself out of commission. I couldn't think and needed space to just sit and be with all I was feeling.

We — all of us — felt tormented, betrayed, and powerless to stop the assaults. Ever since the arrest, we'd all been seeing Mary for intensive therapy; we were working hard to heal. Yet to even begin healing we needed space, time, and peace. But having lost the battle, Vinyard was now storming the gates. The invasions were escalating. It never stopped. It just *never* stopped!

The package soon arrived. It was from a music store in Denver and when I looked at the label, I froze. "To: Kaia Anderson."

Kaia. How does he know that name? He had just penetrated my last sanctuary. I was devastated.

Greg responded and opened the package. It was a music CD bearing the title *Kaya* and, with it, a small scrap of paper with another rambling, quintessential Vinyard stream of bizarre thoughts and pleas. "Run for the shadows. You'll finish and I'll respond passionately."

I felt sick. These "romantic" gestures were grotesque. And he'd exploited my name, as if he was entitled to.

No. It was my identity apart from him.

The timing concerned me. "Tomorrow's my birthday, but there's no way he could know that," I told Greg, doubt streaming into my gut.

Greg made a note of it, and his investigation soon revealed that Vinyard had sent the music store specific instructions to attach his handwritten note and be sure it arrived by the date of my birthday.

In the same batch of mail was a letter from the court. It was a copy of an order to deny dismissal of my restraining order. I hadn't even known Vinyard petitioned to have it dismissed. Maybe it was better this way, learning about it only when the magistrate denied it.

Just before Christmas, Tim, Greg, and I convened for a meeting. All the charges were class 4 felonies, Tim assured me. There were two counts of stalking with a maximum sentence of sixteen years each and a maximum of twelve years for one count of tampering, for a total maximum of forty-four years. Numerous counts of violation of protection order tacked onto the cases would also add time, he said. I barely listened. No way would we get anything near that.

The next day, Tim provided me with a copy of a second letter from Vinyard to the magistrate, appealing the decision to deny dismissal of the restraining order. Citing case numbers and criminal code, it read like an attorney, "to wits" and all. I soon received a copy of the same letter directly from the magistrate, stamped "Denied." I don't remember Christmas.

12/27/2003

Another letter soon arrived, stamped "Uncensored Inmate Mail." The return address announced, "Inmate Name: <u>Robert Vinyard</u>." It was addressed to a fictitious name. Greg responded and opened it.

"I am writing this to you because I want you to know that this letter and others and other gifts recently sent to you to make-up is my last try to, my last effort to take action, to reconcile, make-up with you."

Good, he admitted he'd sent them.

Begging me over and over not to prosecute, he claimed that if I didn't respond in a positive way, he'd "for <u>sure</u>, <u>positively</u>, <u>absolutely</u>, <u>certainly</u>" never contact me again. "I'm not like calling or writing to you every day. The few times I have I absolutely had to. I have been like 99.9% compliant."

There was not a hint of comprehension that he alone was responsible for his choices and their consequences. And there was no remorse. Not that I expected it. Despite his apologies read aloud in court five years before, I'd long suspected that his particular psychosis rendered him incapable of empathy.

He would be re-arrested in jail, Greg said, and I asked him to tell the jail staff to check the address, not just the name, on outgoing letters and to hold as evidence any more letters intended for me. It had to stop. We desperately needed it to stop.

12/31/2003

New Year's Eve, 9:00 PM. The unpublished phone rang and Sophie answered it, heard the recorded introduction, and shoved the phone at me. Both our phones were supposed to be blocked. Livid, I accepted the call to record it at the jail but said nothing.

> Yeah, hello, yes. Hello. Peggy? Ka-ee-ah? What, uh, can we just have a conversation? I mean, you're really turnin' loops. First of all you block your calls, now you have unblocked calls. You know, what's, what's — I don't wanna really have a monologue here, can we have a dialogue? Hello, I'd like to hear your voice. Oh, come on. Who is this? Is your name Ka-ee-ah, K-a-i-a? …
>
> Why? Okay, why? Why am I calling you? 'Cause I want to talk to you. I want to see if there is any way that — if you

could drop the restraining — I can't drop the restraining order. I've already tried, I've written to the courts twice now. I can't drop the restraining order. You have to drop the restraining order. That's what I'm trying to accomplish. Why, why did you unblock your phone number? You had it blocked for a while, now you're unblocking it. Why? Do you want me to call? Uh-huh. ...

His delusions looped endlessly. "You seemed always thrilled when I came over to visit you. You always seemed thrilled when I called you. You were always happy to see me back then. Now, why? Why, why are turning your cold shoulder to me?"

I hung up and he called right back:

Yeah, let us have a conversation. Um, all right, you wanna — you wanna know why? Just drop the restraining order, that's why. Ya know. I still have feelings for you, that's why, okay, isn't that enough? What else do you need? I can't be — I can't — all you have to do is drop the restraining order. Just drop the restraining order. You do it, and I've done everything I can. I wrote two letters this past month, both denied. Now they're not going to deny you. This is a woman's county; they'll do whatever you want, ya know. So, you, you drop the restraining order. I can't see — I can't — I don't understand — I can't see — to go through all this effort I'm going through for nothing. I can't understand that. And I put a lotta effort into this. And I'm just not going to give up. I'm not going to give up. I'm not gonna quit.

With that, he hung up.

I unplugged the phone and called the jail from the other number. It was New Year's Eve and all I could do was leave a message.

I then left a message for Greg. "Do what you can to stop this at the jail," I demanded, rudely. I was not myself.

Finally, pacing feverishly again, I was so distraught, I called Tim at his home.

"Oh, my God," he said and promised to contact the jail immediately. "I know he goes into lockdown between 10:00 PM and 8:00 AM, so you should at least have some peace then."

Another call came in on New Year's Day. I didn't accept it.

This was torture — for all of us. A living hell. Every new contact pulled the trigger, and rage rocketing through my system, the chain reaction raced toward my inevitable demise. And all the stress symptoms I'd had while Vinyard was out persisted and worsened.

I could not stop the unwanted thoughts chasing around in my head. Spinning out of control, I felt I was going crazy. Even steel bars had not stopped the assaults; we were constantly bombarded. And every day, in one way or another, the pervasive, interminable judicial proceedings invaded my life.

Infuriated, despondent, I sank into a deep, dark depression. No matter the outcome, I would never be free of him and his maniacal obsession. I had no interest in life and at times, I admit, felt death would be a welcome release. But I could not abandon my children.

Stop! Shift your focus. Look within. Breathe.

It's not about him; it's about me. What needs attention? What needs healing?

I knew that between throwing up my armor, putting my head in charge, and the short circuits in my brain, I had succumbed to old habits, shut down, and thrown away all my power again. But I was so disoriented, I couldn't remember what to do. I needed help.

*   *   *

"Relax, let go, open your heart," Mary reminded me.

I knew her counsel was true. I'd experienced the truth of it myself, and yet overcoming my instincts while continually under fire felt impossible. Why was this so hard?

Every instinct told me to fight, not surrender; to be rigid, not soft; to erect walls, not hold boundaries and connect; to shut down, not open. Tempered by decades of emotional assault and my desperate attempts to stop the pain, my defenses were hardened steel.

"The feminine aspect of power lies in softness and receptivity," Mary said, "but of course these are the very places where we — all of us, women and men alike — have been so violated for thousands of years."

After pausing a moment to let that sink in, she said, "You feel you are hitting bottom because you're not opening to higher powers."

I sighed. "I'm being pushed to my limit to let down my guard."

It seemed a cruel and backward way to approach the lesson, but the insight offered a spark of hope. My own strength of will and mind were working against me.

"It's the Chinese finger puzzle," I recalled and pictured it in my mind. *Stop fighting it and relax. Trust, have faith. Feel the resistance then let it go. Surrender.*

"That's right," Mary said. "You know this is the process of surrender. If we hold barriers to love, we're not safe. The universe is battering your shields to teach you that the only way to deal with the world is with an open heart. The only way to be powerful is to be totally connected to yourself, to others, and to higher powers. When you are defended and shut down, when you close your heart and resist your power, you are at risk of harm. Only when you're open and connected can you connect to the situation and be powerful."

I flashed back to the moment Vinyard ambushed me with my young son. Terrified, I froze. Then suddenly, surrendering my fear, I was overcome by the sensations of peace and love pouring into me. I'd felt immensely powerful, and opening my heart and connecting with the stalker, he backed down, and Ian and I escaped. I shared the story with Mary.

"Exactly!" she said. "You released your barriers to love and surrendered your fear. You connected to higher powers and opened your heart. And open, connected to yourself and the situation, you embraced your power." It was the only way Ian and I could have been safe, she felt.

At the time, I'd been stunned by both the contradiction and the familiarity of the experience. Now it was beginning to make sense.

"If we dim ourselves down, if we are defended and shut down, we don't have access to and support from higher powers," Mary said. "You know how powerful you are, but you're not trusting it and you're not feeling safe."

It was true. I still didn't trust my own power. More, I feared it.

Feared, not integrated, my personal power was still locked in the basement, imprisoned in shadow. After all this time, it was only in extreme crisis that I set foot lightly on the stairs, accessing just enough power to get me through the moment. Why?

Long ago I'd learned to shrink-wrap myself in deference to others and, I believed, to be safe. Then the stalking began and the question that was the mortal wound followed: "What did you do?" others had asked, implying I was responsible for the stalker's obsession.

So I bound myself into an even smaller package, knowing full well I'd become so much less than I truly was. I felt wasted. I knew better now, but the wound ran so deep for so long. So long in fact, that I'd seen myself, centuries ago, killed for simply being all that I am, for being in my power. Or was I?

At the moment of my violent death in that past life, I was in the grips of fear. The only thing that had healed the experience was just what Mary was now encouraging me to do. Softening, I had opened my heart, surrendered fear, accessed higher powers, and received the love poured into me.

Yet the compulsion, still, to contain my personal power and lock it down was overwhelming. But in doing so, I'd once again reached the breaking point.

I had to surrender my resistance. I had to embrace my power. It was the only way. And hard as it was, from the beginning of this whole ordeal, I was determined to find the gift in this, to learn the lessons this decades-long nightmare offered me. It was this quest, to find that pinpoint of light in the black abyss, that had pulled me through my darkest hours. I could not abandon it now. The lessons learned had never failed me.

My power was mine to own and take responsibility for. Shoved into the unconscious, it would not be contained. The dragon in the basement, it would only thrash and act out in ways that did not serve. But brought into consciousness and integrated, how it was used would be my choice. My conscious choice. I journaled:

> I've been working all this time to become all that I am and be in my power. It is time to own whatever abilities I have. The trial a few months away, I now realize all the work I have yet to do. I must rediscover that part of myself I may never have truly known but only been vaguely aware of and feared my whole life. It is urgent that I discover all that I am, integrate this power, emerge from the chrysalis.

Who are you? What are you capable of? Tell me, show me. You are not responsible for anyone else's choices or actions. You just are. And I want to know you. I want to own you and love you. Be seen. Be heard. Be with me.

*   *   *

In a mad dash to keep up with the blizzard of contacts, Tim was trying to amend the charges and group the three cases into one. Then he received a letter from Vinyard declaring his plan to represent himself in one of the stalking cases; his attorney was still on the other.

"Mr. Johnson, I'll be going Pro Se in 03 CR2052. I need Discovery and have a right to Discovery prior to the Preliminary see C.R. Crim. P. Rule 16 Part I(a)(1) … ," Vinyard wrote.

Now it was even more urgent to combine the cases and prevent this from happening.

In the meantime, I was ignoring the hearing notices filling my mailbox. It was all becoming a blur, and until Tim said I was needed, I was just riding it out — engaged but not controlling. Tim always informed me of the results, and all they'd been so far was moving targets with further delays.

The only thing on my radar was a trial or two in April, and I was skeptical even of that. One of the preliminary hearings delayed at least twice before was now scheduled for February 6, but Tim had agreed my testimony wouldn't be needed.

2/5/2004

Trying to catch up, I was working late when, at nine o'clock, the doorbell rang. My heart leaped and shot out of the gate.

I didn't recognize the man in the peephole and cautiously opened the door a crack. Verifying I was who he was looking for, he shoved an envelope into my hand.

"Have a good night," he said and rushed into the darkness.

I had just been served.

As a witness, I was required to report to the preliminary hearing the next morning. It was the second case involving all the contacts from jail: one charge of stalking and multiple protection order violations. The subpoena was signed by Vinyard's attorney.

I dug in my heels. *No way.*

There was no reason for me to attend. I was sure Vinyard just wanted me there in the same room. For the judge to force me to be stalked in his courtroom would be the height of insanity. *Throw me in jail for contempt,* I thought.

I called Tim's office, certain he would check his messages before going to court.

2/6/2004

The next morning, pulling on my jeans and an old sweater, I was preparing for work when Tim called.

"There's no reason for me to be there. He just wants to stalk me in court," I declared resolutely.

Tim agreed that I shouldn't have to testify. He'd ask the judge to quash the subpoena first thing. "But," he said apologetically, "you should definitely be here, just in case."

Dammit. I rushed back upstairs, tore off my sweater, and, refusing to go too far, threw on some slightly more appropriate clothes.

I barely had time to make it. Wheels skidding over pavement, I reached into my toolbox: *Breathe. Drop, ground, center. Open. Light, boundaries, fill. Expand. Help!*

Still working on grounding, centering, and opening, I sat quietly outside the courtroom, waiting for word I could leave. The minutes crawled by, and with too much time on my hands, I imagined refusing to testify and being escorted to jail in protest. But the bottom line was, nothing could jeopardize the case. Nothing.

Finally, the doors opened and I stood to receive the news. The judge didn't quash the subpoena; I had to testify. And Vinyard was representing himself.

A burst of shock and outrage scorched the air around me, my wrath not just aimed at Vinyard. The judge too was engulfed in the flames.

CHAPTER 24

Ascent

"We can only be what we give ourselves the power to be."
~ Native American Proverb

Why didn't the judge quash the subpoena? Not only was he sanctioning this predator's stalking, he was enabling it, aiding and abetting the crime.

Stop! Right now his reasons are irrelevant.

I now needed more time to prepare myself again. The doors of the theater opened, and with each step the aisle before me seemed to tunnel, stretching longer and longer.

Diving, my awareness plunged into my center and down, deep into the center of the earth, where I consciously released all negativity. Dark, amorphous blobs dropped, one after the other, into the incinerator at her core. Anchored there, the connection holding, I trusted that all that did not serve my highest and best interest would continue to be sucked into the earth's center and transmuted.

When I drew my breath and awareness back up to my center, to my astonishment, a tremendous power was drawn up with it, firmly grasping my lower chakras. *You are supported.* Thoroughly rooted deep in the earth, I felt stable, unmovable. And tremendously grateful.

Surrendering more and opening my heart, I then sent my awareness up and out into the ether. Breathing deeply, I drew the glistening light and all benevolent forces I touched down into my center. The power drawn in overwhelmed me. *We are here with you. You are beloved.*

Awestruck, I softened, released, and surrendered completely to these unfathomable powers. Body and soul, partner and beloved child, I was steadfastly held in a circle of protection, and an outpouring of love and comfort penetrated my heart. I was safe.

Suspended in these exquisite sensations, I was firmly anchored in a vibrating column of energy pulsing between heaven and Earth, my body merely a small node on this living trunk line — a node distinct and yet not. And in my center, the energies swirled as if waiting, and I knew. My center was the lens through which all this power could be focused and used according to my own free will. I was entrusted with this unfathomable gift.

Breathing deeply, I stepped up into the witness box. With each breath in, these forces were drawn in, filling my space. With each breath out, my space expanded, pushing my boundaries outward. Pumping this energy with every breath, I grew larger and larger until, as I took the oath and sat down, my space encompassed the whole front of the courtroom.

Sensing this energy pulsing through me and vibrating the air around me, I gazed across the room then locked onto Vinyard and connected. And the power pouring into me reached out from my heart, solidly holding that connection. Only in love lies truth, and I was firmly anchored in love's power. Delusions, distortions, non-truth were no match for this. Sitting tall, leaning forward, focused on the stalker, I felt no fear.

"Questions, Mr. Vinyard?" the judge asked, and I realized this was the same judge who'd heard the case the first time I'd testified in court, more than six years before.

Vinyard stood, and while he shuffled to the podium, I found myself calmly calculating both my own leap over the witness box wall and his.

"Hello, Ms. Anderson," he began and looked up at me. Holding him firmly in this unwavering force, my glare was riveted on him. His shoulders dropped and he glanced at the floor.

"It's kinda unusual circumstances to see me this way," he said, snickering awkwardly.

Fumbling to frame his questions, he began walking back and forth behind the podium, and first breaking eye contact, then slouching and studying his shoes, he was visibly diminished.

> Vinyard: There's some question about your name change. Why did you change your name to Kaia Anderson?
>
> Anderson: I changed my name to Kaia Anderson for several reasons. One of them was to protect myself from you and provide some anonymity because of all the ... media coverage that's surrounded this case and

to protect my professional reputation as apart from this case.

Vinyard: Is there any particular reason why you chose the name Kaia?

Prosecution (Tim Johnson): Objection. Not relevant.

Judge: Sustained.

Vinyard: Did you ever receive a musical cassette in your mailbox [called] *Kaya* besides the date of December 10, 2003?

Prosecution: Objection, not relevant.

Judge: Sustained.

Vinyard: You allowed me, Your Honor, quite a bit of leeway when [my attorney] was questioning the witness. I'm trying to make some points about our past relationship and how it evolves into today.

Judge: The objection is sustained.

Vinyard: What does that mean, sustained? I'm not a lawyer by —

Judge: The last question will not be answered by Ms. Anderson. Move on to a different question.

Vinyard: And you don't have to state why or —

Judge: No.

Vinyard: Is, is the CD or cassette *Kaya* familiar to you in any way? ...

Anderson: Yes, it is familiar to me.

Vinyard: And what — in what way?

Anderson: I've heard many types of music over the years and am familiar with it. The spelling of the name of the CD is different than my name and has nothing to do with my name.

Vinyard: And you like reggae music?

Prosecution: Objection, irrelevant.

Judge: Sustained.

Time seemed fluid. I found I could step back from the moment and take in the larger picture at will without missing a beat. I also, at will, could shift my point of view, seeing the scene from above me while, simultaneously, seeing it through my own eyes. It was not dissociation. I was fully present. Connected to cosmic consciousness and my own celestial soul, which exist outside of time and space, I was experiencing multiple dimensions at once.

This is our truth. It's always our truth. Blinded by the material world, we perceive the ethereal and physical realms as separate, but we are so much more than our mind, our ego, wants us to believe we are.

> Vinyard: Started today I guess, the criminal Complaint lists the dates started on Saturday, October 25th and ending on Thursday, January 1st. What makes you believe the call on Saturday, October 25th was from Robert Vinyard?

I couldn't place the call he was referring to. I turned and looked daggers at the judge:

> Anderson (to the judge): I don't — I don't have my notes with me. I wasn't expecting to testify today. I'm not sure what happened on October 25th.
>
> Vinyard: Will you allow her access to her notes, or may she, judge?
>
> Anderson (to Vinyard): Can you tell me what happened on October 25th?
>
> Vinyard: Well, that's the first date on the criminal Complaint. First date listed for this offense of stalking is listed as October 25th, which happens to be a Saturday.

His questions continuing, I discovered that when called upon, the warrior within me moved to the foreground. This was not the warrior of legend or myth; there was no rage or desire for vengeance. This was calm, centered, pure, grounded power rising in defense of my boundaries and truth. And as appropriate, vulnerability then compassion for all present swam forward. Reaching within, I was pulling every facet of myself forward as needed, and often, seemingly disparate aspects were held in my awareness at once. And in a way I had not fully comprehended before, I understood: Only when opposites are integrated can truth be known, can duality cease, and balance and wholeness be attained. I grew still larger.

My mind was clear and sharp but was not in charge. My mind was the servant, my heart the master, and all of it — all of who I am — was fluid and working in harmony. Centered, integrated, powerful beyond anything I could have imagined, I felt I commanded the space. He could not get in, could not push a single button.

> Vinyard: Okay. Now, do you know what other dates specifically you are alleging that I called on?
>
> Anderson: I do not have all of those dates in front of me.
>
> Vinyard: Is there any way you can access your notes?
>
> Anderson: I did not bring my notes with me. I haven't gathered them. I wasn't expecting to be here today.
>
> Vinyard: Okay. On the other calls of this same relative period of October — late October to January 1st, 1994 —
>
> Anderson: 1994?
>
> Vinyard: January —
>
> Anderson: Of 2004?
>
> Vinyard: I guess, yes. 2004. I'm a little out of date, I guess. What was said that — what was said that you believe I was calling you? What was said that made you believe that I was calling you? On what — how many calls?
>
> Prosecution: Objection to the compound nature of the question. I don't understand the question.
>
> Judge: Please rephrase the question. Make sure you —
>
> Vinyard: On the other calls that you received, how did you positively identify me as the caller, and what did I say to make you believe that I was — made that particular call?

The question was wide open, and I intended to take advantage of it:

> Anderson: When the first one or two calls came in that I did not accept, I called Officer (Greg) Malsam. I also believe that I notified Mr. Tim Johnson, the (Deputy) District Attorney, that these calls were happening. I also called the gentleman who handles the phone system at

the jail — I'm familiar enough with this; over the years I've talked to him many times — and asked if he could determine who the calls came from. He said he could limit it to five potential prisoners at the time, inmates, but not specifically one.

As we discussed it further, because this phone call — all of these phone calls came in on a line that was unlisted and unpublished, and therefore, I had not — no one had made an effort to block ... it. I also did not have access to recording equipment on that line as I did on my other phone line.

As a result of that, we talked about the potential — I realized that there was some question as to whether the calls were from you or not, and I knew that I needed more evidence to prove beyond a shadow of a doubt that they were from you. Therefore, he did describe to me that if I accepted a phone call, it would be recorded at the jail automatically, thereby proving who the call came from. Subsequent calls after that, therefore, I accepted and allowed them to be recorded at the jail for evidence.

Vinyard: Subsequent to what date?

Anderson: I don't know the dates specifically. Subsequent to the calls that I did not accept the charges.

Vinyard: And on how many of these calls can my voice be identified?

Anderson: I don't know, but they are recorded, so I assume that is available to the Court.

Vinyard: How well do you know Robert Vinyard's voice?

Anderson: Extremely well.

Vinyard: Extremely well from — would you say intimately?

Prosecution: Objection. It's argumentative.

Judge: Sustained.

Vinyard: Why not intimately?

Judge: I sustained the objection. I don't care to argue with you about it.

Vinyard: What would your — what is your definition

for intimately, Ms. Anderson?

Prosecution: Objection.

Judge: Sustained. Don't ask any more questions with the word intimate in it.

The whole situation was so bizarre, the scene felt surreal. Scanning the faces of the audience, I was struck by the sense that everyone in the courtroom seemed caught up in a mass delusion, calmly accepting the scenario as perfectly sensible and pretending not only that this predator should be questioning me, but that this clearly insane man could function in the courtroom. How on earth had we gotten here?

Vinyard: Explain to the Court your serious emotional distress that you have suffered this particular episode. Since they've changed the law to a new legal phrase — credible threat to serious emotional distress. Go ahead and tell the Court how you've suffered.

Appalled, I waited for the objection that never came then turned to the judge. "May I ask a question?"

"Why don't you just answer the question," the judge replied.

The question, posed so bluntly and insensitively by the very person who inflicted the pain, was obscene. Was I the only one who saw this?

The face of the warrior swam forward, and I found myself perched on the edge of my seat, leaning so far toward the stalker that I felt my knees press into the wooden wall of the witness box.

Anderson: All right. I feel terrorized. I feel extremely angry every time I have a contact from you and unable to do anything about it other than to work through this justice system, which is exactly what I've done.

Vinyard: So — you mean is — you testified you felt terror? Is what you're testifying to?

Anderson: Yes. ... If [these charges] are specifically beginning at the phone calls and any contact that I had after you, Mr. Vinyard ... were incarcerated, I did not feel as terrorized as when you were out and not incarcerated.

However, I feel shocked when I get a contact. I feel extremely distraught, distressed, very concerned about my family, the violation of my privacy, the violation of my life. And *extremely* angry.

Vinyard: Do you — do you like scary movies?

Prosecution: Objection.

Judge: Sustained.

Vinyard: Well, some people like to be scared.

A stunned silence fell over the room.

Vinyard: Do you remember making the statement on a telephone conversation with me that said you did not know I — that I was fond of you until I beat on your windows and knocked on your doors in the middle of the night? Do you remember making that statement?

Prosecution: Objection, Your Honor. I believe this is predating what's been charged in this Complaint.

Judge: Sustained.

Vinyard: This goes to the whole background. This is what we're trying to get at is the background of this case.

Judge: No, we're not trying to get at the background of this case. Sustained.

Vinyard: You allowed [my attorney] leeway.

Judge: Sustained.

Vinyard: You're not giving me the same leeway you gave [my attorney]?

Judge: As I warned you, I may not. I don't have a clue what I let [your attorney] do eight, seven years ago —

Vinyard: He went back into the —

Judge: But I am not allowing you to do it, sir.

Vinyard: — past. Can we bring up our college together? That we went to CU together?

Judge: When I speak, you don't. I'm not allowing you to do it. Sustained. Ask your next question.

Vinyard: Well, that's the main purpose I'm up here for, Your Honor. Is to elicit past — our past —

Judge: Then go to your secondary purpose.

Vinyard: Secondary purpose? I, I don't see any purpose. You can dismiss the witness. If I can't ask her questions about our past relationship, if our relationship was intimate, if the relationship — what is the meaning of intimacy to her, what's the — what's the purpose of this for me? You know, I'm basing my behavior on what — how close I was to her in '78, '79.

Judge: The only purpose — I don't know what the purpose is for you. The purpose is for me to determine if there's probable cause, to see if you've violated count one, the stalking statute.

Vinyard: The purpose for me is to get on testimony how she's conflict — she's in conflict.

Judge: Right. So you lose that argument. I win that argument.

Another question, objection, sustained, and Vinyard relented to consulting with his attorney. Though he represented himself, it appeared she was allowed to advise him. I wondered why she was even there.

More questions and objections, sustained. Blocked at every turn, Vinyard was obviously getting frustrated.

"I'm disappointed that I'm not allowed to ask questions about or concerning our past. And that's all I really got here is my past," he said. "So if I can't ask questions concerning my past with Ms. Anderson and elicit some, you know, truth on the issue, there's really no purpose for me. And I've already asked the questions I wanted answered. … "

In cross-examination, Tim asked more about the emotional impact of Vinyard's contacts and delved into the effects on my children. I was hesitant. I didn't want Vinyard to know much about them. Mentally blocking him out, I focused only on Tim and the judge:

Prosecution: Do they see how the contacts from Mr. Vinyard affect you?

Anderson: Yes, they do.

Prosecution: And how do they respond?

Anderson: They're emotionally distraught as well

and have even some physical symptoms as a result of it: nausea, headaches, lethargy, things like that.

Tim's final questions turned to my reasons for getting the restraining order. I was relieved. I hoped the change in subject would turn Vinyard's attention away from the children. Then the judge offered Vinyard the chance to question me again. Breathing deeply, holding my space, I let go of my anxiety and surrendered it all to Source.

> Vinyard: Do you — you said that your children suf-
> fered. Did they go to the hospital?
> Anderson: No, they did not.
> Vinyard: Did they go to any kind of doctor?
> Anderson: A physician, no. A therapist, counselor, yes.
> Vinyard: And what — do you have doctor bills, ther-
> apist bills for suffering serious emotional distress?
> Prosecution: Objection.
> Judge: Sustained.
> Vinyard: Well, I don't have any questions.
> Prosecution: No further questions.
> Judge: Thank you, Ms. Anderson, you can step down.

Still held firmly in this pulsating column of energy, I consciously disconnected from Vinyard and left the courtroom. The advocate escorted me out then paused and, wide-eyed, exclaimed, "I don't know how you do it!"

That's a long story, I thought.

Walking down the hall, I was absorbed in the sensations. Fully aware of the floor beneath my feet and the walls around me as well as the higher vibrations and dimensions I moved through, I was walking in both worlds at once. It was as if the cells of my organs and skin were not solid at all, the cosmic energies moving freely in and out of my body. Perhaps if I were a poet, I could find the words to fully describe the experience.

Gratitude radiated from every fiber of my being. Being linked to this presence, this loving Force, was the single most humbling experience of my life. The overwhelming power I'd experienced was in no way mine. Yet a small part of it was.

It was as though there'd been a code inside of me, a program lying dormant, just waiting to be switched on and connected. And I realized that, working with these powers and all that I am, I was consciously co-creating.

This is what it feels like. This is who I truly am, what I'm meant to do, what we're all designed to do: to be here now in human form, drawing in Spirit to manifest on Earth. You are made in God's image. Gnothi seauton: Know thyself.

Step upon step, I reflected on the experience. *Trust. Perfect trust.* Though horrified and furious at the injustice of the encounter, it was also a gift, the answer to my desire to know my power and to own it.

All the work I'd done had led directly to this — this initiation. Not initiation into something new, but something lost and long forgotten, severed from my consciousness. Suppressed and under pressure, once I finally tapped into that power, like a flood of water breaching a dam, it rose up, re-awakening with tremendous force.

Trust that at every moment, dark as the path ahead may be, I am guided. And trust not only higher powers, but myself. For body, mind, and soul, the key is in me.

Finally, once I felt ready, I released the intense connection I'd called upon. My heart remained open and full.

The euphoria lingered as I headed home. For the first time in my life, I felt wholly liberated. This was true freedom. A freedom no one else can give.

*   *   *

That night, amid the constant stream of nightmares I'd had in recent months, I had a dream. A house dream. Nothing in the home was familiar, but I knew it was mine. It was evening and friends appeared. They were not faces I recognized, yet I knew they were friends. Mingling and moving among them, I soon found myself alone in a hallway and came across an odd clue that this was my home, for I almost always dreamed that items were left by the people who lived there before me.

It was an old wall hanging like none I had ever seen before. Painted figures of angels and beautiful script encircled a pocket filled with slips of paper. Curious, I pulled the papers out and slowly sifted through them. Also beautifully embellished with images of angels, they contained names, dates, and narrative. Each was a remembrance of one who'd passed on and was, undoubtedly, dear to the former occupants.

As one would read headstones in a graveyard, I read the slips one by one with reverence, reaching out to those souls who had moved on. Then it dawned on me. These were not tributes to others. They were markers of the chronological passing of my former selves. The whole memorial was a loving gesture honoring those earlier expressions of myself that passed on each time I shed the old — old limiting beliefs, old patterns of thinking and being in the world — and became more and more my true, authentic self.

There was nothing sad in this small memorial. In fact, it had the appearance of a gift created for the birth of a child, a celebration of new life. Indeed, that's exactly what it was. Each time one form of myself passed, it was to allow for the birth of the new, a little more conscious, a little more mature and evolved.

* * *

The irony of the judge forcing me to be confronted by Vinyard in the courtroom was not lost on the reporters. "**Accused stalker allowed to question victim.** A man accused of stalking a woman for 25 years got to face her — and question her — in a court hearing Friday," the *Daily Camera* reported.

Between news articles and the transcript, the events surrounding my testimony unfolded. Tim had begun by bringing the court's attention to a couple of issues, the first being a motion filed by the defense to seal the hearing.

Citing the pertinent statute, Tim argued against it. "I think that the court is without statutory authority to close this hearing. I, personally, am concerned about closing the hearing. I believe that when we start doing things in secret that that's a bad precedent to set ... ."

I couldn't have agreed more.

The judge turned to Vinyard and asked if he wanted the hearing closed or open.

"No, I'd like this particular hearing to be closed, because it's got a lot of confidential and private — "

"Okay," the judge interjected. "The motion is denied. I see no authority in the rules or the statutes. Next?"

"Your Honor, … I received notification this morning, approximately 7:00 AM, that the victim in this case … has been subpoenaed by the defense to be compelled to testify at the preliminary hearing," Tim said. Pointing to two rules, he argued, "I will tell the court that the purpose of the preliminary hearing is a screening device. It is not meant to be a mini-trial."

Tim assured the judge that he would provide sufficient evidence to find probable cause for all the charges: Greg would testify and all the evidence would be presented in full.

"The use of the subpoena power at the preliminary hearing is the use of a discovery-type tool," Tim added. "While the defense is allowed some limited discovery (information the prosecution has that must be shared with the defense), nothing is going to be gained from allowing the defendant in this case, who the allegations are has been stalking this victim for twenty-five years, to have a direct face-to-face and questioning contact with the victim at this point in time. The People feel that the purpose of that part of the subpoena is harassing, it's retaliatory, and it's unduly unfair to the victim in this case." He asked the judge to quash the subpoena.

When asked to respond, Vinyard said his intention was to elicit testimony regarding "our past involvement, the nature of our relationship." He claimed he would show he had not been stalking me.

"The court will not quash the subpoena," the judge said, adding, "The court is not giving wide latitude to you to question her."

At the close of the hearing, the judge found probable cause and bound the case over. Tim asked for an increase in bond in this case alone to $150,000. The judge granted it.

Then, to give us peace, Tim asked the judge to restrict Vinyard's phone and letter-writing privileges to communications with his family and his attorney, who could screen and forward letters.

"The People feel that Mr. Vinyard's unfettered access to both phone and letter writing is a continuing cause of these new charges. Mr. Vinyard, in his last phone call, stated that he is not going to stop, he is not going to quit," Tim said.

When asked her opinion, the defense attorney said there was no case law supporting Tim's request and that she, personally, didn't want that burden. She also claimed it would be an extremely difficult burden to impose on the jail.

"[W]hat are we gonna do, duct tape him and tie his hands to a chair?" she asked.

If that's what it takes, I thought.

She then drew the court's attention to the question of where Vinyard got my unlisted number — the number that evidence now showed he'd called twenty-eight times while in jail.

"He gets it right from the discovery, the discovery that's provided from the district attorney's office," she exclaimed. "Here is a 1997 report … There's the phone number that he called was on. In this particular document — "

"Thanks for the gift," Vinyard injected.

" — where it, the phone number — "

"I told you somebody gave it to me," he said.

I was no lawyer, but it sure seemed to me that both Vinyard and his attorney just admitted he'd made the calls and sent the CD; my new name and birth date were listed in the same report. Although it was shocking to learn that my confidential information had not been redacted in discovery, I didn't blame the police or the DA's office for it. It was just further proof that it was impossible to hide from a stalker. And it wasn't right that I should. He, alone, was responsible for his monstrous behavior. It just had to be stopped.

Yet still arguing against the restrictions, Vinyard's attorney declared, "That would be, in my opinion, cruel and unusual punishment" at a time when his cases were pending. "And I think we know also that, that we've already talked about it — Mr. Vinyard has some mental health issues and problems. I could see this sort of thing spiraling into a situation that will cause him severe destruction — self-destruction — if he's not allowed to have any contact with the outside world."

If he's not allowed to have contact with me, you mean. She had no comprehension of the destruction he had and still wreaked on us.

The judge then made his ruling. "The court is going to amend the criminal protection order to as follows: The defendant may not use the telephone at the jail except to call [his attorney] and his immediate family members. … Defendant may write letters only to his attorney … . The letters can be addressed to anybody else, but [his attorney] will be the screener of letters."

Instantly, Vinyard leaped to his feet and pointed at the judge. Three sheriff's deputies swooped down on him and chained the one hand he'd had free for the hearing.

> Vinyard: That's a violation of civil rights. I'm gonna sue your fucking ass.
>
> Judge: You know, if it would make any difference to hold you in contempt and put you in jail, I would, but it doesn't make any difference at this stage.
>
> Vinyard: That's a gross violation of civil rights. And you know it. You're a fucking asshole.
>
> Judge: Behave yourself, sir. You'll find yourself — I could do something at the jail, I could put him in the hole, couldn't I?
>
> Sheriff: You just did it.

The trial for all three cases combined was scheduled for April, in two months. Next came the motions hearing.

You have the right "to be treated with fairness, respect, and dignity and to have a swift and fair resolution of your case," the brochure said. With nine delays of the motions hearing alone, it would be another year before the case moved to the next step, a full year and a half before it went to trial. Between Vinyard's refusal to accept the consequences of his illegal behavior and the judiciary indulging his every desire, the defendant's due process consumed my life. And while the case was side-winding its way through court, the stalking never ceased. It was a serial nightmare.

Arraignments, hearings, and status conferences were scheduled and rescheduled. Motions and counter-motions were filed, followed by supplements and briefs in support of counters to the counter-motions. And the defense attorneys played musical chairs.

I have no idea why the motions hearing was delayed the first time. Tim assured me he wouldn't need me to testify. "The defense, on the other hand, may try to call you," he said.

As the judge had promised, Vinyard's outside communications were restricted. But the phone log at the jail showed my blocked number was still being called from the administrative unit, where Vinyard was housed.

Then his attorney filed a motion claiming the restrictions required him to be segregated — a punitive sanction against him for conduct of which he was presumed innocent — thus violating his constitutional rights.

Tim filed a response arguing that, while there was a presumption of innocence until found guilty, the judge had already found probable cause. "The People have taken steps to try to ensure the Defendant is restrained from attempting to contact the victim ... but clearly, the Defendant has been able to circumvent those protections," he wrote. "The Defendant, through letter writing and phone calls, has continued to terrorize the victim."

The case was now in Judge Daniel Hale's hands. He modified the restriction. Vinyard would be allowed to send mail, unsealed for inspection, with the jail's return address. His telephone privileges were restored. Fortunately, both my numbers had been successfully blocked at the jail again.

In the meantime, the case dragging on, the judge granted a request by Vinyard for access to the jail's law library seven days a week. Worming his way out of consequences had become his career; it had always worked before. Finally, the jail staff asked the judge to restrict his access to five days a week, when a librarian was on duty who could obtain the legal information Vinyard wanted and could supervise his activity. The judge granted the staff's request.

March brought an arraignment for the most recent contacts. Afterward, Tim told me that Vinyard decided he needed more sleep and refused to come to court. I asked what would happen if I was subpoenaed and refused to come to court.

"Good question," he replied. "You could be jailed up to six months and fined $500." The arraignment was continued.

When the continuance arrived, Vinyard didn't enter a plea. Instead, the defense moved for dismissal, claiming the statute was unconstitutional again. It was upheld when he'd challenged it before, and the court of appeals had declared it constitutional just one week earlier. Tim challenged the motion and called to update me.

If Judge Hale upheld the statute, the defense planned to plead not guilty by reason of insanity and Vinyard would be sent to the state hospital to be assessed, Tim said. "And when he is found sane, we'll go to trial."

I wasn't so sure about that. Clearly he was insane. The question was, was he criminally insane?

In April, the jail staff intercepted a letter Vinyard had written to me. He'd addressed it, stamped it, and coerced another inmate to slip it into a letter he gave a visitor — to be mailed from the outside. Tim emailed me and suggested that if I wanted to see it, I come in and view it with an advocate.

"It is sexually vulgar and obscenely graphic (imagery). It is a fantasy of a rape," Tim wrote. "It is eight pages single-spaced typed plus handwritten parts — ninety-five percent is sexually vulgar. I think I can say I suffered serious emotional distress by reading it."

I was already struggling to function. Now, just hearing Tim's description was so disturbing, it haunted me for a week. I didn't look at it.

Vinyard was moved back to the disciplinary module, and Tim planned to add more charges for the letter: counts ten and eleven in the second stalking case.

"I know it is the umpteen-hundredth offense," he wrote, "but the charge is for second and subsequent offenses." The trial would now have to be pushed to June or July.

By now, my nerves were shot and fear was getting a grip on me again. Afraid that when Vinyard finally realized he wasn't going to squirm out of a long sentence no matter what he did, he would post bail and bolt, I asked Tim to request a higher bond when the new letter was charged. The total bond for all three cases was already $400,000, he assured me.

When the motions hearing came around again, Vinyard's attorney had a potential conflict of interest: She'd represented the patsy Vinyard used to smuggle the letter out of the jail. The hearing was continued again, and when Greg helped the sheriff's department return Vinyard to jail, he asked Greg to send me his best wishes.

"I can't do that," Greg said and added another charge for attempted contact through a third person.

Vinyard's maniacal obsession at the helm, the judicial process had, once again, become an unsolvable Gordian knot. All I wanted was to "pull an Alexander," wield my sword, slice right through it, and be done.

I must say, Tim was tremendously patient with me. We were constantly in contact and I was losing it. Often, I emailed long lists of "whys" and "what ifs." Sometimes I just ranted:

> My frustration with all this is almost unbearable. Just
> have to rave a little again. Why isn't my need for closure
> considered in any of these absurd delays? Why is it all
> about the defendant's rights and not the crime victim's?
>
> I know there's an explanation for almost every delay,
> but the big picture is this guy is keeping a stranglehold on
> my life, keeping me engaged and involved. And all I want
> is to stop it. I want my life back. I want him out. My God,
> twenty-five years. No one can understand how this has
> affected me. This is so unjust, and I'm sick of it beyond
> description.

Both Tim and Greg understood completely and confessed it was their biggest frustration, too, that the rights of the defendant far outweighed the rights of the crime victim.

All I could do to stay sane was keep my sense of humor. "I've come up with a new description of being a crime victim in American courts: Roadkill Beneath the Wheels of Justice," I wrote. "Would love to see this in the header of the next letter I get from your office saying I have the right to be informed or that the next hearing is rescheduled. And on the little flyer that says 'Victims Have the Right to be Heard.' I have a file drawer full of these."

The goal of all the motions and delays, Tim reminded me, was to get an airtight conviction. But I had seen too much for too long. There had never been an airtight conviction for any of his offenses, and I had no faith whatsoever in the system.

The defense made a motion for a protective/gag order and the judge partially granted it. Both parties, including me, would be prohibited from giving case facts to the media, and all exhibits would be placed under seal.

At the next court date, citing her conflict of interest, the defense attorney withdrew from the case. The hearing was continued.

When the continuance arrived, Vinyard was on suicide watch at the jail and was not transported. It was continued again to later that week.

Later that week came and went. It was continued again and when that day arrived, Vinyard complained of having a bad back. The judge postponed it.

May arrived. The judge found that the defense attorney did have a conflict. She would be removed from the case but stay on the motion to dismiss on constitutional grounds. A new defense attorney was appointed, and the judge rescheduled the hearing to see if he'd settled in.

When the time came, he had not settled in and the hearing was continued. Time marching on, the trial would now have to be rescheduled again.

In the meantime, Tim received a typed letter from Vinyard, offering a plea agreement:

> RE: Plea Bargain
>
> Sir, Seeing this is Mother's Day Weekend let's settle this without much more hassles, acrimony, and fighting; not to mention the considerable cost in time, energy, and money an additional attorney, appointed at state expense, would be. We could do a plea bargain with [the prior defense attorney], before the conflict of interest issue.

As if ordering from a lunch menu, he proceeded to list his terms: "I'll plead guilty to the first episode of stalking from June 7 [2003] thru June 20th [2003] in exchange for a deferred sentence or probation being transferred to Montana or Idaho."

Then — light on the mayo — he said he'd even be willing to wear an ankle bracelet. It was one of his "better points to bargain with," he wrote.

"Mr. Johnson, I do not think I am responsible for the 2nd episode of alleged stalking from Nov. 25, 2003 thru Dec. 31st 2003 and will not plead guilty to it," he declared. "Without the phone # that you gave me that whole episode would never had happened." He claimed it was entrapment.

Turning to the constitutional challenge, he cited sections of the stalking statute and several cases as precedence then argued that the state Supreme Court had not issued a decision.

"But anyway let's do something cordial for each, May is a nice month to be out … ."

Tim didn't bite, of course, and two weeks later, Judge Hale heard the constitutional challenge, upheld the statute, and did not dismiss the case. The motions hearing was continued to August. The jury trial was rescheduled for September 2004.

It was June 2004, one year to the day that Vinyard was released from prison. I picked up the mail and was stopped in my tracks by an envelope bearing an elaborate drawing of a tiger's head, baring its teeth, its tongue hanging out. The hairs on my neck stood on end.

"Jail art," Greg said, donning his gloves and slicing it open. With a Denver postmark, no return address, and no jail stamp, the letter had obviously been smuggled out and mailed from the outside.

Reading silently, Greg's face contorted into a grimace. He asked, as he always did now, how much I wanted to know. Only the general tenor and any specific plans or threats, nothing more, I replied. It was more of the same, he said: hand-written, sexually explicit, and vulgar. I stopped him there.

August arrived and Vinyard wanted an attorney with experience in the insanity defense. According to the judge, there were only a handful of those and they were private attorneys.

Not guilty by reason of insanity. It chilled me to my bones.

Two months passed and in October, two more letters addressed to me, with bogus return names and addresses, slipped through the screeners and landed in my mailbox at once. Both thick and heavy, they each bore underlined, hand-written warnings to open them carefully. That was alarming.

Cautiously, I slipped them into a manila envelope, called the police and emailed Tim.

Tim was rushing off to court but wrote, "Yikes!!! Call Longmont PD immediately, have the officer call me when they arrive, and don't open anything (you know that — don't know why I am saying that)." My nerves in knots, I chuckled through clenched teeth.

Greg wasn't available, but another officer quickly arrived and took the envelopes. They would open them at their headquarters, he said.

One letter included two letters. His time, it seemed, was spent indulging in erotic fantasies — fantasies that had progressed from sexually explicit to sexually violent. Later, the police turned his cell and found and confiscated copies of all the letters he'd written me from his jail cell. I felt sick.

In December, the arraignment for the new letters was combined with the motions hearing and continued again. Vinyard had filed two motions asking the judge to dismiss his attorney and appoint new counsel with experience in mental health defenses. His attorney related that Vinyard had become exceedingly argumentative, progressively distrustful, and difficult to communicate with. His underlying hostility raised concern of irreconcilable conflict, he said and concluded that further representation would potentially be unethical. He did not object to Vinyard's motion and said he'd be willing to stay as co-counsel.

The judge appointed another attorney with experience in mental health cases. He would take the lead; the other attorney would assist him.

The now January 2005 trial date was vacated. It would likely be moved to April or May. As always, I had no say in any of it. I was just dragged along for the ride.

*   *   *

Throughout all of these delays, I was plagued with the same stress symptoms I'd had through the years and they were evolving. And I was just so angry. Again, it felt impossible to open, connect, and surrender when I was pounded by a battering ram.

I had come so far, but the hits never stopped. Every one of Vinyard's sick, ruthless invasions, and every delay, twist, and turn in the court dealt a blow, pummeling old wounds that had never healed.

By now, life was reduced to day-to-day survival. Panic attacks came out of nowhere at any time of day, and the only way to stop them was to sleep and "reboot." But sleep was a nightmare.

Over and over, I dreamed I was struggling against impenetrable barriers. Exerting every ounce of energy and ingenuity I had, I still could not overcome them. Then came the fighting dreams. I'd had these dreams before, where it was hard to move and every move I made was blocked or wriggled out of. But until now, I had never seen the face of my enemy. I'd never seen Vinyard's face.

Then one night, there we were, standing eye-to-eye, arms outstretched, holding guns to each other's chests. We fired simultaneously.

He fell to the floor and I fell back against a wall then slowly sank to the floor. Glancing down, I touched the hole in my shirt and watched in horror as a dark stain spread over my heart.

Don't die, I told myself. *Don't die. I need to be here for my kids.*

Mary knew it was the trauma — repeated trauma that now spanned twenty-five years — that was blocking my way. With all the damage embedded in my nervous system coupled with the unceasing assaults, everything I'd learned and integrated simply could not break through and flourish.

Over the years, I'd talked with practitioners who specialized in various therapies for PTSD, but the one thing they all agreed on was that no therapy would work until the cause of the trauma stopped. And it *never stopped.*

Then Mary made a suggestion. The past-life regression I'd had years ago had, in the end, been deeply healing. Now Mary, herself, was certified in regression hypnosis; it was a tool she used in conjunction with therapy. She suggested we try it again.

CHAPTER 25

Eye of the Needle

"Compassion is the chief law of human existence."
~ *Fyodor Dostoyevsky*

Sheer desperation overrode any fear of seeing my past. I agreed to Mary's suggestion of hypnotic regression, but before we began I told my guides firmly that I wanted to see only what I needed to see, and I asked for emotional detachment when needed. I did not want to feel the horror and anguish I had the first time I'd stumbled upon a former life. I just couldn't take it.

Over a period of months, I saw a handful of my past incarnations, both as men and women, in several regressions. Each time, we set a specific intention to help me heal what most needed healing in the moment. Overall, our goal was to release blocks to higher love and transform anger, fear, and pain into love.

My wish was fulfilled. In each regression I was guided and protected, and I experienced exactly what, and only what, I needed to. In some, I reached across time to heal both the past and the present. In others, I reached far, far back in time, meeting more ancient expressions of my soul — to remember. To dive beneath my life experiences, tap lost wisdom, and remember who I am. To experience what it felt like to be whole, powerful, and connected — to Spirit and myself, to the world around me, and to my fellow man — at all times. To remember what it felt like to live fully in the embrace of love and compassion, even in the midst of tremendous upheaval and brutality.

It was those ancient selves, feeling what it was to embody a different paradigm — a culture of love not fear, a culture in which we honored all emotions and supported one another in all life experiences — that were the most healing and transformative. Something deep inside me shifted, aligning with the sensations experienced.

As, one by one, I pulled these manifestations into my consciousness,

I was expanding so rapidly that my system struggled to contain this new state of being, this higher, broader, larger vibration. And I felt spread across time, not always certain I was fully in the present tense.

It was then I consulted a naturopathic physician, and the synergy of the regressions and homeopathic support was incredibly powerful — alchemical, it seemed. The remedies and essences she chose seemed to snap my nervous system into place, not only restoring my natural state of being, but supporting this higher, more expansive energy. I felt I'd finally emerged from the chrysalis a larger, more whole, and much more evolved being.

The pummeling by the stalker and the courts did not subside, and neither did some of the effects. But though fear, anger, and grief persisted, I was able to let them flow through me and be released. Deep in my core, a gentleness and calm sustained me.

As the months passed, the case still slithering through the court, I continued to experience spontaneous releases and felt freer and freer. And feeling clarity and wholeness, feeling connected and empowered became not merely a sensation of the moment, but a way of life.

*   *   *

Soon after the new attorney was appointed to the defense, Tim met with Greg and me to discuss the potential pleas and outcomes. It was a morass of possibilities. Tim was still pushing for a trial; it would be easy to prove guilt, he said. But the insanity defense was a problem, and Vinyard could always ask for a trial by judge — no jury.

In all these years, none of the cases had ever gone to trial. A jury had never heard them. Hiding behind curtains, lurking in shadows, this predator had never been fully exposed. Secrecy protected him. The cloak of darkness fueled his perverse behavior. The defendant had the right to a jury trial, but I was the one who wanted it. I wanted the truth to ring out.

I knew both Tim and Greg were working extraordinarily hard on the case and were doing their best to bring us, if not justice — it was far too late for that — at least peace, and I was sincerely grateful to them. But through all these years, I felt I'd been shoved into a box labeled "victim." Then, with the powers that be comfortably relieved of the burden of seeing my full human dimension, I was conveniently shoved aside and stripped of my power. Until I was called upon, I was not seen or heard in court. While the DA's office was planning its strategy, I was informed, not involved. The entire judicial system, it seemed, under the guise of defending me, did everything in its power to keep me powerless, firmly locked in the box. "Re-victimizing the victim," others called it.

I was not powerless, and I was not a victim. I looked Tim and Greg in the eyes and said, "I don't want to be rescued. I want to be empowered."

I'm sure that from their point of view, it came out of nowhere.

"I have been stripped of my power at every turn. I want to be involved in decisions and speak in open court," I said.

Comprehension dawned and they nodded. From that point on, Tim consulted me when strategizing and asked how I felt about options. We made decisions together, as a team.

The year turned and on January 27, 2005, as I browsed the papers in a newsstand, a headline grabbed me and would not let go. "**Disorder in the court**: Recent Supreme Court decisions could impact how Colorado offenders are sentenced" was splashed across the cover of the *Boulder Weekly*. The article, "**Justice reconsidered**: Colorado courtrooms could be in for a change thanks to recent Supreme Court decisions," was more than I could handle. Panic swelling, I grabbed the paper, rushed home, studied the article, and called Tim.

It was true, he said. The Supreme Court ruled that the way judges had been sentencing — adding time to some prison stays — was unconstitutional. Everyone was scrambling to sort out the ramifications, but the decision directly affected the potential sentence in this case. Until the state legislature addressed the issue, discretionary aggravators could not be applied. The bottom line was, the U.S. Supreme Court had just cut the potential sentence for this predator's crimes in half, and when the state legislature revised the sentencing system, the "fix" wouldn't be retroactive. It couldn't be applied to this case.

Filling my lungs with oxygen, coaxing my heart to slow down, I asked Tim what the potential sentences were now.

First subtract two years from each charge for the two years Vinyard had been in jail since he was arrested, he said. Then subtract another two years for "good time," which had nothing to do with good behavior while incarcerated; it was just a credit given for being in jail and calculating the parole eligibility date, which occurred when 50 percent of the original sentence was served.

His setup rushed right past me. I was waiting for the punch line.

So, if Vinyard was convicted of all charges pending, the maximum he could get with consecutive sentences was twenty years and he would be eligible for parole in seven years, he said. I knew that wouldn't happen; judges never gave the maximum time for all the charges. If he got the maximum with concurrent sentences, he'd be sentenced to six years and already be eligible for parole. And if he got the minimum concurrent sentences, he would have already served the full two-year sentence and would be paroled immediately.

I couldn't take it in. I couldn't accept it. Suddenly, an insanity plea sounded a lot more appealing.

Another deputy DA, Bruce Langer, who had experience with insanity cases, was brought in to assist Tim. If Vinyard pled and was found not guilty by reason of insanity, there would be no conviction and no sentence; he would be transferred to the state mental health institute indefinitely, Langer said. But, he added, we could probably only count on five to ten years; the hospital didn't warehouse people anymore since it was successfully sued.

I refused to accept that and asked to see the law governing release in insanity cases. Soon the statutes dropped into my inbox. "A little light reading," Tim wrote.

When the arraignment and motions hearing came around again, the new defense attorney wasn't ready. It was continued again. And again.

"Speedy trial continues to be tolled," the judge noted.

I was confused and Tim explained that when mental health issues were raised, it tolled the defendant's right to a speedy trial. I was quite sure the defendant had no desire for a speedy trial anyway, but what happened to my rights?

Then one day, Tim asked to meet me. Langer and Greg joined us. Wary, I eased into a chair and Tim gently broke the news. Vinyard's attorneys were now considering the "Hendershott" defense. There were few cases on the books and no precedent had been set, but basically, for the defendant, it offered the best parts of the insanity plea without the worst. If the defense was successful, Vinyard would simply be found not guilty. I was on the verge of crashing again and chose to believe that wouldn't happen.

In February, the defense and the DA's office filed a joint motion for one expert to perform an evaluation to determine Vinyard's sanity and the existence or non-existence of the Hendershott defense. His attorneys said if Hendershott didn't apply, they may or may not enter a plea of "not guilty insane." More uncertainty.

The judge granted the motion. The psychiatrist's evaluation would be reviewed in April. But before her report was finished, another letter arrived. The envelope was handwritten, had fictitious names and, this time, bore the county jail stamp.

"It's seven pages long and extremely sexually explicit," Greg said and gave me the option of reading it, but discouraged me from doing so.

I didn't want to hear any more, much less read it, and Tim and I agreed not to charge the letter. A stalking charge included two or more offenses; it didn't matter how many more there were. So nothing would be gained by adding the letter and delaying the case further.

The psychiatrist completed her report. In her opinion, Vinyard was criminally insane at the time the crimes were committed. I heard no more about the Hendershott defense.

The arraignment finally occurred in April, but when the time came, Vinyard refused to enter the insanity plea, declaring he couldn't enter a plea that wasn't true.

"Either the defense attorney or the judge could legally enter the plea on his behalf if he refuses," Tim assured me. The arraignment was continued to May.

On the morning of the continuance, I anxiously awaited the news from Tim. It was delayed again, he wrote in an email, and he related the events of the day. In the parking garage, Vinyard screamed at the top of his lungs at the jail deputies escorting him — there were six of them, Tim wrote. Evidently, it only got worse from there. In court, he yelled at his attorney and the judge, and he demanded that more motions be filed, including another motion to have the stalking statute declared unconstitutional.

Of course. Now that he's finally not getting his way, he threw a tantrum.

The judge reset the hearing for the next week and said that, at that time, either Vinyard would plead insanity or he would enter the plea for him.

"I am SO sorry that nothing (again) seems to be happening," Tim wrote. "The judge will force the issue next Thursday."

To my great relief, when Thursday came, Vinyard entered the plea: not guilty by reason of insanity. A short, half-day trial before the judge — no jury — was set for the first week of August 2005.

"And the defense filed another motion challenging the constitutionality of the statute and moving for a judgment of acquittal," Tim said. The judge would hear that issue separately in June.

When June came, his attorney called in sick. It was continued to July.

Now that the insanity plea was agreed upon and we knew there would be no jury trial, I told Tim I wanted to be allowed in the courtroom for the whole trial. I felt it was the least the court could do. He soon filed a motion to allow it. The defense filed a motion opposing it. The judge hadn't decided.

As the trial drew nearer, I also told Tim I wanted to present a statement to the court. No one expected me to. With the insanity plea, there would be no conviction and so, no sentence.

"It won't affect the outcome," Tim said.

I would not be swayed. "I want to have my voice, and I believe it is my right."

Tim understood. "If he's found insane, you would get a chance to make as long a statement as you want. There'd be an agreement to that."

Then, preparing me for trial, he explained that before the judge found Vinyard not guilty insane, the prosecution would have to prove he committed the crimes. In other words, Vinyard would have to be found guilty before the insanity defense kicked in. I would need to testify.

Tim gave me some sample questions to review and suggested I refamiliarize myself with all the evidence. I obliged and read through his questions then listened to copies of the phone recordings. Finally, after preparing myself and feeling a healthy degree of detachment, I read all the letters charged. Fortunately, for various reasons, the most sexually violent letters were not charged. But I scanned the letters to be prosecuted, skipping like a stone on water over the grotesque sexual references. Even then, the letters were deeply, horribly disturbing.

But while I reviewed the questions and evidence, it was my statement that I focused on. I had much to say.

On July 6, 2005, the motions hearing and the hearing for the defense's latest constitutional challenge combined finally occurred. I wasn't there.

The next morning, I was greeted by the *Times-Call* headline, "**Stalking law ruled constitutional**: Defense attorney wants proof of 'emotional distress.' " The good news was Judge Hale upheld the statute again and did not dismiss the case. The shocking news was the defense wanted my mental health records released in discovery.

My mouth fell open. In all these years, my right to privacy had been trampled by the stalker. Now the defense attorney was picking at the carcass like a vulture. I couldn't believe he would be so cruel.

I thought of all the times, all the years I'd asked for any information about the stalker's mental state to help me protect my family. That information was confidential, they all said; protecting his right to privacy, they would tell me nothing. Yet now the defense attorney would gladly invade my privacy and parade the torture I'd endured at the hands of his client just to exonerate him, knowing full well he had stalked me for decades. Where was sanity?

Tim argued that the disclosure would violate my right to privacy and said the law itself stated that a victim need not show that he or she received professional treatment or counseling to show he or she suffered serious emotional distress.

The judge didn't make a decision. He told the defense to file a brief.

Moving on to the constitutional challenge, Vinyard's attorney argued that the stalking law limited speech, thus violating the First Amendment.

"The more I look at this, the more I think we're prosecuting words," he opined.

From his seat in the jury box, Vinyard called out, "Even if it causes severe emotional distress" men should have a chance to express themselves. The stories in *The Graduate* and *As Good As It Gets* involve lovestruck men and initially uninterested women, he said. "Finally they get together at the end of the movie and it has a happy ending. We're guys, we like to pursue woman. We should have that right."

I must say, there were two things Vinyard did well. One was exposing every single crack in the system. The other was tapping into distortions buried deep in the collective unconscious and defiantly stating them out loud.

He was virtually the embodiment of the collective shadow that, Mary confirmed, permeated our culture. The feminine aspect within rejected, repressed, and distorted, the inevitable projections were aimed directly at women. The result? Hideous, barbaric abuse: both wanting women and dismissing them entirely; objectifying, owning, and violating them.

Fortunately, once Vinyard dredged these distortions up from the shadows and exposed them to the light of day, it was obvious to everyone how sick that line of thinking was. Or so I thought.

Then the defense concluded, "He's being prosecuted for relentlessly professing his love for this woman."

Aghast, I resolved then and there to revise my statement and address his premise directly.

In the end, Judge Hale rejected the defense's argument for the second time, stating, "It's not the speech that is punished; it's the conduct that is punished."

Amen.

August 2, 2005 – Trial to the court, day one

Nearly four years from the day Kathy told me the assault conviction had been overturned and he would be released, nearly three years since he was released from parole and the stalking resumed, and twenty-six years from the time his stalking campaign began, Robert Vinyard was finally brought to trial for two counts of felony stalking, twelve counts of misdemeanor violation of protection order, and one count of felony tampering with a witness.

I had no idea what was going on behind closed doors while I sat in the hall, waiting to testify. I consciously let go of it.

The court was attending to business. First, Judge Hale made sure Vinyard understood his right to a jury trial and asked again if he was willing to waive that right to proceed to trial before the judge.

He'd talked with his lawyer, Vinyard replied, and, "Yeah. I take it that I would get a better result with a judge."

I didn't know if I'd be allowed to remain in the courtroom after my testimony; the judge still hadn't decided. The issue was discussed while I waited.

The defense attorney was still opposed to it but told the judge his client said he wanted me in the courtroom.

"So, is it your desire Ms. Anderson stay in the courtroom during the entire trial?" the defense asked Vinyard again.

"Yeah. I would like to have her here."

This would include testimony from a psychiatrist about your mental state, your background, your mental issues — all of that testimony, his attorney explained.

"Um, yes, I wouldn't mind sharing."

Once that was decided, the defense brought up the unresolved issue of disclosing my therapy records, and the judge finally gave his ruling. The records privilege set forth under HIPPA was not waived because a person was a victim in a criminal case, he said. My records would not be released.

The defense then raised the issue of the term "serious emotional distress," the element of the statute critical to proving the crime of stalking in this case. He had filed motions asking for a clear-cut definition and had challenged the law on the grounds that the term was unconstitutionally vague. In response, Tim had crafted instructions for a jury that he said, though not exhaustive, did include factors cited in other cases. Now the judge addressed the issue in some detail and said serious emotional distress was a term that was commonly understood. But the defense was not going to let go of that bone.

Tim waived opening argument. In his opening, the defense made it clear he was contesting all the charges and moving for a judgment of acquittal; the prosecution had not proven every element beyond a reasonable doubt, he declared. Then he promised to renew the issue of the statute's constitutionality. If the court, however, found beyond a reasonable doubt that Vinyard committed these crimes, he would ask for a verdict of not guilty by reason of insanity, he said.

Given the short trial, Tim had whittled down his list of witnesses from sixty to three — Officer Sloan, Greg, and me — but assured me he wouldn't shortcut the evidence. All the phone recordings and all the letters charged would be entered into evidence, and CDs of the recordings would be played aloud in court, in full.

I was the first witness Tim called. The doors opened and I stepped into the arena. While I recognized a few reporters in the front rows, I had no idea who most of the people were and, searching for familiar faces, finally found my small, solid cluster of friends.

Before the trial came to order, I had studied the layout of the room, but I didn't know where Vinyard would be seated. Now I discovered that, dressed in dark blue jail garb, wrists chained to a waist chain, he was seated in the first row of the jury box. And the only direct path to the witness box was right in front of him. *This is not a problem*, I coached myself, and mentally blocking him out and owning my space, I assumed an easy, confident gait.

I settled into my seat and was quickly sworn in. Vinyard sat to the left of me. As had become standard procedure, soon after my testimony began, the defense asked to have one of Vinyard's hands uncuffed so he could make a few notes. Judge Hale, to my right, granted the request.

After briefly reviewing the stalking history, Tim's questions turned to the current case, focusing on how I felt and how I altered my routine when Vinyard was stalking me. Then one by one, each phone call and letter was discussed, and Tim asked how I felt after receiving each contact. I understood the need to discuss the contacts as they were entered into evidence, but describing my emotional response to each discrete one was jarring, if not impossible.

Then Tim approached a CD player prominently placed in the center of the courtroom and pressed "play." Suddenly, the audience was transported to the moment — feeling the tension, malevolence, and insanity; the outrage and fear captured in the phone recordings. It was chilling. The sea of strange faces turned to me and stared, wide-eyed and horrified. If there was ever any doubt as to the meaning of "serious emotional distress," in that moment it completely vanished.

Eventually, we reached the letter of June 2004 (the one adorned with the tiger's head) and Tim asked me to describe my emotional response. By now I was so frustrated, I ignored the disjointed nature of the questions and blurted out my truth: "I felt the way I always do with these contacts. Violated. Angry. Very, very angry that the contacts were continuing."

We'd already passed the half-day trial mark and broken for lunch, and still on the witness stand, I began to wonder if we'd finish by the end of the day.

Presently, cross-examination was offered to the defense. He wouldn't review individual contacts, the attorney said. Instead he would talk trends, beginning with the late 1970s.

Quickly, the terrain he was leading me through came into sharp relief. We were traversing the land of his client's delusions.

Before long, his questions turned down the path of Vinyard's conviction that there was a romantic relationship, and I fumed. *As if that would excuse his behavior.* But the attorney was obviously just Vinyard's mouthpiece. I was sure he had to ask the questions or run the risk of Vinyard claiming inadequate defense counsel again and stopping the whole process. That was the last thing I wanted. *Breathe. Let it go.*

> Defense: And these are — pardon me for these questions, but I have to ask them — were there ever any hugs between you and him?
>
> Anderson: I don't think so. Honestly, I was never comfortable with him. So I doubt that there were hugs.
>
> Defense: Were there ever any kisses?
>
> Anderson: No.
>
> Defense: Were there ever any plans to go out together or do anything together?
>
> Anderson: Not that I recall.
>
> Defense: Do you remember him once saying to you that he had, I think, come back from Idaho or something and wanted to travel with you or something? Do you remember that?
>
> Anderson: I remember he made an allusion to something like that in recent contacts.
>
> Defense: Okay. And did you respond to him, "Well, I would like to but I can't," referring to your current relationship with somebody else?
>
> Anderson: I have no idea if I responded to this, if this event ever occurred or anything. I have no recollection of it whatsoever. That would have been prior to 1979.
>
> Defense: Okay. So your answer is, "I don't think I said that. It's possible, but unlikely." Is that right?
>
> Anderson: No. My answer is I have no recollection of any such conversation. …
>
> Defense: So in your memory of things, you don't see anything in that time period where you either flirted with

him or in some way led him to believe there was affection from you flowing toward him?

Anderson: No, I did not.

Defense: That did not happen. Okay. But that was a recurring theme in his various communications with you?

Anderson: That's correct.

Defense: And another recurring theme is that he wanted to rekindle that in some way — "Why didn't we get back together, let's just get together," that sort of thing. Was that a recurring theme?

Anderson: That's correct.

Defense: And another theme was if you just talked to him, just let — just get together and talk, that somehow he could overcome those barriers that you have toward him if he could just talk to you, get alone with you, that sort of thing?

Anderson: That is a recurring theme.

Defense: How did you respond to, in general, to those overtures that he made?

Anderson: I refused him and told him to leave me alone.

Defense: So over and over and over again, it's your testimony that you said, "I don't want to have a relationship with you, I don't want to have contact with you, don't contact me?"

Anderson: Yes, that's correct.

Defense: But he continued to try to contact you?

Anderson: Correct.

Defense: Under the apparent belief that if he could talk to you, he could rekindle the relationship?

Anderson: That's what he expressed, yes.

Defense: Now, in a lot of these things we have heard here and the letters and whatever, it's almost like he's begging you, "Please listen to me, please whatever." Is that a fair statement that he is always begging, like pulling at your sleeves — "Listen to me, come meet me, come see me," that sort of thing?

> Anderson: It's fair that that is what he starts out doing, begging me —

Interrupting, he abruptly changed direction then changed direction again:

> Defense: And you're fairly familiar with that (stalking) statute, aren't you?
>
> Anderson: Yes, I am.
>
> Defense: More than the average person?
>
> Anderson: Yes.
>
> Defense: So in the early days, when you felt he was stalking you, the problem was, there was no credible threat, correct?
>
> Anderson: According to the definition of a credible threat, yes. ...
>
> Defense: ... And isn't that part of the justification where you wanted to get involved in this committee to say we need another form of stalking that doesn't involve credible threats, is that right?
>
> Anderson: I wouldn't phrase it that way. May I phrase it my way?
>
> Defense: Phrase it your way.
>
> Anderson: It was very apparent that in prior cases, justice was not served — that there was no understanding of what a victim of this kind of activity goes through. It was not even recognized as stalking at the time. And that was appalling. That was appalling. So it was apparent that the statute needed to be expanded beyond just a credible threat to include serious emotional distress — activities that would cause serious emotional distress.
>
> Defense: Okay. So you were very much involved in that process?
>
> Anderson: I worked on the subcommittee that did revise the statute. ...
>
> Defense: So, when you're saying that you knew that when this prosecution commenced, that your serious

emotional trauma would become the focus of the prosecution — would be one of the elements that the DA had to prove?

Anderson: I knew that it was one of the [elements], that's correct.

Defense: So this is something that you went in eyes wide open, knowing that your emotional state — and it has been today and I apologize for that — is out there, and it's something that the DA has to prove?

Anderson: That's correct. ...

Defense: And when the prosecution was initiated, it was done with your full consent?

Suddenly, I saw where he was headed. He wanted my therapy records disclosed and insinuated that I'd given my consent. I had not consented to release my records. I had consented to prosecuting Vinyard. Of course.

"Yes," I replied.

"If not you being the motivating person behind it?"

"Yes."

He went on to ask me about therapy, when it started and how often I saw my therapist while Vinyard was in prison and during the current case. Then he brought up the issue of my records again to the judge.

"All right," the judge replied. "And I'm still denying the request for the release of Ms. Anderson's therapy records, despite the testimony that's been elicited on both direct and on cross up to this point in time. Even though Ms. Anderson consented to and wanted prosecution of Mr. Vinyard, I find that by her being a willing and active participant in the prosecution, she did not compliedly or specifically waive the privilege that she has."

A small flame of hope ignited in my chest. After all these years, perhaps this was a judge I could trust to see clearly and do the right thing.

The defense turned his attention back to me and, subtly, the issue of serious emotional distress:

Defense: Now, in terms of your reaction to this — and I know these get to be personal questions but I have to ask a few — I'm sort of hearing you say two things. One is that you were scared, you were frightened. But then I hear you say, "I'm ready to fight, I was ready for war, that I was defiant." And that you were going to stay strong. And part of me is wondering whether this became an almost life-and-death duel between the two of you. Does that sound true at all?

A duel. He was twisting my words to make it sound as though we both freely chose to engage in battle.

> Anderson: Those are your words, not mine.
>
> Defense: Okay, well I'm asking you, and I'm hearing you — when you say you're ready for war, what does that mean?
>
> Anderson: The Defendant specifically said that it was like he was a warrior ready to fight the last battle on Earth. I felt fully threatened, fully threatened. I was terrified and I was ready to defend myself. Basically, all I can tell you is that in the face of fear, we have a choice. We can embrace the fear and live it, or we can choose courage. I chose courage. ...
>
> Defense: Because you sound to me like a very strong person.
>
> Anderson: I am a very strong person.
>
> Defense: That's what I thought. A person who is willing to try and change the law, right?
>
> Anderson: Yes.
>
> Defense: A person who will stay at home at night sleeping on the couch in her clothes and shoes just in case somebody comes because there might be a confrontation?
>
> Anderson: That's correct.
>
> Defense: Okay. And a person who, even though the envelopes come and you don't open them, when [Officer Greg] Malsam shows up, you open them together and you still choose to read them?
>
> Anderson: I chose to read most of the letters, not all

of the letters. I chose to read them because in order to fight an enemy, I have to know an enemy. And the more information I had, the better I could be prepared.

Defense: I think I understand that. ... But you want to know something about the enemy, because you felt you were still at war with the enemy?

Anderson: I felt that I was threatened. ...

Our sparring match continued — with interruptions by Vinyard coaching his attorney from the sidelines — until at last, the defense's questions were exhausted.

Tim didn't have many questions for me on redirect, but he did clear up one important thing:

Prosecution: Ms. Anderson, [the defense] started asking a question about Mr. Vinyard, saying it was like he was tugging on you, saying, "Please, please, please?"

Anderson: Yes.

Prosecution: And you said it started out that way, and it sounded like there was a kind of a hanging second part of that answer. Can you complete that answer, please?

Anderson: In the past, I've had the experience of him face-to-face begging me, begging me, begging me, and I refused. He becomes extremely angry and extremely volatile and frightening.

Finally, there were no further questions and the judge addressed me directly, "You may step down. Ms. Anderson, I've indicated you can stay in the courtroom, but I don't know if it was conveyed to you that I also stated you would not be able to be called as a rebuttal witness if that became necessary. Do you understand that?"

I paused. The condition concerned me. But inhaling and exhaling deeply, I surrendered my anxiety and gave it all to Source.

"All right. Thank you, Your Honor."

Climbing down from the witness box, I chose a seat in the back of the audience, at some distance from my friends. With the whole audience in Vinyard's line of sight, they understood why.

Soon the judge said that, in all likelihood, he wasn't going to be able to rule that day, and he called for a brief recess. Upon our return, the now ancient assault case — the one reversed by the court of appeals — was revisited. I had no idea it was still in play.

If Vinyard agreed to the *new* plea offer, the felony conviction of attempting to assault the officer would be dropped and he'd plead guilty to third-degree assault, a misdemeanor. A four-year sentence would be imposed with credit for time served, and the case would be closed.

Vinyard asked if he'd have a felony on his record if he accepted the offer.

No, the judge said, not from that case.

"All right. Great," Vinyard replied with glee. It was a deal.

The evaluating psychiatrist for both the prosecution and defense was called to the stand. Her credentials in criminal forensic psychiatry were impressive.

The defense questioned her first. Her diagnosis included layers of thought disorders, with the qualifiers "either-or" and "may have." Later, she testified that, the layers interacting with one another, Vinyard was a difficult person to diagnose. But, she determined he fit both prongs of the legal definition of insanity: He did not know the difference between right and wrong, and he was unable to form a culpable mental state. At the time the crimes were committed, she concluded, Vinyard was legally insane.

When asked about medications (past, present, and recommended), she described her findings in great detail. Her testimony dragging on, I found myself drifting, unable to make sense of all the medical psycho-speak. *What is the point of all this? What does it mean to me or the case?* Then suddenly, a beacon was flashing in the fog.

She described an interview she had with Vinyard before he took the lithium prescribed. His thinking was disorganized, he broke into two different songs unrelated to the topic, and almost continually from the time she entered the room, he intermittently touched his foot to hers, she said. It turned my stomach.

Then Vinyard told her of an incident he imagined happened — I was sure it never did — in which he invited me to go canoeing. We both agreed to go, he told her, but there was a problem and we ended up not going. He insisted this meant I wanted to go on a date with him.

"He demanded that I confirm that that is, in fact, what she wanted to do," the psychiatrist said. "When I refused to do as he wished, he began to scream at me using extremely foul language, leaned forward, and began pounding on the desk firmly with his fist multiple times. He was able to calm himself. I was not assaulted. But it was a fairly impressive display."

After he took lithium, she saw none of those behaviors, she said, though when asked, she confirmed that it didn't affect his delusions. And when asked about Vinyard's past compliance with court-ordered treatment, she conceded that she didn't see anything in his history where he followed through for a significant period of time.

Then the defense asked if Vinyard could benefit from the administration of anti-psychotic medication in a closed treatment facility, a locked facility like Orion and Iverson had recommended seven years earlier.

"In a closed or open treatment facility," she replied.

My jaws clenched. *As an outpatient? Why would she volunteer that?*

When the prosecution was given the floor, Langer took over for Tim and pressed her on the subject. Would the mixed bag of symptoms make treatment more difficult, he asked?

Yes, she replied and said, "Delusional disorders tend to be difficult to eradicate even with aggressive treatment."

Langer then asked more about Vinyard's history of refusing medication, including lithium, and his history of assaultive behavior both out in the community and in locked facilities.

"Okay. So, when I consider what the risk is, and of course that wasn't the question I was asked; the question I was asked was to determine the sanity or insanity in the legal sense. But reviewing all of these documents, it was impossible not to notice that Mr. Vinyard had a history of assaulting staff and attempting to assault a physician at the state hospital during two different admissions."

He ended up in seclusion and restrained, she said then went on to describe some other examples of his violent history: He attacked the officer in Boulder, had a weapon when arrested, and he stalked and threatened to kill his victim in Aurora. After an angry outburst by Vinyard, she continued, adding that Vinyard confirmed he'd kicked our house and the record showed he had fought with Bruce.

Lithium alone probably wasn't enough to stabilize him, she concluded, adding, "With a history of medication noncompliance, since 1981 anyway or 1982, I would be concerned — since, of course, we're always looking toward the least restrictive setting — that Mr. Vinyard — that somebody ought to consider the possibility of using an injectable medication so there isn't the risk for Mr. Vinyard forgetting his medication, or losing his medication, or deciding not to take his medication."

I felt blindsided. She knew his decades-long history of stalking, assault, and refusing to comply with treatment. She knew the delusional disorder was notoriously unresponsive to treatment. And hunting me across a quarter century, he had severely harmed me and my family. But the goal was the least restrictive setting?

Langer drew her attention to some examples that didn't seem to fit her finding and, instead, showed that Vinyard understood I wanted no contact with him.

> Witness: … He doesn't hear. He's not accepting when she says that, that that is what she means, regardless of how many times she has said it, or how many times he's had the police investigate, or how many times he's been incarcerated.
>
> Prosecution (Bruce Langer): So, essentially, there is nothing she could say, there is nothing she could do, nothing anyone could do to make him stop?
>
> Witness: Of his own volition?
>
> Prosecution: Yes.
>
> Witness: Probably not.

Langer then backtracked to the interview when she refused to confirm that I wanted a date with Vinyard and he'd exploded, enraged:

> Prosecution: What was your reaction to that?
>
> Witness: I need to qualify that by stating that I specialize in working with extremely violent men, clinically. And having worked in places like … maximum security forensics, violence is not something I'm unfamiliar with. So my reaction may not be the reaction of the average person on the street. Had he stood up, I would have considered myself to be in extreme physical

danger. But he didn't. And I knew — I watched carefully. He was between me and the door. I was right outside the control module. I didn't think it likely that he would actually assault me, but it crossed my mind that that was a real possibility.

Prosecution: And still speaking about that and what you have described — and I'll just use the term "fight" that was going on during this interview — have you ever seen or experienced anything like that in your —

Witness: In many, many years, no. ...

My head shook involuntarily. *And she's talking about treatment as an outpatient, the least restrictive setting.* It was mind-boggling.

Prosecution: Now, as part of your evaluation, you reviewed voluminous police reports, you've reviewed records of various types of communications from Mr. Vinyard to the victim, phone conversations, letters, etc.?

Witness: Yes.

Prosecution: Would you agree with me that over time those became more sexualized?

Witness: Yes.

Prosecution: And that even within that category of sexualized communication, they seemed to escalate?

Witness: Yes.

Prosecution: To the point where it would be fair to say that they were rape fantasies?

Witness: They appeared to me to be just that.

Prosecution: There was also some mention repeatedly throughout the information you reviewed about Mr. Vinyard's desire to finish the relationship?

Vinyard: Can I make a request? I want to go back and talk to Ms. Anderson. Can I sit beside her? I spent over seven hundred seven days in jail.

Judge (Daniel Hale): Mr. Vinyard, either be quiet —

Vinyard: You can even handcuff me — just to be closer to her. Come on.

Judge: Please be quiet.

Witness: Mr. Langer, maybe I ought to restate that. My concern was that they were rape fantasies. I think in his mind he wanted to finish the relationship by having a sexual relationship with his victim and — but did not — but that it being a consensual thing. In his mind, she wanted this. From reading what she had written, and, of course, because she is pursuing this and doesn't seem to want a relationship with Mr. Vinyard, I have to assume it would end up being a rape situation.

Prosecution: Based on your evaluation of Mr. Vinyard, do you think that's something, given his mental illness at this point, that he is capable of?

Witness: Yes.

Officer Sloan and Greg both testified. When the assistant defense attorney cross-examined Greg, he quizzed him on what he observed about the level of my emotional distress when I received a letter.

Greg said he read the letters first and that, though he felt I was an extremely strong person, the more sexually provocative the letters became, the more he was concerned about my well-being.

"In fact, most of the time when you met with Ms. Anderson — as you said, she is a fairly strong person — her demeanor was more or less calm, isn't that true?" the defense asked.

"Calm, quiet, reserved. But she gave the appearance of being distressed, of being concerned about what she had just received," Greg replied.

The defense leaned harder on my reaction to the letters, and Greg said if he was offended by the language, he strongly encouraged me not to read it unless in the presence of a therapist or counselor.

"What was her response?"

"She respected my request," Greg said. "I don't know if she has read them to this day."

Did I read them in front of him, he was asked again? No, Greg replied.

When questioned again by Tim, Greg clarified that the most sexually graphic and violent letters were not charged and he'd never inferred that I'd read them. In fact, I never did.

Tim rested his case.

The judge advised Vinyard of his right to remain silent or testify on his own behalf and said that since he had no prior felony convictions — the last remaining felony having just been dropped — he couldn't be asked about prior convictions. Vinyard said he understood his rights. The judge asked if he wanted to testify.

"Yeah, I would really like to present my case and my side of the story and have a contest out of this, what appears to be very one-sided. So I'm leaning towards testifying. But — "

The judge interrupted and continued the trial to the next afternoon, to allow Vinyard time to testify if he chose to.

Then as the judge reached for his gavel, Vinyard called out, "This has been an extraordinary case."

"Pardon me?" the judge replied.

"I know this has been an extraordinary case. I sure would like to talk to Ms. Anderson for five minutes, Your Honor, please."

His attorney jumped in, "That is not going to happen. Stop making the request. It's not going to happen, okay?" Then turning to the judge, he said, "I'll make my motion for judgment of acquittal tomorrow … "

"We'll make that first thing tomorrow," the judge said, and court was adjourned for the day.

*   *   *

Driving home, I was a stew of emotions. In my mind's eye, I saw the whirlpool swirling in my gut. Detritus floating and spinning, nausea was setting in. Something was up and I wasn't quite sure what it was. But rather than drawing it up into my head for analysis, I sank into the vortex, allowing myself to just feel it all, then asked to know what my gut was telling me. Soon the churning bubbles converged and rose to the surface.

I was deeply troubled by the psychiatrist's testimony. Her suggestions for treatment seemed made in a vacuum, the focus only on Vinyard, with little, if any, consideration for the victims of his crimes or for public safety.

And throughout my testimony, while I'd been asked about my emotional distress, all the exchanges seemed to swim around the edges of my experience, never diving into the heart of it. Why? I'd seen it so many times before.

Beyond a doubt, I'd just witnessed the distortions and illusions created by shadow projections again. But there was something even more basic at work here. While there was some level of understanding, others never quite grasped the horror and anguish I'd experienced for so long. *Imagine how you'd feel in my place,* I thought.

Then it dawned on me. I had just witnessed firsthand what happened when the head was in charge, not the heart.

The law, legal proceedings, the arguments — it was all such a head game: intellect pitted against intellect, strategy not truth. I felt I'd been smeared onto a Petri dish and observed from every angle by those who studied the clinical characteristics of emotional distress but could not comprehend its essence. If the heart wasn't fully engaged and guiding, the agony I'd felt could never be understood.

It wasn't anger I now felt, but sorrow. I was deeply saddened by the state of our criminal justice system.

Arriving home, I rushed through the door, reached for my keyboard, and gave voice to my thoughts:

> Law and the legal system were born of our humanity. And in the collective body of society, our humanity is the heart and the systems and institutions we create to serve it, the mind. But we have allowed the mind — the system — to rise to the level of master, with devastating results for those who seek justice.
>
> The heart is always connected to truth; it is the mind that confuses and distorts truth. And the system now in control, law upon law, precedent upon precedent, the slightest distortions have spun off into oblivion, removing us further and further from the justice system's very purpose: to serve our humanity.
>
> Which will we choose? Will we continue to submit and surrender control to the system, thus crushing our humanity? Or will we ensure that the system submit and serve our humanity?
>
> Our humanity must guide the law and when applying it, it is our humanity we must always answer to.
>
> Our humanity recognizes and will not abide cruelty

or abuse. And our humanity — compassion — does not distinguish between one and another. It does not judge people as good or bad or see the world as either-or, perpetrator or victim, insane or sane. This is duality, the mind's distortion, and it is not the truth. Compassion encompasses all.

I thought of my own hard work to take the leap from my head to my heart and the clarity that unfolded each time I'd achieved the shift. How could I now reach beyond the mind's interference and open the hearts of those who would not see? How could I invoke our humanity?

"Your power is in your emotions. This is what they're not seeing. Give voice to your emotions," Mary had said long ago.

That night, heart fully open, tears streaming down my face, I revised my statement. The tragedy of it all was overwhelming.

CHAPTER 26

Summit

"Speak without hatred and without fear; tell that which thou knowest."

~ Pierre-Joseph Proudhon

August 3, 2005 – Trial to the court, day two

Morning broke, and like the day before, the sky was bruised and the rain steady — an unusual occurrence in the semi-arid West.

Clearing and preparing myself, I stood in the shower for a long time, feeling the pulse of steaming hot water beat softly against my skin. Then gently patting my body dry, I found I was focused on every nuance of movement. Every act had become part of a ritual. It wasn't a conscious intention; it was instinct. My soul was guiding me, and I followed without question.

I dressed and, gazing at my reflection in the mirror, felt a strong impulse to paint my face. There must be a reason this tradition crosses cultures and spans the ages. Helping us shift out of the mind's limitations (the ego's constricted sense of self) and into pure potential, ritual is universal.

In this ritual, I was embodying the warrior I intended to be.

Be with me today. Help me be Your messenger.

I chose essential oils, invisible to others, known only to me. Intuition guiding me, I slowly drew three stripes at once across each cheek. Another stripe followed the bridge of my nose. Then my forehead and the top of my head were anointed.

I studied my creation. Straight on, the paint was invisible, but turning my head from side to side, it caught and reflected the light. *Perfect.* It was the foundation beneath color and powder, the soft face of the feminine.

Appropriate, I thought. *She is so much more than her stereotypes. So much more than meets the eye.*

* * *

It was in closing arguments that I first saw the attorneys' passions. Tim went straight to the heart of the charges. Between September 12, 2002 and July 15, 2003, Vinyard blatantly violated the restraining order many times, causing me serious emotional distress, he said.

"She testified that this affected her personal life, it affected her family, it affected her ability to sleep, her ability to eat, her ability to function. This had a profound, major impact on her life."

This distress was not caused by my desire to stay informed about the case, Tim emphasized, but rather was caused directly by Robert Vinyard. Stressing Vinyard's persistence and determination to have contact with me, Tim said there was ample evidence to prove he was guilty of all the charges. Then Tim clarified that serious emotional distress was not a single emotion that could be assigned to each individual contact, but that it was the impact of all the contacts in the sense that the whole was greater than the sum of its parts. *Yes!*

He asked the judge to find Vinyard guilty of all the charges then weigh the evidence regarding "not guilty by reason of insanity" and render an appropriate verdict, taking into consideration the fact that he, on behalf of the People, was not disputing the insanity plea.

The floor was then given to the defense. The defense attorney argued against the tampering charge. With regard to the other charges, he said his client wanted him to raise the defense of "mistaken belief of fact." I was sure it was some obscure defense Vinyard had excavated while mining the jail's library. But the judge, prosecution, defense, and defendant had all agreed beforehand that, rather than have Vinyard take the stand to present his own version of the past, the judge would privately read a document Vinyard had prepared himself.

His attorney continued:

> Defense: ... I think [Mr. Vinyard] still has a subjective belief that, if he can just get alone with Ms. Anderson and talk to her for five minutes, as he requested a couple of times in this trial, that this would all go away because he can talk her out of it. So certainly that belief is there in —
>
> Vinyard: I'll do it right now, Your Honor. Give me a chance. I'm going to ask her to marry me.

> Judge (Daniel Hale): Mr. Vinyard.
>
> Vinyard: Let me ask her to marry me.
>
> Judge: Mr. Vinyard, if you're not quiet I'll have you removed.

The defense then launched into the issue of serious emotional distress with zeal, claiming that no appellate cases had defined it.

> Even the definition that you came up with, lifted from the civil instructions, tries to quantify how much distress there has to be, and there's a lot of language in there that no person in a civilized society should have to deal with this kind of emotional distress.
>
> But the thing that's interesting in this case, from a factual point of view, is that Ms. Anderson presents in a very unique way. She told us about all of the fear and those types of emotions, but what I heard her say the most was she was not going to let this man pull her down. That she was going to be in control of this situation. She's a very strong person. She said so and [Officer Greg] Malsam said so. She's a very strong person.

I was struck by the irony. As a victim of a violent crime, I'd been given the chance to work with Mary just to help me cope with the relentless, terrifying invasions. And now all the work I'd done, all I'd achieved was wielded against me. It was the defense's weapon of choice, it seemed.

He tightened the vise:

> So she decided that when that letter came in 2002, "I'm going to the cops." Okay, it wasn't enough. Now, the very next contact she's — she got the statute passed — she goes to the cops and now, "We've got enough, let's lay a trap, let's get him." Now she's justified, totally justified in her feelings, but is that serious emotional distress as you're defining it or as the statute contemplates?
>
> And the acid test is — the acid test is those letters at the end. [Officer] Malsam opens up those letters and she

has the option of looking at those letters or not. And if this were a civil case — no one is talking about intentional infliction of emotional distress — and the person said, "I realized I had the option, I didn't have to open those letters, but I chose to do it." Why? "Because I am strong. I can do this. He has not damaged me. I will rise above this."

Now, that is a fair statement of [Ms.] Anderson. She is a strong person. Now, she shouldn't have to go through all of this, but one of the elements of the statute is how is it affecting someone. And the fact that she can look at those letters and voluntarily read them and then say, "When I read the letter it caused me serious emotional distress" — this is a person who is at war, and she won the war, and I don't believe it fits the definition under the statute, and it underscores the problems with the constitutionality of the statute.

Basically, anything goes. If you're weak and you cower in the corner, that qualifies. If you're strong and you rise up and you fight, that qualifies. What doesn't qualify? How do you cross-examine somebody when they say, "I was angry, I was distressed, I was fearful." That's the end of the case. ...

And I want to say again, that's not to say that what she's been through is something that any of us would wish upon her. But her response to it, her individual response was to rise up and fight and win. And she has survived, and she is strong, and I don't believe that the prosecution has proven [serious emotional distress].

Eventually, he moved on to the issue of insanity. First the court needed to find the defendant guilty of stalking beyond a reasonable doubt and then, and only then, turn to issue of insanity, he said.

"The truth of this case is that he's psychotic. He's been psychotic for a long time, and he needs help," the defense proclaimed.

Then he added, "I want to say something else. I want to address [Ms.] Anderson for a minute." And he turned to face me.

Indignation flared in my gut. I was not on the witness stand. I was an observer and did not want to be addressed directly by the defense, especially with no opportunity to respond. Torn between objecting and not wanting to give the judge cause to remove me from the courtroom, I glued myself to my seat and glared at him. He persisted:

> You are a strong person, and somebody needs to tell you, "I'm sorry." Now, I'm sorry. Okay, I know what you've been through. It is unjustified. You don't deserve it. It just came out of nowhere, and I'm sorry that you have been through this. My hope is that someday he can say these words to you because he can't, but for now I hope you accept my words.

In fact, I recoiled at his words, as if I'd been slapped in the face. He had no comprehension of what I'd been through. "I'm sorry" couldn't begin to touch this. And I didn't ask for an apology. All I'd wanted all along was for his client to take responsibility for his actions and for the courts to hold him accountable and stop his ruthless, savage hunt.

But this maneuver seemed designed to undermine all that, to leverage sympathy for his client and absolve him of all responsibility. Then to dismiss it, to just sweep it all away with an apology.

"In the final analysis, there's no bad person here," he then said to the courtroom. "He's not a bad man. He's an afflicted man. He's been psychotic for years but we hate everything that he's done, and people hate him as a human being, but actually he's a pretty decent human being when you get down through all of his layers."

Finally summing up his argument, the defense claimed this case was about the ravages of mental disease and what it did to the afflicted, as well as the people around them. That was why Vinyard needed to go to the state hospital and, perhaps, get some help, he concluded.

Tim had a chance to reply and returned to the serious emotional distress element, citing three cases in which the state appellate court had already addressed the issue.

"Ms. Anderson not only suffered, again, emotional distress that affected her family and forced her to send her children away and forced her to delay her work, but it also just struck her with such terror in her soul that she could not function. None of the other cases talk about that. ... And I find [the defense's] argument about [Ms. Anderson's] strength against her as disingenuous," Tim said.

Before retiring to his chambers to deliberate, the judge, unexpectedly, made one ruling: "The motion for judgment of acquittal on all counts is denied."

I breathed a deep sigh of relief. The motion had been made on the grounds, again, that the stalking statute was unconstitutional. Judge Hale had just disagreed. Once more, he was upholding the law.

The judge returned to the bench far sooner than I expected. Taking my seat in the back of the audience, fully aware of how monumental this moment was, I closed my eyes and, breathing deeply, strengthened my connection with the earth and higher powers. Then opening my eyes, my heart reached out to the judge.

Vinyard was presumed innocent of all charges and the prosecution was required to carry its burden of proof, he said. "I find the following facts beyond a reasonable doubt."

My pulse quickened.

After meeting at CU in 1976, the defendant developed a belief without any basis in fact that the friendship was more than that of a friendship between fellow students, the judge said. "Ms. Anderson never acted in a way to encourage the defendant that any kind of a romantic relationship was even remotely possible. I find Ms. Anderson's testimony in that regard was wholly credible with regard to her being a friendly person and being a person who didn't want to hurt somebody's feelings, in a nutshell."

A swell of hope filled my chest.

Based on the "defendant's invasive interference with her — Ms. Anderson's — life, she sought a restraining order on September 2, 1997." The defendant knew of the order when it was granted and later sought to modify it, further demonstrating his knowledge of it, he said.

"I find that on or about September 12, 2002, the defendant sent a letter to Ms. Anderson from the Department of Corrections. This was the first communication relevant to the charges in the three cases that I've had before me for trial. I find that the defendant wrote and mailed the letter to Ms. Anderson, and I find that Ms. Anderson suffered serious emotional distress upon receipt of the letter."

Suddenly, tears filled my eyes and spilled over. In all these years, in all these cases, I had never heard a judge say the words so clearly and forcefully: that Vinyard did, in fact, stalk me and that his crimes had a devastating impact. For the first time, I felt understood, validated by the court. "I see you. I hear you," his words said to me. The healing power of this simple gesture was so profound and, sadly, so rare.

At that point, the judge paused and said he would talk more about the serious emotional distress later in his ruling, then he moved on:

> That letter let Ms. Anderson know that the Defendant was still obsessed with her and that she was still the target of his unwanted contact. She knew that this letter was sent by the Defendant despite the existence of a permanent restraining order. I find that Ms. Anderson was terrified the Defendant was again in contact with her.
>
> The letter was in itself sexually suggestive and in that letter the Defendant described himself as a warrior who was unable to control what would happen. The Defendant stated that he would get together with her in the form of a promise to her that he would be in contact with her. In the letter, Mr. Vinyard acknowledged that his contact with her may lead her to call the police. This further corroborates my finding that he was well aware that his contact was prohibited by the permanent restraining order of September 19, 1997. Ms. Anderson's serious emotional distress was corroborated by the fact that she called the police to report the contact, contacted Mr. Vinyard's case manager, and I find that any reasonable person would have suffered serious emotional distress upon receipt of the letter.

Contact after contact, the judge stated clearly that he found Vinyard did commit the crime and that we had experienced the impacts I'd described, then he explained his reasoning. He didn't miss a detail.

Like a warm viscous liquid, his words poured into me, soothing the raw, deep gashes. With each finding, the knot in my stomach relaxed and unwound more and more.

Presently, the judge revisited the question of serious emotional distress:

> I think that serious emotional distress is a phrase that can be comprehended by a person of normal education and understanding, and I find that that includes Mr. Vinyard, who is a college graduate. And from the various letters I've received from him and reading the letters that he sent to Ms. Anderson, there's no doubt that he's an intelligent individual. ...
>
> I find ... that serious emotional distress consists of highly unpleasant mental reactions amounting to more than simply fright or shock. That mental reaction includes feelings of anger, fear, feeling unsafe, vulnerable, threatened; fearful for the safety of loved ones or one's self; inability to function normally, altering one's way of life, and suffering emotionally to such a degree as to physical symptoms of illness appear. ...
>
> [S]erious emotional distress is distress that is so extreme that no person of ordinary sensibility should be reasonably expected to tolerate and endure.
>
> It also has to do with the intensity and the duration of the distress. ... There's no way to quantify and categorize the emotional distress felt by Ms. Anderson with regard to each contact that Mr. Vinyard had with her. ... The repeated contacts had a cascading effect, heaping emotional distress upon emotional distress and causing serious emotional distress to become more and more serious as time went on, given the nature and number of contacts that Mr. Vinyard had with Ms. Anderson.
>
> I find that any reasonable person that receives the phone calls, letters, and visits that Ms. Anderson suffered at the hands of Mr. Vinyard would [feel] serious emotional distress.

Gratitude was now pouring from my heart.

The judge then began listing the corroborating evidence, including the fact that I slept on the couch fully clothed, with footwear, so I could hear and fight Vinyard if he entered our home, and more:

> She suffered from loss of appetite. She kept her shades drawn so no one could see into her home. She would drive in a pattern which — basically described by her as a square around the block to be sure that she was not being followed by Mr. Vinyard. She would walk the premises of her residence to make sure no one was lurking in the area.
>
> The contact of Mr. Vinyard, which escalated and deepened the serious emotional distress, culminated in June of 2003 when Ms. Anderson separated from her children because she had to take them to a safe location to protect them from genuine reasonable fear of harm. I find that was particularly credible because, while Ms. Anderson remained composed throughout her testimony, that was an area of testimony when she became quite tearful talking about the separation from her children, and she did so, as any reasonable person would do, because of the serious emotional distress from which she suffered.
>
> I find from June of 2000 through September 2002 onward, that Ms. Anderson was reasonably and genuinely in fear for her life and the life of her children as a result of the Defendant's act and contacting her and, on occasion, having contact with her children by phone. So with regard to the stalking charges, I find beyond a reasonable doubt that the prosecution has satisfied the element of proof beyond a reasonable doubt as it relates to serious emotional distress.

Count by count, the judge read his findings, clearly leaving no room for successful appeal of his verdict. The tampering charge was not proven beyond a reasonable doubt, he said. On all twelve counts of violating the restraining order and on both counts of stalking, Vinyard was guilty.

"The fact that she's a strong woman," the judge added, "that she went through whatever it is she went through that I didn't hear much about that led to her becoming involved in being on the subcommittee to change legislation shows that she's a strong person. But strong people evidence strength but yet suffer from serious emotional distress, and I find that's the case with regard to Ms. Anderson."

He then addressed the "mistaken belief" defense raised by Vinyard. "Whatever Mr. Vinyard believed regarding how he viewed Ms. Anderson and her view of him does not negate any elements of the offenses," the judge said. "Further, to the extent that and if such a defense existed, that defense was, I think, greatly undermined in 1979 when Ms. Anderson told Mr. Vinyard she would call the police if he didn't stop contacting her."

Mistaken belief, he concluded, was completely abrogated in 1997 when I obtained a permanent restraining order.

Finally, the judge turned to the insanity plea. "I find the (expert) testimony ... has created a reasonable doubt regarding the sanity of Mr. Vinyard and that, in fact, he is insane."

Not guilty by reason of insanity.

The judge then asked Tim if, before moving to commitment proceedings, there was anything he wanted to do. In response, Tim asked the judge to hear a statement from me. Judge Hale granted the request.

Quickly composing myself, I stood and, stepping into the aisle, heard the muffled sounds of people shifting positions. Glancing up in the direction of the noise, I found myself caught in the large, dark, vacant eyes of several cameras. Drawing deep breaths, I filled my space more and turned to face my destination — the witness box.

I didn't acknowledge Vinyard, didn't even look at him. But the cameras did, and the *Daily Camera* photographer captured him gaping at me, mouth slack, as I passed by.

Stepping up into the witness box, my heart reached out to all present, including Vinyard. But strengthening my boundaries, I also blocked him from my space completely. After settling into my seat, I glanced at the startlingly rapt faces of the audience then nodded at the judge and began:

> Your Honor, I am speaking now to further inform the court of the impact this has had on my loved ones and me. Although this will have no effect on the outcome of this trial, I do this because I feel it is essential that the truth be told, that the perpetrator's actions and devastating effects

be exposed. I also do this to inform those who will, in the future, evaluate the stalker for change in security status or release. These people … hold the key to our future safety and peace.

But before I begin, I want to make one thing perfectly clear.

The term "love" has been used many times to defend the perpetrator's actions. This is a vile, grotesque distortion. It is not the truth.

The truth is that stalking is a narcissistic, predatory violation of another human being. Stalking has nothing to do with love and everything to do with obsessive self-gratification at any cost.

The use of fear, intimidation, coercion, and threats is abuse, not love. The stalker's actions terrorize his target. The hunt is, to him, an addiction. The target is merely prey for the predator, a sacrifice to serve his own desires.

Stalking is a taking of another's life energy, freedom, safety, and happiness against their will. And it deeply affects not only the one hunted, but loved ones, friends, and neighbors.

Like domestic violence or rape, to refer to stalking as an act of love is an abomination, a complete perversion of the word.

As I continue, I ask that this criminal act be seen clearly for what it is: a demented, intolerable violation; predation and abuse of another human being.

Do not be deluded. This is *not* love.

Drawing a slow, deep breath, I felt this proclamation hover in the air. Then, like a heavy, comforting blanket, the truth of it softly drifted down and settled over the courtroom.

To even begin to comprehend the impacts on my family, one must look beyond the current case and understand recent events in the context of the whole. For us, this has been one endless living nightmare that, absurdly, has plagued me more than half my life and my children, nearly all their lives.

In this trial, I have been asked how I felt after receiving this phone call or this contact. But the truth is that the effects of continued, repeated invasions and violations are cumulative, long-lasting, and life-altering.

We are emotional beings and cannot dissect and compartmentalize the impact of events. The traumatic memories of past events are deeply embedded, and those memories — both conscious and unconscious — are triggered with each new strike. And with each new violation, the banked memories of terror grow larger. They persist in our psyche. They permeate our lives every day. This is the very reason that the current stalking statute addresses "totality of conduct."

This stalking saga, unbelievably spanning more than a quarter century, has reached mythic proportions. To describe it in any detail would take hours. Instead, I will condense the episodes to provide context and then focus on a few, specific events that I hope will illuminate our experience to some degree. This summary, however, does not fully describe the impacts. I ask that those who review this also read my [timeline] to get a clearer picture of the horrors we have endured. ...

While relating the history of invasions, I unexpectedly broke down in tears several times. It wasn't until after the hearing that I learned why. A friend who had come to support me and bear witness said, "Did you know that every time you cried, you were talking about your children?" I hadn't known, but it made perfect sense. The horrific impact on them was always the source of my greatest pain.

In this trial I have described at length the emotional distress my children and I suffered while we were stalked. But the emotional and psychological impacts linger long past the events. The emotional fallout and aftershocks persist.

To protect my children's privacy, I will not discuss the effects on them further. But I will describe some of my experiences.

More than a month after the arrest in June of 2003, I still could not focus well and often lost track of my thoughts mid-sentence. This was immensely frustrating and severely affected my ability to work. I was physically and emotionally exhausted and sought extensive therapy for my family and myself.

Over the last two years, while the contacts continued and while this case has been pending, my symptoms persisted and evolved. I have continued to feel uncontrollably hyper-vigilant. Exhaustion persisted and I felt disconnected and "spacey." I lost interest in life.

The sleep disorder continued, and I experienced recurring dreams of fighting and insurmountable obstacles. At times, I dreamed of fights to the death. Upon waking, I felt more exhausted and disturbed than the night before.

Some symptoms worsened over time, some improved, some evolved. I experienced frequent panic attacks: My heart raced and I felt short of breath for no apparent reason. Every morning, upon waking, I felt riveted to my bed, frozen, my nerves tingling and my heart pounding as if I was in imminent danger. I have struggled with long periods of grief and depression. My quality of life and ability to function have been severely affected. My work has suffered. At this point, I feel my career is in jeopardy.

As yet, I have not addressed the financial impact of being stalked for more than two decades. Honestly, the costs are incalculable. Not only was there time lost during stalking episodes and recovery after. My professional reputation is built on the creativity, quality, and efficiency of my work. The amount of work I receive is a direct result of this, and it has been seriously compromised each time my life energy was stripped from me. The financial impact is tremendous and unquantifiable.

With continued, multiple forms of therapy, I am finally experiencing some relief. But the healing continues for all of us. There has been no closure, yet we are working to heal.

With all these words, I still cannot express the depth to which this has affected us. So much of our time, our existence, has been devoted to defending ourselves and our rights. So much of our lives lost. And this, in our country that holds freedom and human rights as its highest ideals. ...

That we have been repeatedly, knowingly subjected to these horrors is unconscionable. I still grieve deeply for all we have endured. It is tragic. It must stop.

Throughout the history of this case, we have been promised peace and safety many times. We trusted that promise, only to be invaded and violated again and again and again. I have worked immensely hard for justice and peace, and I have, many times, felt betrayed by the criminal justice system. It is very difficult to now trust that we will be protected. And so, I would like to talk now about this plea and the future.

I feel the not guilty insane plea is a compromise. Is the stalker insane? No doubt. Is he criminally insane? I accept the conclusion of the psychiatric evaluation that he is. But the crimes were committed. The impacts on us are the same regardless of the perpetrator's mental state.

I doubt anyone who has attended these court proceedings would deny that the perpetrator's miserable existence is tragic. And as a compassionate culture, it is makes sense to help *if* the perpetrator chooses to accept it.

But to compound the tragedy by endangering, by sacrificing others to his mental illness is — excuse the expression — truly insane. This serves no one and inflicts indescribable harm on the victims of the perpetrator's criminal abuses. As I have said, to have repeatedly, knowingly subjected my family or anyone to these true horrors is unconscionable and unjustifiable.

I agree that, of the two possible outcomes of this trial, not guilty insane has the potential to provide us greater relief and peace than a prison term. However, it also has the potential to put us and the community at greater risk.

Recent news articles have said this plea could mean a life sentence in a state mental hospital. To clarify, because the plea is not guilty, there is, in fact, no conviction and no sentence. I have no guarantee of safety or peace for any length of time.

I understand that it is uncertain if mail and telephone calls can be screened. And it has been explained to me that a stay at the Pueblo psychiatric institute is phased with increased privileges, the goal being to eventually release the perpetrator. He is assessed, treated, and then phased from maximum security to reduced security levels. I am uncertain if the Pueblo facility has a security fence. I understand that reduced security means the predator would first move across the campus with a guard and then with no guard. Eventually, work release would occur then conditional release and finally, unconditional release. Because there is no conviction, there would be no probation.

Although the length of stay cannot entirely be predicted, I have been told that between five and ten years is probably a reasonable estimate. And again, during this period security levels will gradually be reduced. This provides very little comfort.

There is a fatal flaw in this standard procedure. It assumes that the perpetrator is treatable, that the problem can be fixed by fixing him. Since the earliest hearings in the 1980s, this has been the court's approach with devastating results for my family. In lieu of incarceration, all types of mental health treatments have been mandated, the focus on fixing him at the expense of protecting us and the public.

And ironically, after twenty-six years, we have come full circle. He will be treated. Our safety is uncertain.

Previously, during the course of his stalking campaign, experts have testified that while there are medications to treat some of his diagnosed mental conditions, the delusional obsession cannot be treated. From my perspective, treatment has never curtailed the stalking, and in fact, the deviance and intensity of the conduct has only escalated in time. What's more, throughout the history of stalking, the perpetrator has, without exception, refused to continue treatment of any kind when released.

There is a stark contrast between this phased, standard procedure and the law. The standard procedure is designed to fix and release the perpetrator. The law is intended to protect those who would be endangered by his release.

Colorado statute 16-8-120 is the key to our safety and peace. It defines the criteria for conditional release and release and states: "(3) the test for determination of a defendant's sanity for release from commitment, or his eligibility for conditional release shall be: That the defendant has no abnormal mental condition which would be likely to cause him to be dangerous either to himself or others or to the community in the reasonably foreseeable future, and is capable of distinguishing right from wrong, and has substantial capacity to conform his conduct to requirements of law."

It is very doubtful that anything will ever cure "the abnormal mental condition that would be likely to cause him to be dangerous." Paraphrasing, the key words then are "would be likely to be dangerous in the reasonably foreseeable future."

How do we define "danger?" Dictionary definitions include "a cause of injury, pain, harm, or loss." Danger is commonly associated with physical assault. That is one aspect of danger, and the threat of physical harm intensifies my emotional distress. But the definition is not limited to physical danger. A physical injury — a broken bone or even loss of limb — the body heals relatively quickly. Emotional "pain, harm, loss" has much more long-lasting and life-altering effects.

When one is physically attacked, it is the violation sensed emotionally that haunts them. And the trauma caused by repeated emotional assaults is cumulative. As soldiers who have suffered trauma on the battlefield know, ghosts of trauma permeate our being and affect every aspect of life. Post-traumatic stress is very challenging to heal. It takes a great deal of help and work, and cannot be fully healed until the cause is stopped.

Experts in the treatment of stalking victims have referred to stalking as "an act of terrorism" and "psychological rape." These describe my experience precisely. The pain, harm, and loss suffered by those of us subjected to such violations repeatedly is devastating. This is the very reason that the current stalking statute recognizes causing serious emotional distress as a very serious crime.

The danger is not just some possible future physical assault. The danger, the emotional injury has been inflicted again and again and again, and the wounds run deep. If this predator is not behind bars, the assaults will, no doubt, continue.

The history of this case and others involving this stalker have proven time and time again that he is, by all standards, extremely dangerous. Knowing the risk of physical harm heightens the anticipation and terror. To expand on this, apart from this case:

- Three 1994 arrest reports for various offenses committed by this perpetrator in Colorado noted that at the time of the arrest he was armed with an automatic weapon.
- Also, as mentioned previously during expert testimony in this trial, in 1994 the perpetrator was arrested for stalking a woman in Aurora. The police report noted that he attempted to take an infant from the woman and to enter her home forcibly —

Suddenly, Vinyard launched out of his seat in the jury box. Chains clanging, his face pulsing red, it was the same specter of crazed rage I'd seen so many times before.

His voice — that voice indelibly etched in my memory — howled through the chamber: "That's — "

Jerking his chains taut, the deputies leaped on him, and a dark mass streaked into my line of sight. A deputy I hadn't known was standing behind and to the left of me, had rushed forward, thrusting his body between Vinyard and me. His back to me, his arms and legs were spread wide in a protective gesture. The impact that image had on me was indescribable.

He's protecting me. Tears swelled and filled my eyes. *Thank you.*

> Judge: Okay. Would you have Mr. Vinyard go out of the courtroom?
> Anderson: Shall I continue?
> Judge: Yes.
> Anderson: The police —
> Judge: Just a minute.

"You're a liar!" Vinyard roared as three deputies hauled him out of the courtroom. "I'd like to state my view of the facts, not listen to your lies, bitch. She's a fucking liar." And the door clicked shut behind him.

Once the room had settled, I pressed on, listing the evidence of physical danger presented episode after episode, year after year, then continued:

> These are merely examples that I know of. I have not done further research. I have known what I needed to for a very long time: that this predator is, by all definitions, extremely dangerous.
>
> The other key phrase of the statute, "in the foreseeable future," is very subjective and hauntingly vague. To predict the future, one must look at the past. The whole history of this case clearly demonstrates that nothing — not arrests, medication, therapy — nothing will even curtail the stalking except imprisonment. Even then the conduct did not stop, and the desperation and depravity have continued to escalate. ...

I ask that those who will determine appropriate security levels and those who will evaluate the stalker for conditional release or release in the future review this statement, review my personal [timeline], and weigh the risks very carefully. Look at the record — when he is free we are imprisoned, we are in danger. And we have already been harmed far more than anyone should ever have to endure when it is possible to stop it.

To conclude, today we hear news of global terrorism daily. We spend billions of dollars and risk young lives to fight the "war on terror." Yet the fact that we knowingly, repeatedly allow this kind of personal terrorism to continue within our own borders is beyond my comprehension. We must wake up and see the truth. Predatory violations of other human beings, in all forms, must be stopped. Sanity and conscience — our humanity — must prevail.

At that point, uncertain how to proceed, I turned to face the judge and said, "I wanted to address the perpetrator one last time in person, but I will go ahead and make this statement."

"Well, if you want to, what's your schedule tomorrow? Because I'm not going to bring him in this afternoon."

"No, that's all right. I'll just make this statement and it will be on the record." In my mind's eye, I saw him clearly, and consciously holding my boundaries and opening my heart, I connected:

I would say to him, Robert Vinyard, *never* contact me or anyone close to me directly or indirectly again.

In the recorded messages of June 2003 you said, "Let's finish this." Hear me now. This – is – finished. It is done.

And for myself, I say this. I will not be sacrificed for anyone, nor will I allow those I love to be sacrificed. I will live according to my own free will and no one else's. I will not live as a victim. I will defend my life and my freedom in whatever way I must. I will not run and hide and become invisible. I will be seen and heard.

*   *   *

At four o'clock the next day, Judge Hale would commit Robert Vinyard to the Colorado Mental Health Institute in Pueblo, the state hospital that houses, among others, the criminally insane. I had no intention of attending; I'd said all I needed to say.

Finally, my work was done.

CHAPTER 27

Return

"We shall not cease from exploration, and the end of all our exploring will be to arrive where we started and know the place for the first time."
~ *T. S. Eliot, Little Gidding*

When I opened the door and emerged from the justice center, there was no fanfare. No cameras, no throng of reporters or well-wishers. No dramatic score played by the orchestra that accompanies the lives of film. Only the rhythmic patter of raindrops hitting the pavement, the subtle metallic scent of ozone, and the sound of my own footsteps splashing in shallow puddles filled the air as I walked to my car. It was an appropriate end for what was, in essence, a solitary journey.

I passed people walking, shopping, laughing. Cars moved in all directions, transporting people to their daily destinations. The world around me did not stop and take notice of the moment. I felt as a soldier must, returning from war. I had been on a journey few had experienced, and those who hadn't could never understand. I returned to a people I could not relate to, nor they to me. We walked in parallel worlds, it seemed, a gossamer veil draped between us.

One of my friends who accompanied me that day planned to meet me at a restaurant to celebrate once the trial was over. She left before me, giving me time to say my goodbyes, and as I drove back alone, the sky pressing in deepened to an iron grey, warning of the gathering storm.

Fortifying ourselves against the damp chill, we ordered Irish coffee and shared a treat: lava cake, the center a rich molten fudge. But when our forks penetrated the sumptuous reward and the sweet taste hit our tongues, the celebration felt starkly incongruous.

Together we sat in companionable silence. Then suddenly, the steady rain beating softly on the windows swelled and broke in a deluge. Staccato splashes pounding the panes commanded attention, and the murmur around us was silenced. I turned to gaze into it, and as if from someone else's mouth, the words walked out of mine: "And then the rain came."

My friend nodded quietly. The depth of my grief, it seemed, had waited for this day. The tangled jungle path I'd been traversing suddenly opening up, I found myself standing at the edge of a yawning chasm of sorrow.

The local papers reported the story the next day, and the *Daily Camera* published a weekend spread. By the next week, the story was old news, and the stream of notes and calls from friends ceased. The world had moved on. But I did not. As the days rolled into weeks and on into months, I felt myself sinking deeper and deeper into a darkness like none I had ever known.

In all these years, I had never fully grieved for all the suffering, all the loss, the years that could never be recovered. Now, in the long silence of the aftermath, my sorrow grew and grew. It was as if a powerful, invisible undertow had swept my feet out from under me and sucked me down with no air to my lungs. And the harder I struggled against it, the further I was pulled from the shore.

I grieved for my children. I grieved for myself. I grieved for the ignorance and cruelty that still lived in our courts and our culture. I grieved for all who suffered at the hands of their fellow man, for all those tormented still by tyranny, oppression, and injustice in this world. I grieved for the state of humankind. All the sorrows of the world seemed to pour into my heart, and like a lead weight, they lay so heavy on my chest that I struggled to breathe.

In time, my grief became so profound, so all-consuming, I could barely function. All I wanted to do was sleep, to be whisked away into a dreamless state. I couldn't bear this agony anymore, didn't want to be here anymore.

I never considered suicide, but I no longer had the will to live. I felt I had done what I was meant to do; my work was complete. So, why was I still here? I was ready to leave this life, but one thing held me back: my children. I would not abandon my children. Still, life held nothing for me.

With all the work I'd done and all the epiphanies I'd had, how could it be that, at the end of it all, I did not want to live? How could it be that at the end of the road was not joy, not happiness, but only an eternity of despair? Thoroughly disappointed in myself, I thought, *I know nothing.*

The months stretching into a year with no relief, I realized there was another face of this darkness I hadn't at first been aware of. For the first time in my life, I felt completely disconnected from Spirit: cut off, walled out, abandoned; my pleas for help echoing in the void. Then one evening, consumed by the pain, feeling utterly lost and alone, I confided in a friend.

"It sounds like the dark night of the soul," she said. I'd never heard of it. "Some say it's the death of the ego."

Curious, I did a quick search online and discovered it was considered the spiritual crisis in the journey toward union with the Creator and reflected one step on the ladder toward mystical love. Apparently, many who devoted themselves to the spiritual life had experienced it.

Mary confirmed that it was the dark night of the soul but assured me it was I who had disconnected, not Spirit. Now in its death throes, in a last gasp of desperation, my ego had cut me off from Source and convinced me I was abandoned, that I was not worthy. If I released my grip and let go, there would be nothing to catch me, it warned; the pain would be greater than anything I could possibly imagine.

But Mary was telling me otherwise. The more I held on and resisted going into the depression, she said, the more I prolonged it and suffered.

"Go into your feelings. Trust them. They are your truth, and only by feeling them without judgment can you let them flow and be released. Only by embracing them can you heal," she reminded me. "Do not fear the dark. Be with it. Listen."

In darkness lies illumination, I recalled. Finally, truly afraid I would lose myself completely, I loosed my grip, surrendered my fear, and descended into black despair.

There is a wonderful old story told of Ananda, cousin and disciple of Gautam Buddha. For more than forty years, he was at Buddha's side, accompanying him while he preached and attending to his every need. When Buddha died, the other disciples found Ananda weeping and scolded him.

"Buddha died completely fulfilled. You should be rejoicing," they chastised.

Overcome with despair, Ananda replied, "You misunderstand. I do not weep for him. I weep for myself. For in all these years I have been at his side, yet still I have not attained."

That whole night, Ananda meditated deeply, feeling his sorrow and pain. When morning broke, it is said, he was enlightened.

My own grieving ran the full course of the long, dark night. For nearly another year, powerful waves of despair rose up and submerged me. But as each wave pulled me further and further down, the pain of deeper and deeper wounds was released until finally the tide turned, I slowly emerged, and the promise of dawn colored the horizon.

If it was the death of my ego, it did not cease to exist. Where there is death, there is transformation and rebirth.

My ego wasn't the enemy. Its purpose self-preservation, it helped me survive in the world. It was my ego that warned me of danger. It was my ego that, when all hope was lost, still fought to live. But when in control, my ego — my mind — led to confusion and kept me in bondage to beliefs that do not serve: not myself or others, not my soul or the higher purpose. When in control, my ego condemned aspects of myself as unacceptable and cast them out, chaining me to an identity, a sense of self, that was far less than who I am, far less than my Creator intended me to be.

And finally, when its very survival was threatened, in its final hours it enslaved me to the ultimate illusion: isolation, separation from the Divine.

At last awakening, transformed, my mind has assumed its proper place and serves me heart and soul.

Death, transformation, rebirth. It is the way of life, the path of consciousness. The phoenix rises from the ashes.

Fire, after all, does not consume. It transmutes.

*   *   *

Looking back on my long journey down dark and twisted paths, as order emerges from chaos, I see where all my searching, seeking truth in the dense fog of distortions, was leading me. All paths — *all* paths — led home, to love.

My soul, at one with higher powers, was guiding me, holding up mirrors for me to discover who I truly am and find my way home. Bringing me messengers, friends, and my mentor, my soul was calling me back: *Remember. Return.*

The way, it called to me through the darkness, *is love, not fear.*

The path, it whispered, *is through your heart, not your mind.*

Open your heart, surrender your fear, have faith, it assured me.

Trust yourself. Know yourself. Love yourself — all of who you are — as you are so beloved.

The answers are within you. For, never separate, we are one.

CHAPTER 28

Dawn

As I closed the last chapter on this part of my life story, feeling content and at peace, I picked up my journal and walked into my garden. It was a beautiful summer day, and preparing to recline, I opened my chair. Then settling comfortably into it, I closed my eyes.

Soon I was so captivated by the warm caress of the sun, the cool breezes gently stroking my skin, the vibrant song of life all around me, that I sank into the moment and allowed myself to just feel it all. Then, with no effort, I let all interference — tension, distractions, thoughts — drift away. I emptied myself, and like water poured into a pitcher, the message poured into and out of me:

> You are children of the Divine, whole and perfect expressions of creation. To be loved is your birthright. It is given unconditionally. And all that is asked of you is — hearts open, receiving the limitless love poured out to you, and love flowing through you — that you co-create, manifesting on Earth the boundless potential of all that serves love.
>
> Love is the only truth and the only thing worth serving. It is what you all yearn for and what you are given. You are incarnations of love, and serving love, you are infinitely powerful. To believe anything else is distortion.
>
> Given free will, it is your choice to accept this gift or not, to trust it or not. But know this:
>
> If it nurtures and heals, it serves love. If it inflicts harm, it does not serve love and only love will heal it.
>
> If it comes from fear and wields fear, it is false power and does not serve love. Only in love lies true power, and only love can free you from the shackles of fear.
>
> If it heals duality and restores wholeness, it serves love. If it divides and entrenches duality — good or bad,

win or lose, you or me — it is an illusion that does not serve love, and only love will disperse it.

If it is unloved, feared, or shamed and condemned to the unconscious, it is projected onto others, wounding both others and yourself. Only by bringing it to the light of consciousness and love and integrating it will the wounds of all be healed, will all be empowered, and all be set free. Then, and only then, will heaven be manifested on Earth.

*   *   *

"The day will come when, after harnessing space, the winds, the tides, gravitation, we shall harness for God the energies of love. And, on that day, for the second time in the history of the world, man will have discovered fire."

~ *Pierre Teilhard de Chardin*

Epilogue

Within a month of the trial, the defense filed a notice of appeal to the Colorado Court of Appeals, contending once again that the stalking statute was unconstitutionally vague and overbroad. Two years later, in August 2007, the attorney general's office notified me that the court had issued its decision. "I am pleased to let you know that the Court has affirmed (upheld) the trial court's judgment," the letter read. "This means that the People have won."

The defense then petitioned the Colorado Supreme Court to review that decision, and in March 2008, its petition was denied: The court would not revisit it. The statute would stand.

Because Vinyard was found not guilty by reason of insanity rather than guilty, just how earnestly the state hospital would enforce his communication restrictions was, at first, unclear. Then, although the permanent restraining order prohibited Vinyard from contacting me, I occasionally received phone calls and letters from him through 2009. When questioned by local reporters, a hospital spokeswoman said the hospital was bound to protect a patient's right to freely use the phone and mail services, despite knowing what he might do with them. Those rights could only be restricted by the treating psychiatrist or a court order, she said, but only in "extreme cases."

When I called the hospital to report the contacts, citing patient privacy laws, staff would not confirm that Vinyard was there. I also reported all contacts to Greg and Tim, whose calls to the hospital were met with the same response. When asked about this by a reporter, Tim exclaimed, "I know he's there; I put him there."

Tim told another reporter that one way to prevent the issues we'd encountered from occurring in future similar cases would be for legislators to change state laws to "reflect a 'guilty but insane' ruling," something Tim and I had discussed at length.

Each time Vinyard contacted me, Greg gathered the evidence, investigated the contact to the extent he could given the hospital's stance on patient privacy, and filed a report with Tim. I never opened the letters, and per my request, Greg did not inform me of the contents. Most of the calls and letters were covered by the press, and finally they stopped.

Tim has left the decision to prosecute any contacts in my hands. If they were prosecuted, in all likelihood, the stalker would again be found not guilty insane and he'd be committed, just as he is now. So to date, I've chosen not to prosecute. Instead, Tim has kept a file to present as evidence in the event of a hearing for change in Vinyard's status, in which case Tim would argue strenuously against it. His opportunity came sooner than expected.

In 2012, I received a letter from the hospital notifying me that because Vinyard was no longer "verbalizing threats of harm" directed at me, his treating psychiatrist discontinued the hospital's duty to warn and protect me. The letter went on to say that the hospital would continue to notify me of any request for progression, such as off-grounds privileges. Then in February 2014, Tim told me the court received notice from the hospital that, barring an objection from the DA's office within thirty-five days, the superintendent planned to grant Vinyard staff-supervised excursions off the hospital grounds. The hospital hadn't notified me.

According to Tim, the notice provided no indication that "staff" would include armed guards, and only two staff members would accompany as many as ten patients on the outings.

To protect the patient's privacy, I was not allowed to see the mental health report submitted in support of off-grounds privileges. But Tim was and, in his vigorous objection, disclosed details about Vinyard's conduct not protected by the privacy provision, including continued "assaultive behavior" against staff and other patients and his attempts to contact me despite extreme interventions. Apparently, he'd continued to write me letters that were not mailed, one dated less than a month before the hospital issued its notice. The most recent assault reported had occurred within the last six months. Without a doubt, the delusional obsession and the danger — to me, my family, and the community — persisted.

Shortly after Tim informed me of the hospital's notice, I filed a complaint with the Colorado Division of Criminal Justice against the state hospital for failing to notify me and for several other possible violations of the state's Victim Rights Act. In June, the subcommittee reviewing my complaint began investigating those issues that it determined fell within the authority and purview of the act.

On July 7, 2014, the day before the hearing to decide if Vinyard would be allowed off campus, the hospital submitted a letter to the judge and DA, asking them to vacate the hearing. No reason was given for abandoning the plan.

Four months later, the Victim Rights Act subcommittee found, unanimously, that "based on a pattern of egregious acts" over the years, there was a basis in fact for my allegation that the hospital had violated my right "to be treated with fairness, respect, and dignity, and to be free from intimidation, harassment, or abuse throughout the criminal justice process."

To help facilitate systemic change and prevent such a violation in the future, the subcommittee required the hospital to explain how it would ensure victim notification and to submit a plan for training staff on victim safety and victim rights; enforcement of court-issued protection orders; and, to the best of its ability, ensuring that patients charged with stalking offenses do not continue to stalk their victims while in the hospital's custody and care. After several rounds of review and revision, the subcommittee determined that the hospital had fulfilled its requirements, and in September of 2016 the case was closed. Two months later, the hospital informed me that it again filed a notice with the court that, barring an official objection, Vinyard would be allowed staff-supervised outings off grounds. At the time of this writing, Tim has objected. The outcome is pending.

Addressing the broader issues raised by my complaint — balancing patient rights and public safety in insanity cases, the criteria for the "duty to warn and protect," the possibility of a "guilty but insane" verdict, and ensuring that victims of crimes committed by mentally ill perpetrators are afforded all the same rights and protections as other crime victims — will require legislative reform.

As it happens, the same week Tim received notice of the plan to grant Vinyard off-grounds privileges in 2014, this case was featured on Investigation Discovery's *Stalked* documentary series.

*   *   *

My children, now young adults, have embarked on their own life journeys. As for me, in those times I'm not confronted by new twists in the case, I focus on the simple pleasures. Visiting with friends at my home, laughing. Dipping my hands into fresh, moist soil as I plant, the sun at my back. Escapes into the mountains, soaking in the clean, sharp scent of pine needles crushed beneath my boots, the dance of shifting winds rustling the canopy overhead, the rush of cool water cascading over boulders then slowly stirring the pools below. And small kindnesses. Gentleness. Those simple yet profound gifts that wash away the heartache of living in the world today — the gifts that connect us to our true nature and renew the soul.

And though there's more of life behind me now than ahead, I am sometimes able to dream again of new adventures, of traveling and experiencing the rich history and beauty of this vast, diverse planet. So much to explore.

I wish I could say the past has healed, but that is not the case. The truth is, the magnitude of the trauma, for me and my children, was simply too great to be easily shed. Thankfully, new ways of healing trauma are emerging, and we work with some of them as we are able. So, our healing continues.

I don't know that the trauma will be completely healed in this lifetime. And when I look into my children's eyes, I only hope the world their children inherit and their children after them will be at least a little kinder and a little more evolved.

I can say I've made peace with the past. And in those moments I feel angry again that the life we should have had was stolen from us, I remember that the universe works perfectly. That, though I may not always see the higher purpose, every life experience presents an opening, a chance to take another step on the path of awakening, of consciousness.

As Mary taught me, I allow myself to feel the bitterness and to release it. And into the space vacated pours such gratitude for the support and guidance given and for the messengers, teachers, and allies who never failed to appear when needed. They are the soft, clear whispers in my heart that are with me always.

Acknowledgments

I count myself extremely fortunate to have worked closely with a number of outstanding public servants. They are the champions of those in need. Words cannot express the depth of my gratitude to then prosecutors Tim Johnson, Kathy Delgado, D.D. Mallard, and Bruce Langer; and officers Greg Malsam, Rachael Sloan, Sharon Schumann, Chet Culley, Linda Arndt, Matt Heap, and Dan Sova. Thank you.

My sincere thanks also to: officers Bruce Vaughan, Chris Schmad, and Connie Buxembaum; the crime victim advocates and crime victim compensation board members of Boulder County; journalists Doug Cosper, Clint Talbott, Christine Reid, Erica Wilner, Shaun Boyd, and Charlie Brennan; the producers at Atlas Media and Investigation Discovery; Ray Slaughter and his associate at the Colorado DA's Council; members of the 1998 subcommittee that reformed Colorado's stalking law and the 1999 state legislature, which passed it; the Rocky Mountain Victim Law Center staff; and, from the Colorado Division of Criminal Justice, Andi Martin and the Victim Rights Act subcommittee members.

For his exceptional insight and clarity, I would also like to express my profound appreciation to Judge Daniel Hale.

To my editor, whose boundless enthusiasm never failed to lift me up and urge me onward, I offer my immense gratitude. For your tireless work and extraordinary skill, my readers and I thank you. The boots are stacked. Time to dance.

To my talented graphic designers with the patience of saints, you have brought my vision to life. For that and for your gentle, unwavering support, I am deeply grateful.

My sincere thanks also to the legal professionals who so generously gave of their expertise. Without their skillful review, this book may never have left my desk.

My heartfelt appreciation is also extended to my friend Bob Howard, who has freely given of his knowledge, wisdom, and guidance, and to all our friends and family members who have stood by us and offered comfort and compassion these many years. You have my undying gratitude.

To Mary and my children, no words. Only heart.

And to my readers, thank you for sharing my journey.

*   *   *

If you found *Trial by Fire* engaging, please reach out to others considering my book by writing an honest review at **amazon.com**.

I also invite you to visit **kaiaanderson.com** and join me and your fellow readers at **facebook.com/kaiascircle**. I look forward to meeting you there.

Bibliography

NEWSPAPER ARTICLES
(Chronological)

Associated Press. "Pig thief who escaped prison in '54 is caught." *Longmont Times-Call.* Print.

Baird, R.E. "Judge 'soft' on abusers? Retiring judge is said to be lenient in battering cases." *Colorado Daily* 6 Jan. 1995: 1, 4. Print.

Cosper, Doug. "Fear like a shadow." *Boulder Planet* 22 Oct. 1997: 1, 20, 21. Print.

Cosper, Doug. "Woman faces stalker in court." *Boulder Planet* 29 Oct. 1997. Print.

Staff reporter. "Inmate charged with assault." *Daily Camera* 23 Dec. 1997. Print.

Associated Press. "HOLLYWOOD. Spielberg stalker gets 25 years in prison." *Daily Camera* June 1998. Print.

Anderson, Christopher. "Stalker gets 12 years in jail." *Daily Camera* 14 July 1998: 1A, 7A. Print.

Associated Press. "Stalking suspect gets jail." *Longmont Times-Call* 14 July 1998. Print.

Cosper, Doug. "Stalking nightmare over for now." *Boulder Planet* 15 July 1998. Print.

Editor. "Get serious about stalking." *Daily Camera* 22 July 1998. Print.

Talbott, Clint. "And it took only 20 years of stalking." *Daily Camera* 17 June 1999. Print.

Reid, Christine. "Habitual stalker may walk free." *Daily Camera* 9 Nov. 2001. Print.

Reid, Christine. "Stalking defendant curses at court over $50,000 bond." *Daily Camera* 10 Nov. 2001. Print.

Talbott, Clint. "A danger, not an idiot." *Daily Camera* 13 Nov. 2001. Print.

Reid, Christine. "DA wants to add assault charge in stalking case." *Daily Camera* 8 Jan. 2002. Print.

Henry, Travis. "Accused stalker gets new trial." *Longmont Times-Call* 8 Jan. 2002. Print.

Reid, Christine. "Judge declines to lower bond." *Daily Camera* 13 Feb. 2002. Print.

Arthur, Amanda. "Broomfield man may face more charges." *Longmont Times-Call* 13 Feb. 2002. Print.

George, Justin. "Vinyard sentenced in attempted assault." *Daily Camera* 13 Apr. 2002. Print.

Henry, Travis. "Stalker gets out of jail after assault plea bargain." *Longmont Times-Call* 13 Apr. 2002. Print.

Reid, Christine. "Accused stalker behind bars." *Daily Camera* 30 Oct. 2002. Print.

Staff reporter. "Colorado, Thursday, October 31." *USA Today* 31 Oct. 2002. Print.

Henry, Travis. "Stalker gets 8 months." *Longmont Times-Call* 31 Oct. 2002. Print.

Arthur, Amanda. "Convicted stalker is sought by authorities." *Longmont Times-Call* 12 June 2003. Print.

Staff reporter. "Police look for man accused of stalking." *Daily Camera* 13 June 2003. Print.

Arthur, Amanda. "Stalker back in custody." *Longmont Times-Call* 23 June 2003. Print.

Heckel, Aimee. "Convicted stalker back in jail." *Daily Camera* 24 June 2003. Print.

Staff reporter. "Convicted stalker bond set at $150K." *Daily Camera* 25 June 2003. Print.

Staff reporter. "Stalker faces charges over letters." *Longmont Times-Call* 18 July 2003. Print.

Reid, Christine. "Suspected stalker accused of contacting victim again." *Daily Camera* 22 July 2003. Print.

Morson, Berny. "Man, 48, faces new stalking charges." *Rocky Mountain News* 22 July 2003. Print.

Staff reporter. "Stalker arrested for contacting victim." *Longmont Times-Call* 22 July 2003. Print.

Reid, Christine. "Stalking suspect OK'd to stand trial." *Daily Camera* 26 Sept. 2003. Print.

Hughes, Trevor. "Stalker to stand new trial." *Longmont Times-Call* 26 Sept. 2003. Print.

Arthur, Amanda. "Serial stalker returns to court." *Longmont Times-Call* 21 Oct. 2003. Print.

Staff reporter. "One charge against stalking suspect dropped." *Daily Camera* 21 Oct. 2003. Print.

Staff reporter. "Longtime stalker may go to prison under plea." *Rocky Mountain News* 22 Oct. 2003. Print.

Staff reporter. "Convicted stalker pleads not guilty." *Longmont Times-Call* 19 Nov. 2003. Print.

Staff reporter. "Accused stalker enters innocent plea." *Daily Camera* 22 Nov. 2003. Print.

Staff reporter. "Suspected stalker arrested in jail." *Longmont Times-Call* 30 Dec. 2003. Print.

Reid, Christine. "Accused stalker stumbles." *Daily Camera* 31 Dec. 2003. Print.

Staff reporter. "Stalker faces new charges." *Longmont Times-Call* 31 Dec. 2003. Print.

Staff reporter. "Stalker to represent himself today." *Longmont Times-Call* 15 Jan. 2004. Print.

Morson, Berny. "Stalker hasn't stopped." *Rocky Mountain News* 16 Jan. 2004. Print.

Staff reporter. "Stalker's lawyers to research rights." *Longmont Times-Call* 16 Jan. 2004. Print.

Reid, Christine. "Accused stalker allowed to question victim." *Daily Camera* 7 Feb. 2004. Print.

Southern, Joe. "Stalker threatens judge at hearing." *Longmont Times-Call* 7 Feb. 2004. Print.

Staff reporter. "Restrictions eased at jail for accused stalker." *Daily Camera* 9 Mar. 2004. Print.

Staff reporter. "Deputies: Serial stalker at it again." *Longmont Times-Call* 8 Apr. 2004. Print.

Staff reporter. "Jail deputies intercept letter to stalking victim." *Daily Camera* 8 Apr. 2004. Print.

Arthur, Amanda. "Inmate claims anti-stalking law illegal." *Longmont Times-Call* 9 Apr. 2004. Print.

Staff reporter. "Vinyard hearing delayed, conflict of interest cited." *Daily Camera* 9 Apr. 2004. Print.

Arthur, Amanda. "Judge issues 'quasi gag order' in alleged stalking case." *Longmont Times-Call* 17 Apr. 2004. Print.

Staff reporter. "Stalker to appear in court again May 18." *Longmont Times-Call* 7 May 2004. Print.

Arthur, Amanda. "Judge backs stalking statute." *Longmont Times-Call* 25 May 2004. Print.

Staff reporter. "Suspected stalker accused of writing more letters." *Daily Camera* 27 Nov. 2004. Print.

Reid, Christine. "Stalker Vinyard considers an insanity plea." *Daily Camera* 2 Dec. 2004. Print.

Turner, Brad. "Attorney appointed for Vinyard." *Longmont Times-Call* 3 Dec. 2004. Print.

Darcangelo, Vince. "Justice reconsidered." *Boulder Weekly* 27 Jan. 2005. Print.

Staff reporter. "Psychiatric evaluation ordered for suspect." *Daily Camera* 16 Feb. 2005. Print.

Staff reporter. "Alleged stalker may plead insanity." *Longmont Times-Call* 20 Apr. 2005. Print.

Staff reporter. "Vinyard delays arraignment." *Longmont Times-Call* 7 May 2005. Print.

Camron, Victoria A.F. "Vinyard enters insanity plea." *Longmont Times-Call* 13 May 2005. Print.

Reid, Christine. "Alleged stalker has pursued Longmont woman since 1977." *Daily Camera* 13 May 2005. Print.

Reid, Christine. "Judge will not dismiss Vinyard stalking case." *Daily Camera* 7 July 2005. Print.

Camron, Victoria A.F. "Stalking law ruled constitutional." *Longmont Times-Call* 7 July 2005. Print.

Dirt staff. "Judge won't dismiss case." *Boulder Dirt* 8 July 2005. Print.

Hughes, Trevor. "Accused stalker Vinyard on trial." *Longmont Times-Call* 3 Aug. 2005. Print.

Reid, Christine. "Vinyard may take the stand." *Daily Camera* 3 Aug. 2005. Print.

Hughes, Trevor. "Vinyard is found not guilty." *Longmont Times-Call* 4 Aug. 2005. Print.

Reid, Christine. "Judge declares stalker insane." *Daily Camera* 4 Aug. 2005. Print.

Talbott, Clint. "The madman's destruction." *Daily Camera* 4 Aug. 2005. Print.

Morgan, Ryan. "Vinyard apologizes to victim." *Daily Camera* 5 Aug. 2005. Print.

Hughes, Trevor. "Vinyard sent to mental hospital." *Longmont Times-Call* 5 Aug. 2005. Print.

Reid, Christine. "Living as the stalker's prey." *Daily Camera* 7 Aug. 2005. Print.

Reid, Christine. "Goal: full release." *Daily Camera* 7 Aug. 2005. Print.

Arthur, Amanda. "Police: Stalker Vinyard contacting victim again." *Longmont Times-Call* 4 Jan. 2006. Print.

Reid, Christine. "Vinyard faces additional charges." *Daily Camera* 4 Jan. 2006. Print.

Arthur, Amanda, and Pierrette J. Shields. "Stalker called victim from hospital." *Longmont Times-Call* 5 Jan. 2006. Print.

Arthur, Amanda. "Stalking victim: I'm not protected." *Longmont Times-Call* 7 Jan. 2006. Print.

Reid, Christine. "Stalker's note sent on state's dime." *Daily Camera* 8 June 2007. Print.

Reid, Christine. "State pays for stalker's note." *Rocky Mountain News* 8 June 2007. Print.

Talbott, Clint. "The lifetime stalker." *Daily Camera* 12 June 2007. Print.

Shields, Pierrette J. "Boulder District Attorney's Office to fight plan to give legally insane stalker time away from state hospital." *Longmont Times-Call* 25 Feb. 2014. Print.

Shields, Pierrette J.. "Longmont woman's stalker dangerous, Boulder County District Attorney argues." *Longmont Times-Call* 10 Mar. 2014. Print.

Camron, Victoria A.F. "Longmont woman's stalker won't leave hospital grounds." *Longmont Times-Call* 9 July 2014. Print.

BROADCAST MEDIA
(Chronological)

Wilner, Erica. Feature Story. *@Issue.* 9News. NBC, Denver, CO. 18 May 1999. Television.

Yao, Christina. Feature Story. CBS4 News. CBS, Denver, CO. 26 May 2000. Television.

Boyd, Shaun. "Stalking Survivor." CBS4 News. CBS, Denver, CO. 8 May 2006. Television.

Atlas Media Corporation, prod. "Hopelessly Devoted," Season 4 Ep. 14. *Stalked: Someone's Watching.* Investigation Discovery, Discovery Communications, LLC. 24 Feb. 2014. Television.

JUDICIAL DOCUMENTS
The People of the State of Colorado v. Robert Vinyard
(Chronological)

Boulder Police Dept. 16 Dec. 1987. Uniform Summons & Complaint. 87M2979. Boulder, CO.

Boulder County Sheriff's Dept. 16 Dec. 1987. Arrest Report. Boulder, CO.

District Court, Boulder County. 16 Dec. 1987-6 Mar. 1991. Register of Actions. 87M2979. Boulder, CO.

District Court, Boulder County. 17 Dec. 1987. Bond and Promise to Appear. 87M2979. Boulder, CO.

Boulder Police Dept. 19 Dec. 1987. Field Index Report. P87-15679. Boulder, CO.

District Attorney. 31 Dec. 1987. Motion to Revoke Bond. 87M2979. Boulder, CO.

District Attorney. 1 Jan. 1988. Joint Motion for 12 Month Deferred Sentence and Defendant's Waiver of Rights. 87M2979. Boulder, CO.

District Court, Boulder County. 1 Jan. 1988. Order for Supervision: Deferred Sentence. 87M2979. Boulder, CO.

Community Corrections Division. 25 Jan. 1988. Termination Report. 87M2979. Boulder, CO.

District Attorney. 26 Jan. 1988. Motion for Hearing to Revoke Deferred Sentence and Summons. 87M2979. Boulder, CO.

District Attorney. 31 Mar. 1988. Motion for Hearing to Revoke Deferred Sentence and Summons. 87M2979. Boulder, CO.

Community Corrections Division. 2 May 1988. Memorandum. 87M2979. Boulder, CO.

District Court, Boulder County. 9 May 1988. Arrest Warrant. 87M2979. Boulder, CO.

Community Corrections Division. 13 May 1988. Memorandum. 87M2979. Boulder, CO.

Boulder County Sheriff's Dept. 12 Jan. 1989. Criminal Charge Disposition Report. S886786. Boulder, CO.

Boulder County Sheriff's Dept. 12 Jan. 1989. Arrest Report. S886786. Boulder, CO.

Community Corrections Division. 13 Jan. 1989. Memorandum. 87M2979. Boulder County, CO.

District Attorney. 13 Jan. 1989. Motion for Hearing to Revoke Deferred Sentence and Summons. 87M2979. Boulder, CO.

District Court, Boulder County. 13 Jan. 1989. Notice of Setting (Criminal). 87M2979. Boulder, CO.

District Court, Boulder County. 13 Jan. 1989. Bond and Promise to Appear. 87M2979. Boulder, CO.

District Court, Boulder County. 20 Jan. 1989. Notice of Setting (Criminal). 87M2979. Boulder, CO.

Community Corrections Division. 17 Feb. 1989. Memorandum. 87M2979. Boulder, CO.

Community Corrections Division. 6 June 1989. Memorandum. 87M2979. Boulder, CO.

District Attorney. 16 June 1989. Motion for Hearing to Revoke Deferred Sentence and Summons. 87M2979. Boulder, CO.

District Court, Boulder County. 2 Aug. 1989. Arrest Warrant. 87M2979. Boulder, CO.

District Court, Boulder County. 6 Mar. 1991. Case Record. 87M2979. Boulder, CO.

Anderson, P. Letter to Las Vegas Medical Center, NM. 14 Nov. 1994. Longmont, CO.

Boulder Police Dept. 23 Dec. 1994. Uniform Summons & Complaint. P94-20401. Boulder, CO.

Boulder Police Dept. 31 Dec. 1994. Case File Report. P94-20401. Boulder, CO.

Anderson, P. Letter to the Court. 94M5365. 6 Jan. 1995. Longmont, CO.

Community Corrections Division. 6 Jan. 1995. Evaluation Report. 94M5365. Boulder, CO.

Anderson, P. 4 Apr. 1995. Impact Statement. 94M5365. Longmont, CO.

District Court, Boulder County. 4 Apr. 1995. Register of Actions. 94M5365. Boulder, CO.

District Court, Boulder County. 4 Apr. 1995. Commitment to Jail, Amended. 94M5365. Boulder, CO.

District Court, Boulder County. 4 Apr. 1995. Probation Order. 94M5365. Boulder, CO.

District Court, Boulder County. 23 Apr. 1995. Register of Actions. 94M5365. Boulder, CO.

Co. Mental Health Institute at Pueblo. 9 June 1995. Mental Health Evaluation. 94M5365. CO.

Vinyard, Robert. 16 May 1996. Motion for Reconsideration. 94M5365. Boulder, CO.

District Attorney. 18 June 1996. People's Response to Motion to Reconsider. 94M5365. Boulder, CO.

Anderson, P. Letter to the Court. 1 July 1996. 94M5365. Longmont, CO.

Boulder County Jail Management System. 3 Oct. 1996. Arrest Reports. 94M5365. Boulder, CO.

District Court, Boulder County. 16 Dec. 1996. Register of Actions, Amended. 94M5365. Boulder, CO.

District Attorney, and Co. State Public Defender. 10 Apr. 1997. Joint Motion for Deferred Judgment and Sentence and Waiver of Defendant's Rights. 96CR1043. Boulder, CO.

District Court, Boulder County. 10 Apr. 1997. Reporter's Transcript. 96CR1043. Boulder, CO.

District Court, Boulder County. 10 Apr. 1997. Minute Order. 96CR1043. Boulder, CO.

District Court, Boulder County. 10 Apr. 1997. Conditions of Deferred Sentence for the Offenses of Second Degree Assault, Resisting Arrest. 96CR1043. Boulder, CO.

District Attorney. 10 Apr. 1997. Notice of Final Action. 96CR1043. Boulder, CO.

Probation Officer. 8 Sept. 1997. Special Security Alert Notice. Boulder, CO.

District Attorney. 24 Sept. 1997. Application for the Entry of Judgment and Imposition of Sentence Upon Breach of the Deferred Sentence Conditions. 96CR1043. Boulder, CO.

District Court, Boulder County. 24 Sept. 1997. Warrant for Failure to Comply. 96CR1043. Boulder, CO.

Boulder County Jail Management System. 29 Sept. 1997. Arrest Report. 96CR1043. Boulder, CO.

Probation Officer. 30 Sept. 1997. Complaint #2. 96CR1043. Boulder, CO.

District Attorney. 30 Sept. 1997. Application for the Entry of Judgment and Imposition of Sentence Upon Breach of the Deferred Sentence Conditions. 96CR1043. Boulder, CO.

District Court, Boulder County. 1 Oct. 1997. Minute Order. 96CR1043. Boulder, CO.

District Court, Boulder County. 15 Oct. 1997. Minute Order. 96CR1043. Boulder, CO.

District Attorney. 13 Oct. 1997. Subpoena. 97CR1990. Boulder, CO.

District Court, Boulder County. 28 Oct. 1997. Reporter's Transcript. 97CR1990. Boulder, CO.

District Court, Boulder County. 20 Nov. 1997. Reporter's Transcript. 96CR1043. Boulder, CO.

District Court, Boulder County. 5 Dec. 1997. Minute Order. 94M5365. Boulder, CO.

Co. State Public Defender. 11 Dec. 1997. Motion to Enter Pleas of Not Guilty by Reason of Insanity. 97CR1990. Boulder, CO.

Co. State Public Defender. 23 Dec. 1997. Motion to Suppress Statements and Evidence. 97CR1990. Boulder, CO.

Co. State Public Defender. 23 Dec. 1997. Motion to Dismiss and Request for Hearing. 97CR1990. Boulder, CO.

Co. State Public Defender. 23 Dec. 1997. Motion for Separate Trial of Charges. 97CR1990. Boulder, CO.

Co. State Public Defender. 23 Dec. 1997. Motion to Dismiss C.R.S. 18-9-111(4)(a)(II) Unconstitutional. 97CR1990. Boulder, CO.

[Name redacted]. 31 Dec. 1997. Impact Statement. 96CR1043. Boulder, CO.

Anderson, P. 1 Jan. 1998. Impact Statement. 96CR1043. Longmont, CO.

Defense Attorney. 5 Jan. 1998. Motion to Withdraw Guilty Pleas. 96CR1043. Boulder, CO.

Defense Attorney. 5 Jan. 1998. Motion to Vacate Invalid Guilty Plea to Second Degree Assault on a Police Officer. 96CR1043. Boulder, CO.

Defense Attorney. 5 Jan. 1998. Defendant's Second Motion for Appointment of Confidential Psychiatric Expert. 96CR1043. Boulder, CO.

District Court, Boulder County. 12 Jan. 1998. Reporter's Transcript. 96CR1043. Boulder, CO.

Co. State Public Defender. 16 Jan. 1998. Motion to Continue to Jury Trial. 97CR1990. Boulder, CO.

District Attorney. 29 Jan. 1998. Motion to Introduce Evidence of Other Crimes, Wrongs or Acts. 97CR1990. Boulder, CO.

Co. State Public Defender. 4 Feb. 1998. Subpoena. 97CR1990. Boulder, CO.

Office of the Co. State Public Defender. 9 Feb. 1998. Interview of: Taped telephone conversation. 97CR1990; 97CR2639. Boulder, CO.

District Court, Boulder County. 11 Feb. 1998. Reporter's Transcript. 94M5365, 97CR1990. Boulder, CO.

District Court, Boulder County. 11 Feb. 1998. Minute Order. 94M5365. Boulder, CO.

District Court, Boulder County. 11 Feb. 1998. Minute Order. 97CR1990. Boulder, CO.

District Attorney. 5 Mar. 1998. Motion to Dismiss Count One. 97CR1990. Boulder, CO.

District Attorney. 10 Mar. 1998. Objection to Defendant's Motion to Withdraw Guilty Pleas. 96CR1043. Boulder, CO.

District Attorney. 11 Mar. 1998. Criminal Complaint, Amended. 97CR1990. Boulder, CO.

District Court, Boulder County. 11 Mar. 1998. Reporter's Transcript. 96CR1043. Boulder, CO.

District Court, Boulder County. 11 Mar. 1998. Minute Order. 96CR1043. Boulder, CO.

District Court, Boulder County. 11 Mar. 1998. Minute Order. 94M5365. Boulder, CO.

District Court, Boulder County. 13 Apr. 1998. Minute Order. 94M5365. Boulder, CO.

District Court, Boulder County. 13 Apr. 1998. Minute Order. 97CR1990. Boulder, CO.

Co. State Public Defender. 17 Apr. 1998. Motion to Dismiss C.R.S. 18-9-111(1)(f), Unconstitutional. 97CR1990. Boulder, CO.

District Court, Boulder County. 24 Apr. 1998. Ruling and Order. 97CR1990. Boulder, CO.

District Attorney. 27 Apr. 1998. Subpoena. 97CR1990. Boulder, CO.

District Attorney. 28 Apr. 1998. Subpoena. 96CR1043. Boulder, CO.

District Court, Boulder County. 28 Apr. 1998. Reporter's Transcript. 96CR1043. Boulder, CO.

District Court, Boulder County. 5 May 1998. Minute Order. 94M5365. Boulder, CO.

District Court, Boulder County. 6 May 1998. Reporter's Transcript. 96CR1043. Boulder, CO.

Vinyard, Robert. 16 May 1998. Motion to Vacate Invalid Guilty Plea to Second Degree Assault Pursuant to Rule 35(c)(2)(I): Based on Grounds of Ineffective Assistance of Counsel. 96CR1043. Boulder, CO.

District Court, Boulder County. 19 May 1998. Minute Order. 94M5365. Boulder, CO.

District Attorney.18 May 1998. Motion to Dismiss. 97CR1990. Boulder, CO.

District Court, Boulder County. 19 May 1998. Minute Order. 97CR1990. Boulder, CO.

Vinyard, Robert. 5 June 1998. Motion to Continue Sentencing Hearing. 96CR1043. Boulder, CO.

Probation Officer. 8 June 1998. Report. 96CR1043. Boulder, CO.

District Court, Boulder County. 8 June 1998. Reporter's Transcript. 94M5365, 96CR1043, 97CR1990. Boulder, CO.

District Court, Boulder County. 8 June 1998. Minute Order. 94M5365. Boulder, CO.

District Court, Boulder County. 8 June 1998. Minute Order. 97CR1990. Boulder, CO.

Anderson, P. 9 June 1998. Memorandum. 97CR1990. Longmont, CO.

District Attorney. 12 June 1998. Opening Brief on Allowable Length of Probation. 96CR1043, 94M5365, 97CR1090. Boulder, CO.

District Court, Boulder County. 19 June 1998. Minute Order. 94M5365. Boulder, CO.

District Court, Boulder County. 19 June 1998. Minute Order. 97CR1990. Boulder, CO.

Probation Officer. 23 June 1998. Memorandum. 96CR1043. Boulder, CO.

Co. State Public Defender. 24 June 1998. Opening Brief on Sentencing Guidelines. 96CR1043, 94M5365, 97CR1090. Boulder, CO.

District Attorney. 25 June 1998. People's Response to Court's Request for Brief on Sentencing Range. 96CR1043, 94M5365, 97CR1090. Boulder, CO.

Neuhaus, Eric. 6 July 1998. Request for Expanded Media Coverage of Court Proceedings. 96CR1043, 94M5365, 97CR1090, 97CR2639.

Anderson, P. 7 July 1998. Impact Statement, Addendum #1. 96CR1043. Longmont, CO.

Co. State Public Defender. 8 July 1998. Objection to Expanded Media Coverage of Court Proceedings. 96CR1043, 94M5365, 97CR1090, 97CR2639. Boulder, CO.

Co. State Public Defender. 9 July 1998. Second Objection to Expanded Media Coverage of Court Proceedings. 96CR1043, 94M5365, 97CR1090, 97CR2639. Boulder, CO.

Anderson, P. 10 July 1998. Response to Request for Expanded Media Coverage. 96CR1043, 94M5365, 97CR1090, 97CR2639. Longmont, CO.

American Broadcasting Companies, Inc. 10 July 1998. Response of American Broadcasting Companies, Inc. to Defendant's Objections to Expanded Media Coverage. 96CR1043, 94M5365, 97CR1090, 97CR2639. New York, NY.

District Court, Boulder County. 10 July 1998. Minute Order. 96CR1043, 94M5365, 97CR1090, 97CR2639. Boulder, CO.

District Attorney. 12 July 1998. People's Exhibit No. 5: Fairplay Police Department, Offense Report. 96CR1043, 94M5365, 97CR1090, 97CR2639. Boulder, CO.

[Name redacted]. 13 July 1998. Impact Statement. 96CR1043. Boulder, CO.

District Court, Boulder County. 13 July 1998. Reporter's Transcript. 96CR1043, 94M5365, 97CR1090, 97CR2639. Boulder, CO.

District Court, Boulder County. 13 July 1998. Minute Order. 96CR1043, 94M5365, 97CR1090, 97CR2639. Boulder, CO.

District Court, Boulder County. 13 July 1998. Minute Order. 97CR1990. Boulder, CO.

District Court, Boulder County. 13 July 1998. Minute Order. 97CR1990. Boulder, CO.

Defense Attorney. 14 July 1998. Motion to Appoint Office of the Alternative Defense Counsel on Appeal. 96CR1043. Boulder, CO.

Defense Attorney. 14 July 1998. Motion to Proceed in Forma Pauperis and for Free Transcript of Hearing and for Appointment of Counsel. 96CR1043. Boulder, CO.

District Court, Boulder County. 14 July 1998. Reporter's Transcript. 96CR1043. Boulder, CO.

District Court, Boulder County. 15 July 1998. Judgment of Conviction, Sentence. 96CR1043. Boulder, CO.

District Court, Boulder County. 22 July 1998. Judgment of Conviction, Sentence. 96CR1043. Boulder, CO.

District Court, Boulder County. 16 Oct. 1998. Judgment of Conviction, Sentence. 96CR1043. Boulder, CO.

District Attorney. Letter to P. Anderson. 97CR1990. 5 Aug. 1998. Boulder, CO.

District Court, Boulder County. 16 Feb. 1999. Judgment of Conviction, Sentence, Amended. 96CR1043. Boulder, CO.

District Court, Boulder County. 20 Sept. 2000. Judgment of Conviction, Sentence, Amended. 96CR1043. Boulder, CO.

Co. Court of Appeals. 28 Dec. 2000. Appeal from the District Court of Boulder County. 96CR1043.

Defense Attorney. 12 July 2001. Motion for Appeal Bond. 96CR1043. Loveland, CO.

District Court, Boulder County. 2 Aug. 2001. Motion for Appeal Bond, Denied. 96CR1043. Boulder, CO.

Supreme Court, State of Co.. 17 Sept. 2001. Order of Court. 01SC407. Denver, CO.

Anderson, P. 25 Oct. 2001. Memorandum. 96CR1043. Longmont, CO.

District Court, Boulder County. 9 Nov. 2001. Minute Order. 96CR1043. Boulder, CO.

Vinyard, Robert. 2 Jan. 2002. Motion for Reduction in Bond. 96CR1043. Boulder, CO.

District Court, Boulder County. 7 Jan. 2002. Minute Order. 96CR1043. Boulder, CO.

District Court, Boulder County. 4 Feb. 2002. Minute Order. 96CR1043.

District Attorney. Message to P. Anderson. 12 Feb. 2002. E-mail. Fremont County, CO.

District Court, Boulder County. 19 Feb. 2002. Minute Order. 96CR1043. Boulder, CO.

District Attorney. 12 Apr. 2002. Plea Agreement, Advisement Pursuant to Criminal Procedure Rule 11 and Plea of Guilty. 96CR1043. Boulder, CO.

District Court, Boulder County. 12 Apr. 2002. Minute Order. 96CR1043. Boulder, CO.

Co. Dept. of Corrections, Victim Services Unit. Letter to P. Anderson. 30 May 2002. Denver, CO.

Co. Dept. of Corrections, Victim Services Unit. Letter to P. Anderson. 12 July 2002. Denver, CO.

Co. Dept. of Corrections, Victim Services Unit. Letter to P. Anderson. 19 Aug. 2002. Denver, CO.

Co. Dept. of Corrections, Victim Services Unit. Letter to P. Anderson. 26 Aug. 2002. Denver, CO.

Co. Dept. of Corrections, Victim Services Unit. Letter to P. Anderson. 4 Sept. 2002. Denver, CO.

Longmont Police Dept. 11-15 Sept. 2002. Field Report 2002052273. Longmont, CO.

Co. Dept. of Corrections, Victim Services Unit. Letter to P. Anderson. 30 Sept. 2002. Denver, CO.

Co. Dept. of Corrections, Victim Services Unit. Letter to P. Anderson. 28 Feb. 2003. Denver, CO.

Co. Dept. of Corrections, Victim Services Unit. Letter to P. Anderson. 31 Mar. 2003. Denver, CO.

Co. Dept. of Corrections, Victim Services Unit. Letter to P. Anderson. 2 June 2003. Denver, CO.

Longmont Police Dept. 7-19 June 2003. Field Report 2003030025. Longmont, CO.

District Court, Boulder County. 10 June 2003. Warrant for Arrest Upon Affidavit. 2003CR1001. Boulder, CO.

District Court, Boulder County. 15 June 2003. List of Cases/Notes. 03CR2052, 03CR1001, 03CR1216, 96CR1043. Boulder, CO.

Englewood Police Dept. 19 June 2003. Offense Report. 03-8594, 2003CR1001. Englewood, CO.

District Attorney. 10 July 2003. Response to Defendant's Motion to Reduce Bond. 2003CR1001. Boulder, CO.

Longmont Police Dept. 15-17 July 2003. Field Report 2003038584-1S. Longmont, CO.

Longmont Police Dept. 30 Nov. 2003. Field Report 2003066748-1S. Longmont, CO.

District Attorney. 3 Dec. 2003. Criminal Complaint. 2003CR2052. Boulder, CO.

District Court, Boulder County. 10 Dec. 2003. Order Denying Modification/ Dismissal of Restraining Order. Boulder, CO.

Vinyard, Robert. 18 Dec. 2003. Defendant's Appeal of Order Denying Modification/ Dismissal of Restraining Order. Boulder, CO.

District Attorney. 2 Jan. 2004. Motion to Amend Criminal Protection Order and Order Jail to Prevent Defendant's Use of Phone, Computer, and Letters Without Specific Screening. 2003CR2052. Boulder, CO.

District Attorney. 2 Jan. 2004. Motion to Amend Felony Complaint. 2003CR2052. Boulder, CO.

District Attorney. 2 Jan. 2004. Motion to Increase Bond. 2003CR2052. Boulder, CO.

District Attorney. 2 Jan. 2004. Motion to Order the Jail to Restrict Defendant's Communications. 2003CR2052. Boulder, CO.

Defense Attorney. 5 Feb. 2004. Subpoena Duces Tecum. 2003CR2052. Boulder, CO.

District Court, Boulder County. 6 Feb. 2004. Reporter's Transcript. 2003CR2052. Boulder, CO.

District Court, Boulder County. 6 Feb. 2004. Court Minutes. 2003CR2052. Boulder, CO.

Defense Attorney. 24 Feb. 2004. Motion to Reconsider Conditions of Defendant in Jail. 2003CR2052. Boulder, CO.

District Attorney. 1 Mar. 2004. Response to Motion to Reconsider Conditions of Defendant in Jail. 2003CR2052. Boulder, CO.

District Court, Boulder County. Re: library access. 2 Mar. 2004. E-mail. Boulder, CO.

District Court, Boulder County. 8 Mar. 2004. Minute Order. 2003CR2052. Boulder, CO.

District Court, Boulder County. 12 Mar. 2004. Minute Order. 2003CR2052. Boulder, CO.

Defense Attorney. 26 Mar. 2004. Motion to Dismiss Harassment-Stalking Charge as Unconstitutionally Overbroad and Vague. 2003CR1001, 2003CR2052. Boulder, CO.

District Attorney. 31 Mar. 2004. People's Notice and Motion to Introduce Other Transactions Evidence. 2003CR2052. District Attorney. Boulder, CO.

Boulder Jail. 1 Apr. 2004. Incident Report. 04-931. Boulder, CO.

District Attorney. 2 Apr. 2004. Response to Defendant's Motion to Dismiss Harassment-Stalking Charges as Unconstitutional. 2003CR1001, 2003CR2052. Boulder, CO.

District Attorney. 8 Apr. 2004. Offer of Proof of Specific Instances of Rule 404(B) Evidence. 2003CR2052. Boulder, CO.

District Attorney. 14 Apr. 2004. Motion to Compel Disclosure. 2003CR2052. Boulder, CO.

District Court, Boulder County. 16 Apr. 2004. Minute Order. 2003CR2052. Boulder, CO.

District Court, Boulder County. 16 Apr. 2004. Ruling and Order. 2003CR1001, 2003CR1216, 2003CR2052. Boulder, CO.

District Court, Boulder County. 27 Apr. 2004. Minute Order. 2003CR2052. Boulder, CO.

District Court, Boulder County. 6 May 2004. Minute Order. 2003CR2052. Boulder, CO.

Vinyard, Robert. "Plea Bargain." Letter to Tim Johnson, Deputy DA. 2003CR1001, 2003CR2052. 9 May 2004. Boulder, CO.

District Attorney. 22 June 2004. Supplemental Motion for Other Transactions Evidence. 2003CR2052. Boulder, CO.

Longmont Police Dept. 22 Oct. 2004. Field Report 2004061845. Longmont, CO.

Longmont Police Dept. Boulder County Jail Adult Custody Form. 04-61845. Longmont, CO.

Defense Attorney. 1 Nov. 2004. Defendant's Response to Motion to Introduce Other Transactions Evidence. 2003CR1001, 2003CR1216, 2003CR2052. Boulder, CO.

Defense Attorney. 4 Nov. 2004. Notice of Intent to Introduce Evidence of Defendant's Mental State. 2003CR1001, 2003CR1216, 2003CR2052. Boulder, CO.

Defense Attorney. 4 Nov. 2004. Motion to Withdraw. 2003CR1001, 2003CR1216, 2003CR2052. Boulder, CO.

District Attorney. 10 Nov. 2004. Motion for Court-Ordered Psychiatric Exam. 2003CR1001, 2003CR1216, 2003CR2052. Boulder, CO.

District Court, Boulder County. 1 Dec. 2004. Minute Order. 2003CR2052. Boulder, CO.

District Court, Boulder County. 1 Dec. 2004. Order Re: Appointment of Counsel at State Expense Other than the Public Defender. 2003CR2052. Boulder, CO.

District Court, Boulder County. 12 Jan. 2005. Minute Order. 2003CR2052. Boulder, CO.

District Court, Boulder County. 28 Jan. 2005. Minute Order. 2003CR2052. Boulder, CO.

District Attorney and Defense Attorney. 15 Feb. 2005. Joint Motion for Appointment of Expert. 2003CR2052. Boulder, CO.

District Court, Boulder County. 15 Feb. 2005. Minute Order. 2003CR2052. Boulder, CO.

District Court, Boulder County. 1 Mar. 2005. Minute Order. 2003CR2052. Boulder, CO.

Defense Attorney. 31 May 2005. Motion for Bill of Particulars. 2003CR1001. Boulder, CO.

Longmont Police Dept. 2-9 Apr. 2005. Field Report 2005021224. Longmont, CO.

Defense Attorney. 1 June 2005. Motion for Discovery. 2003CR2052. Boulder, CO.

Defense Attorney. 1 June 2005. Motion to Dismiss. 2003CR2052. Boulder, CO.

Defense Attorney. 1 June 2005. Motion for Bill of Particulars. 2003CR2052. Boulder, CO.

District Attorney. 6 June 2005. Response to Defendant's Motion to Dismiss Harassment-Stalking Charges as Unconstitutional. 2003CR2052. Boulder, CO.

Defense Attorney. 13 June 2005. Brief in Support of Defendant's Motion to Dismiss. 2003CR2052. Boulder, CO.

District Court, Boulder County. 15 June 2005. Minute Order. 2003CR2052. Boulder, CO.

District Attorney. 20 June 2005. Supplement to Consolidate Motion for Bill of Particulars. 2003CR2052. Boulder, CO.

District Attorney. 29 June 2005. Response to Defendant's Claims III and IV In Its Brief in Support of the Defendant's Motion to Dismiss. 2003CR1001, 2003CR2052. Boulder, CO.

Defense Attorney. 5 July 2005. Reply to Prosecution's Response to Defendant's Brief in Support of the Defendant's Motion to Dismiss. 2003CR2052. Boulder, CO.

District Court, Boulder County. 6 Jul. 2005. Minute Order. 2003CR1216. Boulder, CO.

District Attorney. 8 July 2005. Response to Motion for Discovery to Compel Production of Alleged Victim's Medical Records, Including Therapist Records. 2003CR1001. Boulder, CO.

District Court, Boulder County. 19 July 2005. Minute Order. 2003CR2052. Boulder, CO.

Defense Attorney. 20 July 2005. Motion for Extension of Time. 2003CR1001. Boulder, CO.

District Attorney. 20 July 2005. Bill of Particulars. 2003CR1001, 2003CR2052. Boulder, CO.

Defense Attorney. 26 July 2005. Brief in Support of Defendant's Discovery Request for Disclosure of Victim's Therapy Records. Boulder, CO.

Defense Attorney. 28 July 2005. Renewed Motion for a Definition of Serious Emotional Distress. 2003CR1001. Boulder, CO.

District Attorney. 29 July 2005. Motion in Limine to Allow P. Anderson to Remain in the Courtroom Following Her Testimony. 2003CR1001, 2003CR1216, 2003CR2052. Boulder, CO.

Defense Attorney. 29 July 2005. Objection to Motion in Limine to Allow P. Anderson to Remain in the Courtroom Following Her Testimony. 2003CR1001. Boulder, CO.

Defense Attorney. 29 July 2005. Objection to Expanded Media Coverage. 2003CR1001. Boulder, CO.

District Attorney. 2 Aug. 2005. Motion to Supplement Bill of Particulars. 2003CR1001, 2003CR2052. Boulder, CO.

District Court, Boulder County. 2 Aug. 2005. Minute Order. 96CR1043. Boulder, CO.

Anderson, P. 3 Aug. 2005. Impact Statement. 2003CR1001, 2003CR1216, 2003CR2052. Longmont, CO.

428 TRIAL BY FIRE

District Court, Boulder County. 2 Aug. 2005. Minute Order. 96CR1043. Boulder, CO.

District Court, Boulder County. 2-4 Aug. 2005. Criminal Trial Reporter's Transcript. 2003CR1001, 96CR1043, 2003CR1216, 2003CR2052. Boulder, CO.

District Court, Boulder County. 2-4 Aug. 2005. Criminal Trial Minute Order. 96CR1043, 2003CR1001, 2003CR1216, 2003CR2052. Boulder, CO.

District Court, Boulder County. 4 Aug. 2005. Criminal Trial Minute Order. 96CR1043, 2003CR1001, 2003CR1216, 2003CR2052. Boulder, CO.

District Court, Boulder County. 4 Aug. 2005. Order Committing the Defendant to the Colorado Mental Health Institute at Pueblo. 2003CR1001, 2003CR1216, 2003CR2052. Boulder, CO.

Co. Mental Health Institute at Pueblo. Letter to P. Anderson. 19 Aug. 2005. CO.

District Attorney. "People v. Robert Vinyard." Cover letter to Colorado Mental Health Institute at Pueblo. 22 Aug. 2005. Boulder, CO.

Defense Attorney. 19 Sept. 2005. Appellant's Notice of Appeal. 2003CR1001, 2003CR1216, 2003CR2052. Denver, CO.

Clerk of the District Court. 21 Dec. 2005. Certificate of Mailing Record on Appeal. 2003CR1001, 2003CR1216, 2003CR2052. Boulder County, CO.

Longmont Police Dept. 20-22 Dec. 2005. Field Report. 2005077730. Longmont, CO.

Co. Mental Health Institute at Pueblo. Letter to P. Anderson. 31 Mar. 2006. CO.

Longmont Police Dept. 2 May 2006. Case Reports. 06-31018, 06-31041. Longmont, CO.

Defense Attorney. 20 July 2006. Opening Brief. 05CA1999. Denver, CO.

Attorney General, State of Co. "People v. Robert Vinyard: Case No. 05CA1999." Letter to P. Anderson. 27 Sept. 2006.

Attorney General, State of Co. 18 Dec. 2006. People's Answer Brief. 05CA1999.

Attorney General, State of Co. "People v. Robert Vinyard: Case No. 05CA1999." Letter to P. Anderson. 18 Dec. 2006.

Co. Court of Appeals. 9 Aug. 2007. Order Affirmed. 05CA1999.

Attorney General, State of Co. "People v. Robert Vinyard: Case No. 05CA1999." Letter to P. Anderson. 10 Aug. 2007.

Supreme Court, State of Co. 24 Mar. 2008. Order of Court. 2003CR1001, 2003CR1216, 2003CR2052.

Co. Mental Health Institute at Pueblo. Letter to P. Anderson. 22 Aug. 2012. CO.

Co. Mental Health Institute at Pueblo. 11 Feb. 2014. Notice of Temporary Physical Removal for Treatment and Rehabilitation Limited. 2003CR1001, 2003CR1216, 2003CR205. CO.

District Attorney. 9 Mar. 2014. Response to Notice of Temporary Physical Removal for Treatment and Rehabilitation Limited. 2003CR1001, 2003CR1216, 2003CR205. Boulder, CO.

Anderson, P. "Request for Enforcement of Compliance with the Requirements of the Crime Victims Constitutional Amendment." Complaint to Crime Victim Services Advisory Board, Co. Division of Criminal Justice. 22 Feb. 2014. Longmont, CO.

Co. Division of Criminal Justice, Office for Victims Programs. Letter to P. Anderson. 24 Feb. 2014. CO.

Co. Mental Health Institute at Pueblo. Letter to P. Anderson. 24 Feb. 2014. CO.

Co. Division of Criminal Justice, Office for Victims Programs. Letter to P. Anderson. 18 Mar. 2014. CO.

Co. Division of Criminal Justice, Office for Victims Programs. Letter to P. Anderson. 24 Apr. 2014. CO.

Anderson, P. "Reply to CMHIP Response to Victim Rights Complaint." Letter to CDCJ, Victim Rights Act Subcommittee. 15 May 2014. CO.

Co. Mental Health Institute at Pueblo. "People v. Robert James Vinyard." Letter to Honorable Andrew R. MacDonald and Honorable Stanley L. Garnett. 7 July 2014. CO.

Co. Division of Criminal Justice, Office for Victims Programs. Letter to P. Anderson. 27 Aug. 2014. CO.

Anderson, P. "Reply to Second CMHIP Response to Victim Rights Complaint." Letter to CDCJ, Victim Rights Act Subcommittee. 3 Nov. 2014. CO.

Co. Crime Victim Services Advisory Board, Victim Rights Act Subcommittee. Meeting Minutes of November 21, 2014. CO.

Co. Crime Victim Services Advisory Board, Victim Rights Act Subcommittee. Letter to P. Anderson. 22 Dec. 2014. CO.

Co. Crime Victim Services Advisory Board, Victim Rights Act Subcommittee. Letter to P. Anderson. 21 Sept. 2016. CO.

Co. Mental Health Institute at Pueblo. Letter to P. Anderson. 14 Nov. 2016. CO.

District Attorney. 12 Dec. 2016. Response to Notice of Temporary Physical Removal for Treatment and Rehabilitation. 2003CR1001. Boulder, CO.

SUPPORTING REFERENCES

Co. Const., article II, § 16a - Rights of Crime Victims.

Co. Const., preamble.

Colorado Victims' Rights Act, Co. HB 12-1053.

C.R.S. 18-9-111 - Harassment - stalking (1999).

President's Task Force on Victims of Crime. *Final Report.* Office of Justice Programs, Office for Victims of Crime. December, 1982. ojp.gov. Web 2013.

State of Mississippi v. Byron De La Beckwith. Jackson, MS. 25 Jan. 1994.

"Summary of Constitutional Rights, Powers and Duties." *Constitutional Rights.* Constitution Society, 24 Dec. 2000. constitution.org. Web 2012.

Tucker Davis, Joanna. "The Grassroots Beginnings of the Victims' Rights Movement." *NCVLI News.* Spring/summer (2005). National Crime Victim Law Institute. ncvli.org. Web 2013.

United Nations General Assembly. *Universal Declaration of Human Rights.* General Assembly Resolution 217 A (III). December 10, 1948. United Nations. un.org. Web 1998.

U.S. Const., preamble.

Victims of Crime Act of 1984 (VOCA), 42 U.S.C.A. §10601 (1984).

BOOKS

Brown, Margaret W., and Clement Hurd. *Goodnight Moon.* New York: Harper, 1947. Print.

Hilts, Elizabeth. *Getting in Touch with Your Inner Bitch.* Bridgeport, CT: Hysteria, 1994. Print.

Orion, Doreen. *I Know You Really Love Me: A Psychiatrist's Journal of Erotomania, Stalking, and Obsessive Love.* New York: Macmillan, 1997. Print.